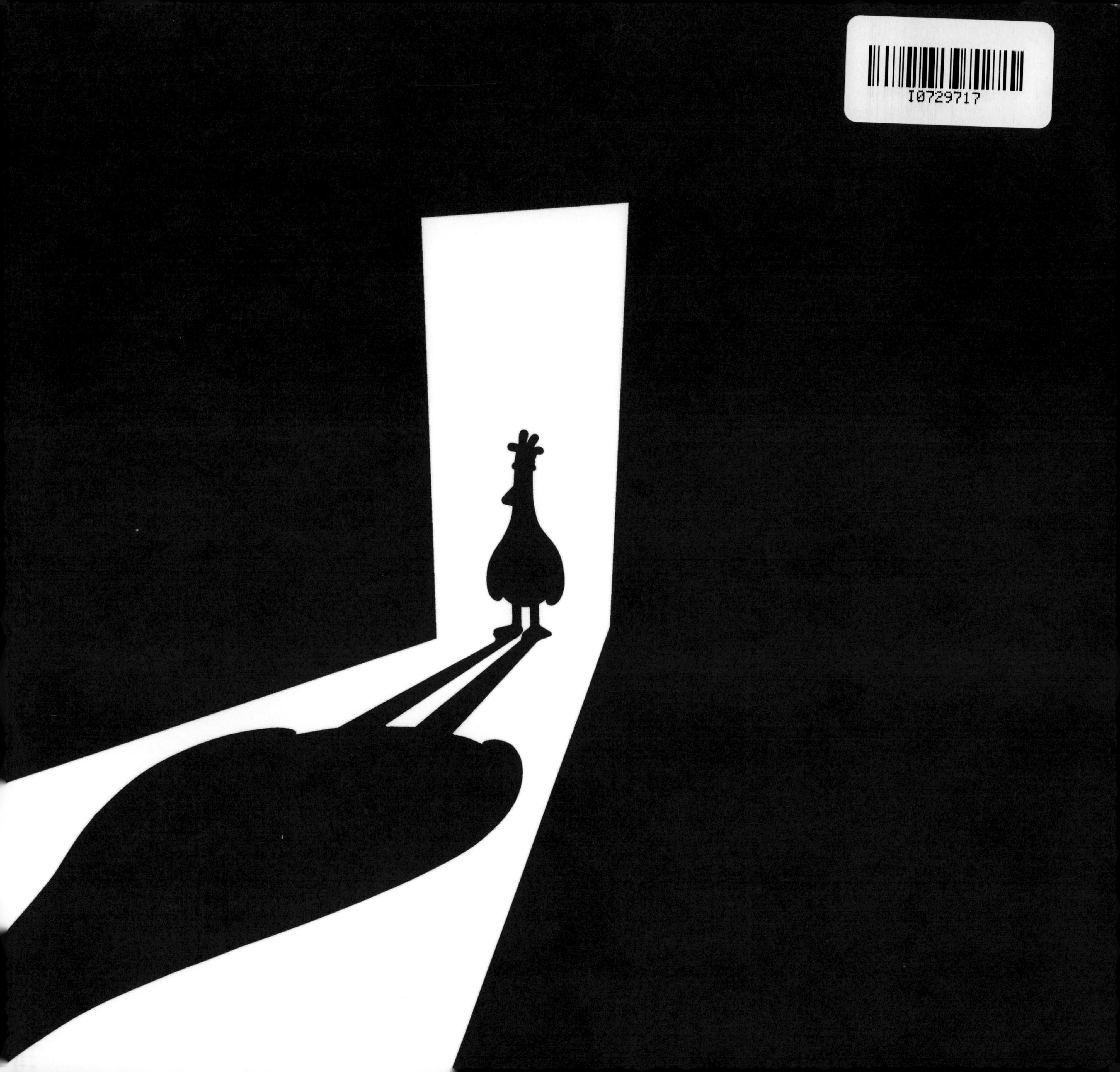

I0729717

THE ART OF Wallace & Gromit™

VENGEANCE MOST FOWL

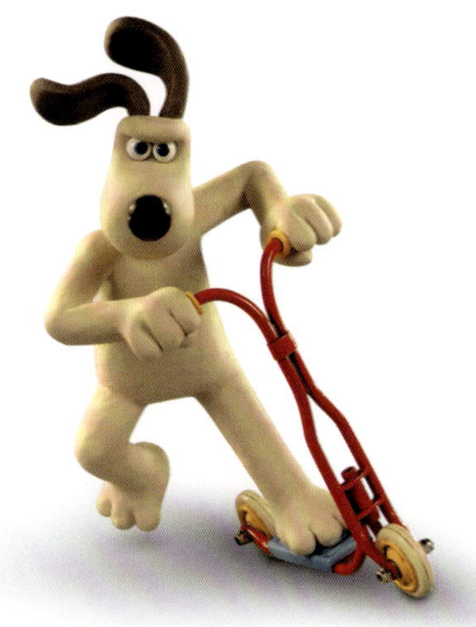

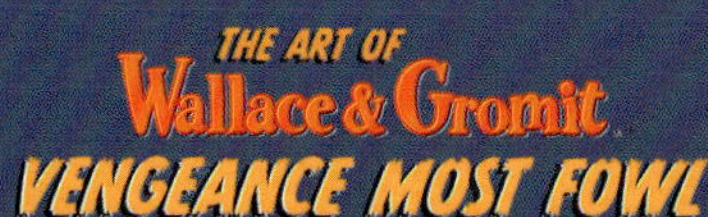

ISBN: 9781835410127

Published by Titan Books
A division of Titan Publishing Group Ltd.
144 Southwark St.
London
SE1 0UP

www.titanbooks.com

First edition: December 2024
10 9 8 7 6 5 4 3 2 1

Did you enjoy this book? We love to hear from our readers
Please e-mail us at: readerfeedback@titanemail.com or
write to Reader Feedback at the above address.

To receive advance information, news, competitions,
and exclusive offers online, please sign up for the Titan
newsletter on our website: www.titanbooks.com

A CIP catalogue record for this title is
available from the British Library.

Printed and bound in China.

THE ART OF
Wallace & Gromit™

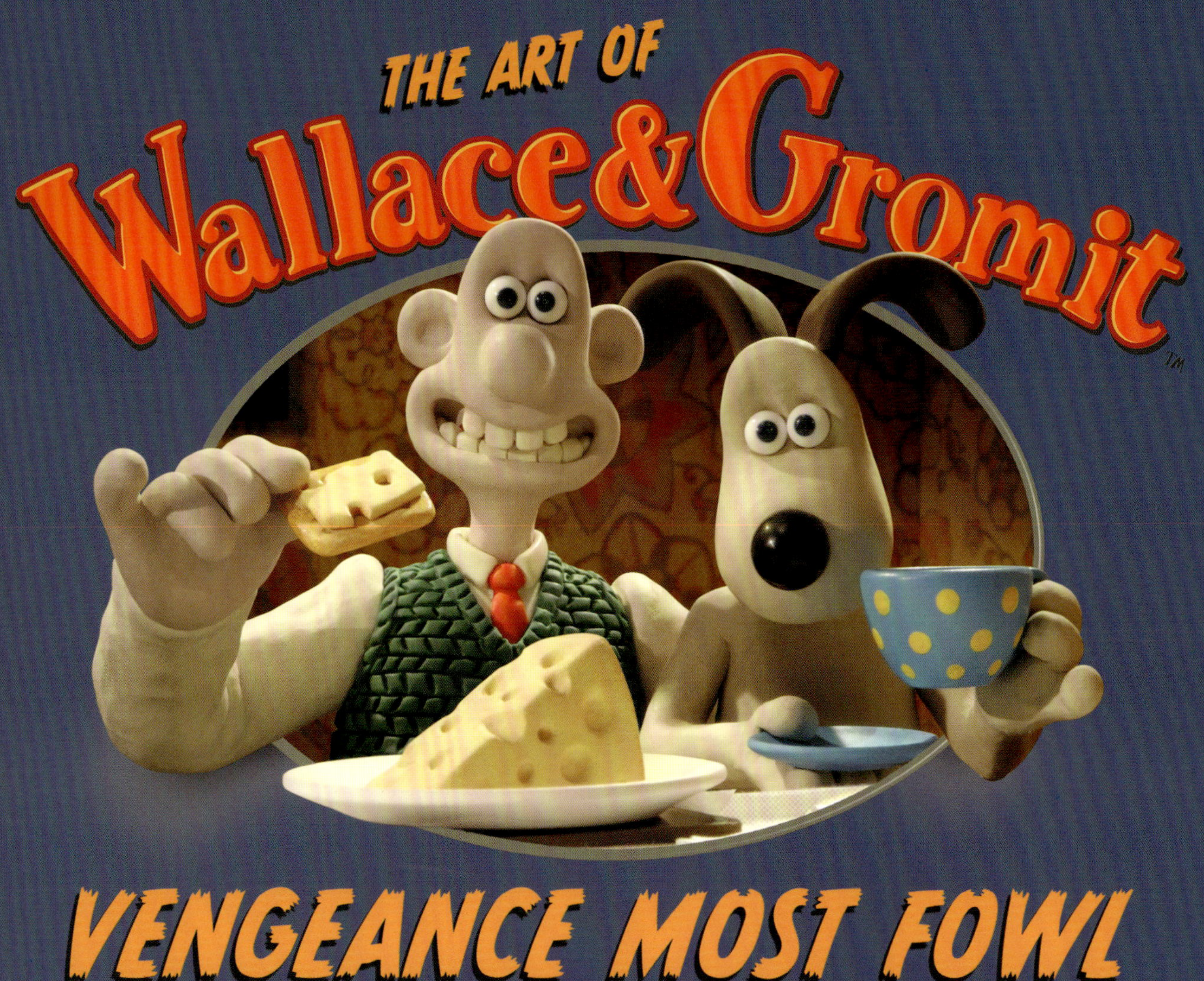

VENGEANCE MOST FOWL

RICHARD HANSOM

TITANBOOKS

Contents

FOREWORD BY PETER KAY   6

CHAPTER ONE   8
Previously on
Wallace & Gromit...

CHAPTER TWO   24
Wake-Up Call

CHAPTER THREE   46
Working From
Gnome

CHAPTER FOUR   76
West Wallaby Street,
We Have a Problem...

CHAPTER FIVE   102
There's Something
Going on in the
Basement...

CHAPTER SIX   122
Making an Exhibition
of Themselves

CHAPTER SEVEN   144
Follow That Barge!

CHAPTER EIGHT   162
Goodbye, Chuck!

**THANK YOU FROM THE
DIRECTORS**   174

ACKNOWLEDGEMENTS   176

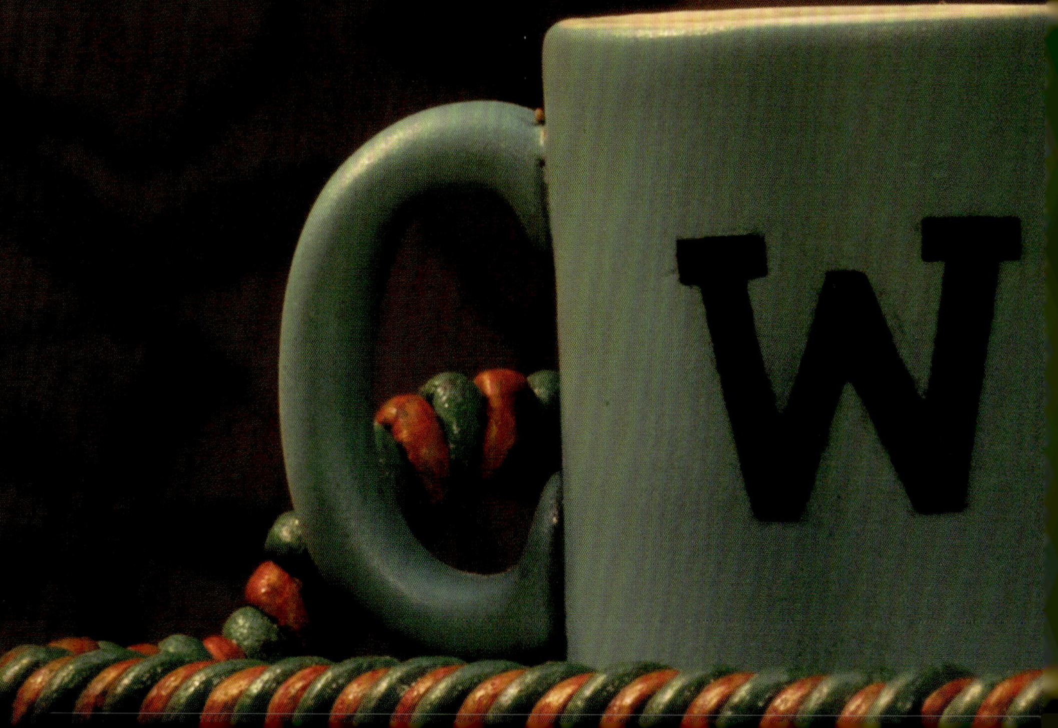

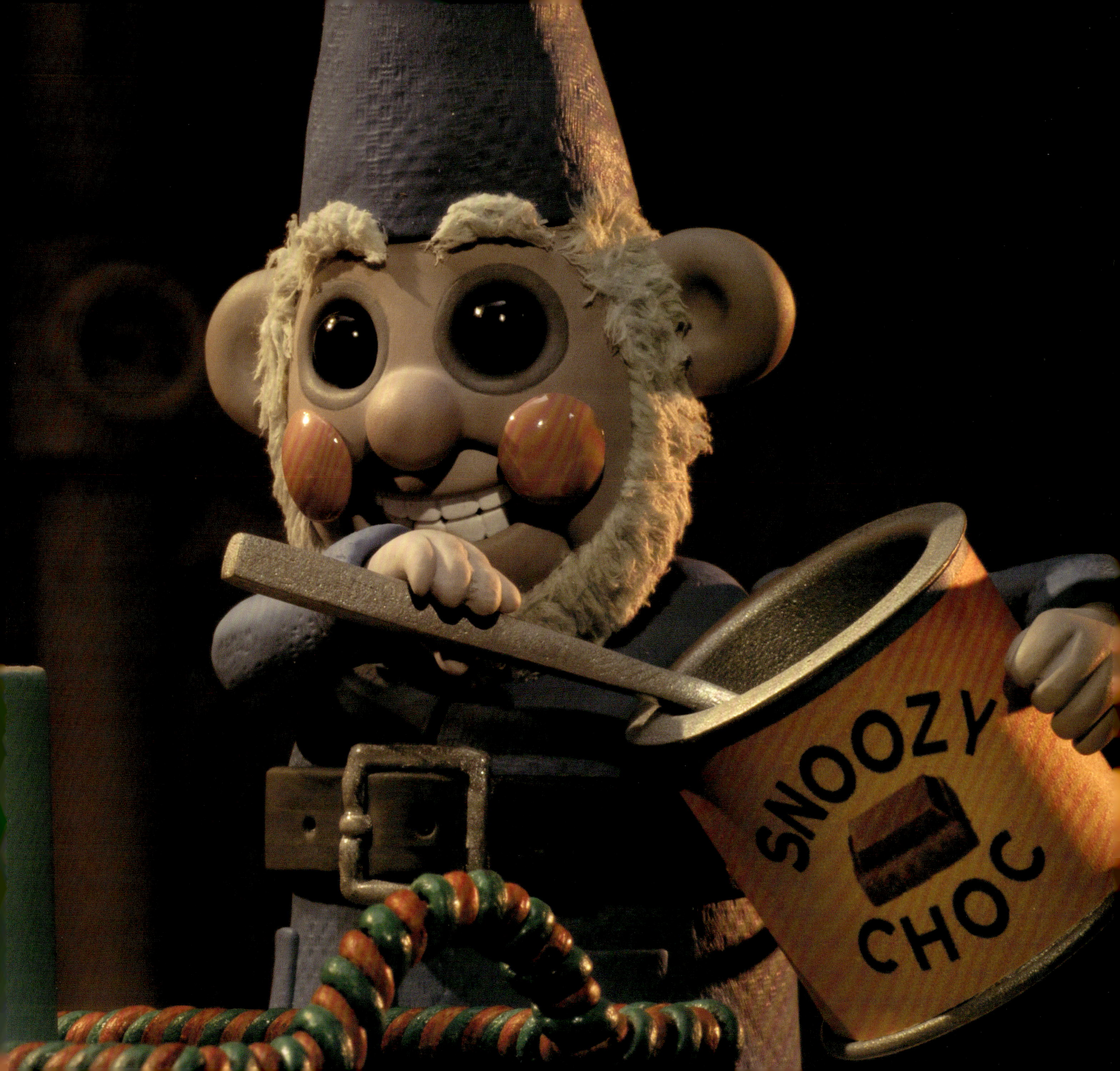

SNOOZY
CHOC

Foreword by Peter Kay

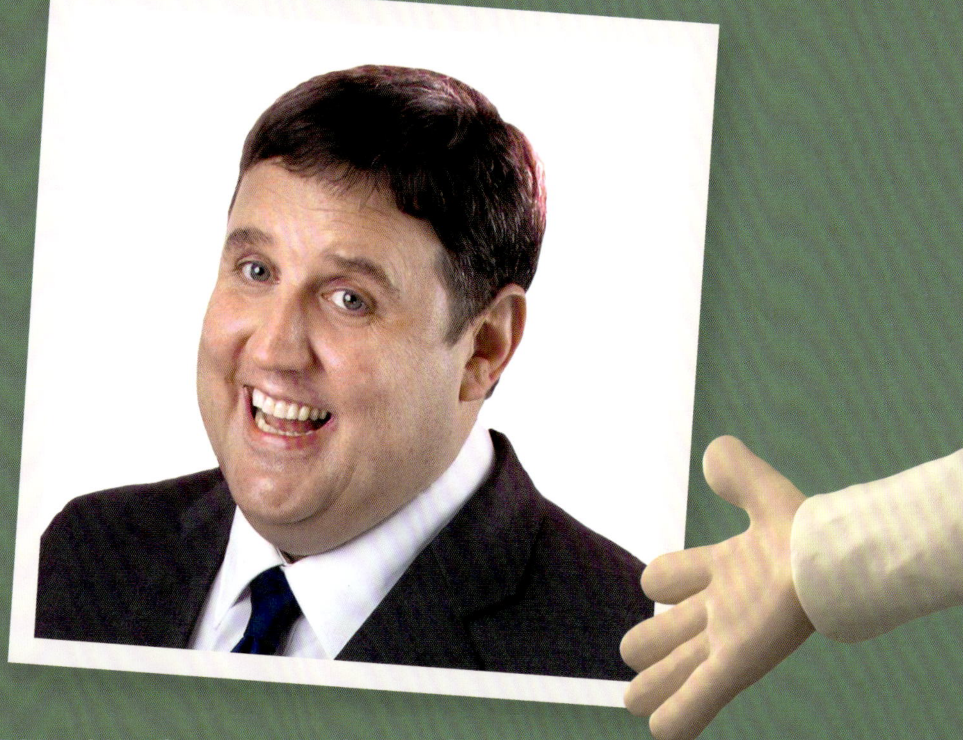

Park to 'do' a voice for *Wallace & Gromit*? They were already firm favourites with my family, watched tirelessly at Christmas or on wet bank holidays. (Also, on a personal note, I was particularly proud as, like Wallace and Gromit, I also hail from Lancashire.)

My first experience was to play the inimitable PC Mackintosh in *The Curse of the Were-Rabbit*, which was deservedly showered in accolades, including an Oscar® and a BAFTA®. More importantly, it successfully introduced Wallace and Gromit to a whole new legion of fans worldwide and turned them into the most unlikely pair of international megastars you could ever imagine.

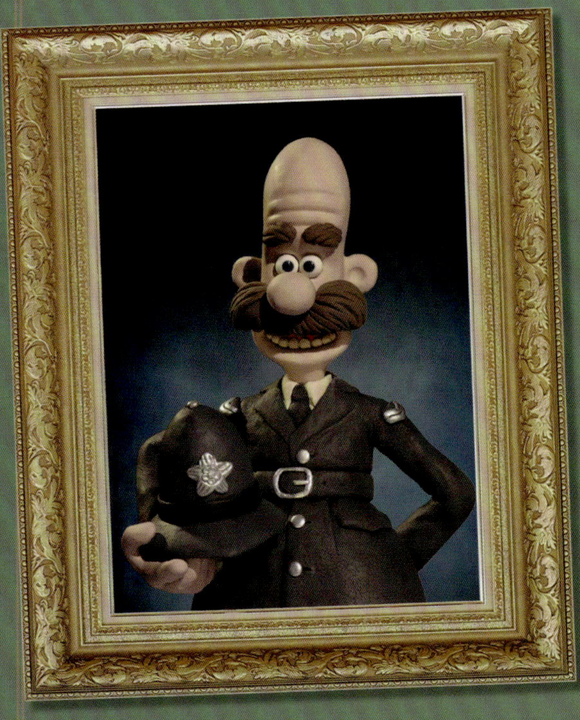

Fast forward almost twenty years and I was over the moon to receive a letter from Nick Park inviting me to return as PC Mackintosh once again, this time for a brand-new adventure: *Wallace & Gromit: Vengeance Most Fowl*. How exciting!

Recording sessions were their usual mix of gruelling fun. I'm always shocked to discover just how many variable ways a single sentence can be uttered. Who knew that "Gromit, the cheese!" can have about thirty different emotional undertones? Reassuringly, Nick and Merlin with the Aardman team know precisely what they're after. It's that scrupulousness, combined with hard work and passion, that makes every project they create look effortless.

Fortunately, I also got the opportunity to visit Aardman's studios during production. It was incredible to see the jaw-dropping attention to detail that goes into producing the sets, the

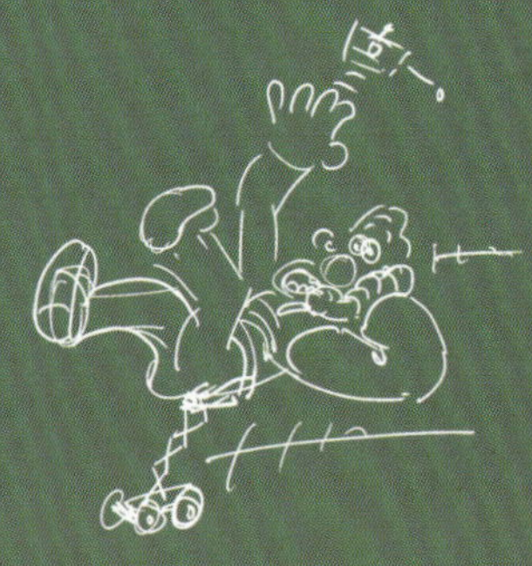

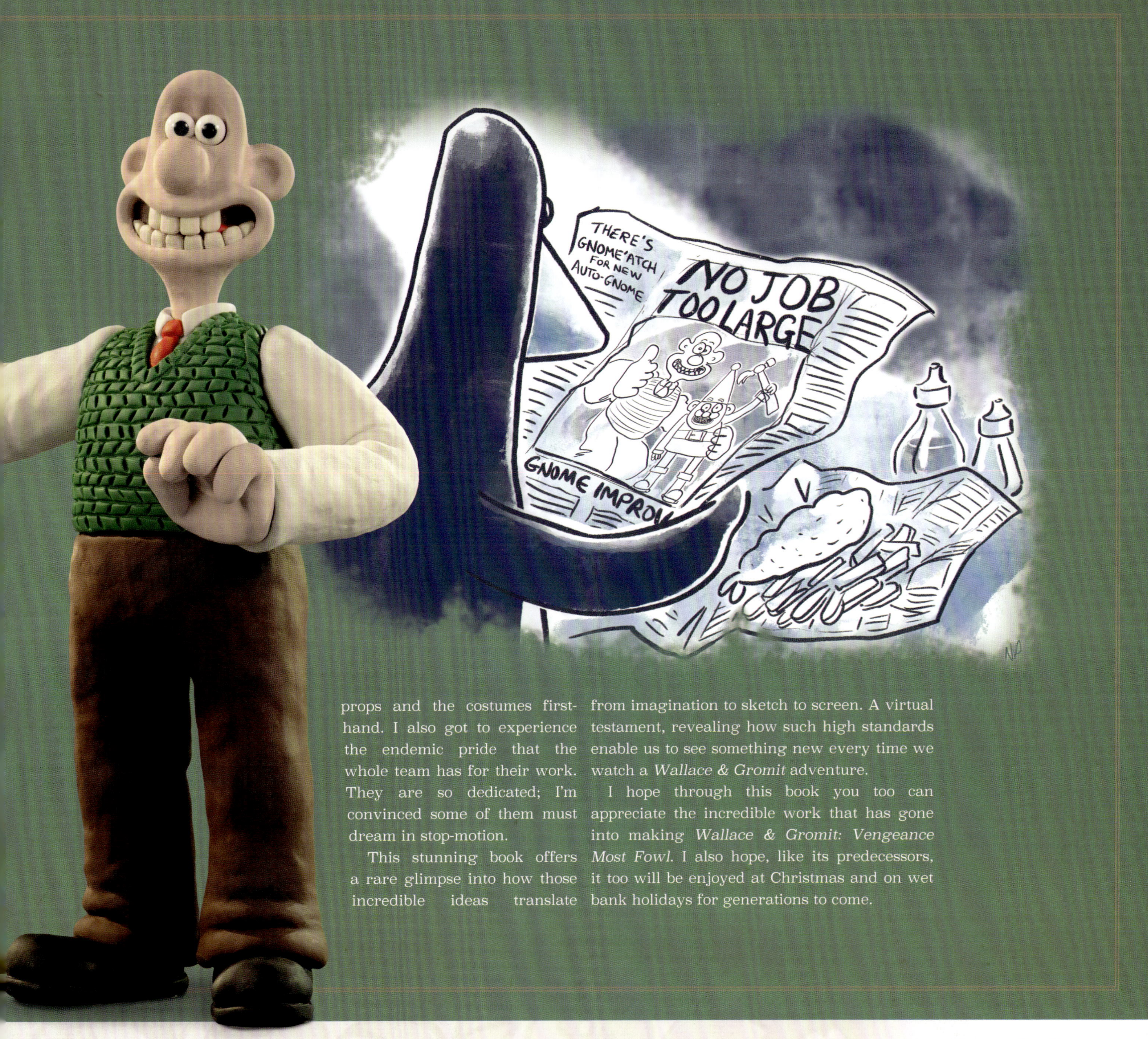

props and the costumes first-hand. I also got to experience the endemic pride that the whole team has for their work. They are so dedicated; I'm convinced some of them must dream in stop-motion.

This stunning book offers a rare glimpse into how those incredible ideas translate from imagination to sketch to screen. A virtual testament, revealing how such high standards enable us to see something new every time we watch a *Wallace & Gromit* adventure.

I hope through this book you too can appreciate the incredible work that has gone into making *Wallace & Gromit: Vengeance Most Fowl*. I also hope, like its predecessors, it too will be enjoyed at Christmas and on wet bank holidays for generations to come.

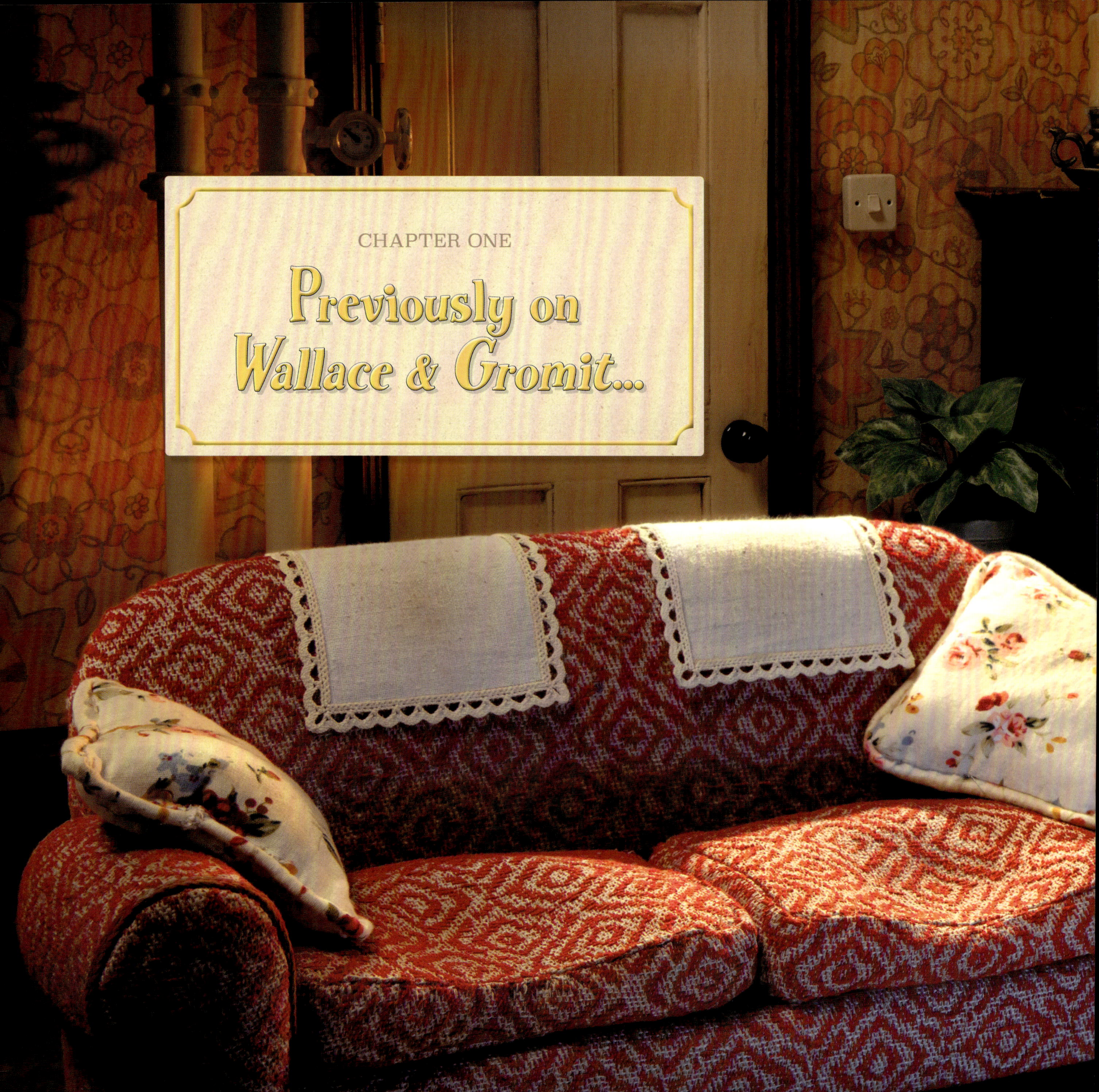

CHAPTER ONE

Previously on
Wallace & Gromit...

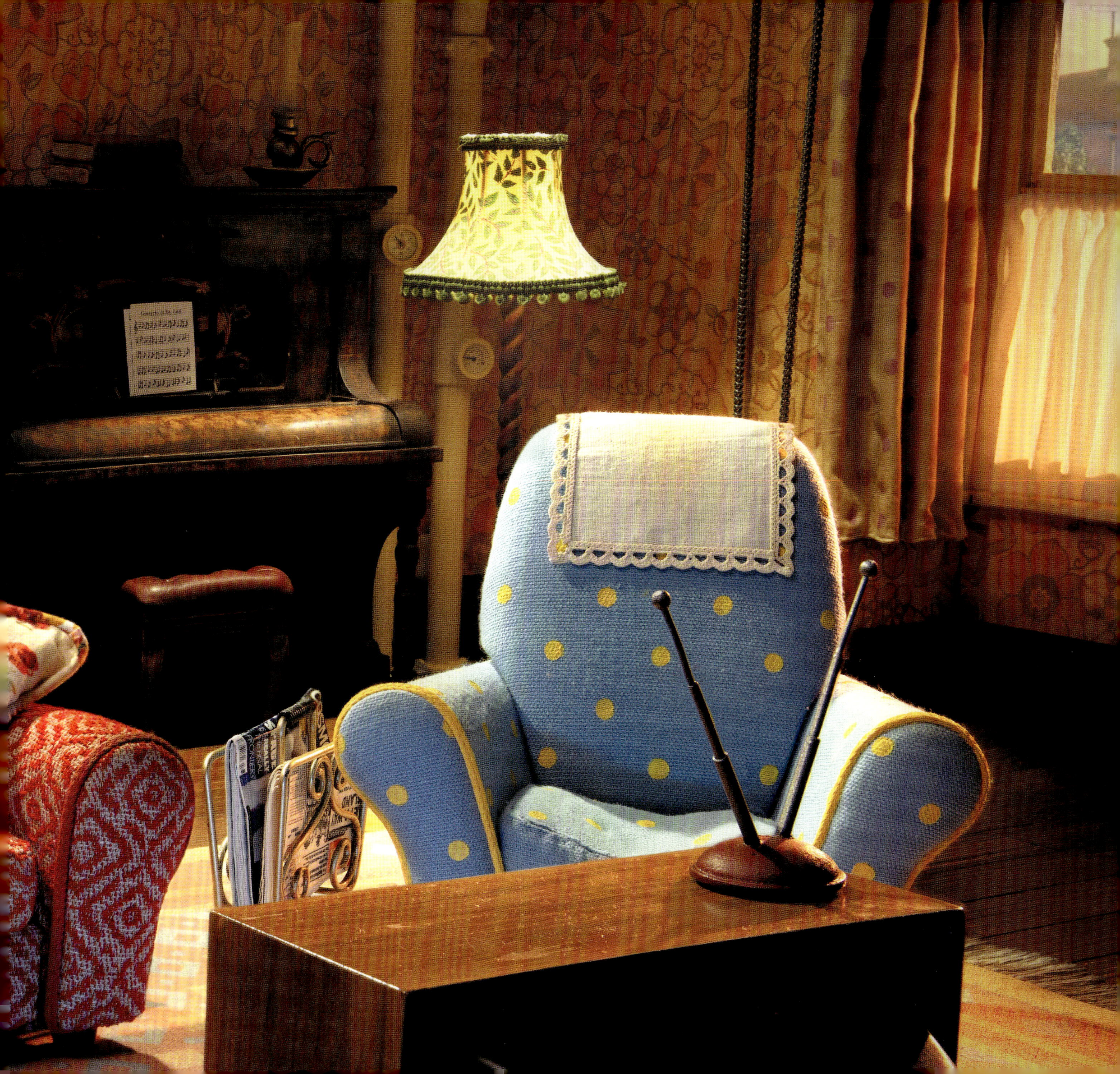

Previously on Wallace & Gromit...

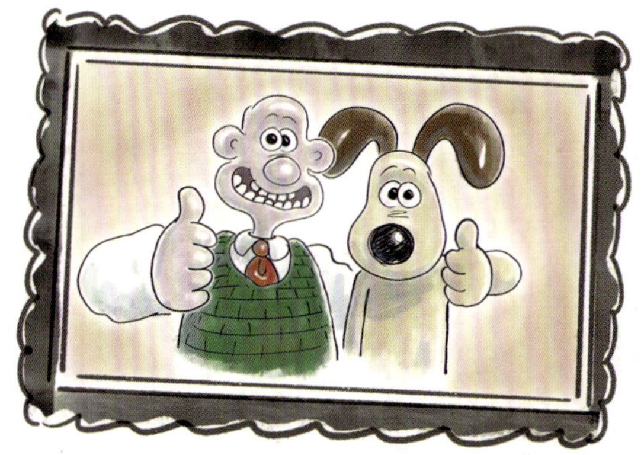

IT SCARCELY SEEMS POSSIBLE, BUT THE premiere of *Wallace & Gromit: Vengeance Most Fowl* comes more than four decades after Nick Park sculpted his first Gromit out of modelling clay. Although *A Grand Day Out* did not premiere until 1989, it began life as a student film eight years earlier when Nick was at the National Film and Television School in Beaconsfield. Its ambitious scale meant that he hadn't finished it when he graduated, so Peter Lord and David Sproxton of Aardman Animations invited him to join their staff,

enabling him to complete it at their Bristol studios while working around other projects. Peter Sallis, the voice of Wallace, famously recalled getting a phone call from Nick many years after he recorded the script, saying "I finished it!"

Its broadcast on Channel 4 in 1990 led to a rapturous reception (including a nomination for an Academy Award® for Best Animated Short Film, only losing out to Nick's other entry that year, *Creature Comforts*), which resulted in Colin Rose at the BBC's animation unit

Above | The Claymation couple as they appear today in an early example from Nick Park's sketch book...

Below far left | ...and in a recent publicity still for *Vengeance Most Fowl*.

Below left | An early sketch by Merlin Crossingham for Wallace's ever-adaptable end-of-terrace.

Opposite | Original concept art for *A Grand Day Out*, which shows Wallace sporting a 'tache and Gromit carrying a few extra pounds.

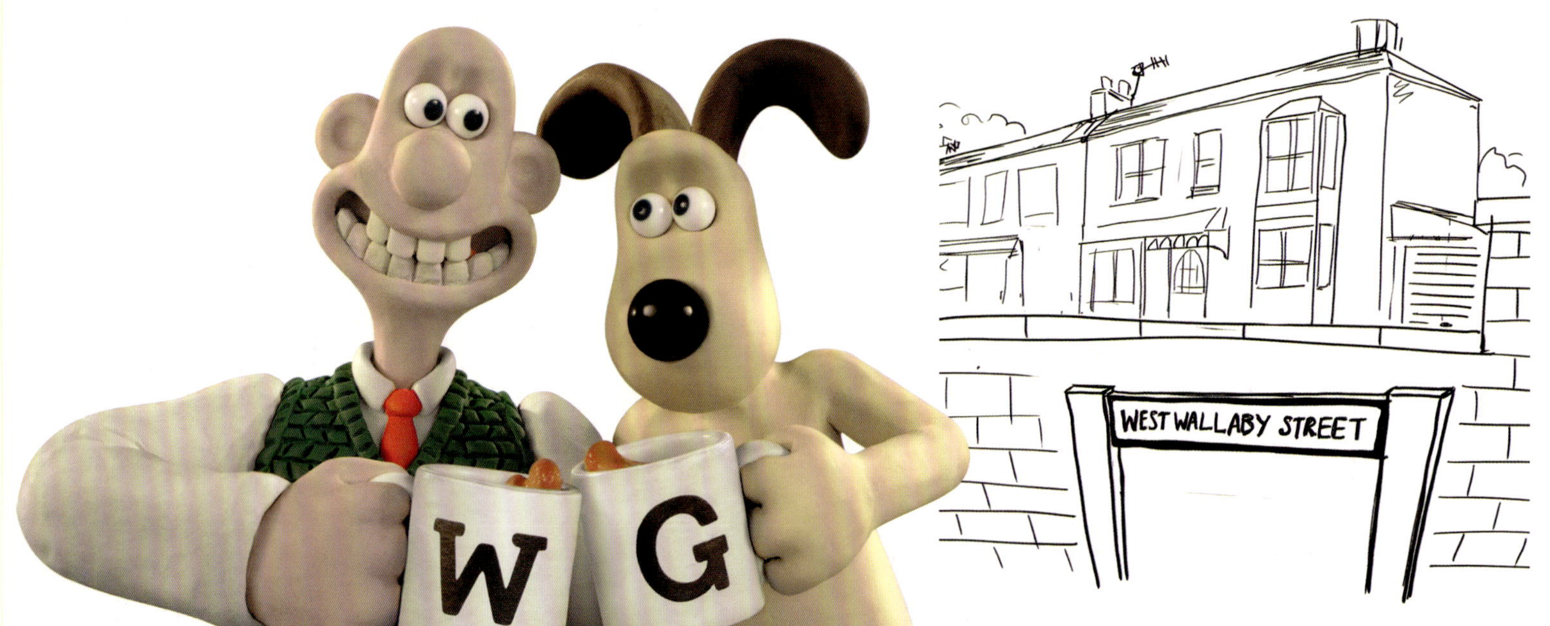

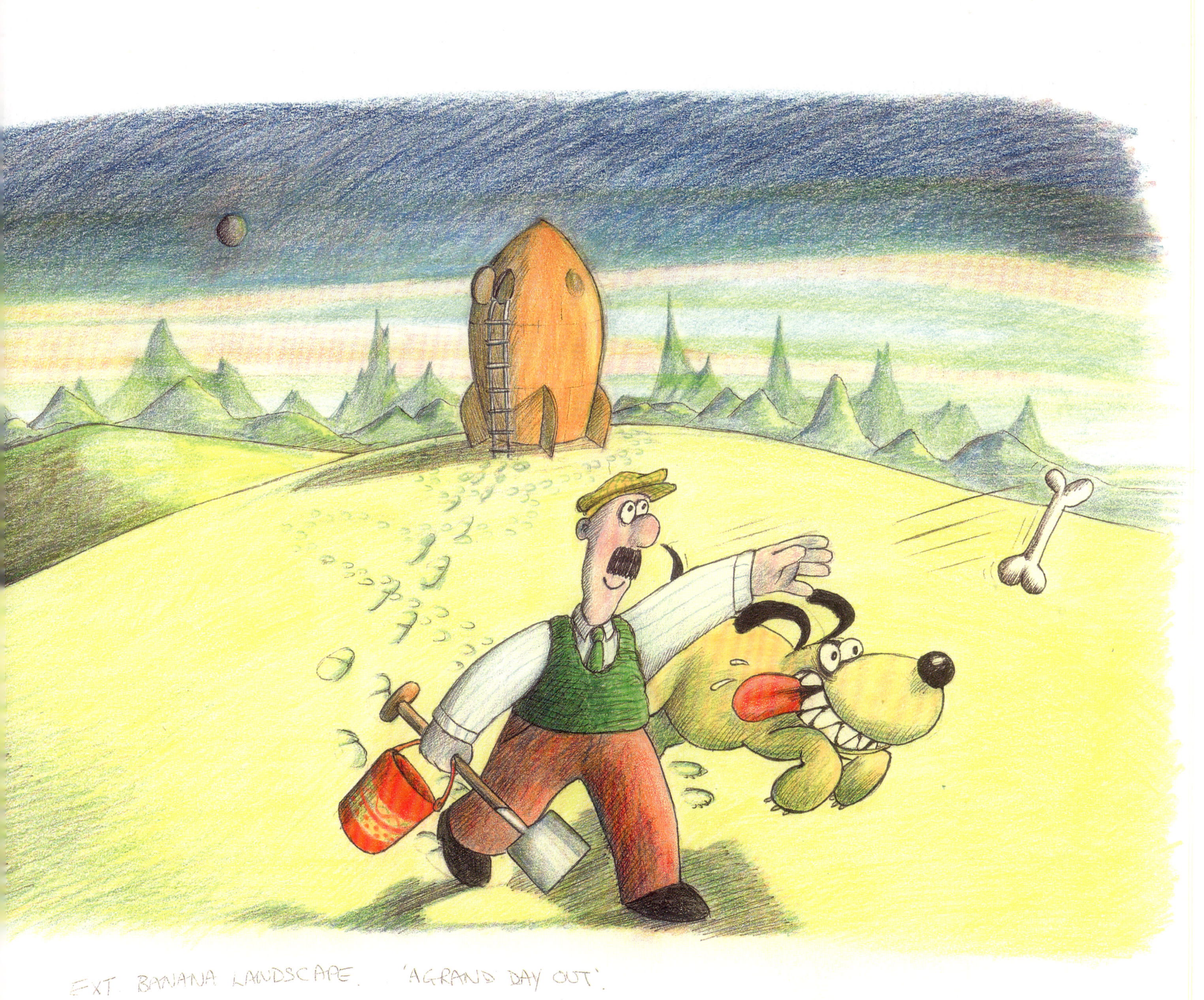

EXT. BANANA LANDSCAPE.   'A GRAND DAY OUT'.

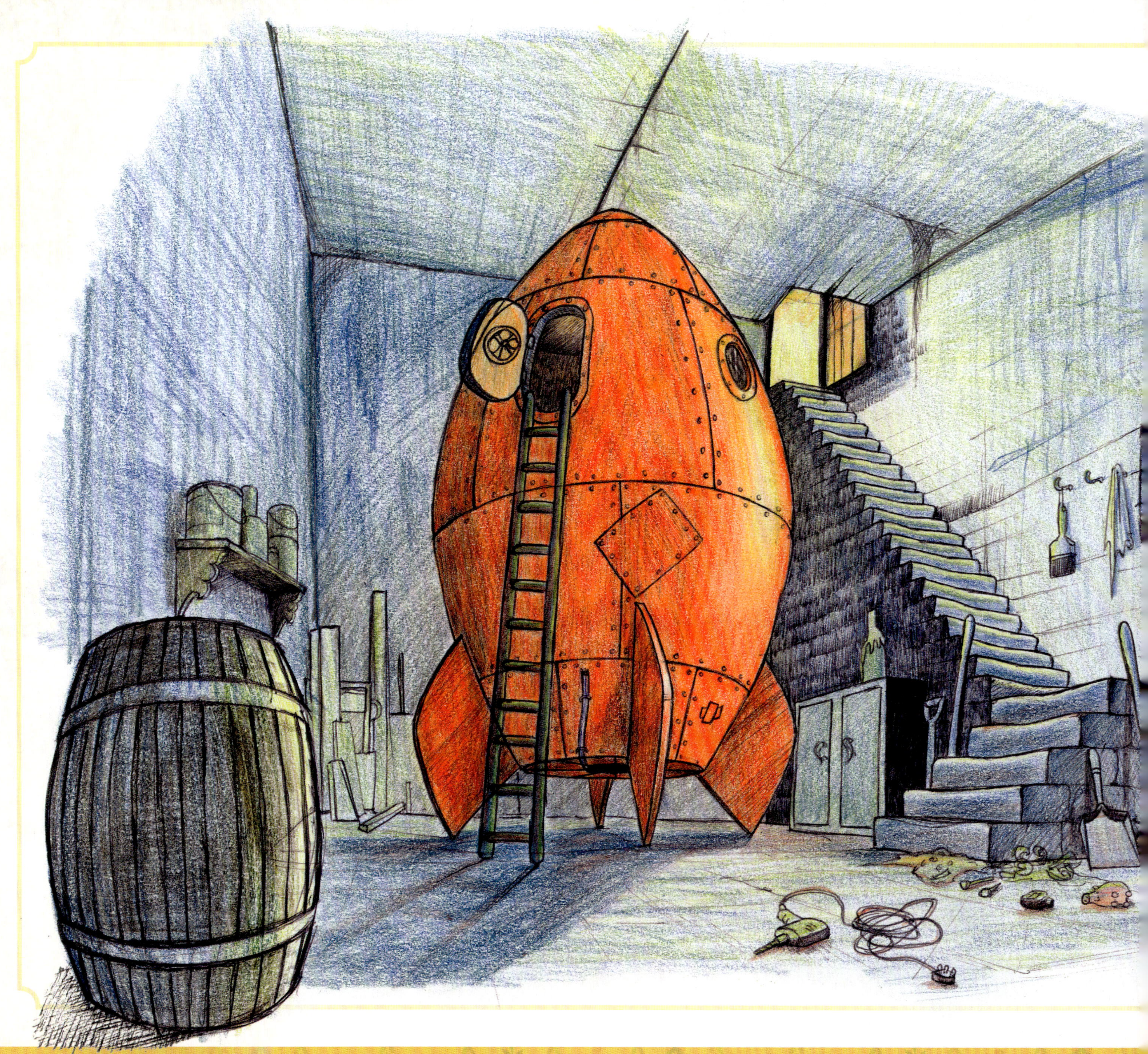

commissioning two follow-up half-hour films, *The Wrong Trousers* (1993) and *A Close Shave* (1995), both of which took Oscar® gold. Needless to say, this brought Aardman's work to the attention of the major Hollywood studios, and a production deal was signed with DreamWorks Animation. This led to a brief diversion into the world of poultry with *Chicken Run* in 2000, before Nick revisited one man and his dog with the feature film *Curse of the Were-Rabbit* (2005), nabbing another Academy Award®, this time in the recently created Best Animated Feature category.

The dauntless duo returned to the short film format and the BBC in 2008 with *A Matter of Loaf and Death*, its Christmas Day broadcast achieving an audience of over 14 million, the most watched TV programme in the UK that year, and Wallace and Gromit continued to entertain audiences in their own documentary series and a plethora of adverts, computer games, exhibitions and theme park rides, even making an appearance at the classical Proms concerts at the Royal Albert Hall. But *Vengeance Most Fowl* marks their first full adventure in over 15 years.

So how did Nick feel returning to his earliest creations after such a long break? "It's like I've never been away," he says. "It's like working with your children, but they're a bit more grown up now! It's great to be working with the old team – the characters, as well as the team in the studio."

And that team has grown exponentially over the years. One person who has been involved from the earliest days is cinematographer Dave Alex Riddett, who remembers hanging some lights for the moon scenes in *A Grand Day Out*, although his first official role was on *The Wrong Trousers*. "Most of the time there were only six people on the studio floor," he recalls, "two of us doing camera, two people animating, a production manager and somebody doing props." But producer Richard 'Beeky' Beek is now helming a crew of around 250 for the new movie, with 40 units and around 25 animators, producing a total of 1,339 shots at the rate of approximately 5 seconds of footage per animator per week, while juggling a budget exponentially larger than that of the early half-hours. Production has moved from Aardman's Gas Ferry Road HQ on the Bristol docks (a barely refurbished banana warehouse when *The Wrong Trousers* was shot) to a vast studio at Aztec West (Aztec being an industrial estate on the outskirts of the city, and not a tribute to Mesoamerican culture…)

Whereas most of the team back in the 1980s were very much 'Jacks of all trades', handling

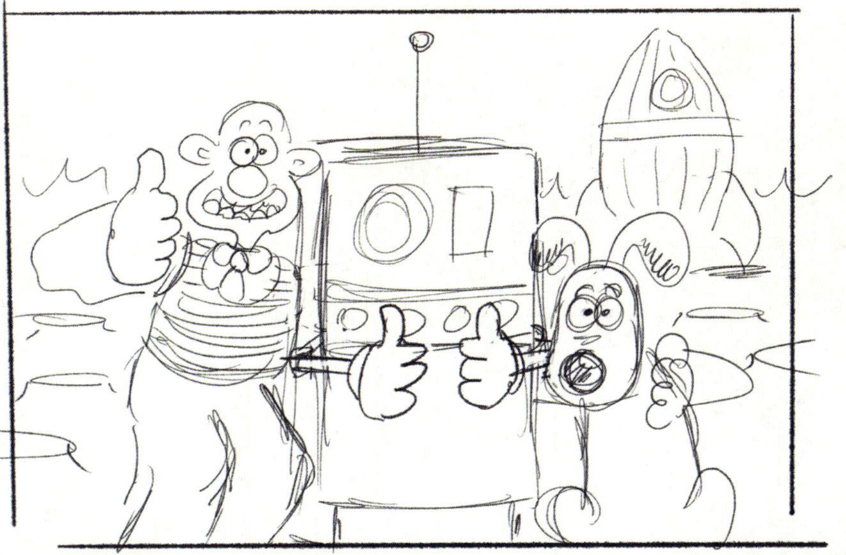

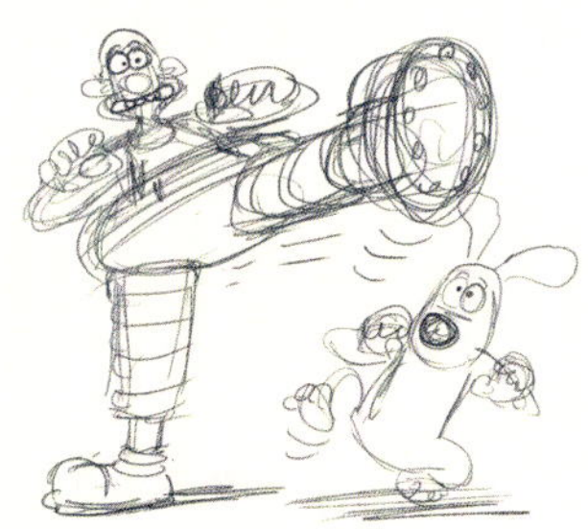

animation, sculpting, prop making and lighting (while farming out some of the bigger tasks like set-building to other local firms), Beeky is now in charge of multiple specialised departments: "We have the production team, the story team, editorial team, puppets, art, animation, rigging, technical team, which then breaks down into camera, lighting, motion control, the CG team, and within the CG team there are sub departments as well – compositing, visual effects, previz… 250 feels like a lot of people, but in terms of Hollywood animation it's nothing. Our credits will probably be five minutes, whereas with most movies from major studios, theirs will be fifteen!"

In this book, we'll be looking at the work of all these departments and what each of them brings to the unique art and craft of *Wallace & Gromit: Vengeance Most Fowl*.

When first conceived, the story was planned as another Christmas half-hour special for the BBC focusing purely on Wallace's latest invention. But as the plot developed and Nick decided to combine it with another idea exploring aspects of the series' history, it expanded into 70 minutes duration. The resulting film manages to combine the cosy homeliness of the TV half-hours and the epic Hollywood scale of *Curse of the Were-Rabbit*: "In terms of its ambition, it's closer to the movie than one of the TV specials," explains executive producer Carla Shelley. "It's still got what's at the heart of all the films, that character relationship and the fun you can have with them, but the chase sequences, all the action events, you can dial up those according to your budget."

From an opening that recalls the domestic eccentricity of *The Wrong Trousers* and *A Close Shave*, the scale of the film expands to include massive set-pieces that could not have been achieved within the half-hour format. "That's very much by design," explains Merlin Crossingham, Nick's directing partner. "Wallace

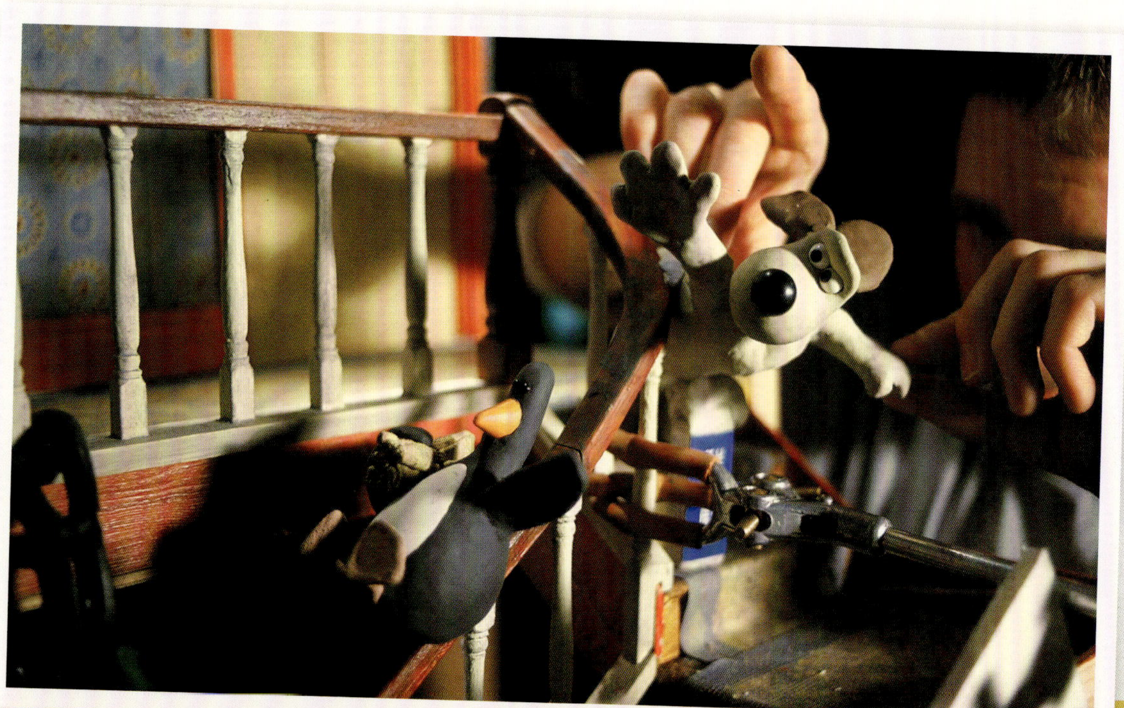

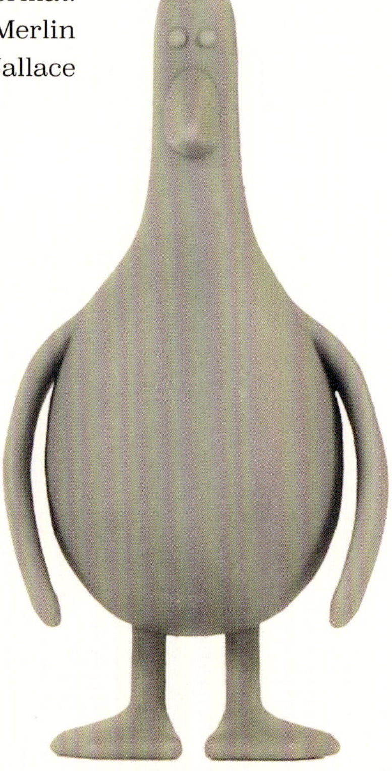

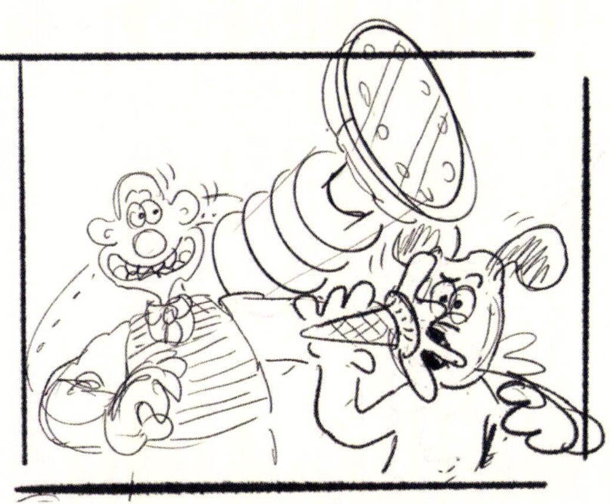

lives in a terraced house in a nondescript place up north, but from this 'normal' kind of place come these crazy inventions. We very much wanted to have a film that was paced with a fairly slow, benign beginning, and grew into something absolutely ridiculous come the end."

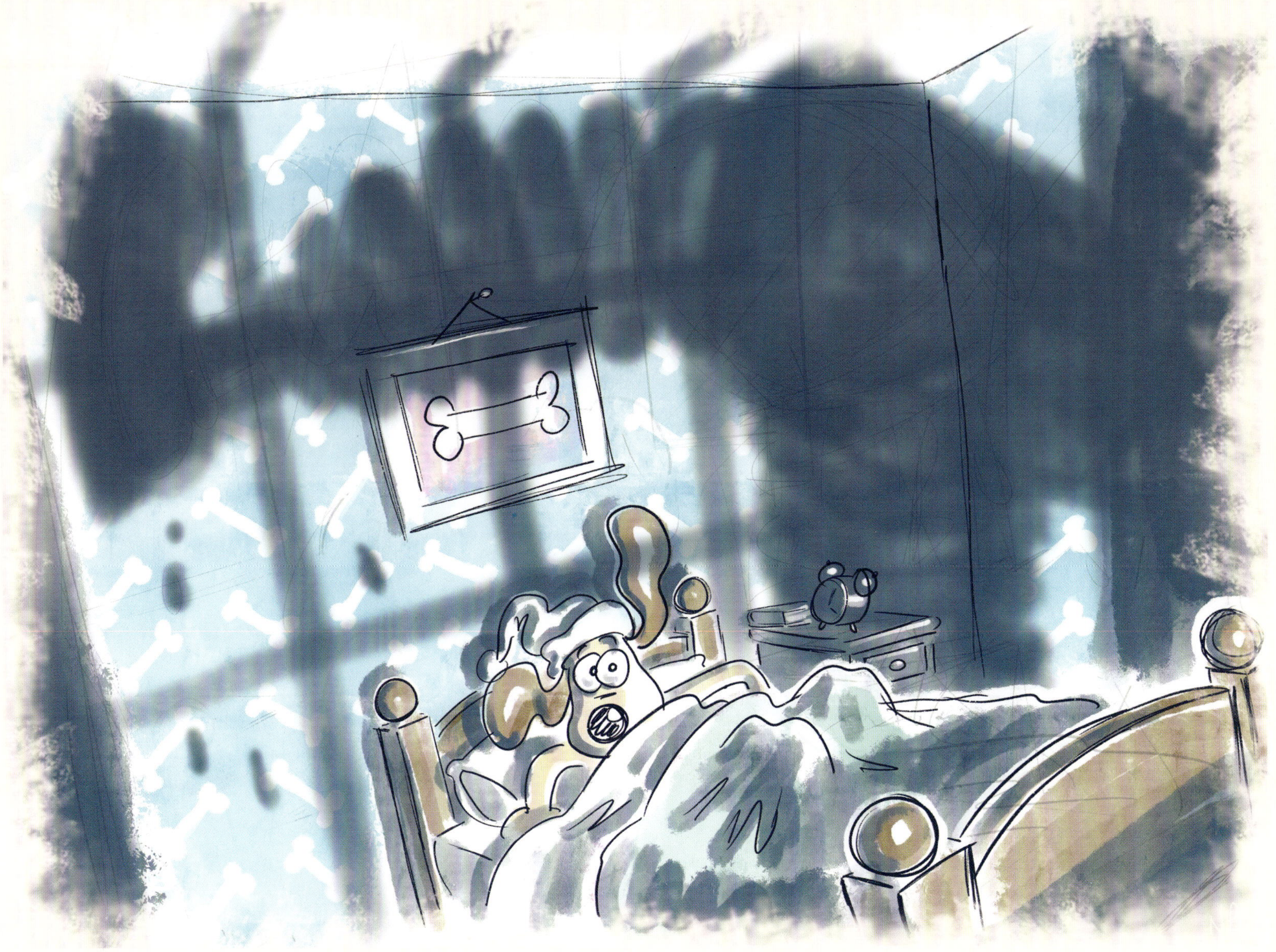

The decision to expand the running time coincided with streaming giant Netflix coming on board as co-financier. "We'd had a really good relationship with them on *Chicken Run:*

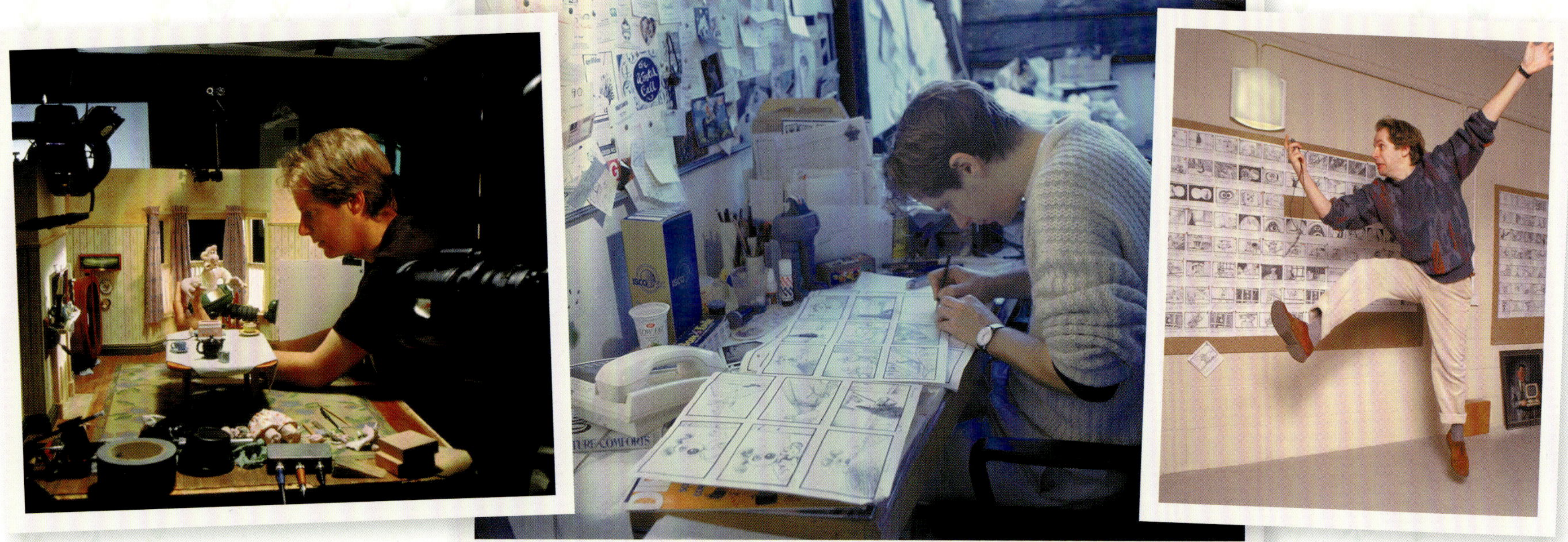

Dawn of the Nugget," recalls Carla, "and it just felt like a natural transition to be working with them on *Wallace & Gromit*."

"In a way it was liberating," agrees Nick. "Now we don't have to watch every single frame count or how many shots because they're open to any length when it's screened."

Not that the transatlantic relationship has been without its confusions. "We had a notes meeting," recalls producer Beeky, "and one of the questions was 'What's a 'Flippin' Nora?'. 'Bog chain' as well… there was a long conversation about people not knowing what a bog chain was. The idea of an outside toilet with a drop-flush was so alien to them. You have to be aware that it's going to be seen around the world, but it's important that it doesn't lose its identity. It's British, it's *Wallace & Gromit*. So the bog chain is still in there visually, but it's not referenced directly as a bog chain!"

As with most of Nick's feature-length projects, he is sharing the director's role, having previously collaborated with Peter Lord on *Chicken Run* and Steve Box on *Curse of the Were-Rabbit*. "It's hard to direct a film of this size on your own," he observes. "It's such an enormous long-haul slog, so it's great to have someone to share that journey." This time his directing partner is Merlin Crossingham, a senior animator at Aardman since *Chicken Run* and more recently animation director on *Wallace & Gromit's World of Invention* and *Early Man*, who has been working as creative director of the *Wallace & Gromit* brand for the last ten years.

"I've been in that role since about 2009," recalls Merlin. "Nick wanted to free his brain up for other things and would ask me to step in and look after this little project or could I direct this commercial. That grew to the point where he wanted to formalise the relationship so he could do things like *Early Man*, and we needed creative oversight over projects like *World of Inventions*, the BBC Prom concert (which was live-event TV with animation). We did a roller coaster in Blackpool, we were going off in so many different directions it needed to have a creative focal point. It's become a great working relationship where Nick still has control over what happens to Wallace and Gromit as the kingpin, for want of a better word, and then once he's signed off the concept of a project I will take it on. It doesn't mean I direct everything, but it means if someone else is I will take on more of an exec role."

"It's great to have someone on board who's so full of energy and knows the characters so well," says Nick, "because Merlin has a lot of history with Wallace and Gromit. Before this he was always a top animator who I always liked to work with. I think it's worked out very well and we shared the vision for the film very much. We worked on it extensively together and with Mark [Burton, Nick's co-writer] developing the script and the storyboards. We're constantly presenting scenes to each other and getting notes back. A lot of it is trying to make the whole thing come together as one. It's like building bridges from two ends – we have to make sure we meet in the middle."

"We are directing half the scenes each, pretty much," adds Merlin. "We make sure we meet every day and talk through what we're doing so we're both making the same film. And we make sure we talk to the people that are doing it. When we go into a set visit or a pre-production meeting or when we talk to the art department, we get asked constant questions, so it's decision, decision, decision."

Was it a difficult task to choose who got to direct which scene? "I love all the scenes," says Nick, "but it's worked out very well. We both first of all said, 'What scenes do we really want to do? Which scenes do we have a real vision for, that we would be miserable if we didn't do?' Then there were a lot of scenes which we didn't care about so much but were happy to take, and we both put full energy and focus into making those scenes work."

This movie also allowed Nick to explore some new aspects of the Wallace and Gromit relationship. "Part of the vision for this was that it's an existential crisis for Wallace and Gromit – which it always is a bit, I suppose. A schism develops between the pair; the premise is about

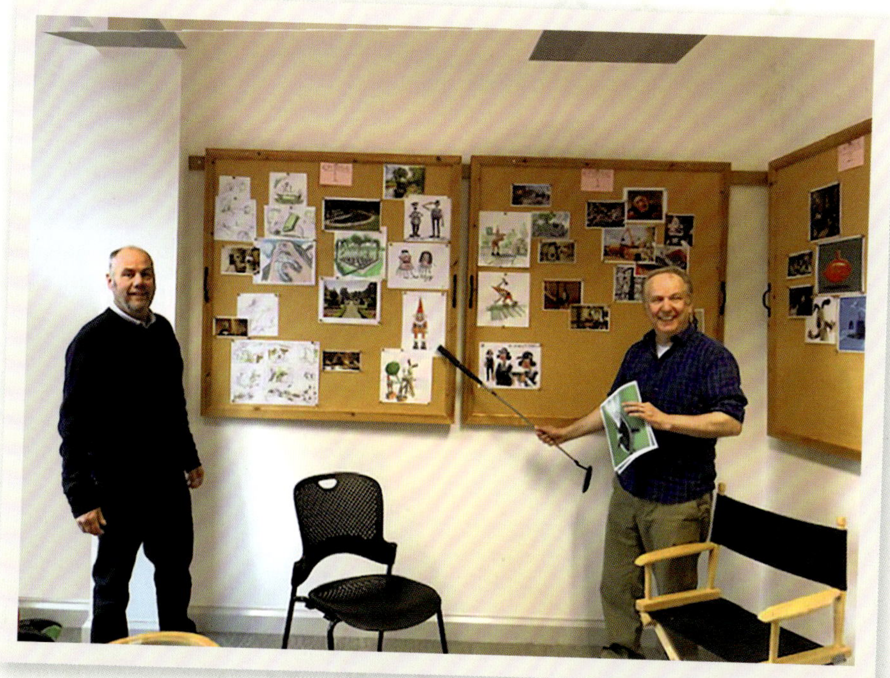

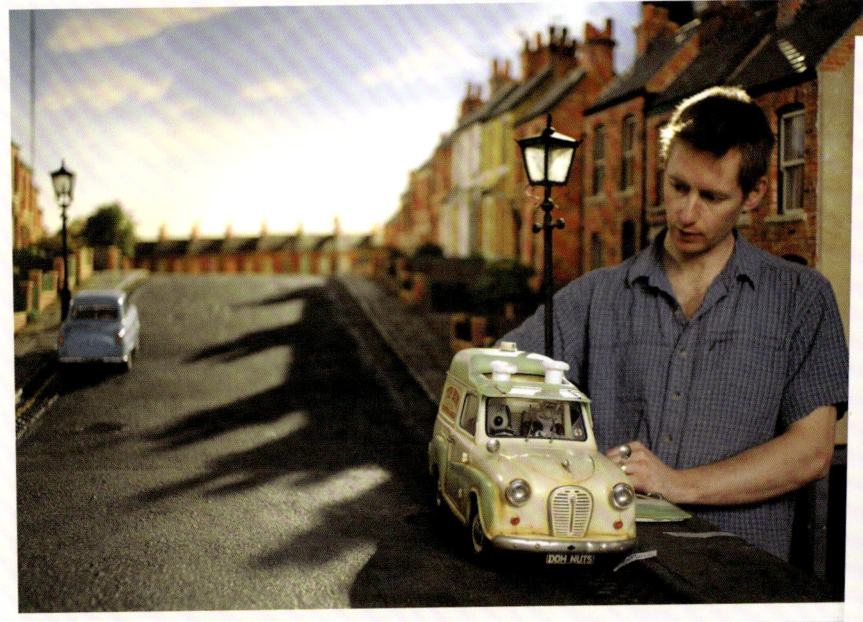

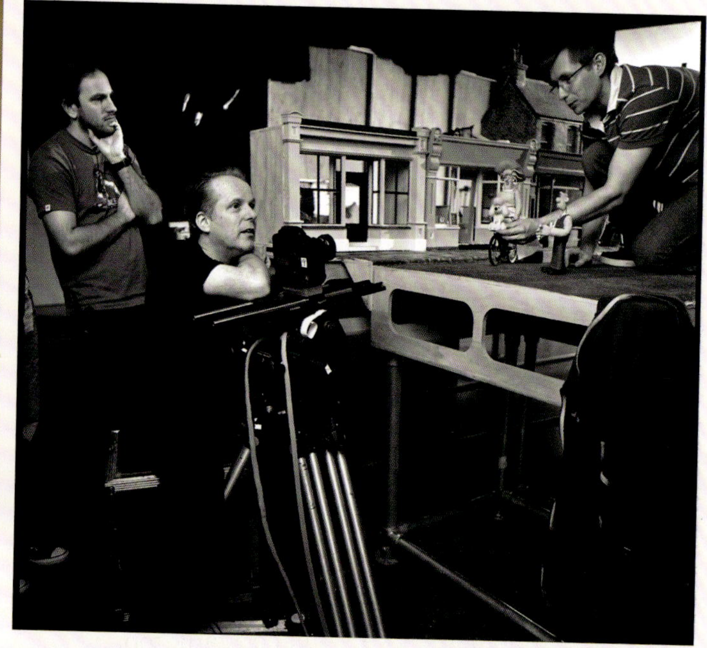

how Wallace's technology is running their lives and it's coming between them. Norbot replacing Gromit and the Norbots getting hacked are the worst thing that could happen, but it turns out to be the best thing because it brings Wallace and Gromit together again through the struggle."

The development phase turned out to be longer than anticipated due to the Covid lockdown in 2020 and 2021. While the impact was greater on *Chicken Run: Dawn of the Nugget*, which was in the studio at the time, the knock-on effect meant that *Vengeance Most Fowl* could not go into production when originally planned. But the creative team agree this worked to the project's advantage: "Normally on a feature film," explains Nick, "the financiers want to get it into production as soon as you've got the vaguest script. It's always felt like being Gromit on the train in *The Wrong Trousers* where you're manically putting down track in front of the train – it's one big scramble and you're trying to re-write scenes while filming other scenes. The delays helped us get much further on with the development – and it was great to do that with the luxury of not actually sitting on the speeding train!"

Nick spent the lockdown in his home town of Preston, so new ways of working remotely had to be devised, one of the most significant of which was his adopting digital sketching rather than pencil and paper. "That was a lifesaver for me," he recalls. "I was able to get on with sketching and designing and thumbnailing storyboards on my tablet, and I could communicate scenes directly to the story artists. Just being able to do things off the top of my head and email them to the relevant people – the sets to the art department or the character designs to the puppet department – that was very

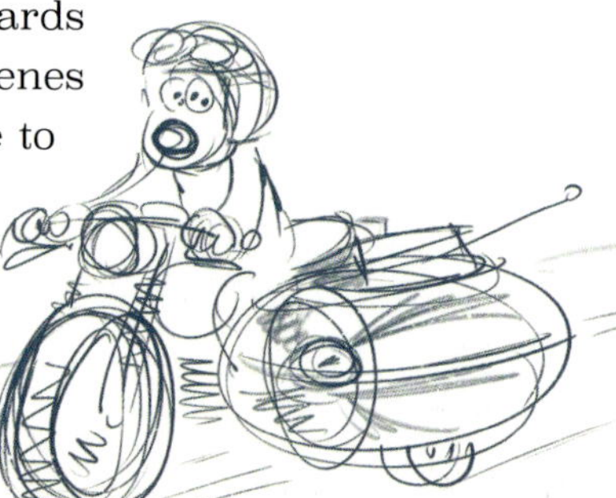

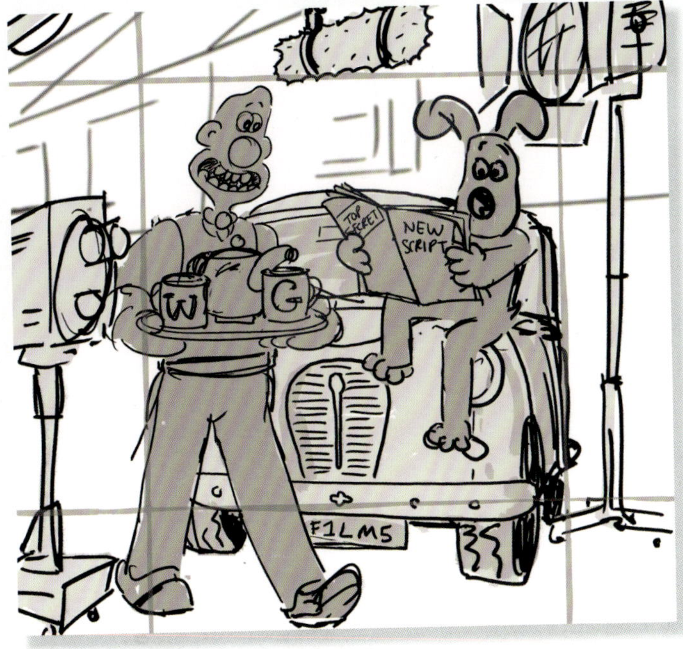

Above | Merlin Crossingham sketch idea for announcing the start of production.

Right | Nick's sketch of Wallace at the control desk for his Gnoming Device.

handy. It was a bit of a learning curve, but it's very user-friendly so I adapted quite quickly. The only downside is that it isn't on paper – the original doesn't ever really exist!"

Work on the story reel also started during lockdown. The storyboards are edited together with 'scratch' performances of the dialogue, often performed by various members of the crew, and the editor puts these together into an 'animatic'. "As soon as we've got a script that we're fairly happy with," explains Nick, "we try to get the whole reel up as the next stage, even if there's still tons that needs sorting out. We worked on it for around a year before production started, but it was by no means finished. We are constantly working up scenes to a finer degree while we're shooting, where we can improve things or make a joke better; it's an ongoing process."

Merlin found remote working far from ideal: "It was very peculiar, and I didn't like it really.

It's the subtleties in the room that make an idea trigger. While those things did happen online, it felt like you had to work harder for them. I think all of us agreed the days where we actually met [up], we moved on much further than on the days we spent together on screen." But the delays did have their upside: "We had Act Three! We started the film knowing the film we wanted to make, and so often I've been involved in projects where that's not the case. We didn't necessarily have it all boarded, but we knew what we wanted to do and we knew where we needed to go. And it's not changed since then. The shots and the order of things has, but the core idea hasn't."

Vengeance Most Fowl also provided the opportunity to re-visit the design of the clay couple – although clay does not play such a large part in their construction these days.

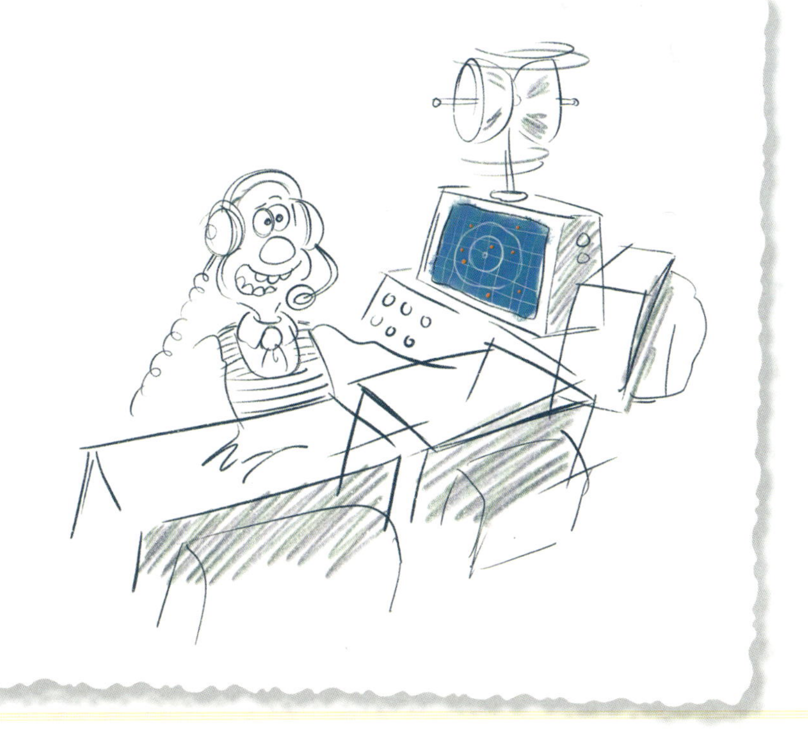

Aardman's traditional animation style is stop-motion (or Claymation as it's known in the US), which involves moving physical puppets incrementally through 12 shots per second, which when speeded up gives the illusion of real movement. Clay puppets lend Aardman's characters their classic home-made look, with the animators' thumbprints intentionally visible in the material. But it's a labour of love and a very time-consuming process to animate them, so any developments that can make things faster are enthusiastically embraced. Steel armatures inside the puppets have been used for several decades now, making them more resilient and easier to pose, while hard resin was introduced for elements like Wallace's tank top.

Head of Puppets Anne King explains: "Originally, all the *Wallace & Gromit* puppets were clay, but the problem is that it's very slow to work with. On the studio floor it takes a lot of sculpting, and for us in model-making it means we have to constantly maintain it. With Gromit, if it's a full clay puppet, you're always pressing out new bits, the animators use them, bring them back, we have to strip it down, re-press it, send it out again, then they have to sculpt it. So on this film we've worked to minimise the amount of clay and go more towards using silicon puppets, just to help that speed of animation." All in all the team produces around 15 Wallace puppets and 20 Gromits, which cover four different variations: a four-legged version, a standing version, a squatted version and a seated version.

There are subtle variations in the design from previous films too – Wallace's tank top is slightly shorter, while his legs are less skinny. With Gromit there has been a minimal change to the shape of his muzzle, and the width of his head has been reduced by a few millimetres on either side. "In every film in the *Wallace & Gromit* canon there's been an evolution in their physical appearance," explains Merlin. "Partly on this film because material technology has evolved, we're using more silicon components than resin or clay. And the interior armatures are much more reliable and advanced. Not that you'd know that, but it does have an impact on

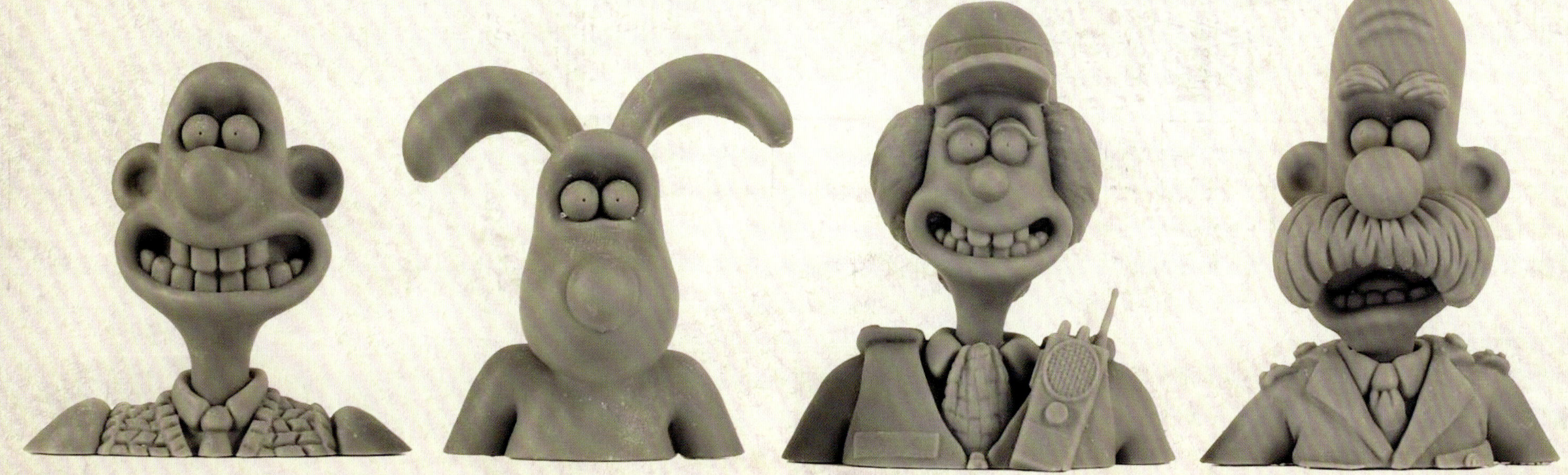

what you can do with the outside. It's not that it changes their DNA, these are minor evolutionary tweaks. The hands and the heads are still clay because they are the most expressive parts. If we could, we would do Gromit in clay the whole time, but the reality is that silicon for the most part looks as good and behaves just as well. The only reason we haven't done this before is that silicon technologies weren't up to it, but now you can see the thumbprints in the silicon from the master sculpt where the light catches it, and it looks great."

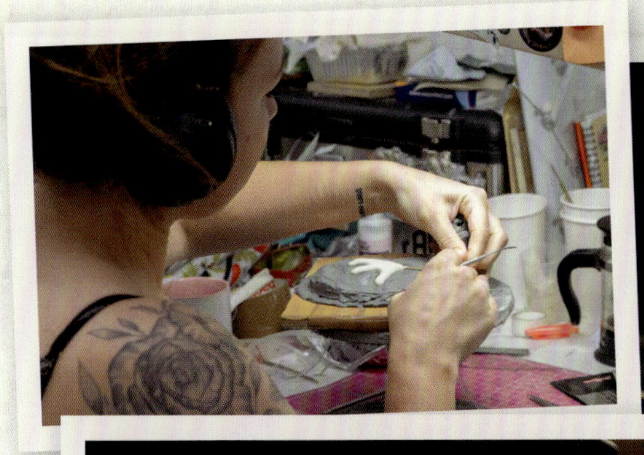

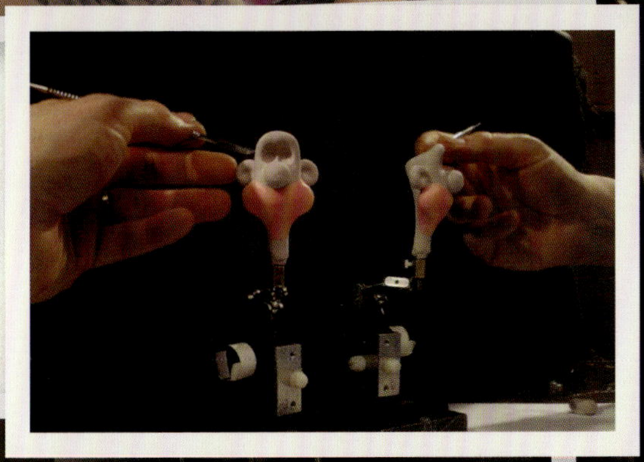

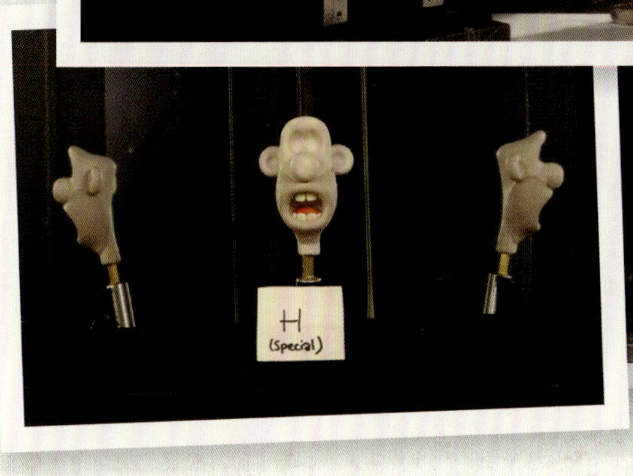

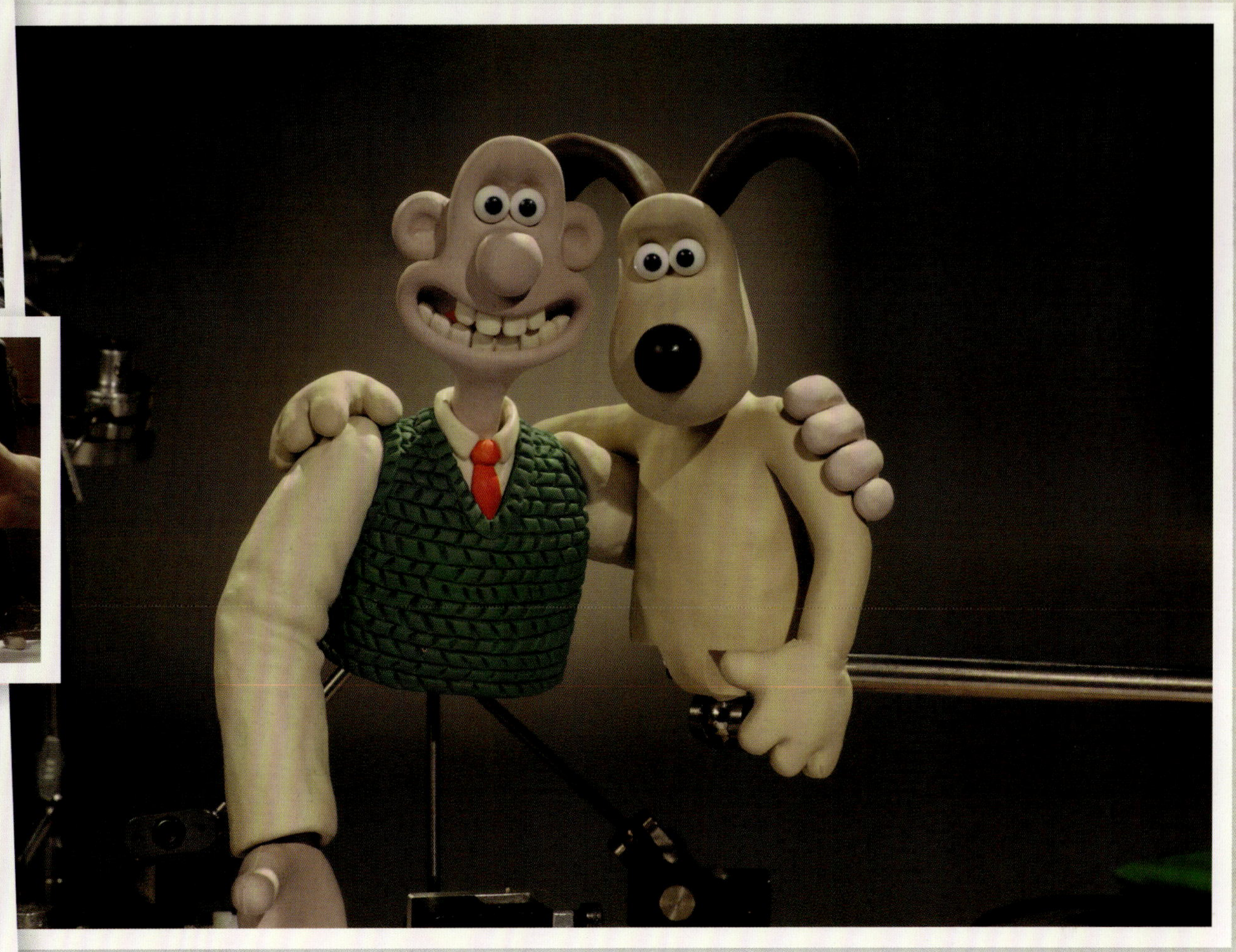

But the premiere of *Vengeance Most Fowl* also marks a couple of sadder milestones in the *Wallace & Gromit* story, with the passing of two key members of the creative team: Peter Sallis, the voice of Wallace from day one, and Bob Baker, Nick's co-writer since *The Wrong Trousers*.

Before agreeing to play Wallace for what was then just a student film, Peter Sallis was a renowned British character actor with credits ranging from all 295 episodes of the Yorkshire-based sitcom *Last of the Summer*

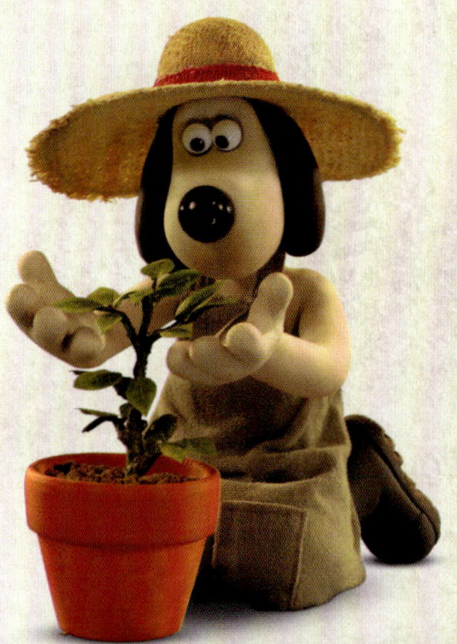

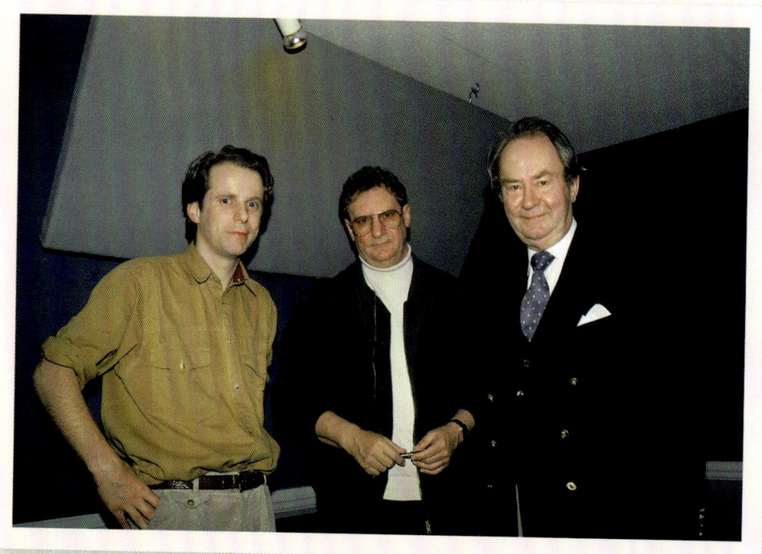

Wine to Hammer Horror films such as *Curse of the Werewolf*. "Peter was well loved by millions and so was in obvious ways a great loss," says Nick. "I remember one quote from a review of *Curse of the Were-Rabbit*: 'Peter Sallis's voice is as welcome as a pair of warm slippers in an uncertain world.' I know what they mean, it's got a cosiness and reassuring tone that takes you into a safe place. He was so much about what made *Wallace & Gromit*. Shortly before ill health meant he couldn't perform any more he said to me: 'It's been such a lovely thing for me. I thought my career was over and that was it really. It came in late in life, but it's been such a joy.' He would say great things like, 'You know, Nick, you can't script charm.' He was just a gem being on board, and when he passed away it all came back how much people appreciated what he brought. You can't really capture it or sum it up."

Despite coming to the role when he was in his sixties, Peter went on to play the part for nearly 30 years, and it often seemed like he would be irreplaceable. "But it was very fortuitous that we had Ben Whitehead," says Nick. "He came in to play one of the townspeople in *Curse of the Were-Rabbit* and sometimes we asked him to read in when Peter couldn't be there. So Ben started mimicking Peter's voice, and we thought 'Ooh, he's pretty good!' And then there were jobs that Peter was happy to pass on, like video games or sat-navs – 'Turn right in 40 metres!', millions of lines like that – so he let Ben do them. That's how it started." Ben went on to provide Wallace's voice for several commercials and spin-off projects, spending many hours in the recording studio with Nick and Merlin to capture the character accurately, with the result that most people don't hear a difference. Peter would undoubtedly be proud to see the baton passed on with such dedication.

Bob Baker was a writer based in the southwest of England, who cut his teeth on local productions such as *Thick as Thieves*, as well as being a regular writer on *Doctor Who* in the 1970s, where he created the Doctor's canine companion K9. He came on board to help Nick with the writing of *The Wrong Trousers* at the suggestion of Colin Rose of the BBC's animation unit, who described Bob's role as giving Nick the courage of his convictions, and the relationship continued on *A Close Shave*, *Curse of the Were-Rabbit* and *A Matter of Loaf and Death*. Nick greatly valued his contributions, particularly to Wallace's character: "There are certain phrases in *Wallace & Gromit* that are called 'Bobisms', things like 'No use prevaricating about the bush'. I think he made some of them up – when Wallace flies through the air he says 'Lummee day!'– I've never heard that said in the North before! It's a mixture of West Country and Northern. Because it was a different generation, I find that he had that

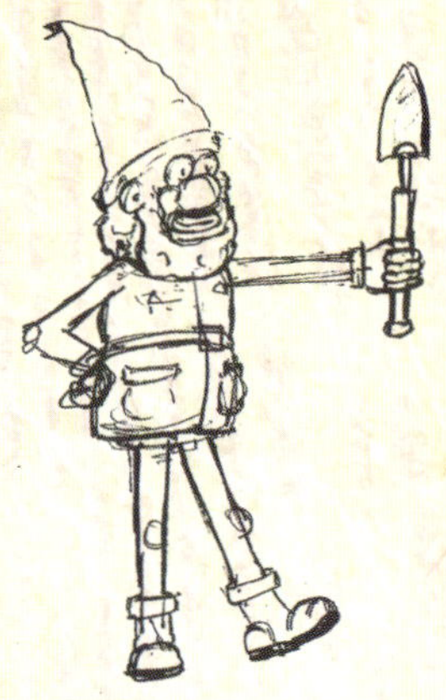

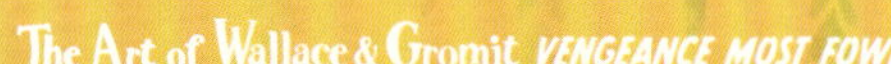

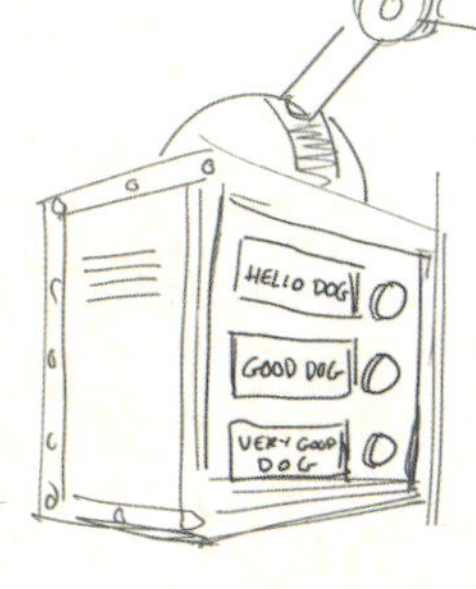

old-school, English way of writing and thinking that helped create the character and the world, giving it that more of that Ealing Comedy style." Bob was even immortalised as Baker Bob in the opening of *A Matter of Loaf and Death*, where he becomes the latest 'John Dough' victim in Piella's murder spree.

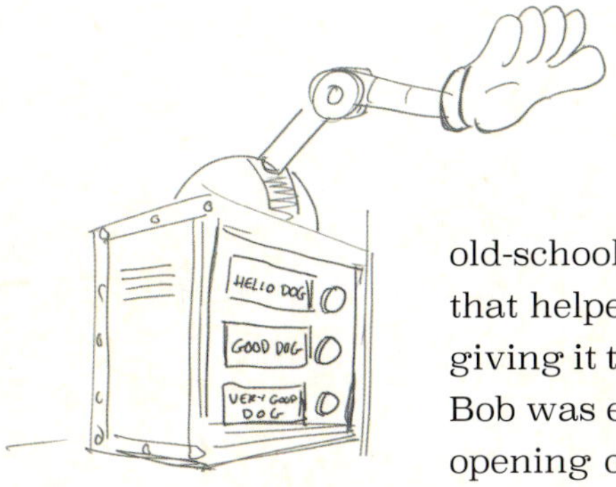

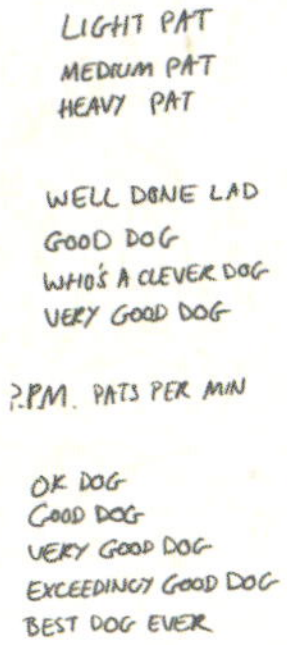

Nick's tradition of co-writing continues with Mark Burton, with whom he first collaborated back on the original *Chicken Run*. "Bob worked on the start of *Were-Rabbit* and Mark came in and helped with a lot of the story issues that we couldn't quite get, and he was good on the gags as well." Mark's relationship with Aardman continued over the *Shaun the Sheep* features, so he seemed a perfect fit to carry on the West Wallaby Street saga. But there are aspects of Wallace that will forever be a testament to Bob: "There was a certain kind of ear that he had," recalls Nick. "Like when Wallace was in trouble in the trousers, he'd say things like 'Good grief, whatever is it?' You don't say that, do you? Or 'I'll be calling my solicitor about that', phrases from the old movies which give a character and nostalgia to everything. Sometimes you can't quite remember who came up with which joke, but you probably came up with it together. It just happened as part of the collaboration, a symbiotic relationship."

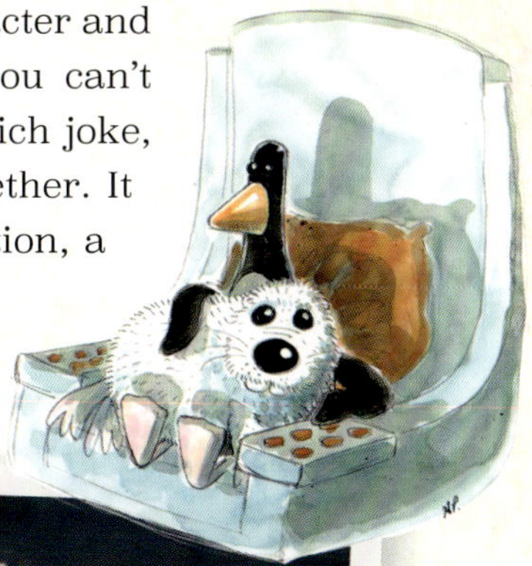

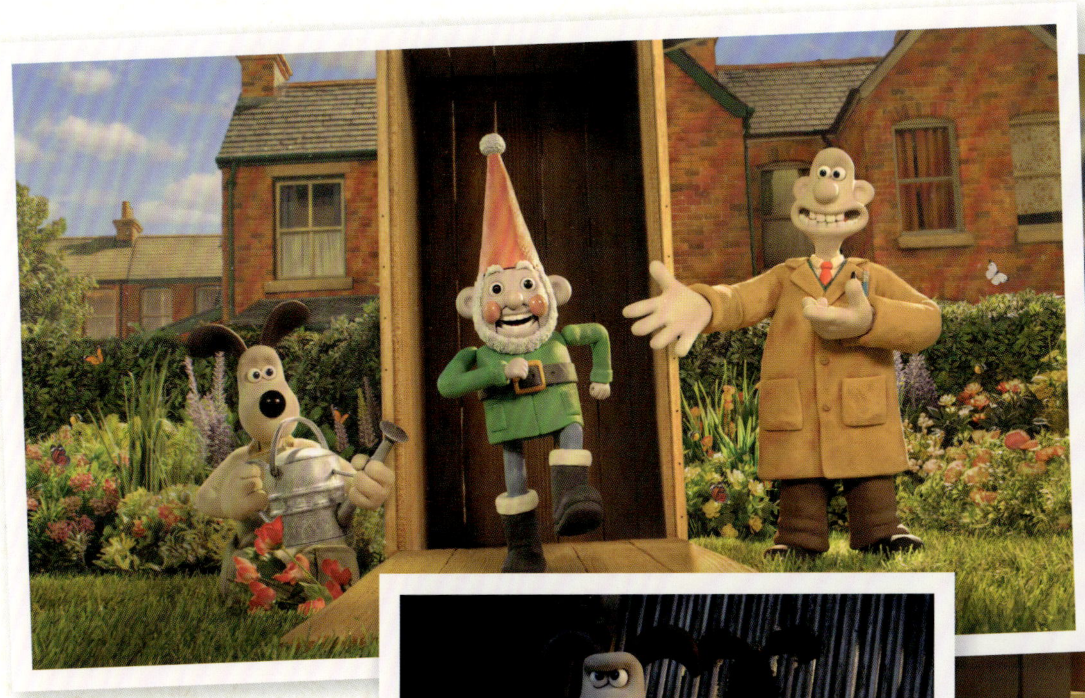

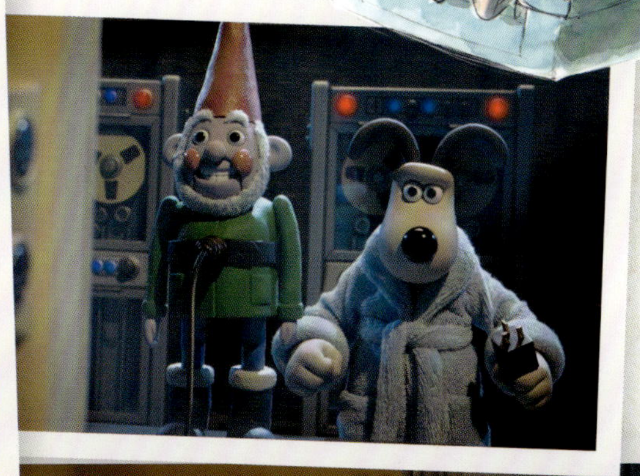

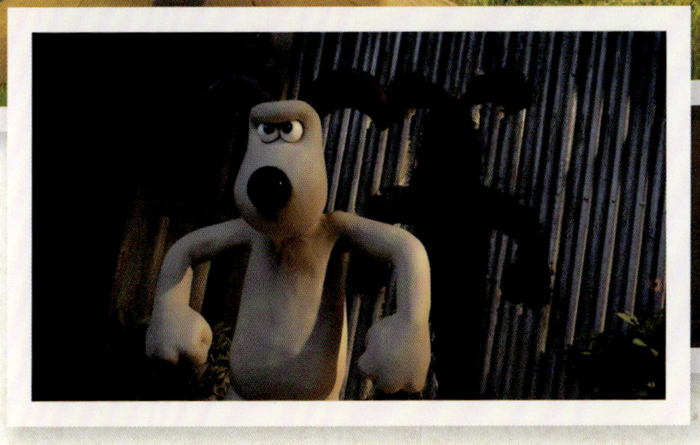

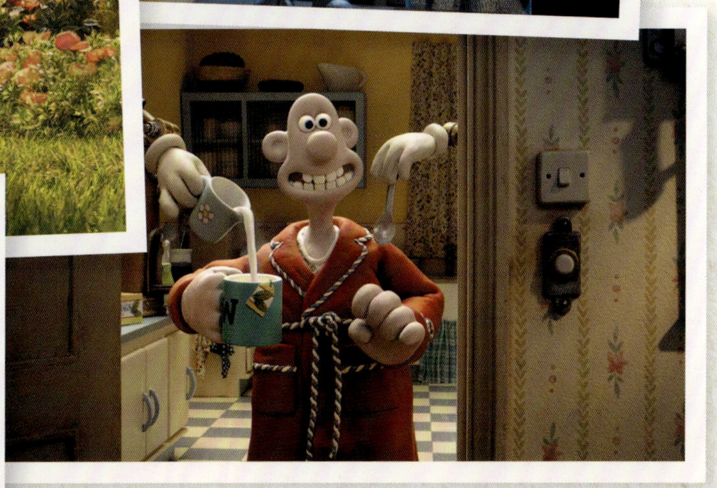

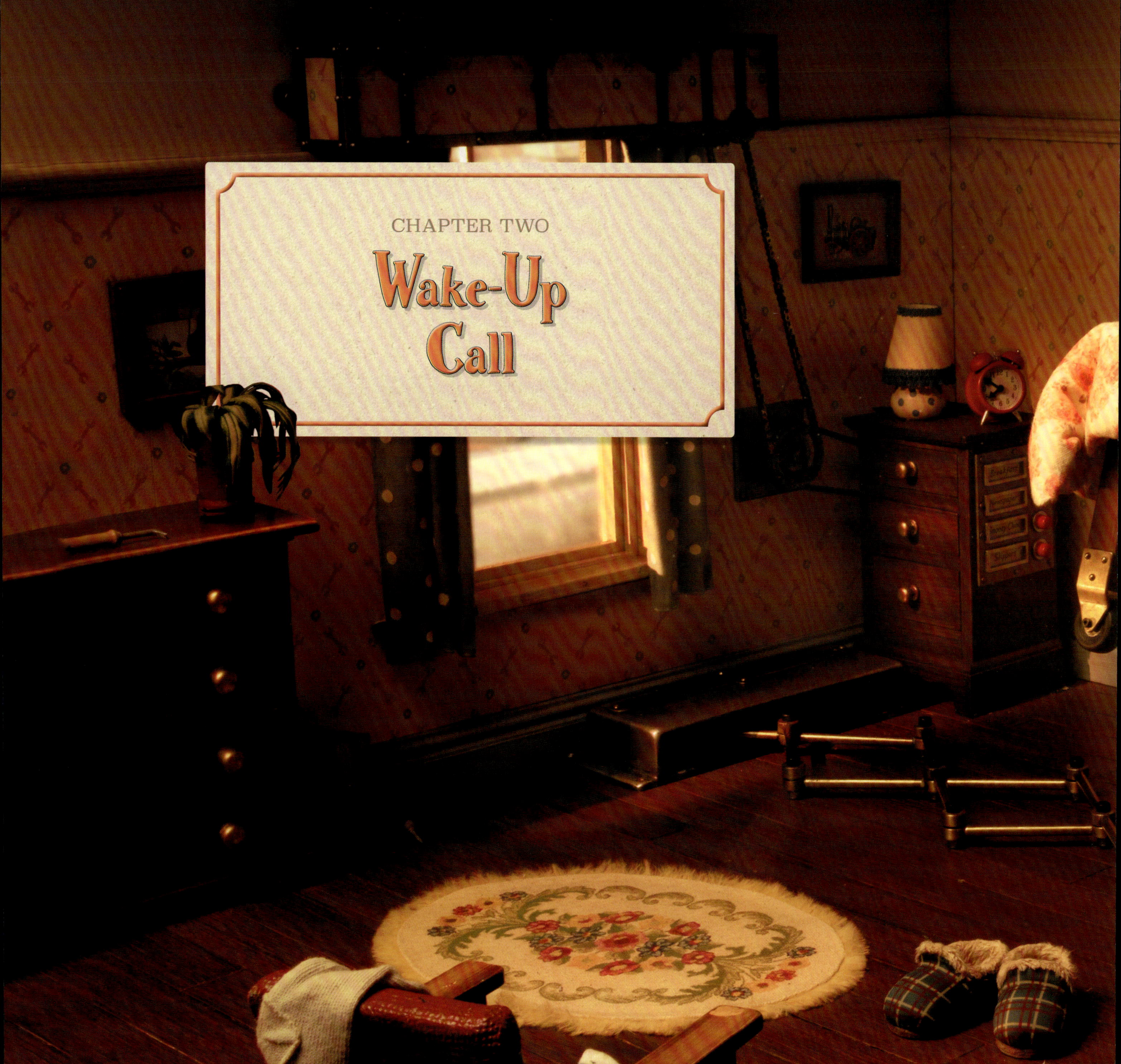

CHAPTER TWO
Wake-Up Call

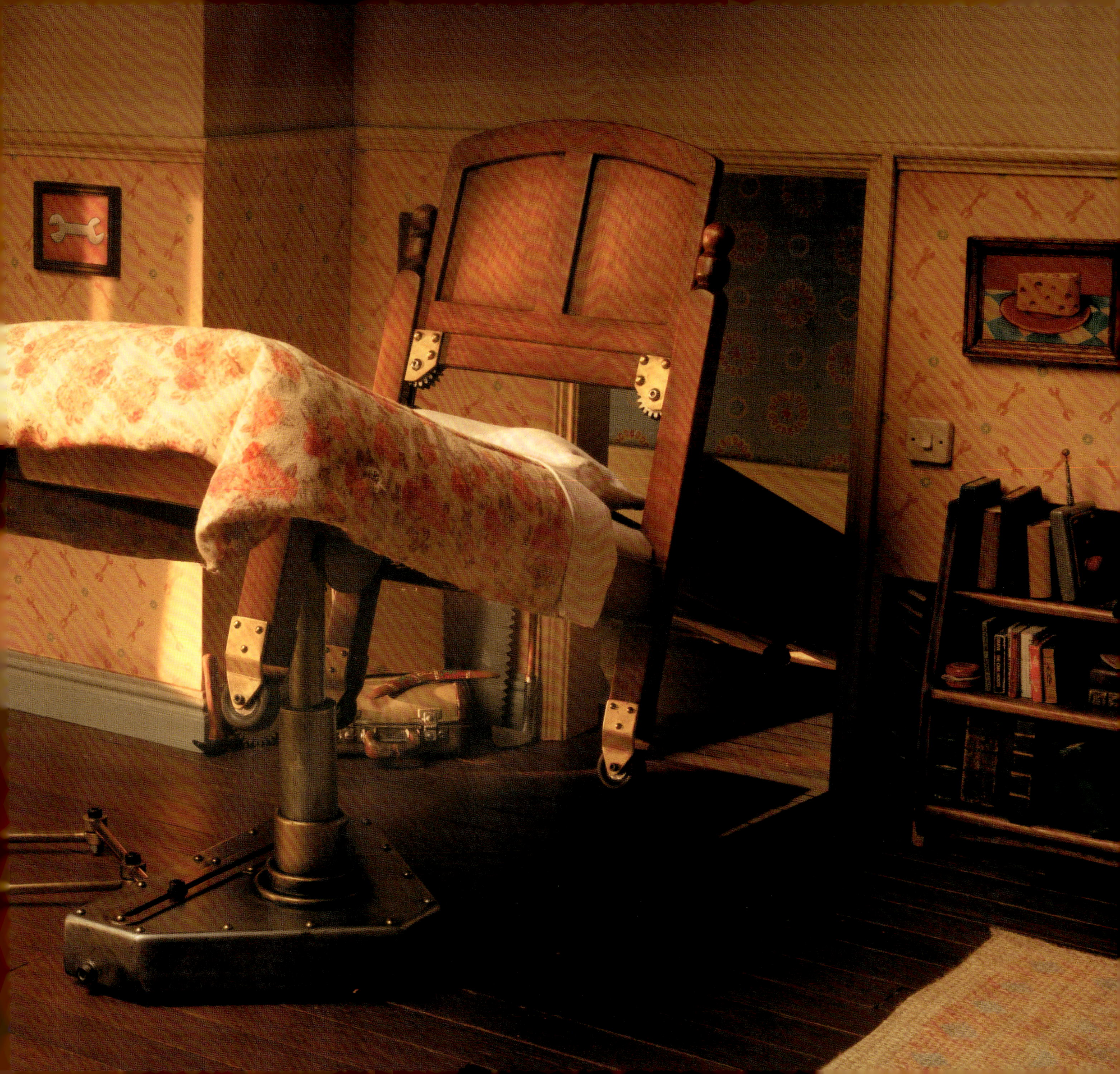

Wake-Up Call

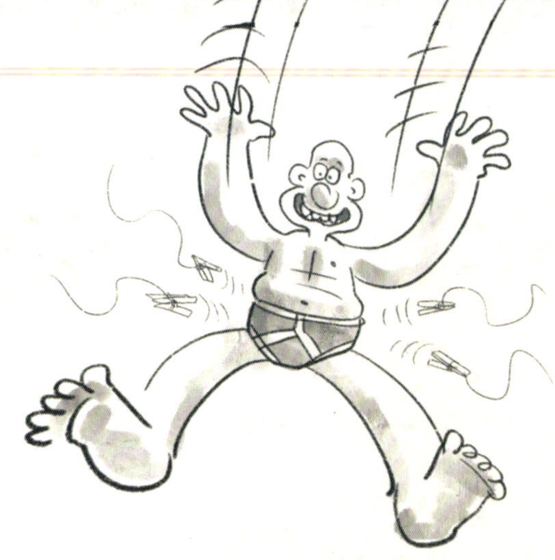

EVER SINCE *THE WRONG TROUSERS*, WALLACE has always made his entrance in a variation of his Get-U-Up contraption. Initially, this was a relatively simple affair, with his bed tipping him through a trapdoor, into his suspended trousers and onto a kitchen chair, where his sleeves and tank top were mechanically added and a ballista device fired jam onto his toast. In *A Close Shave*, this sequence was augmented by a rapid-firing porridge gun, which unfortunately malfunctioned after Shaun the Sheep munched his way through the wiring. Ambitions grew with *Curse of the Were-Rabbit*, as the Get-U-Up was triggered by an Anti-Pesto alarm and delivered both Wallace and Gromit from their beds and into their van, in a sequence

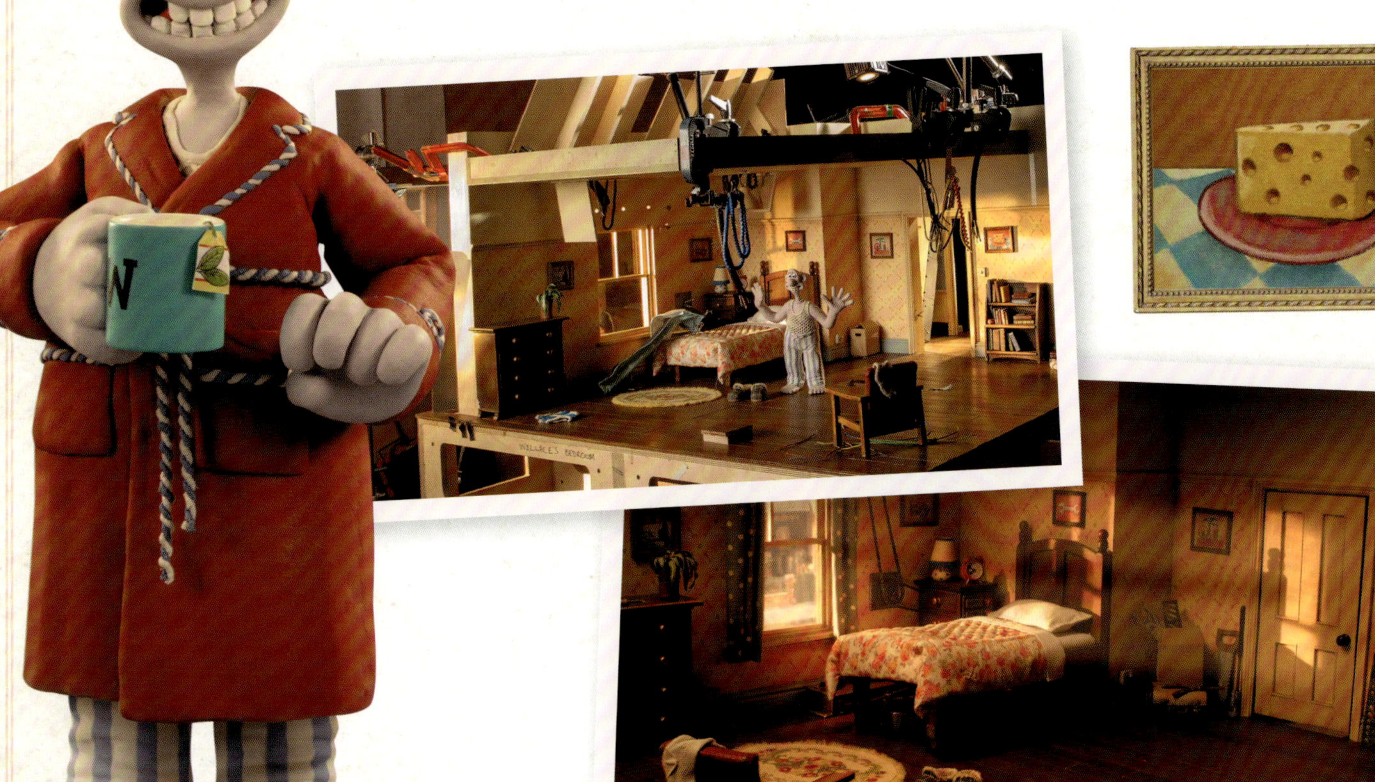

Below left | Behind-the-scenes shot of Wallace in his bedroom (photo by Richard Davies).

Below right | Finished graphic art for one of Wallace's most personal pictures.

Bottom | The new set for Wallace's bedroom.

Far left | Wallace ready to turn in for the night.

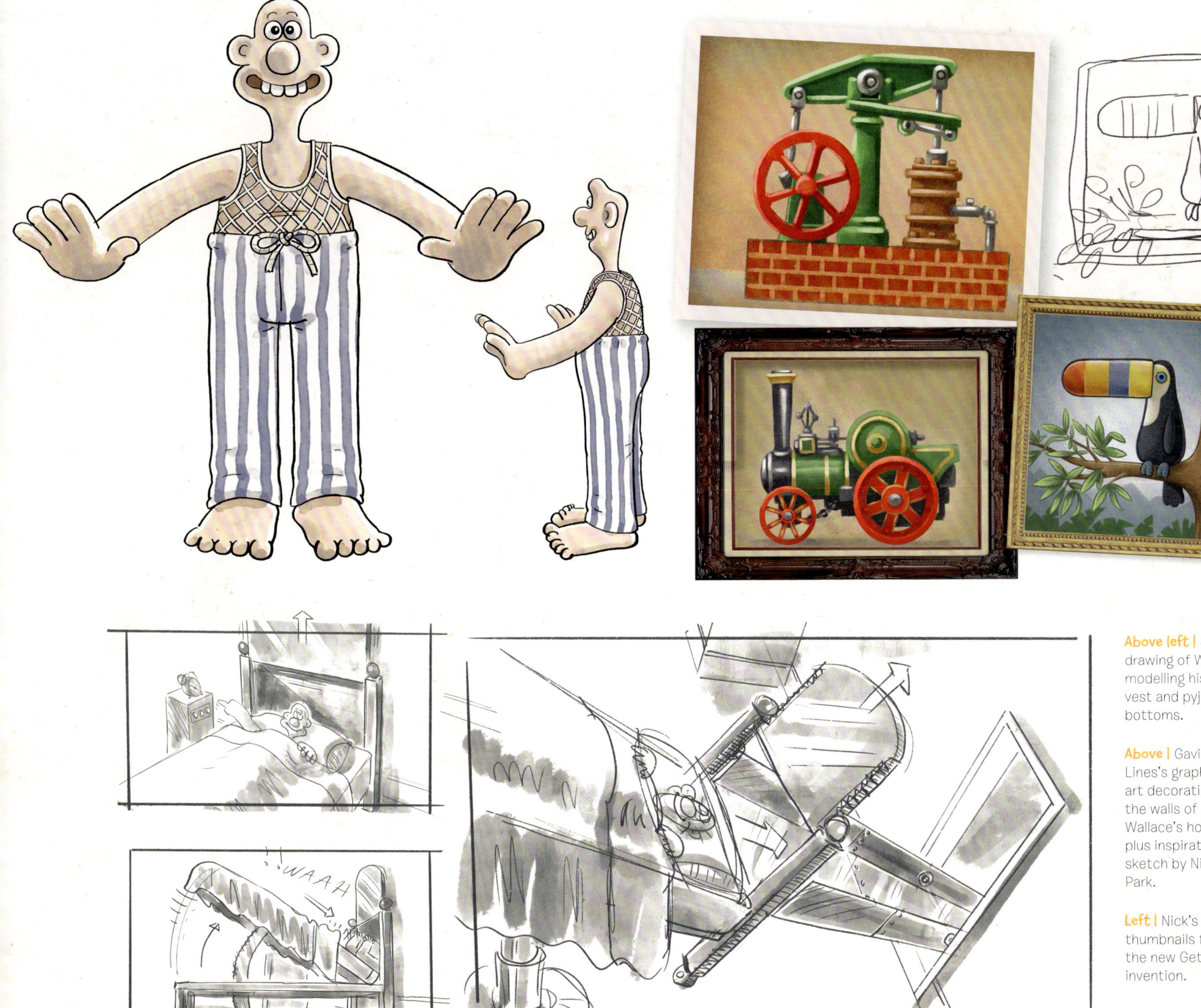

Above left | Scale drawing of Wallace modelling his string vest and pyjama bottoms.

Above | Gavin Lines's graphic art decorating the walls of Wallace's house, plus inspirational sketch by Nick Park.

Left | Nick's thumbnails for the new Get-U-Up invention.

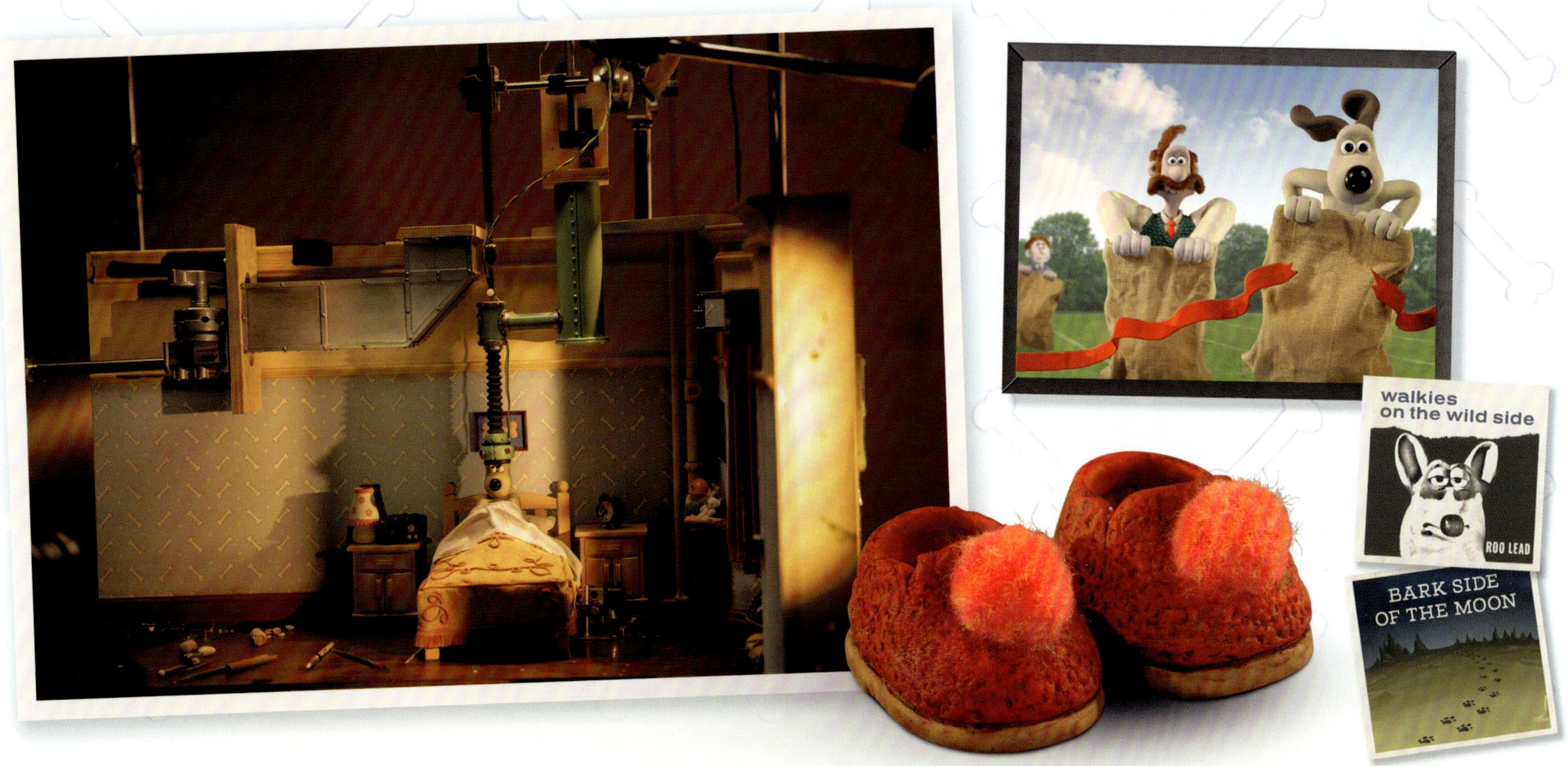

reminiscent of Gerry Anderson's beloved *Thunderbirds* series. And in *A Matter of Loaf and Death* the contraption was combined with the workings of the bakery that Wallace had built in his house, so in a masterpiece of timing he slides through bags of flour and freshly baked bread right into his baker's hat and waiting Top-Bun van (which looks suspiciously like the Anti-Pesto van with some minor modifications and a new paint job…)

Vengeance Most Fowl continues this tradition, in some ways getting back to basics, but in other ways providing the most technically challenging version of the sequence to date. After a 16-year absence from our screens, it felt important to re-establish this classic scene.

Merlin explains: "We're very much aware that there's a group of our audience who know and love *Wallace & Gromit*, and there's also a group who will have never watched it before, whether that's a broad audience around the world or a younger generation. So we needed to find a way of re-visiting how he gets up in the morning and embracing that whole idea of him using a sledgehammer to crack a nut to make existing fans happy while not bamboozling new people."

This Get-U-Up Deluxe sees the addition of several new elements, including a sliding headboard, a bathtub with automated scrubbing brush, a water slide (what else?!) and the most complicated Dress-O-Matic to date. And Gromit is not spared the indignity of a mechanical

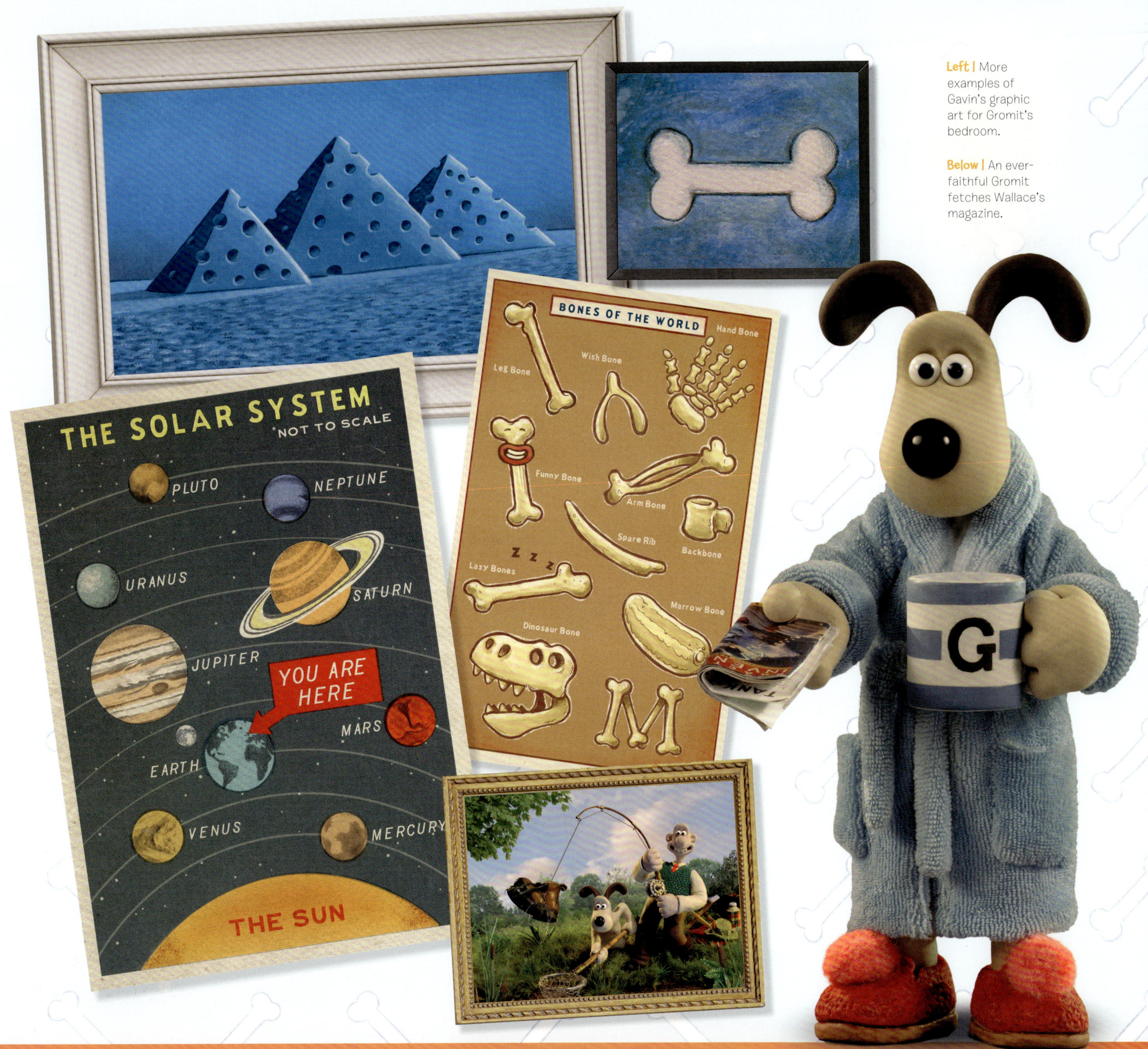

Left | More examples of Gavin's graphic art for Gromit's bedroom.

Below | An ever-faithful Gromit fetches Wallace's magazine.

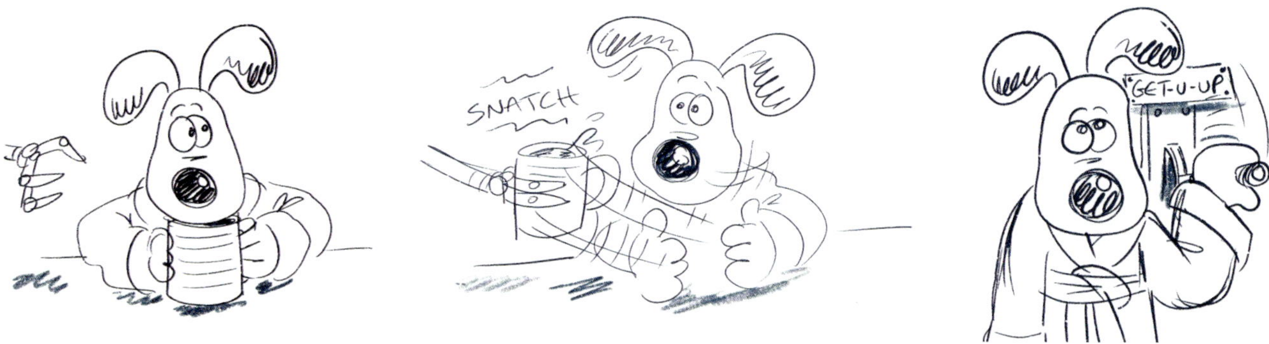

wake-up call himself. But Wallace's ingenuity is only matched by that of the Aardman production team, and this chapter looks at the level of technology and effort required to make the sequence appear so fluid and entertaining, something worthy of an episode of *Wallace & Gromit's World of Invention* in itself.

62 West Wallaby Street has evolved over the years to accommodate these changes. "The house is a more modern variant in terms of set dressing," says production designer Matt Perry. "But we have flashbacks to *The Wrong Trousers*, which means we have to recreate things like the clouds on the wallpaper to be consistent with what we had back then." Advances in camera technology and high definition mean that the original sets probably wouldn't have held up to modern-day scrutiny, and in any case many of these were lost during a fire at Aardman's warehouse in 2005. So the physical set is basically the same one that has been used since *Curse of the Were-Rabbit*, although with modifications for each new film. "We made the back of the house from scratch

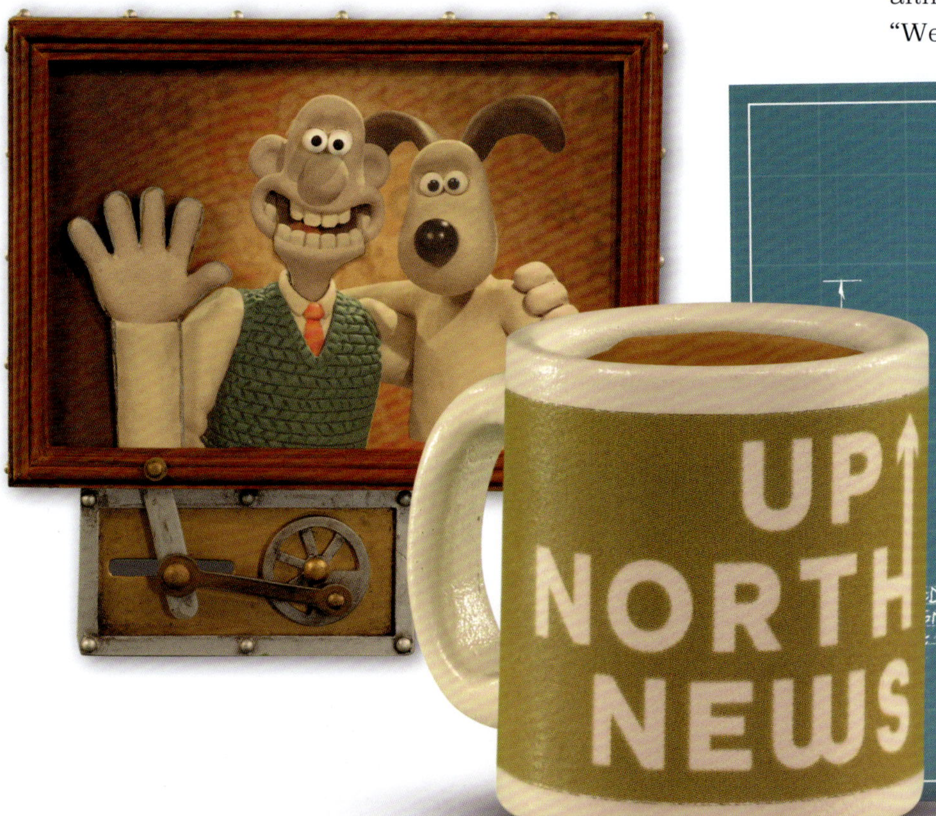

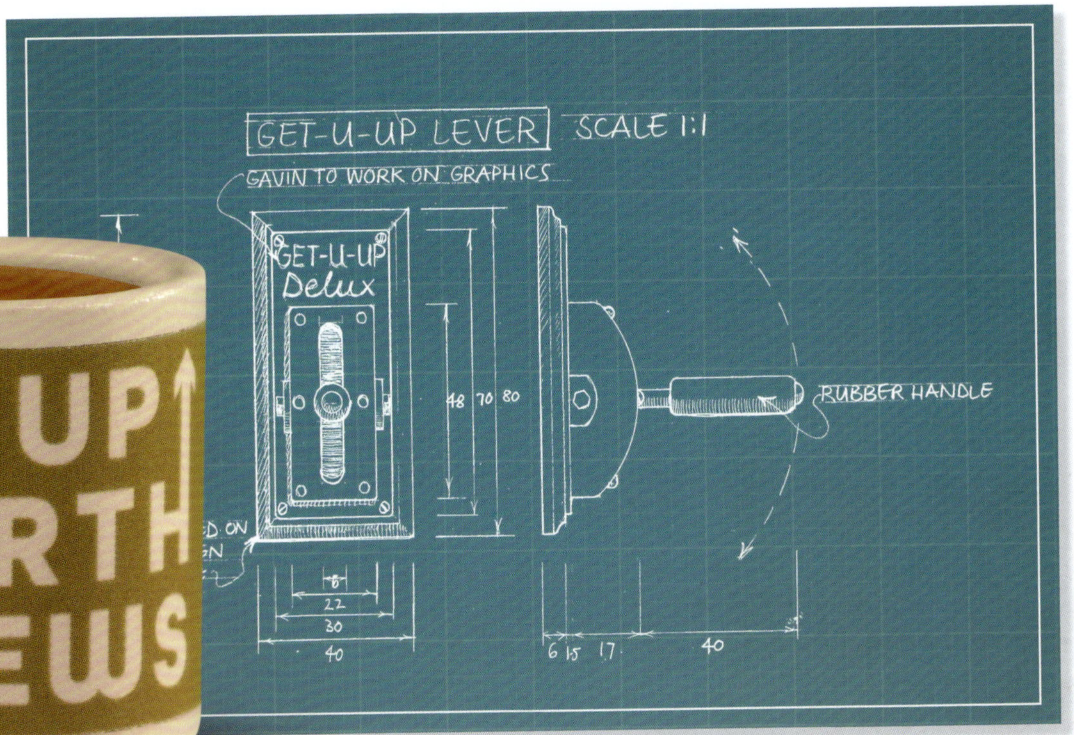

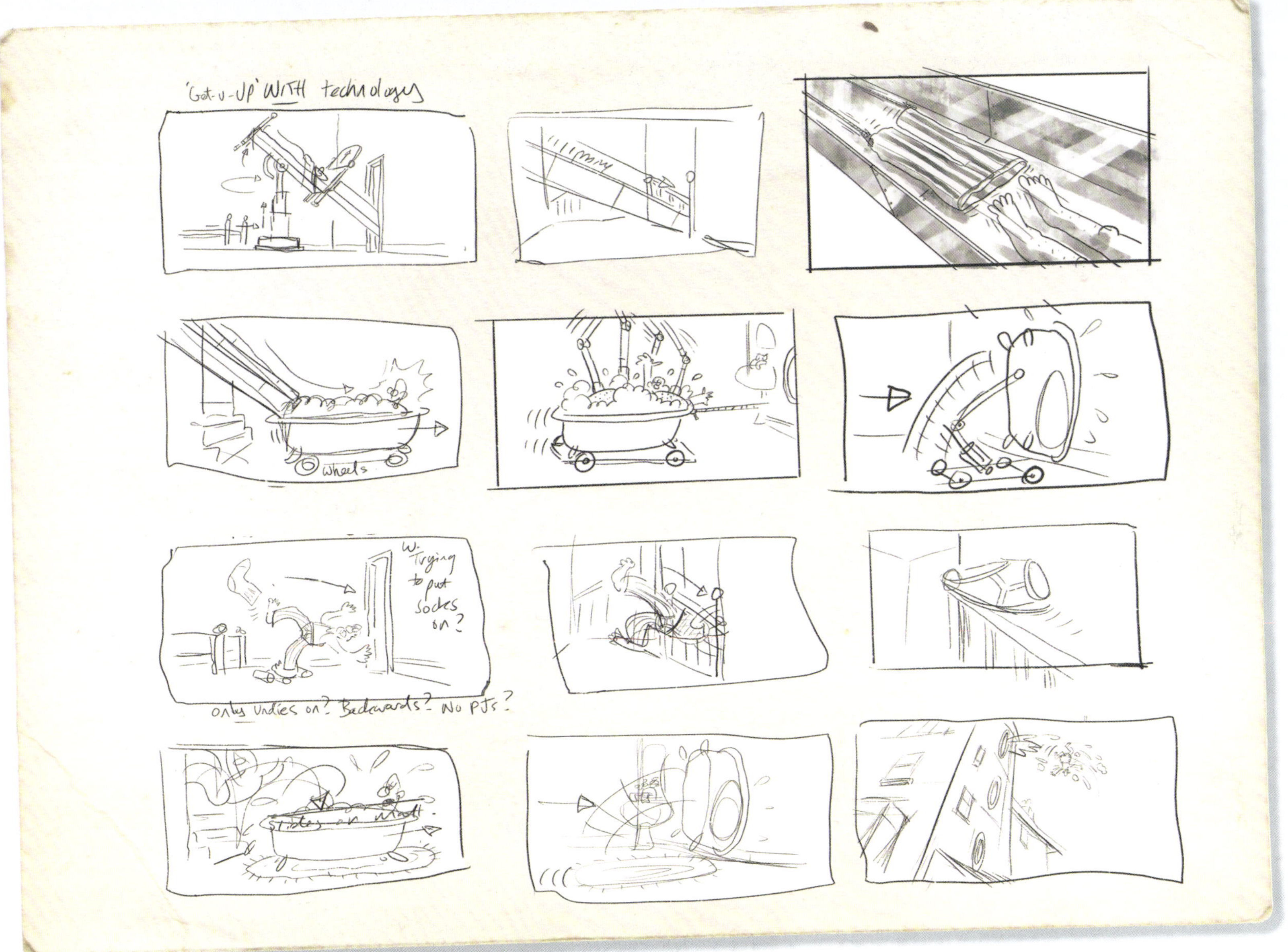

for this film because the windows and doors weren't in the right places for what we wanted," reveals art director Matt Sanders. "And the back has changed for almost every film anyway – sometimes the door's on one wall, sometimes it's on another, things like that. And then we had the water slide, which we had to do at two different scales – one for Wallace to go through and another for the wide shots of the house."

But whatever changes the house undergoes, its atmosphere of cosy familiarity remains the same. "Everything in the house has to feel quintessential," says Matt Perry. "A teapot is what you imagine you always saw at your Grannie's. Whether you did or not, it doesn't matter, but it's that teapot. A proper teapot. There's always a sense of harking back to that nostalgic British feeling."

Dave Alex Riddett agrees: "It's like my Nan's old room. I'm sure there's a genre for that now, but I don't know what you'd call it – postwar utility, old TV sets, tile fireplaces, mismatched

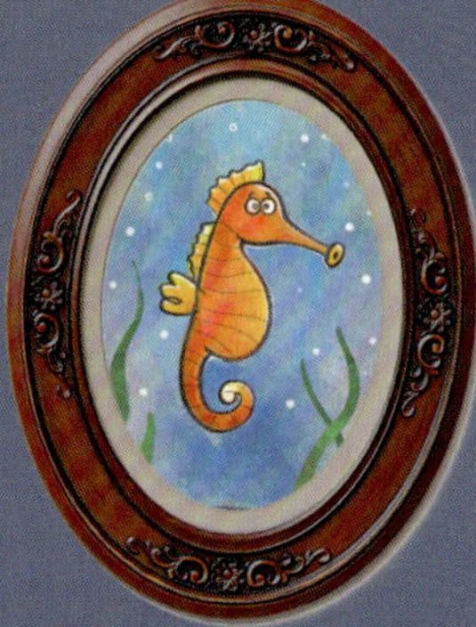

patterns. My Nan had one wall this pattern, that wall another pattern, then this patterned carpet. It's very nostalgic."

Despite the complexity of the latest Get-U-Up scene, it is still rooted in classic stop-motion techniques, although turbo-charged to push the boundaries of what can be achieved. "We've done it fairly traditionally from a filmmaking point of view," explains Merlin. "Even the bubbles in the bath are practical, they're not computer-generated, apart from a few small enhancements. The shot of Wallace getting dressed has around seven different Wallace puppets or component parts to take him from naked through to fully dressed. It's literally the camera pointing at the set, and the animator is figuring out with the rigger and the puppet department all the component parts and animated specials that are needed to achieve the final thing. It happens so abruptly that you can trick the eye."

The Dress-O-Matic sequence was conceived by Nick in a few loose thumbnails, but these posed enormous practical challenges for the team. The scene was shot by James Carlisle, an animator who has proven himself particularly adept at solving complex action problems. "I've been looking at the old films to see how they did it before, and they used a lot of cuts between shots. They'd cut to the other side of the table

Below left | Early colour sketch by Nick Park for Wallace's bath time.

Below | The bathtub sequence as it appears in the final film.

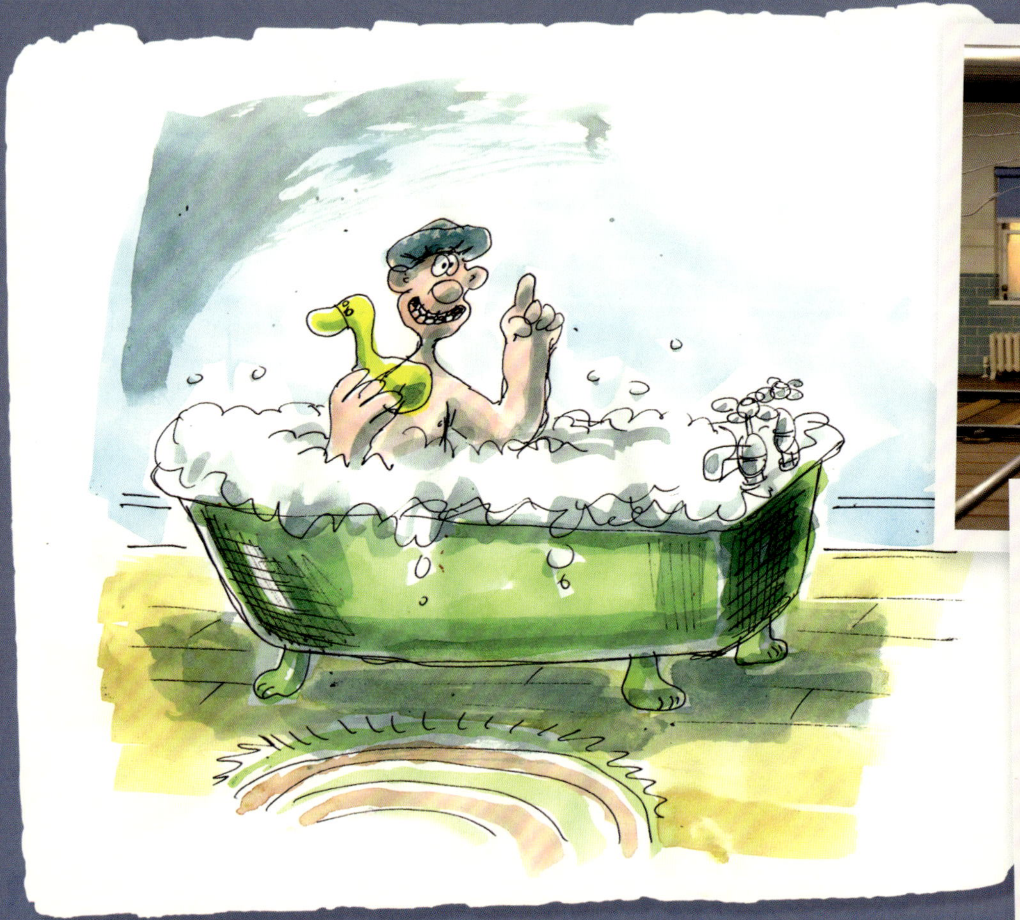

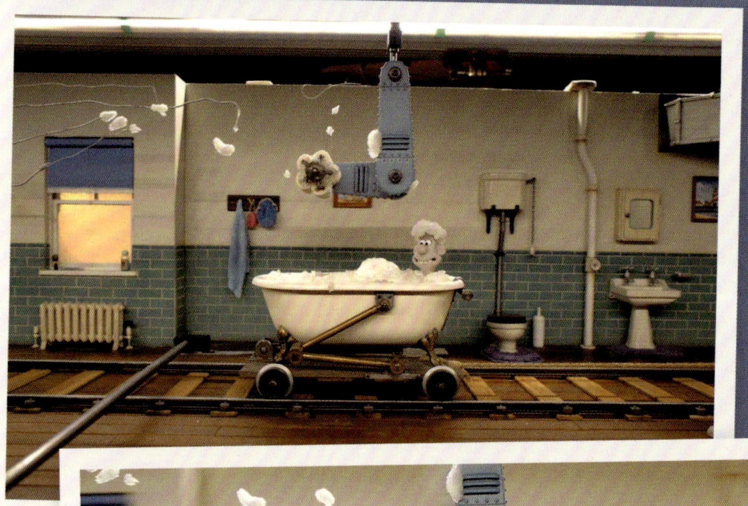

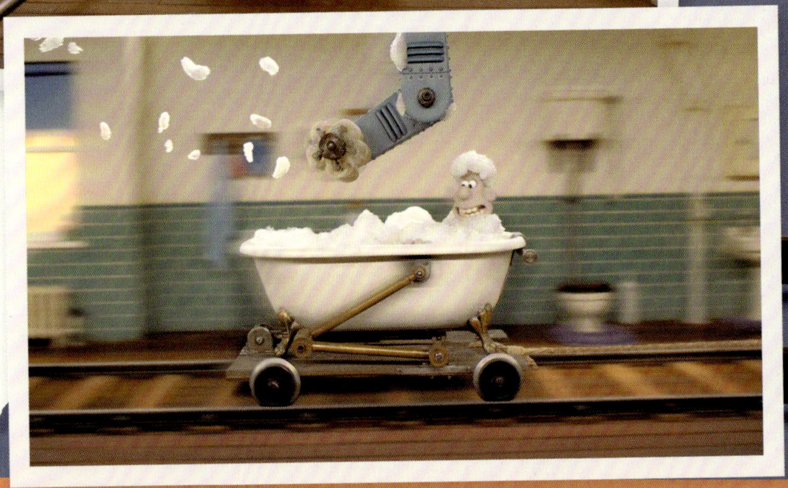

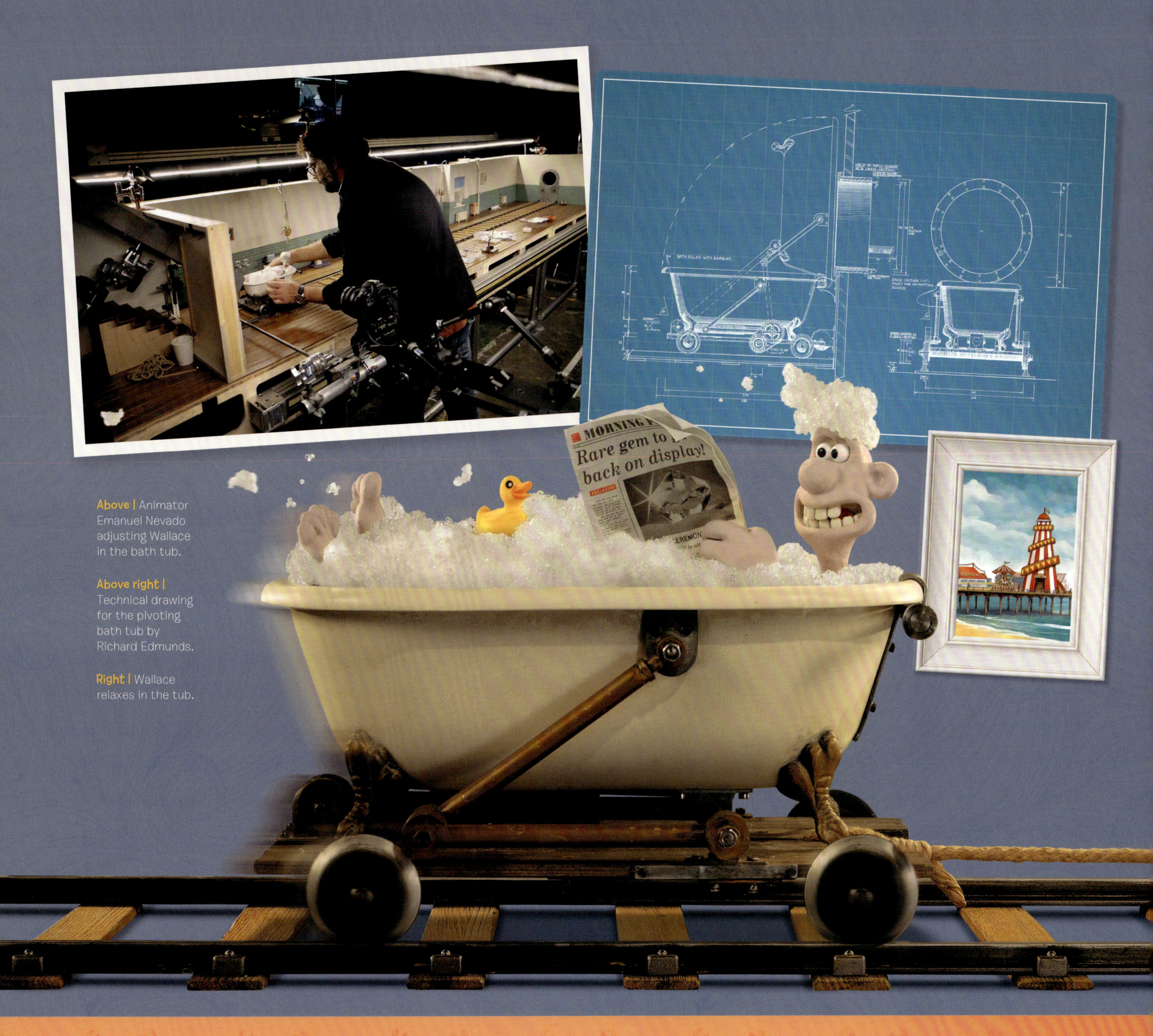

Above | Animator Emanuel Nevado adjusting Wallace in the bath tub.

Above right | Technical drawing for the pivoting bath tub by Richard Edmunds.

Right | Wallace relaxes in the tub.

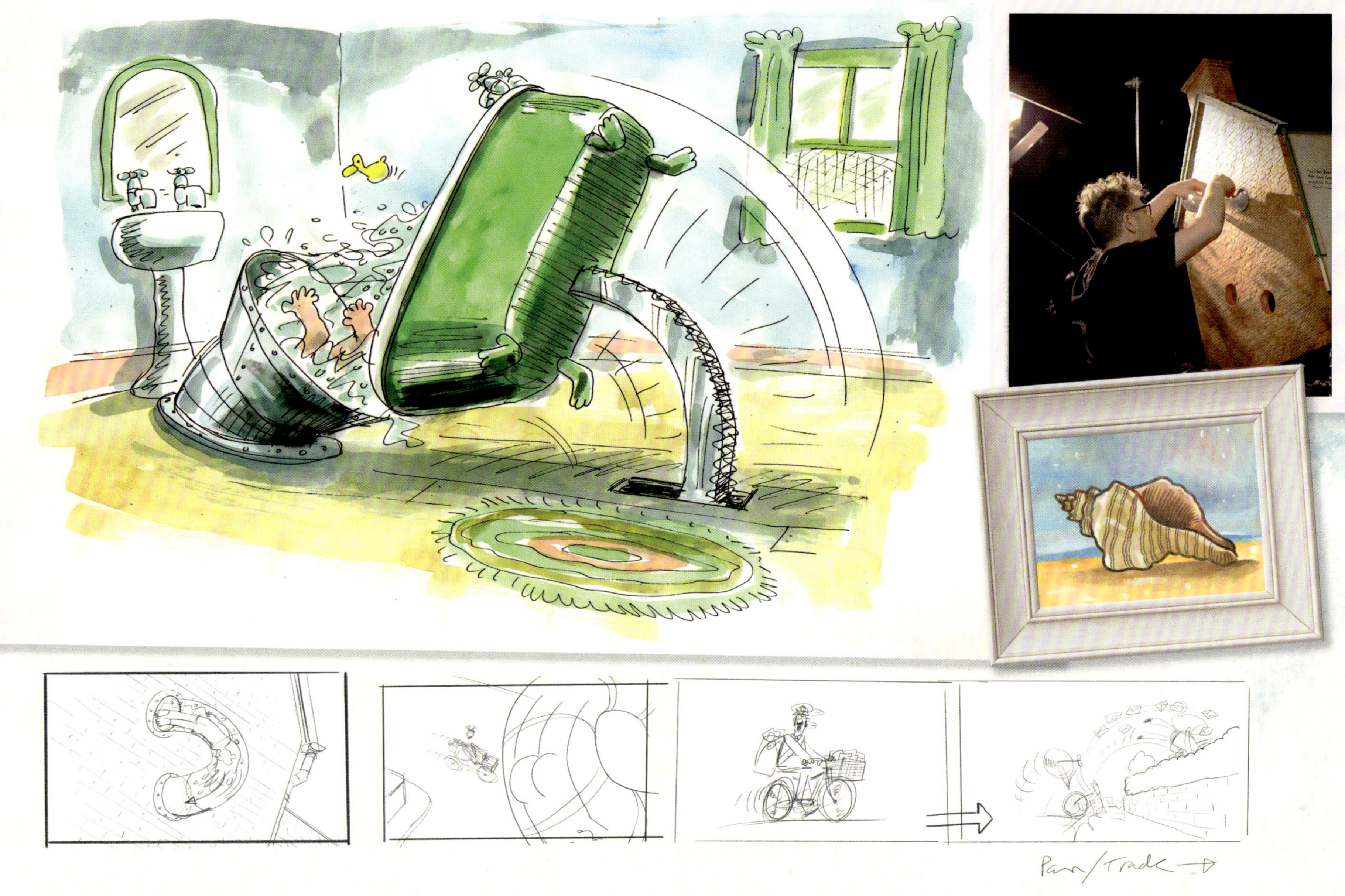

and his trousers would be put on; you'd cut to the top half and his sleeves would get put on. But now it's all happening in one shot – not so easy, but it's very cool." James will first go through the process of 'animation blocking', where he shoots just the key frames as a sort of dress rehearsal, allowing the lighting, set-dressing and other elements to be de-bugged before the animation proper can begin. "It's

about problem-solving," he says, "and seeing what the directors think after that.

"So there's a naked Wallace that comes into shot and drops into his pants, then a version with clay trousers so that they can be animated through. Then the whole bit around his waist comes off, allowing me to swap the pants for a silicon pair. When Wallace falls through, I have to cut that puppet down – it has a rough

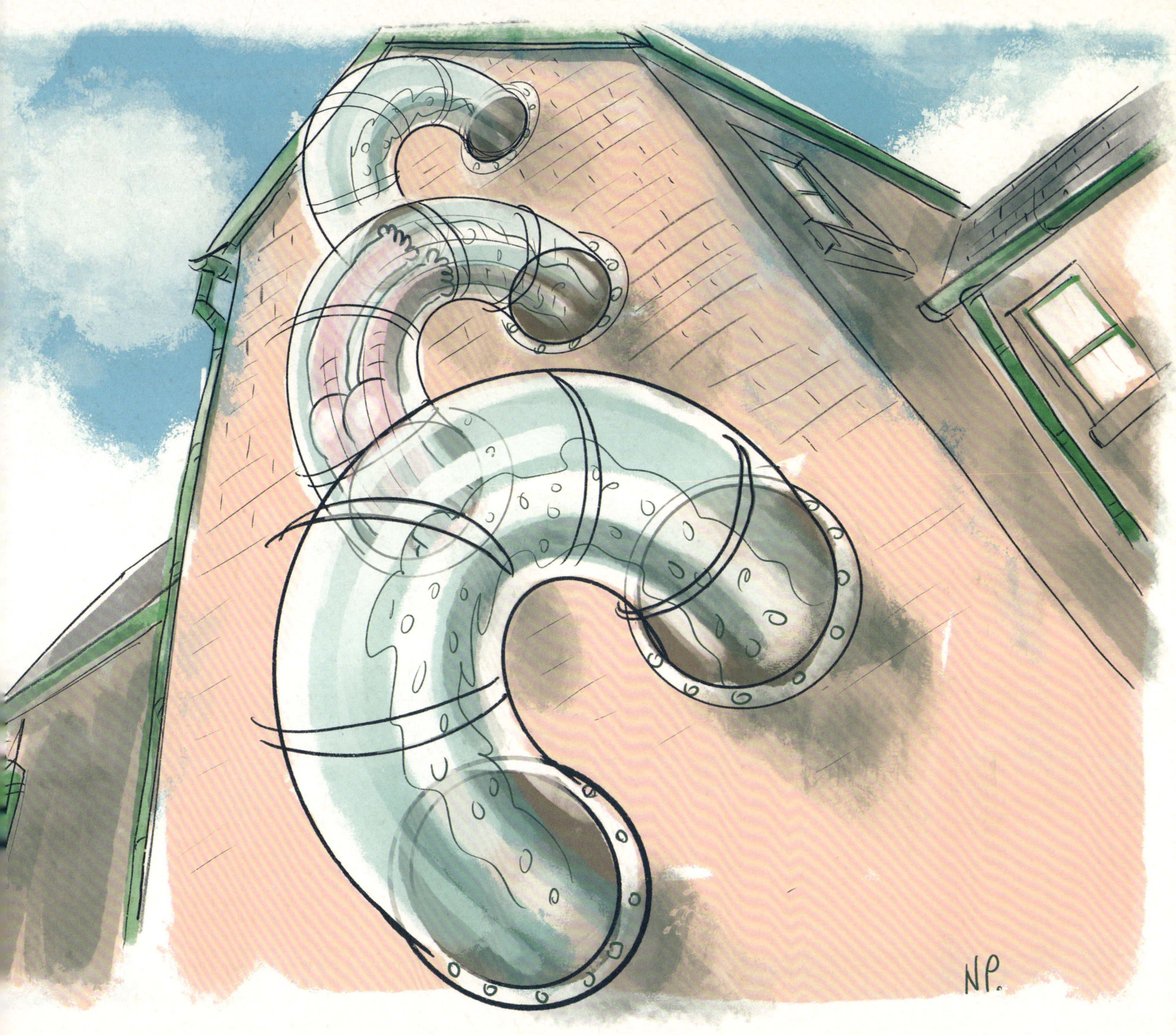

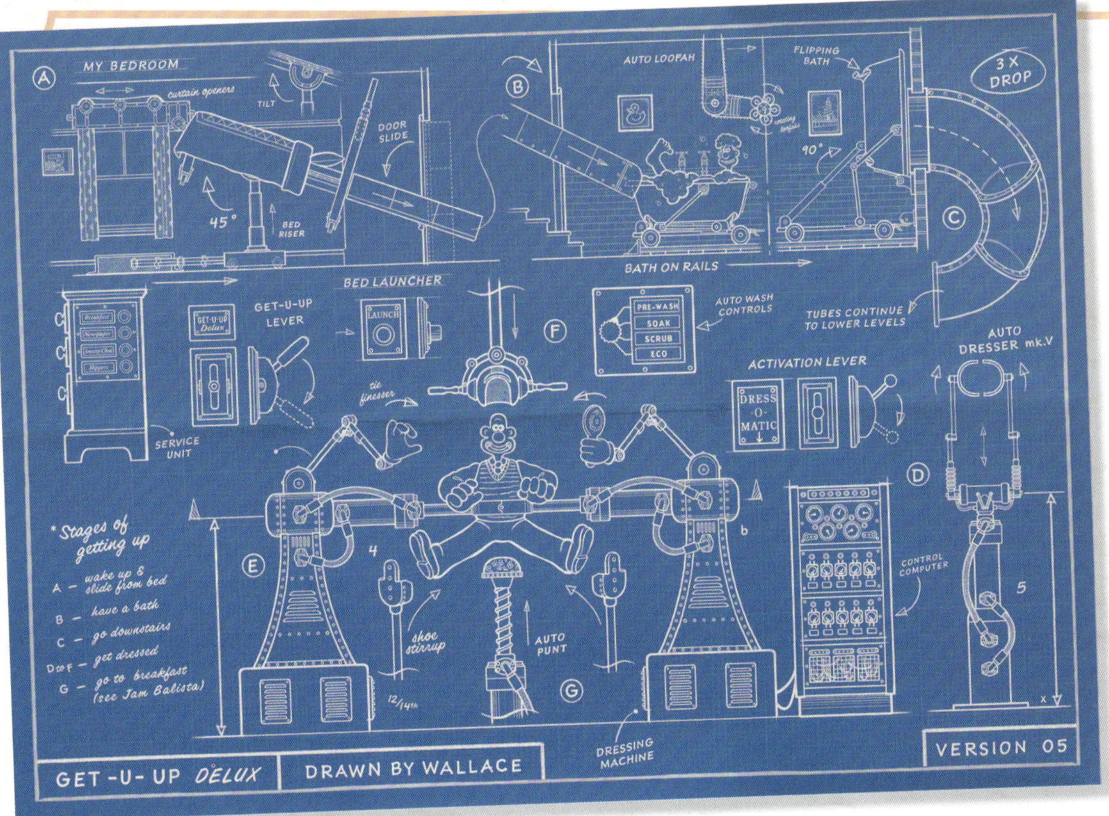

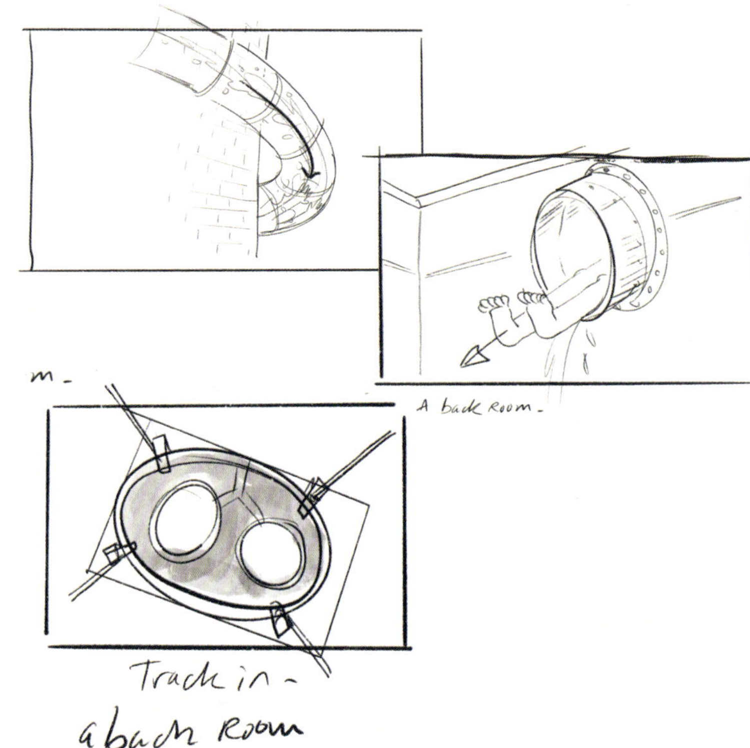

wire armature so you can cut it back. Then I'll sculpt the clay trousers to show his feet coming through, and the clay feet will be replaced as his silicon boots are put on. Finally, mechanical arms pick up a 2D jersey from the washing line and that is substituted for a 3D clay one that goes over his head, so his head stays in then pops out again. The shot is only six and a half seconds long!"

Of course, with a naked Wallace, James's duties even extend to being an intimacy coordinator. "Every shot of Wallace naked has tactically placed hands, or as he falls through he's covered by a prop or piece of the set until he leaves frame. Everything is choreographed so it's decent."

Traditionally, stop-frame animation is shot at 12 frames per second (or 'twos', as each shot is held for two frames), as opposed to the 24 frames per second ('ones') used for live-action filming. There are certain points where James will animate in 'ones' for the faster-moving action, but generally he prefers working in 'twos', "to give it that traditional Aardman feel", he explains. "It makes the machinery a bit robotic and clunky. You have to pick and choose where to spend the time. If you tried to make everything perfect it would take months to do anything. Some of the quicker stuff you can keep really 'thumby' [i.e. with the animator's thumbprints still visible in the clay]. Nick and Merlin like it to stay that way, true to how it was in the early films. Full clay animation really lends itself to that; you can play around with the texture."

As easy as it is to say that Wallace simply 'drops

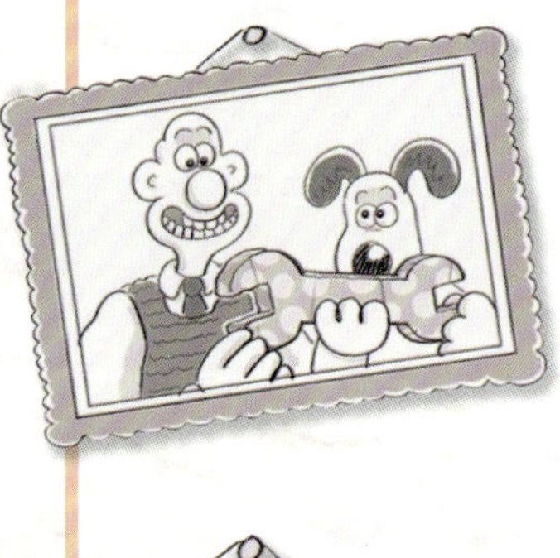

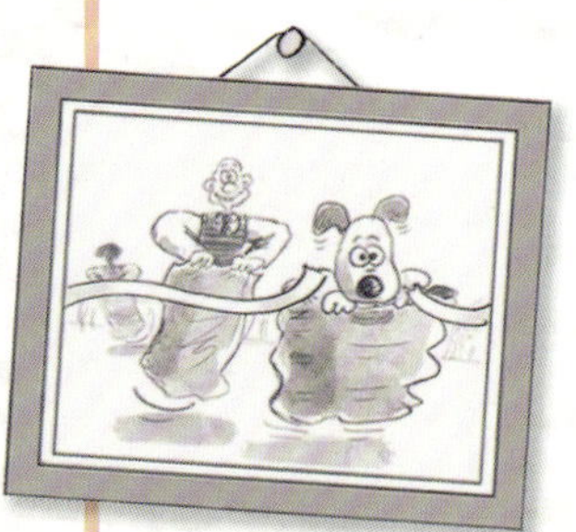

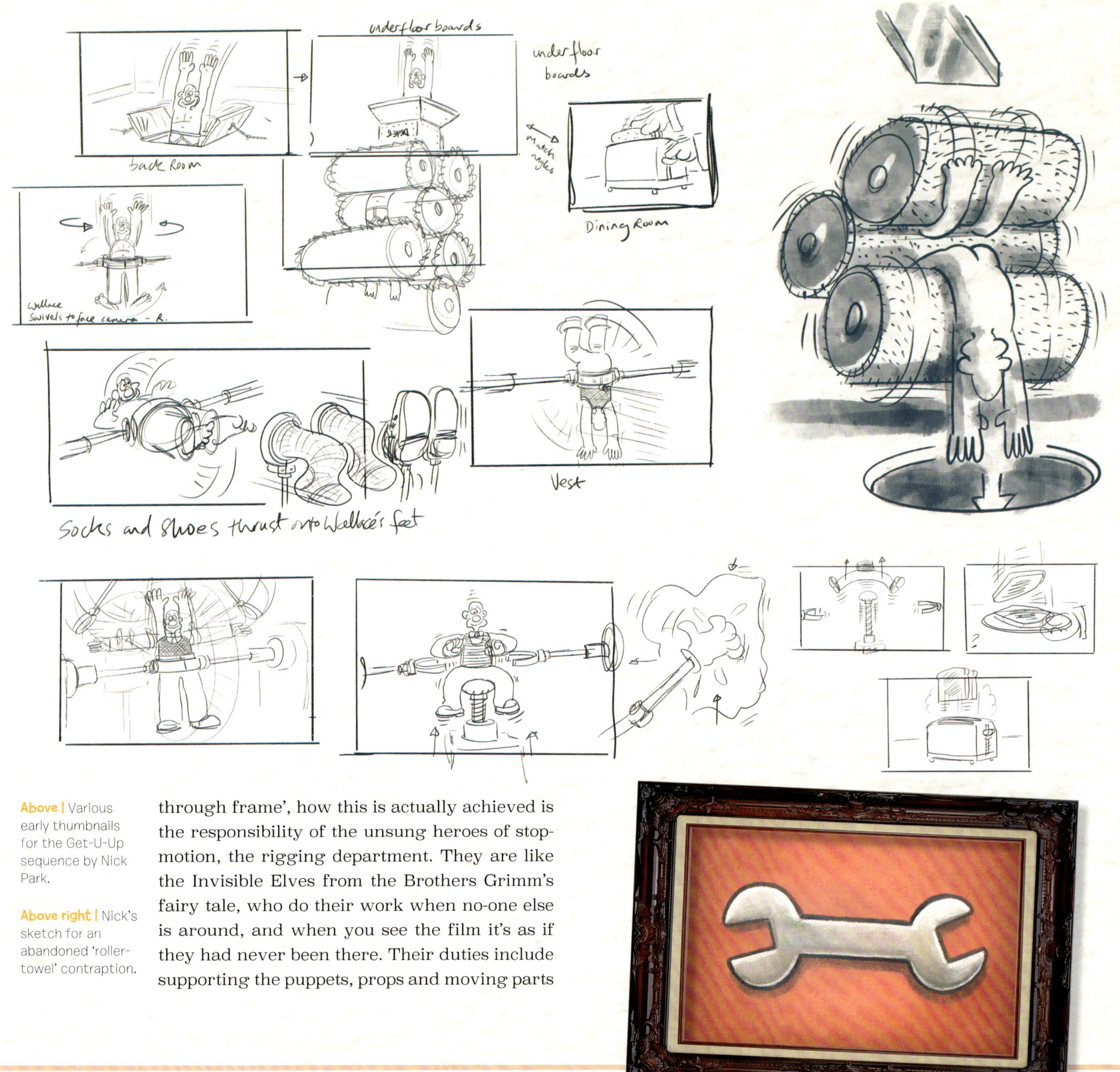

through frame', how this is actually achieved is the responsibility of the unsung heroes of stop-motion, the rigging department. They are like the Invisible Elves from the Brothers Grimm's fairy tale, who do their work when no-one else is around, and when you see the film it's as if they had never been there. Their duties include supporting the puppets, props and moving parts

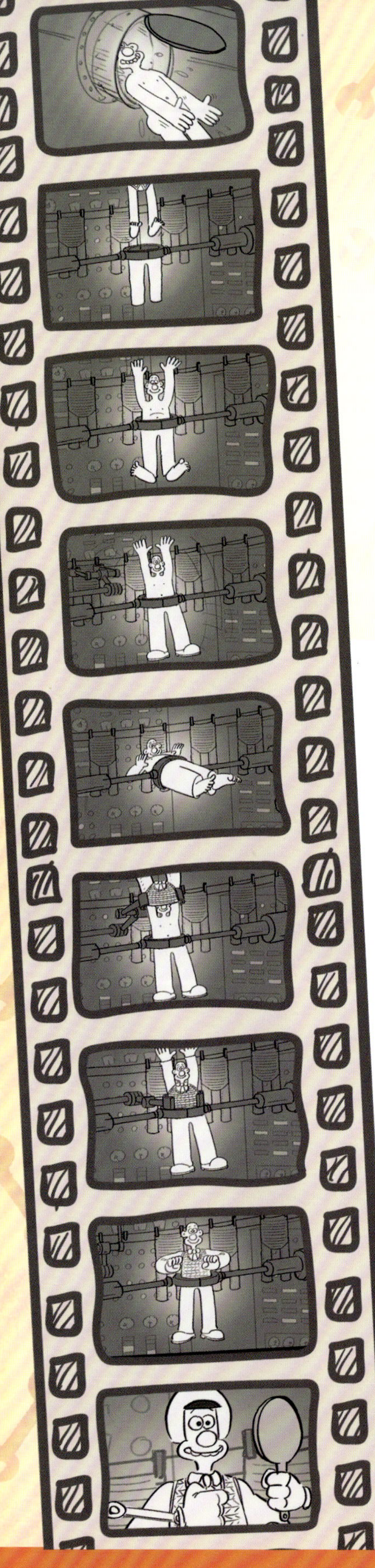

of the sets so that they can be animated in any position. Head of Rigging Del Lawson explains: "You never see what the rigging department brings to a project. We get involved in all the shots to some degree. Some of it might be very simple stuff like fitting something into a character's hand or helping the animator out with 'tie-downs' so they can keep a character attached to the set. But there's a lot of stuff on this film."

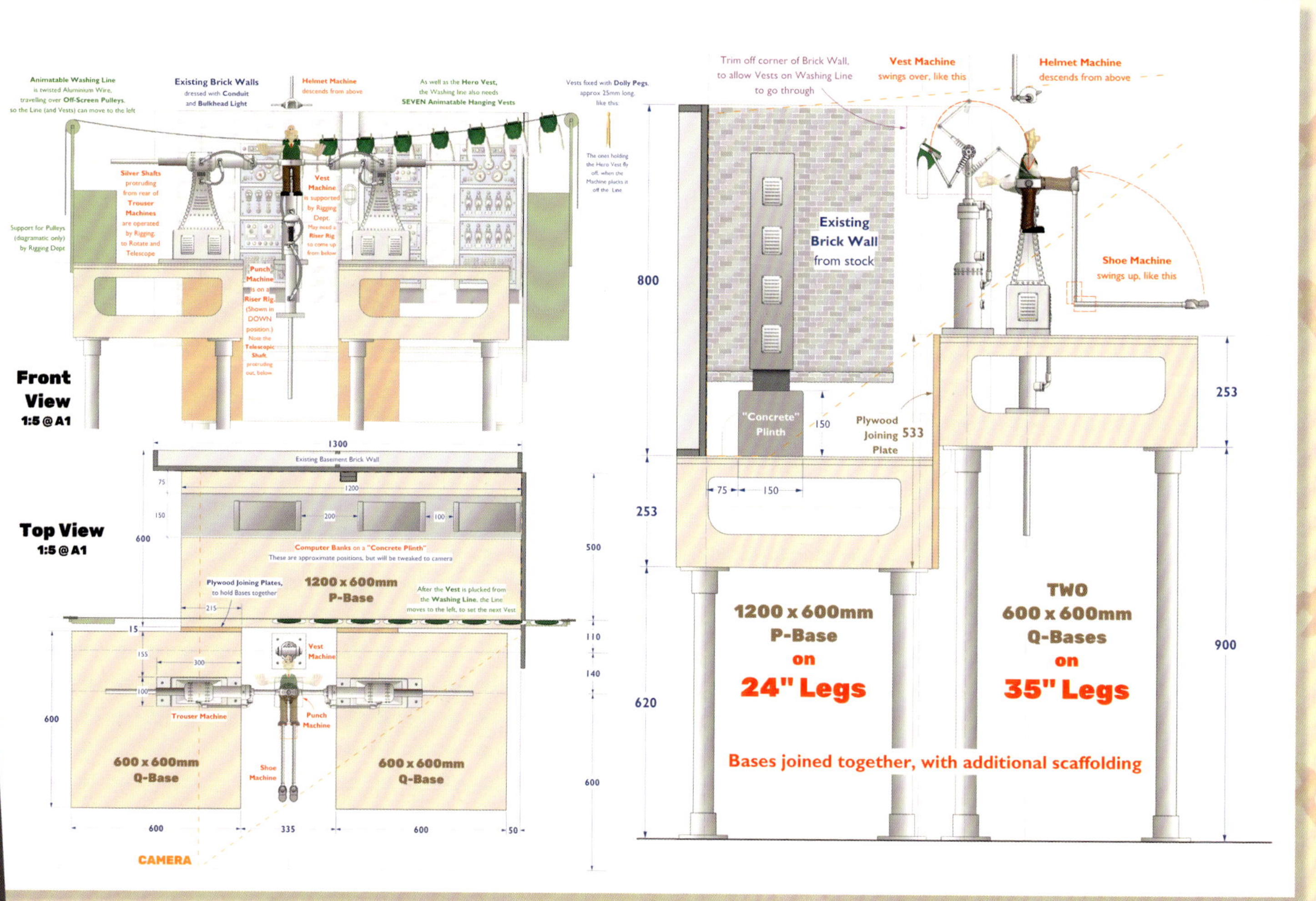

Del has been working with Aardman since the days of *A Close Shave*, so he remembers how effects would be done before digital technology was an option: "When we did the first Dress-O-Matic, it would have just been a clay Wallace, which might have had a hard resin jersey and a couple of special bits. We used a lot of tungsten wire or nylons and it was more about trying to hide the wires, whereas these days you can put stuff in and remove it in post-production." The first *Chicken Run* saw the

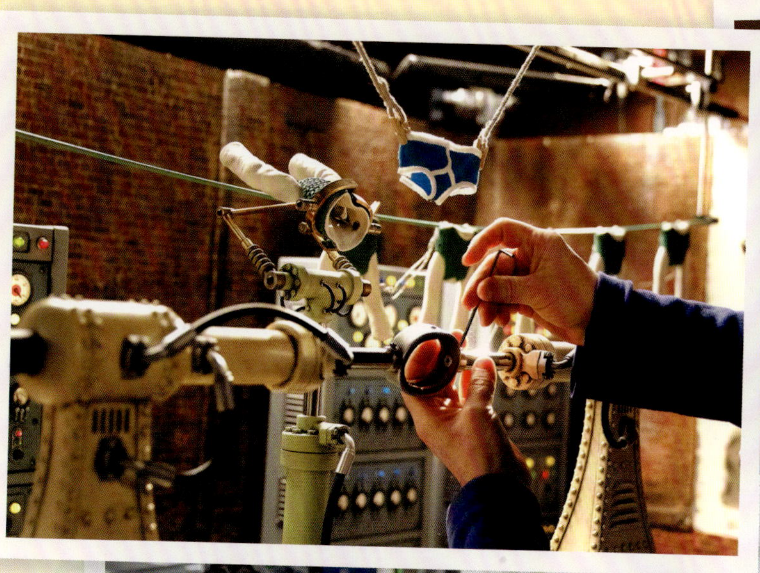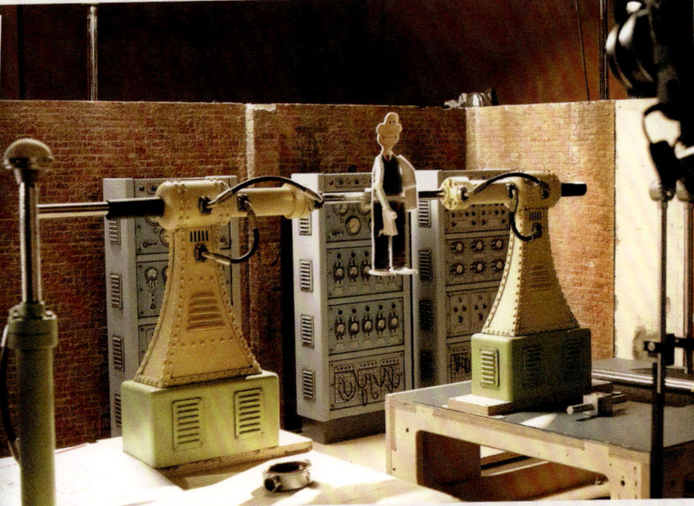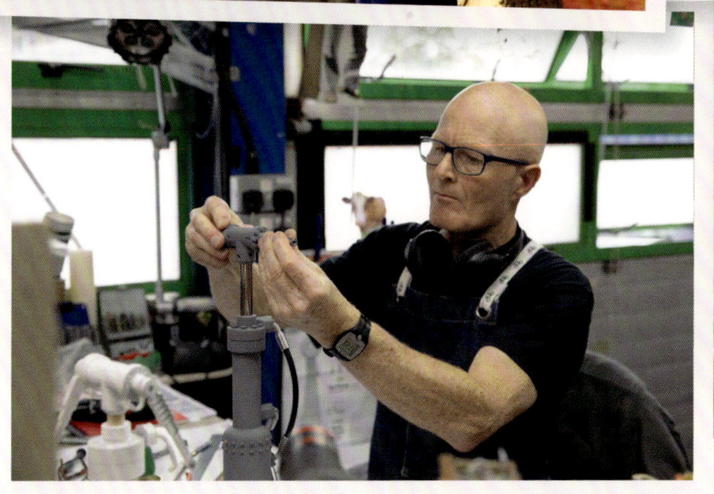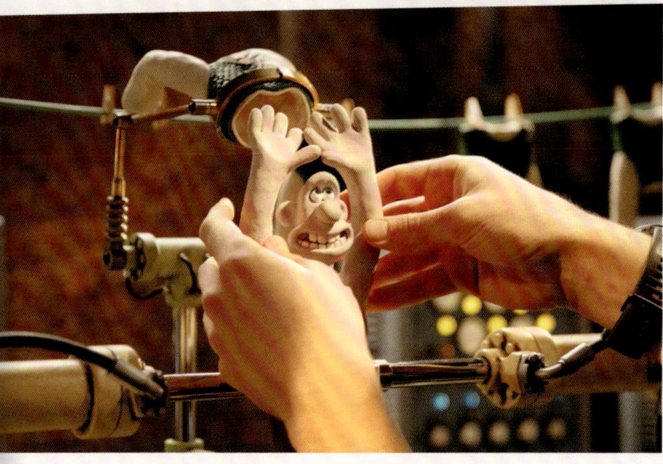

formation of a dedicated rigging department, where Del devised Aardman's tracking system, adapting equipment used on production lines in the food industry. "We use a lot of winding devices, where basically you wind a handle and the pinion moves a rack to which we can attach props, puppets or bits of set, meaning the animator can move them incrementally frame by frame. The tracking systems have motors which can be programmed so that barges, for instance, can move accurately along rails."

This sequence involves even more forms of rigging than it does special puppets. "Wallace has got to spin," explains Del, "so there's a rotation device which allows the animator to spin him back so the shoes can come in and get slapped on his feet – that's another rig. He also needs his jersey putting on, so as we track the washing line across and the Dress-O-Matic picks up the jersey I thought it would be nice to have a bounce on the line, so I put in another winder, which allows the animator to flex the

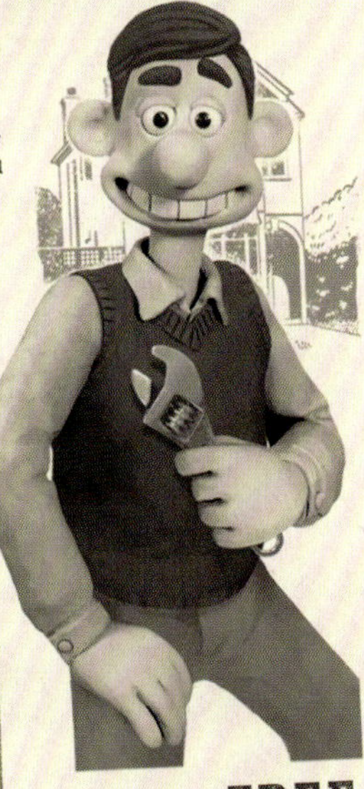

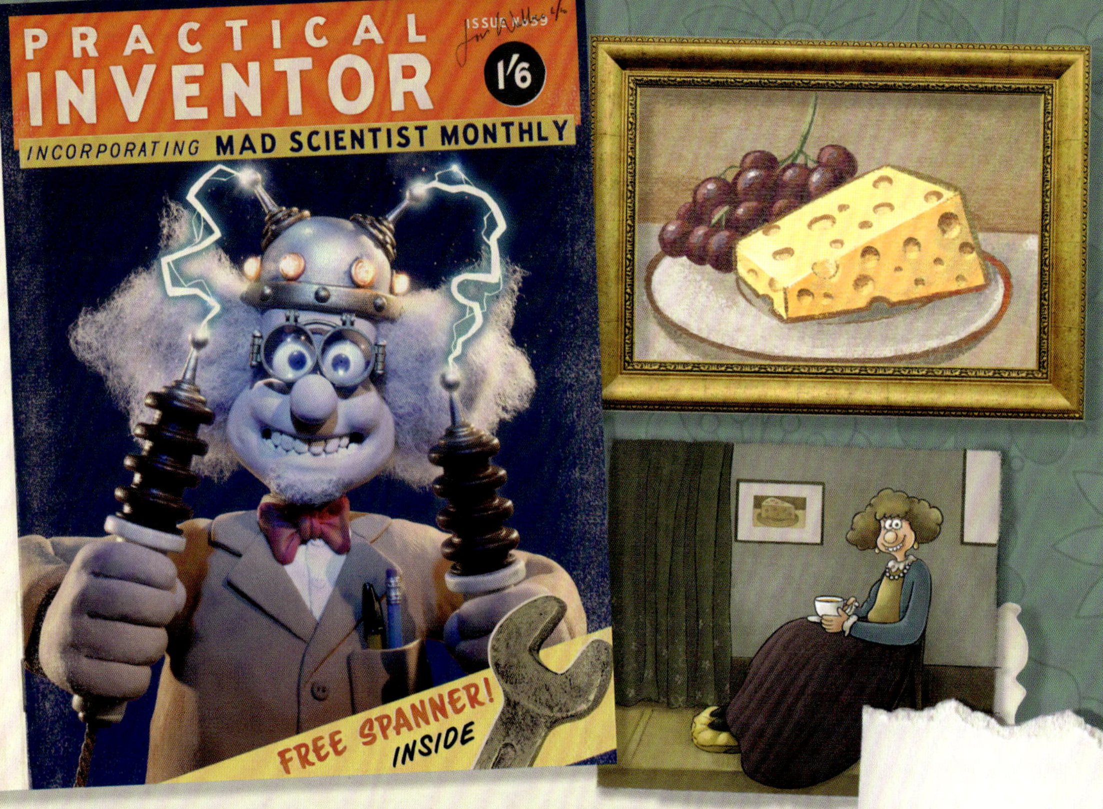

piece of steel that the clothesline is made from. Ultimately, when Wallace is dressed, the solid section that the puppet is bolted to needs to come apart to release him, so there is a rack-and-pinion winder holding the puppet that takes Wallace away." Looking at the live set with all the rigging in position, sometimes it's impossible to tell where Wallace's contraptions stop and Del's equipment begins.

"You're just trying to make it easier for the animator," says Del. "We work closely with the animator, the director, all departments really. The director gives you the vision – this is what we need – and we work out how are we going to achieve it. You make suggestions, the animator makes suggestions and you come to a way of doing it. The idea is to get it done as quickly and efficiently as possible. The audience will just see Wallace getting dressed, but everything that goes in behind that shot is immense. And anything we put in as a rigging department will basically have to be taken out."

Another example of the use of rigging in the Get-U-Up sequence is the automated cereal-pouring device. Each flake of breakfast cereal has to be separately animated, moving them along wires that trace the trajectory of their movement. But, of course, once the animation is complete, someone needs to remove the wires, and that is where the digital clean-up artist comes in. "We are the bane of the digital department's life," admits Del, "creating all these problems, things to remove. Nowadays, we do put stuff in that can be seen in shot, so we have to make a decision

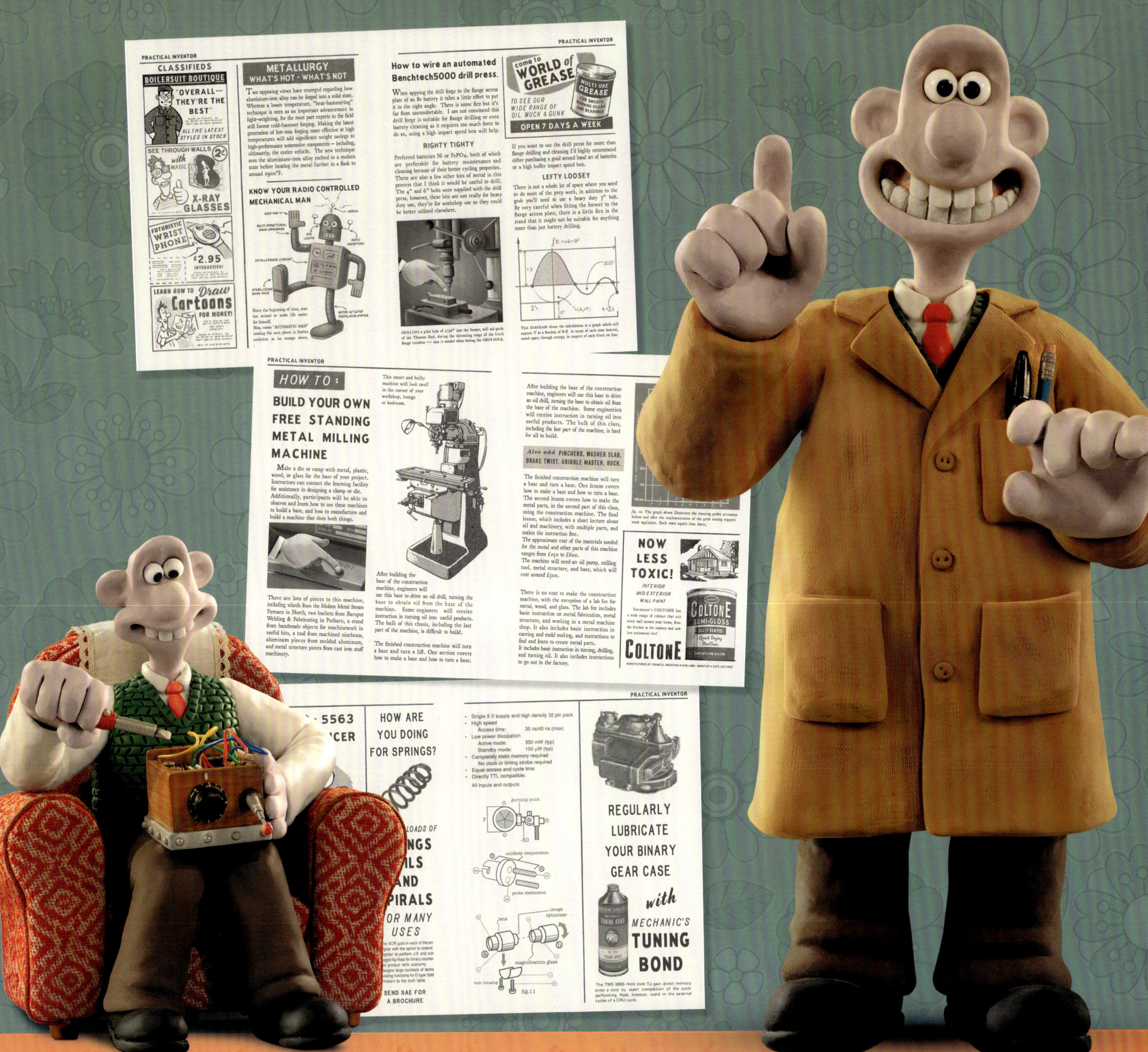

PRACTICAL INVENTOR
CLASSIFIEDS
BOILERSUIT BOUTIQUE
"OVERALL— THEY'RE THE BEST"
ALL THE LATEST STYLES IN STOCK
SEE THROUGH WALLS with MAGIC
X-RAY GLASSES
2'
FUTURISTIC WRIST PHONE
£2.95 INTERACTIVE!
LEARN HOW TO Draw Cartoons FOR MONEY!
METALLURGY
WHAT'S HOT – WHAT'S NOT
KNOW YOUR RADIO CONTROLLED MECHANICAL MAN
How to wire an automated Benchtech5000 drill press.
RIGHTY TIGHTY
come to WORLD of GREASE
MULTI USE GREASE FOR SMOOTH RUNNING GEARS AND BEARINGS
TO SEE OUR WIDE RANGE OF OIL, MUCK & GUNK
OPEN 7 DAYS A WEEK
LEFTY LOOSEY
HOW TO:
BUILD YOUR OWN FREE STANDING METAL MILLING MACHINE
Also add PINCHERS, WASHER SLAB, BRAKE TWIST, GRIBBLE MASTER, RUCK.
NOW LESS TOXIC!
INTERIOR AND EXTERIOR WALL PAINT
COLTONE
SEMI-GLOSS
Quick Drying Non-Toxic
COLTONE
MANUFACTURED BY CHEMICAL INDUCTION IN OUR LABS – MAINTAIN A SAFE DISTANCE
HOW ARE YOU DOING FOR SPRINGS?
LOADS OF SPRINGS COILS AND SPIRALS FOR MANY USES
SEND SAE FOR A BROCHURE
Single 5 V supply and high density 32 pin pack
High speed
Access time: 35 ns/45 ns (max)
Low power dissipation
Active mode: 350 mW (typ)
Standby mode: 100 µW (typ)
Completely static memory required
No clock or timing strobe required
Equal access and cycle time
Directly TTL compatible:
All inputs and outputs
turning point
unlikely conjunction
probe distinction
lens
image optimizer
magnification glass
bolt housing
fig.11
REGULARLY LUBRICATE YOUR BINARY GEAR CASE with MECHANIC'S TUNING BOND

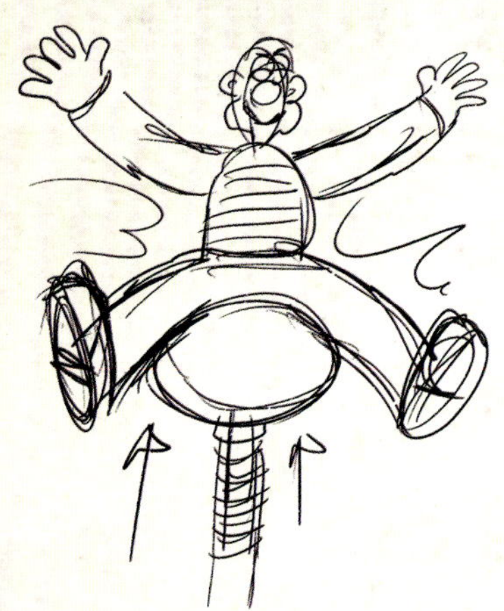

about whether something is going to be an easy removal. But there are things you have to be really careful about, like creating shadows of the rig across practical animation."

There are two basic ways that clean-up can work: one is by 'rotoscoping' – digitally cutting around the key animation – so it can be dropped in against a 'clean' background plate (a plate being a separate shot of the background with no rigging, which can be composited with the animation to make the rig disappear). The second is by using cloning software to digitally 'paint out' the rig in each individual frame. To make life easier in the cereal shot, the wires were the same colour as the flakes. However, painting out the wires is still a laborious process. "It needs a lot of patience," explains Sabby Zola, one of the junior digital artists. "Sometimes you are just in the zone and you put a podcast on or something so your brain can be somewhere else while you're doing it. Other times I need to focus, to know what I'm doing, so it's less auto-pilot."

But the digital artists also make more creative contributions to the final shots. For instance, Sabby used mapping technology to create shadows for each individual cereal flake on the table to give the scene a greater

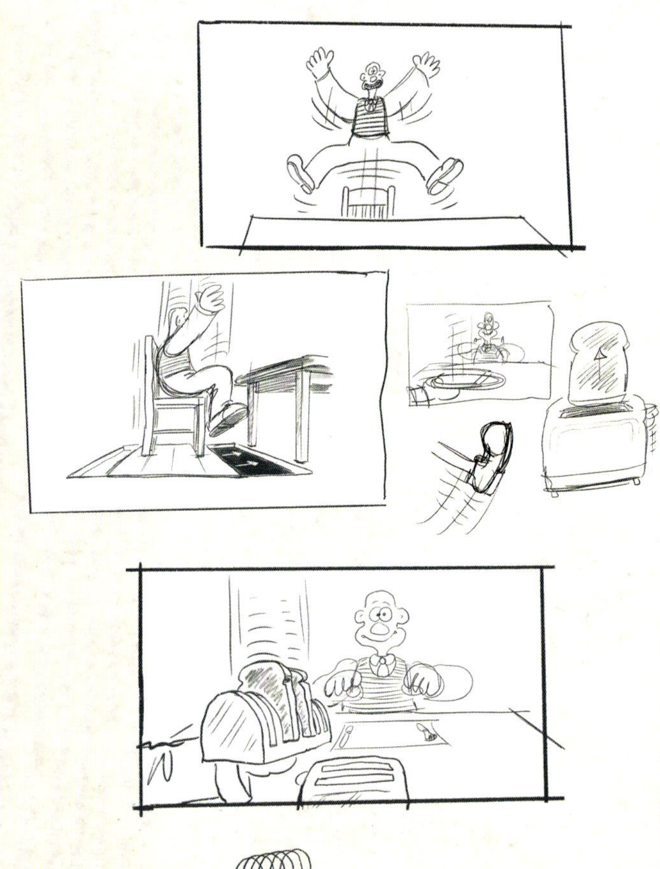

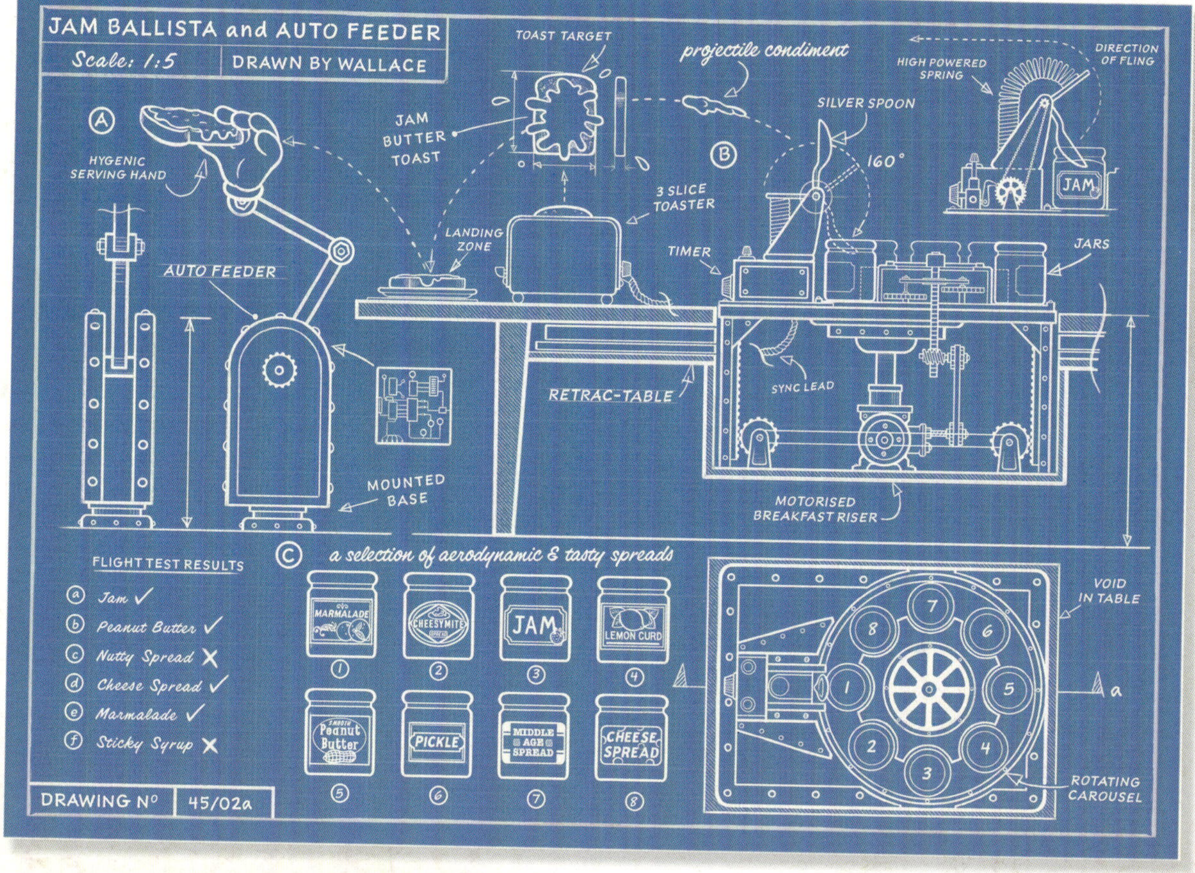

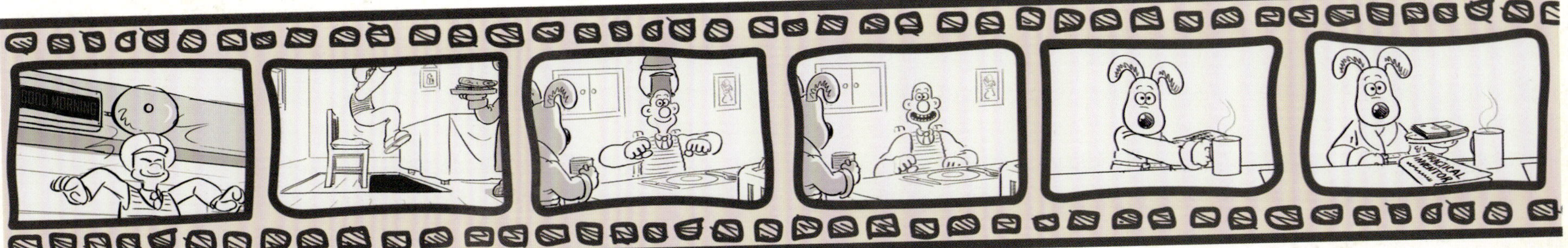

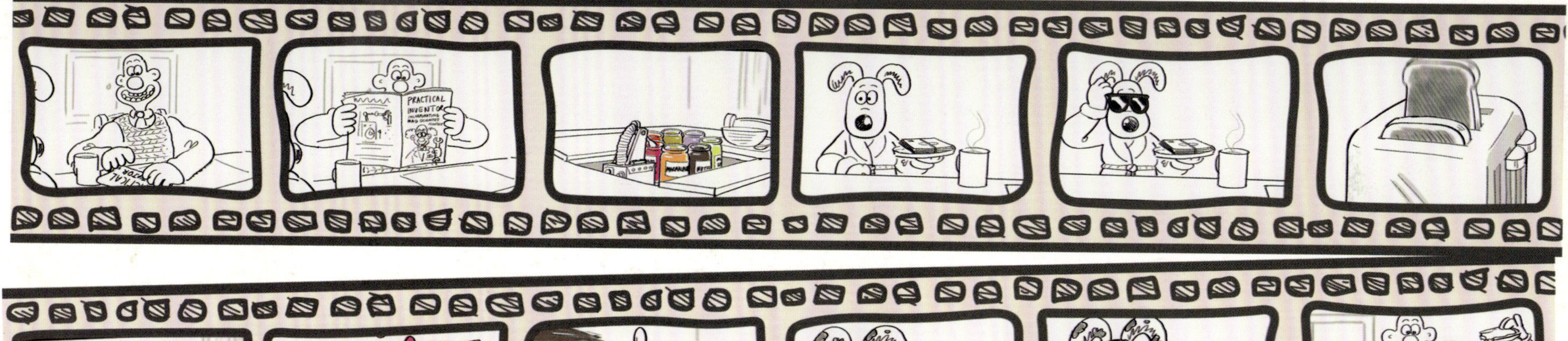

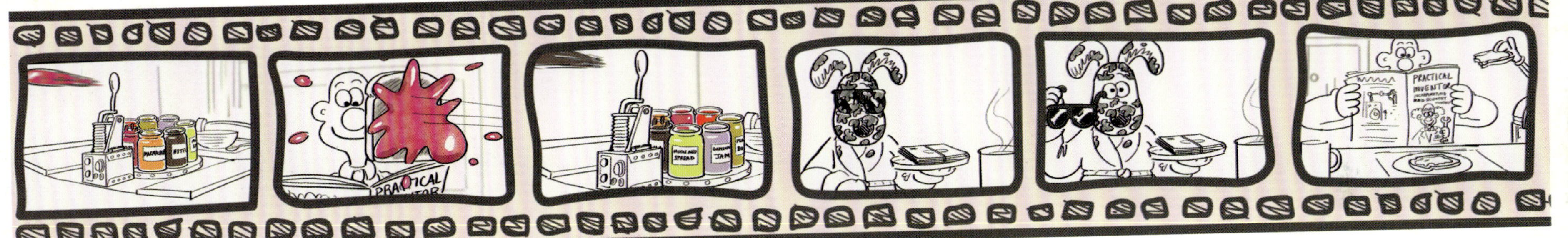

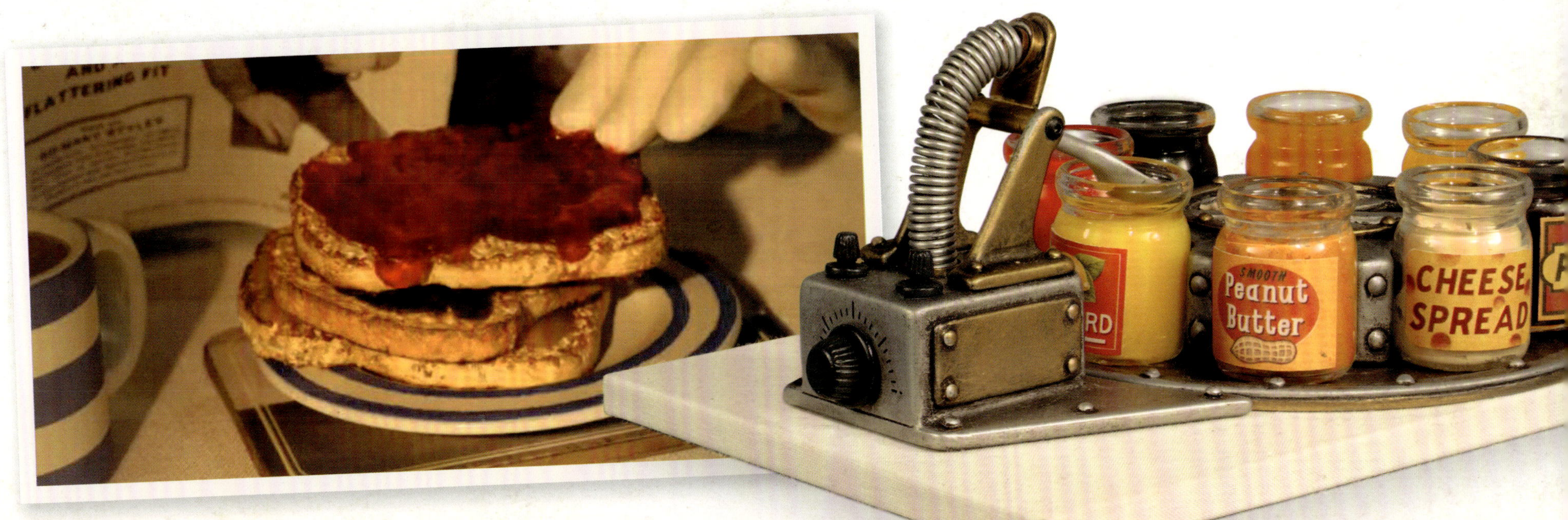

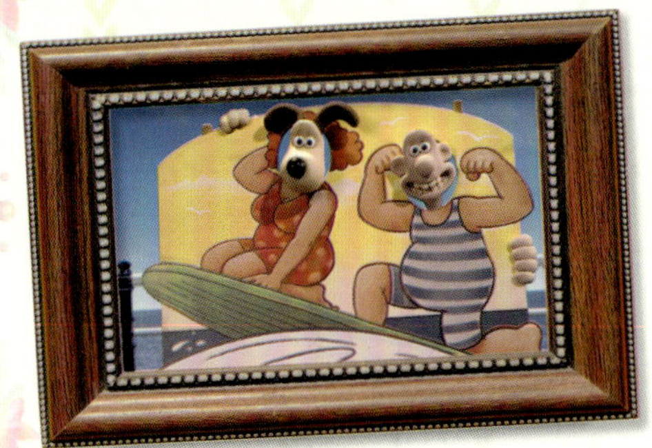

feeling of realism and added digital steam to the cups of tea to create a cosy atmosphere. Digital artists will also clean up some of the puppets, removing hairs and blemishes where necessary, although only if this is something that is distracting to the eye. "We are embracing the whole hand-made look in CG," says Kirstie Deane, VFX producer. "There are only so many units and so many animators, and they just have to get shots done. That's where we can help them by adding bits in."

So the Get-U-Up sequence revisits some classic moments from earlier *Wallace & Gromit* films in a far more sophisticated way, but it is more than just a cracking example of slapstick comedy. As Merlin says, "It's setting up the theme of reliance on technology and the underlying relationship of Wallace and Gromit: Gromit is feeling a bit down and needs a pat, and Wallace even has a machine for that. All Gromit wants is an actual pat on the head. Which happily he finally gets, if that's not a spoiler!"

 The Art of Wallace & Gromit *VENGEANCE MOST FOWL*

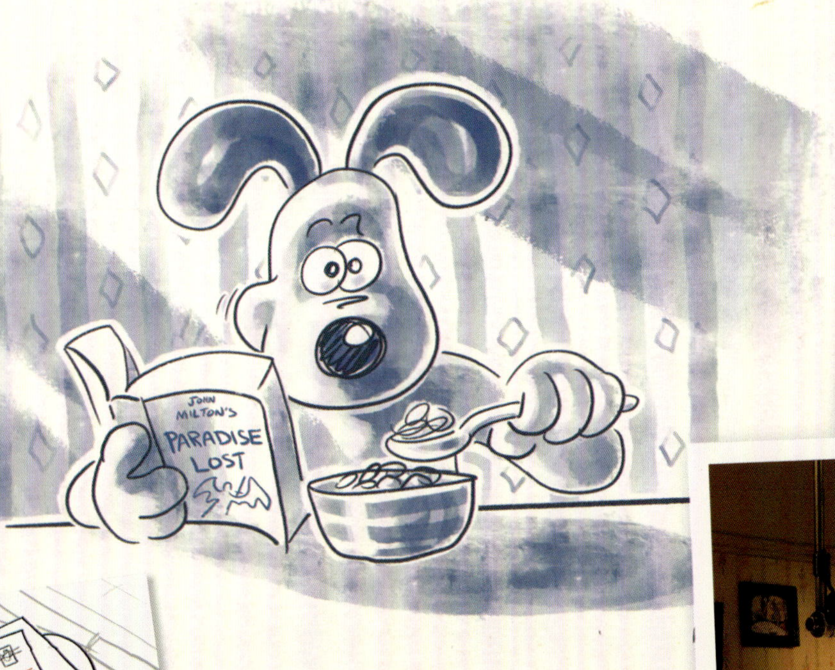

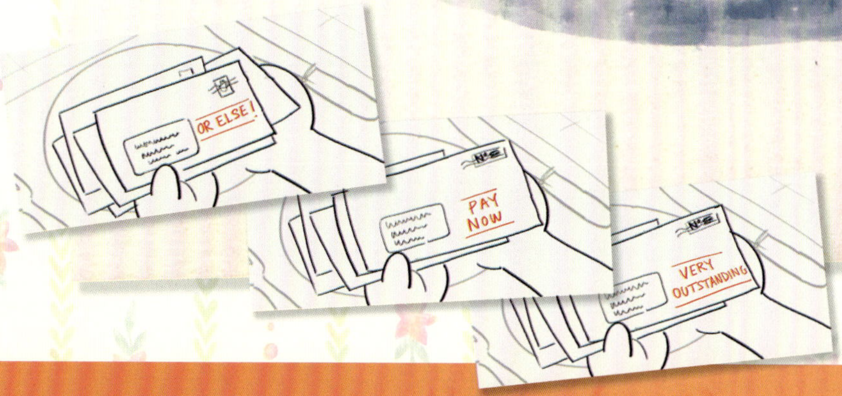

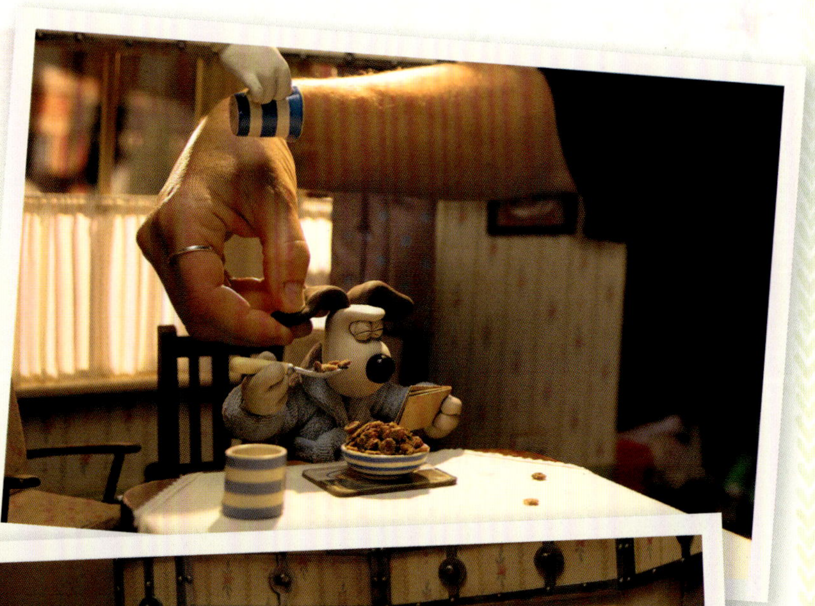

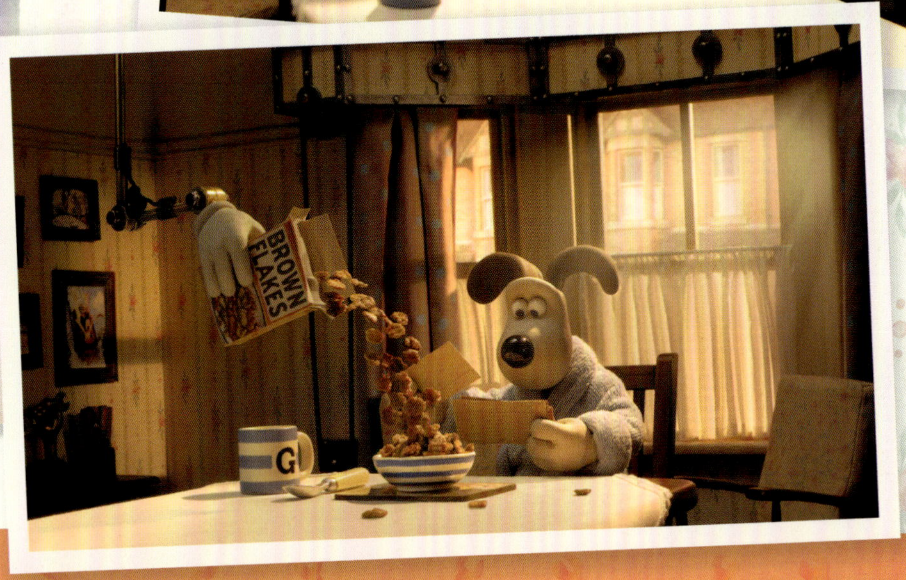

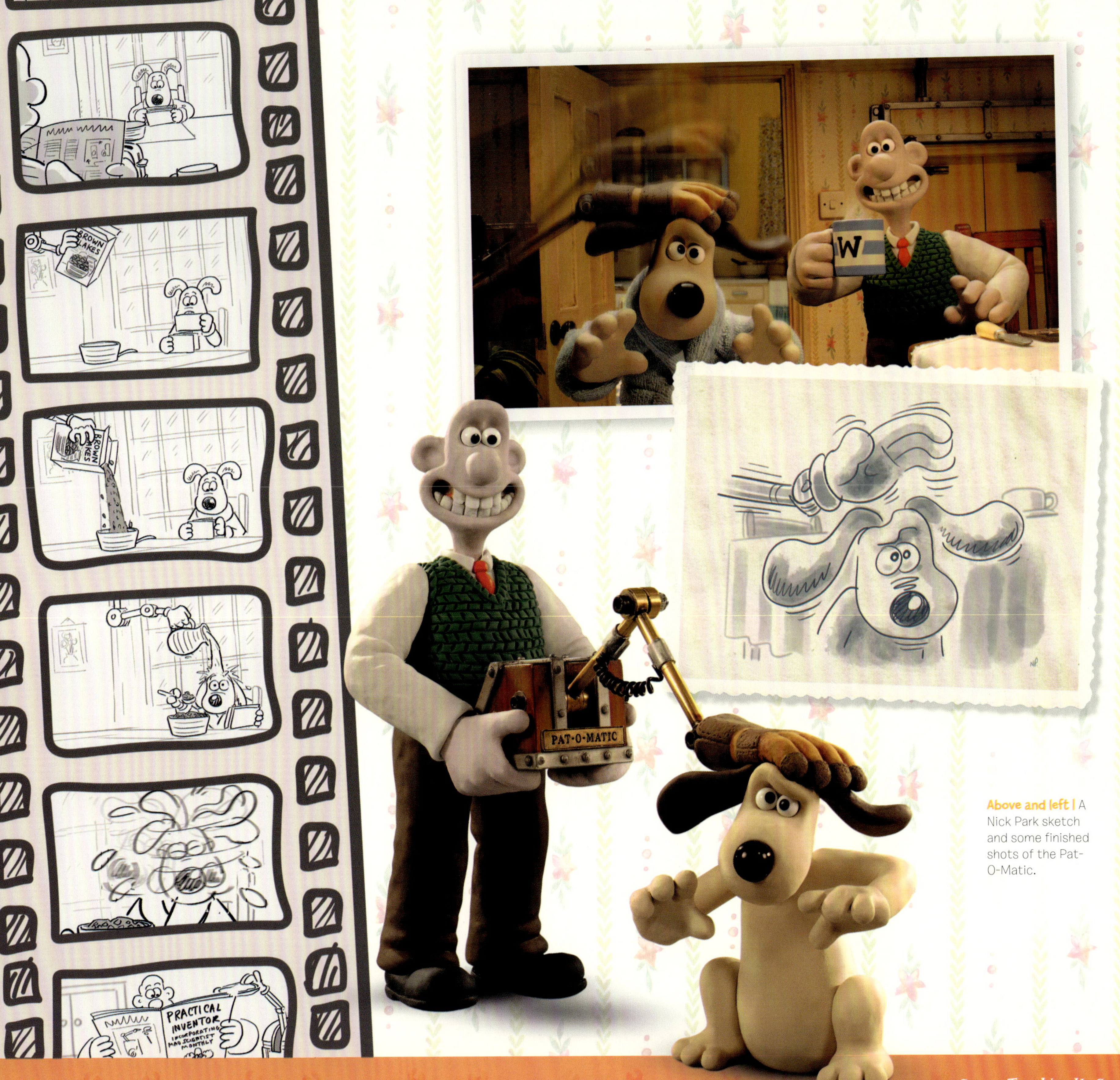

Above and left | A Nick Park sketch and some finished shots of the Pat-O-Matic.

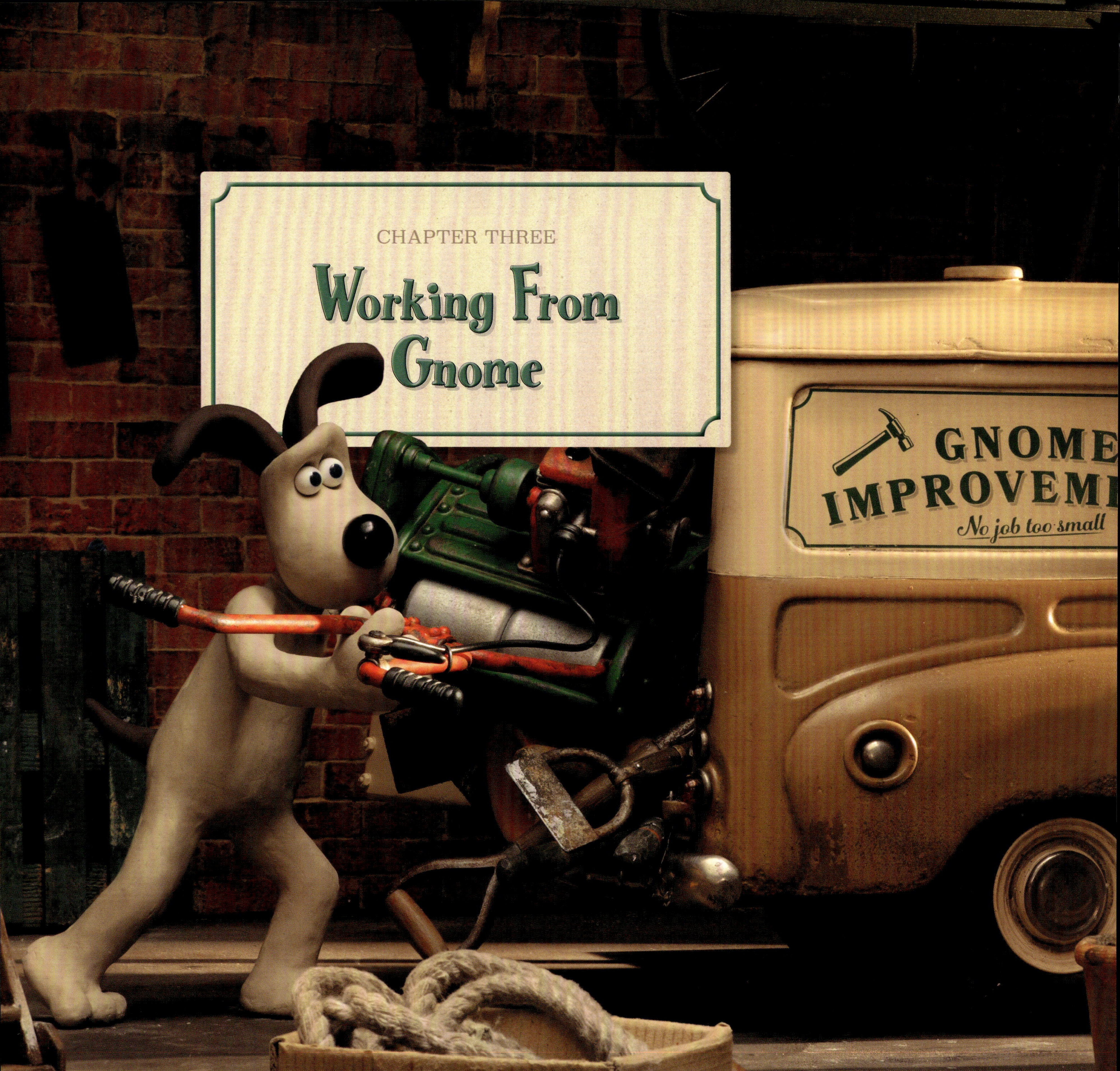

CHAPTER THREE
Working From Gnome
GNOME
IMPROVEME
No job too small

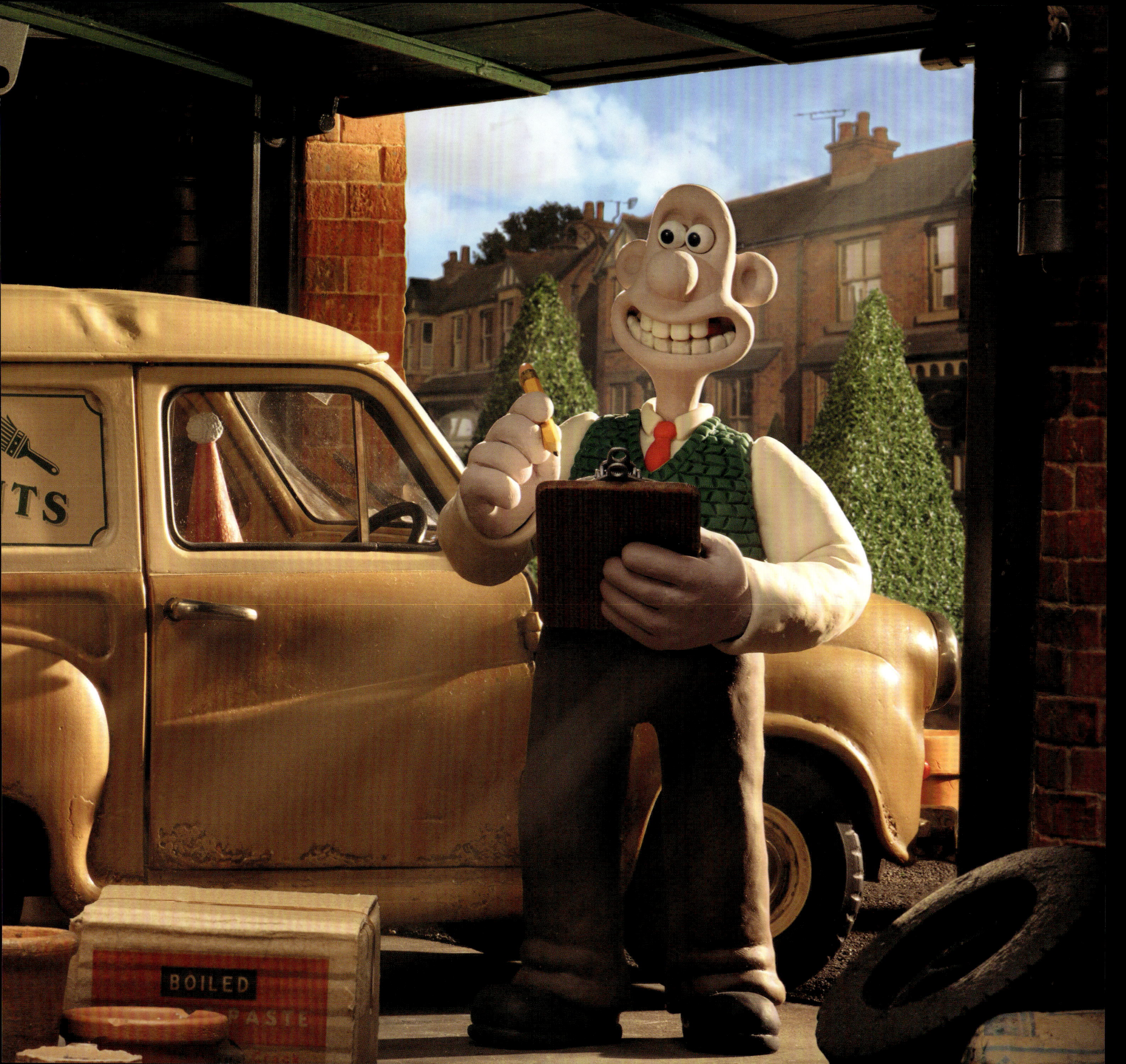
ITS
BOILED
PASTE

Working From Gnome

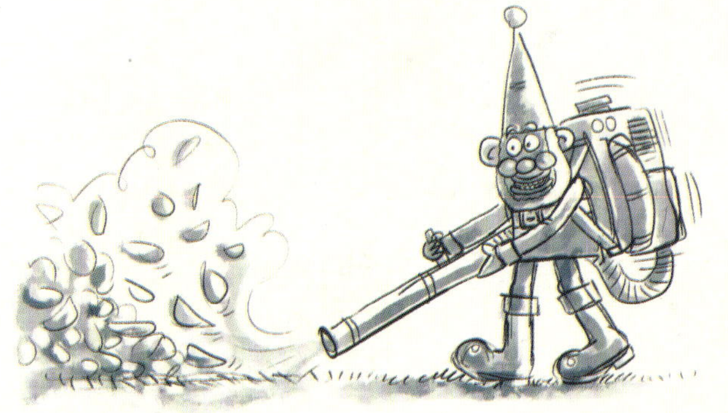

IT HAS TO BE ADMITTED THAT WALLACE HAS a somewhat chequered career as an inventor, but in *Vengeance Most Fowl* he finally seems to strike gold. The Nifty Odd-jobbing Robot (or Norbot for short) proves a hit with his West Wallaby Street neighbours, admired for its enthusiastic gardening skills and relentlessly chirpy demeanour. The 'smartgnome' is suddenly in high demand all over town, and it looks like Wallace's ingenuity has finally paid off... Or has it?

The idea of an invasion of malevolent garden gnomes is one that had been brewing in Nick's imagination (and sketch pad) for years: "It's been around since *Curse of the Were-Rabbit* as the germ of an idea," he recalls. "I find that one film tends to spawn a new idea for the next one, even if you don't know it yet. And gnomes have always been part of Wallace and Gromit's world. A lot of these ideas come from a doodle or a 'what if?' question. What if Wallace invented an automated gnome to help Gromit in the garden?"

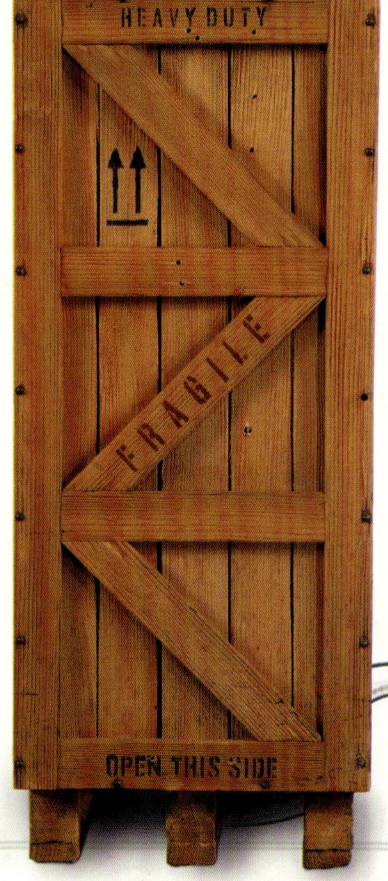

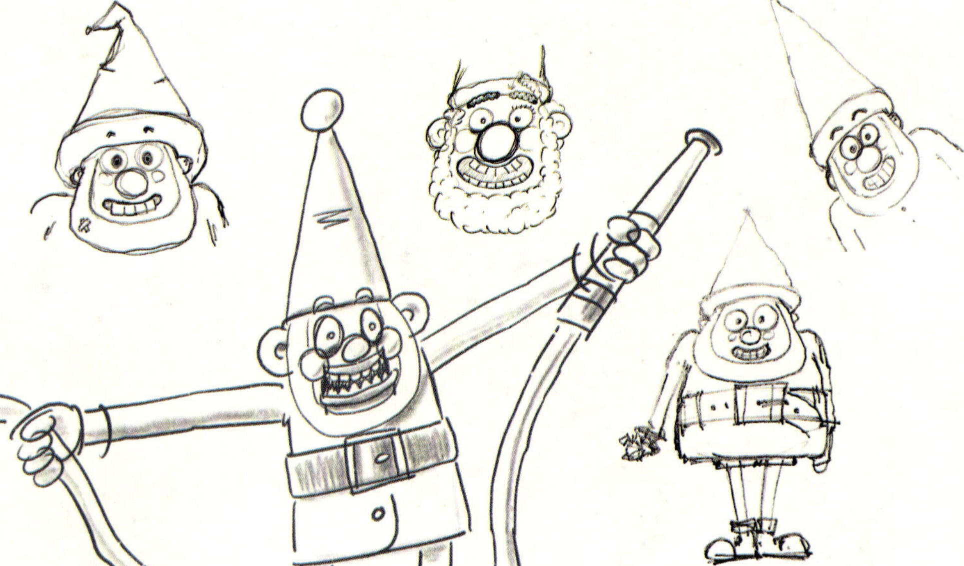

Above | Nick Park's sketch of Norbot 'pointlessly blowing leaves around'.

Below left | Freed from its crate, the Norbot puppet marches off to work.

Below | Various alternative character sketches for Norbot by Merlin Crossingham.

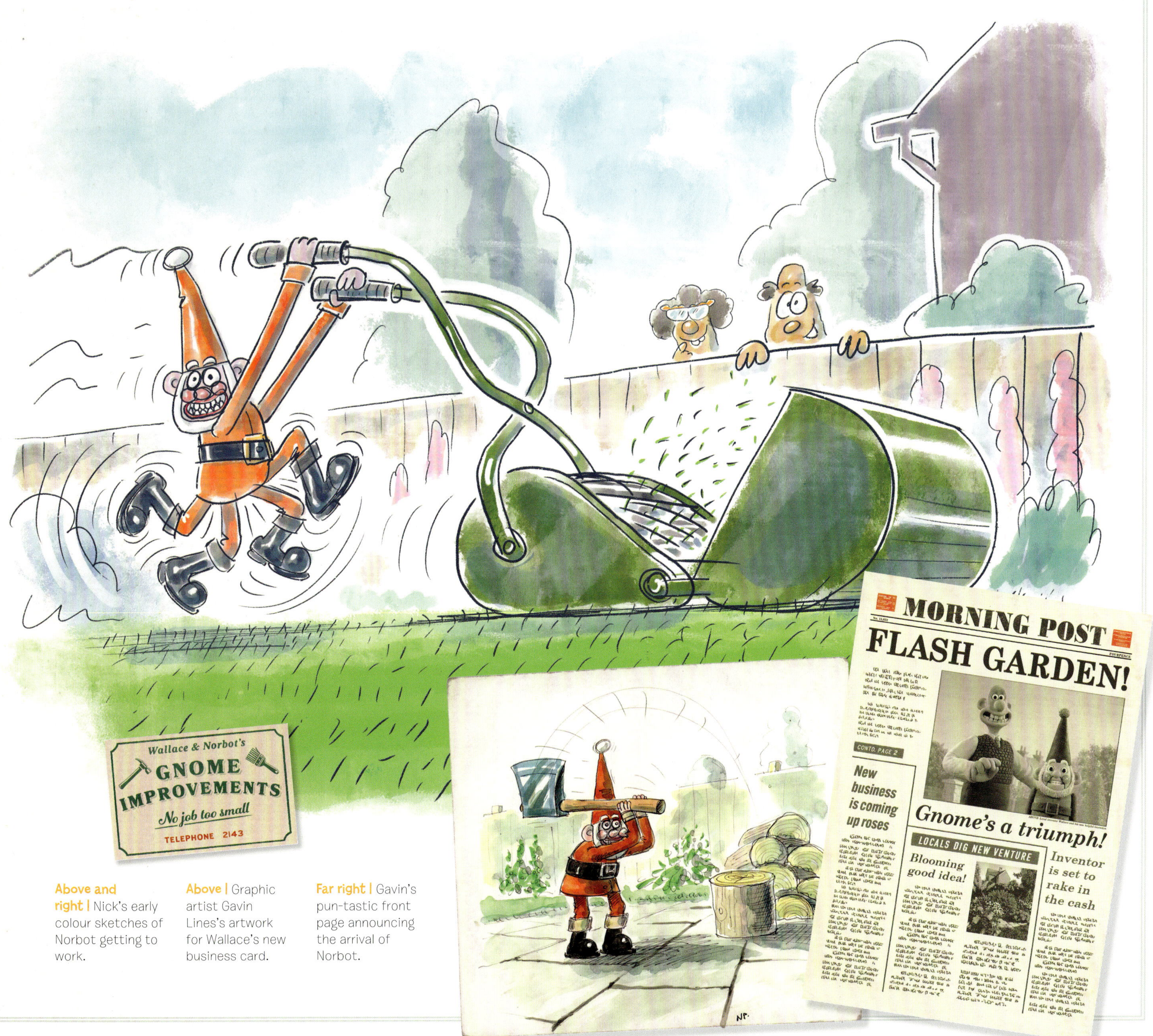

Above and right | Nick's early colour sketches of Norbot getting to work.

Above | Graphic artist Gavin Lines's artwork for Wallace's new business card.

Far right | Gavin's pun-tastic front page announcing the arrival of Norbot.

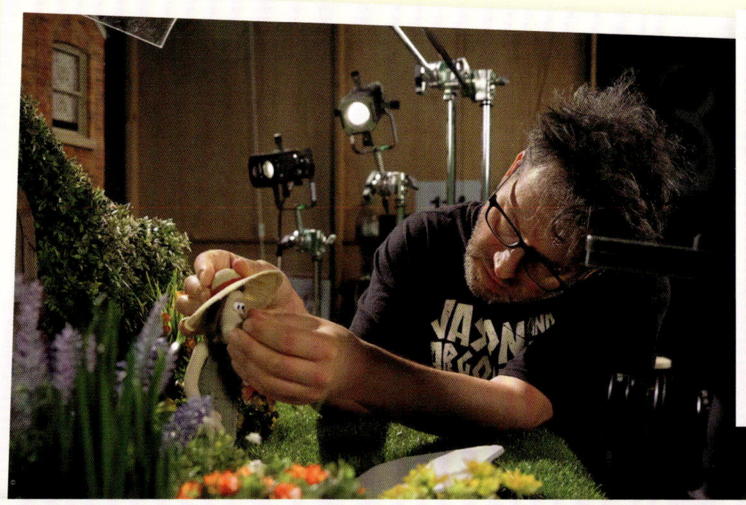
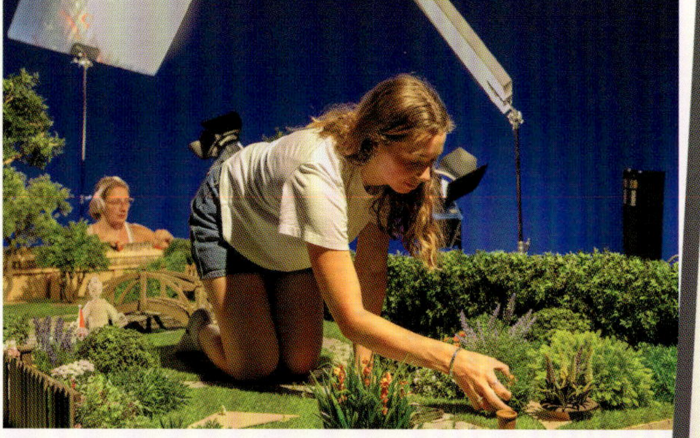
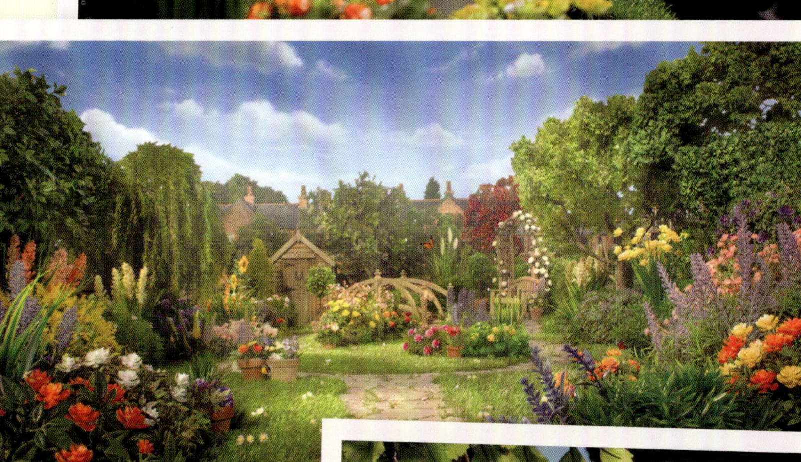
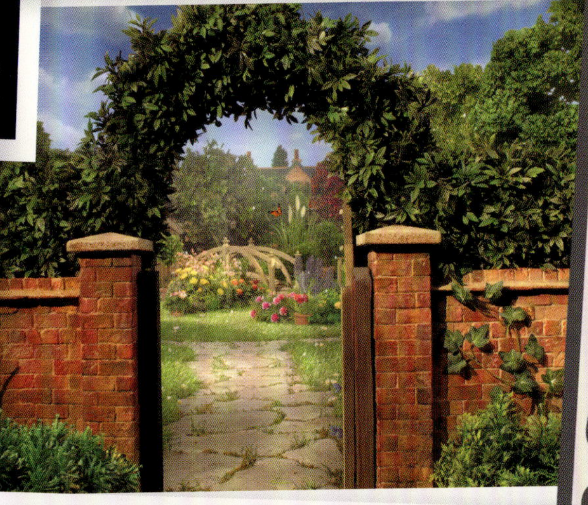
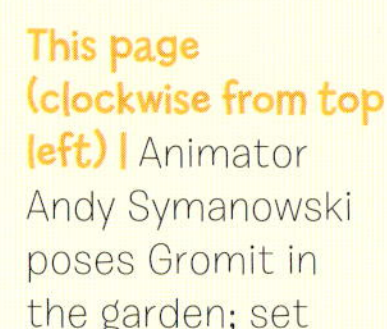
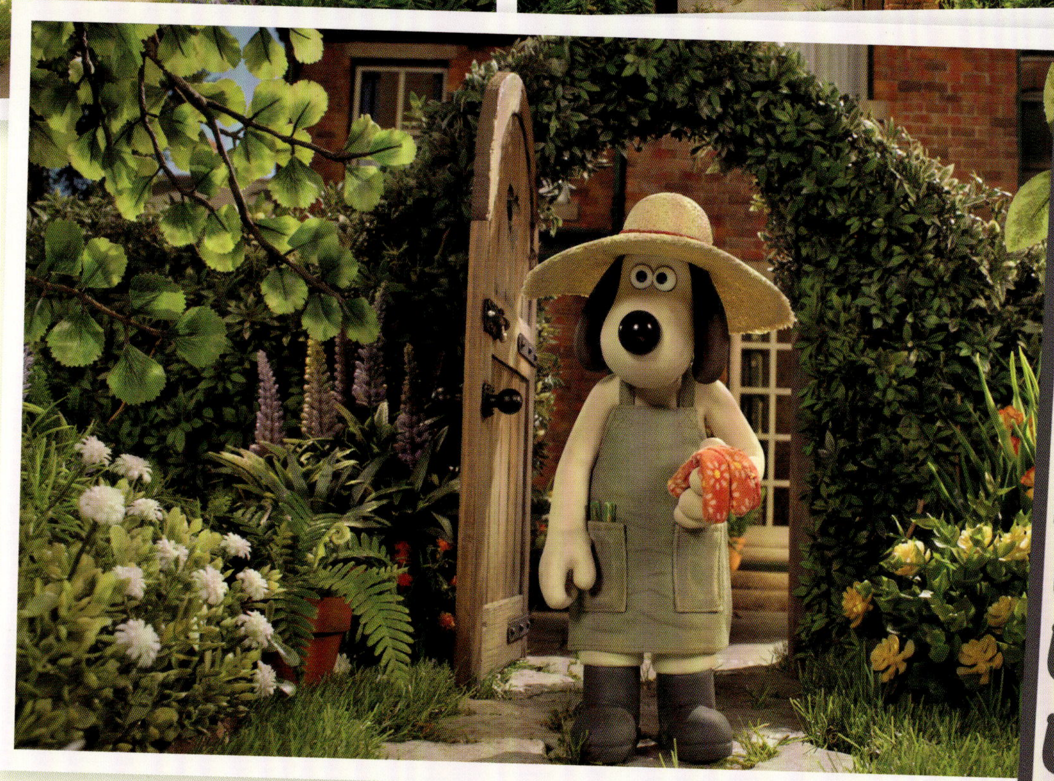
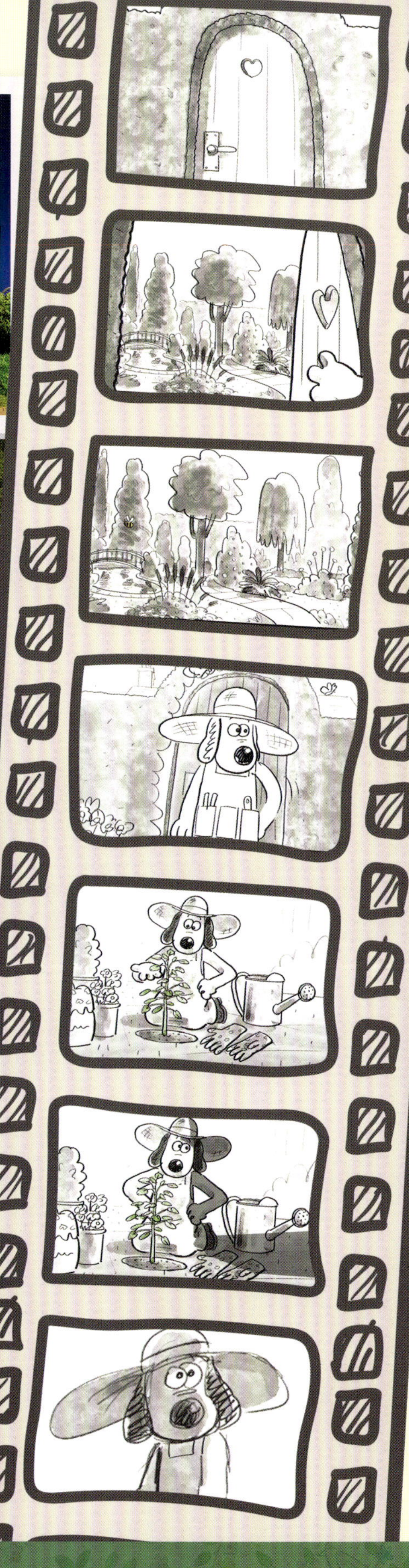

This page
(clockwise from top
left) | Animator
Andy Symanowski
poses Gromit in
the garden; set
dresser Isabella
Gilding adjusts
the shrubbery;
the entrance
to the garden;
Gromit surveys his
handiwork; long
shot of Gromit's
English country
garden.

Far right |
Mike Salter's
storyboards for
Gromit gardening.

Right | Thumbnail storyboards by Nick Park for the arrival of Norbot.

Below | Gromit's gardening days are numbered...

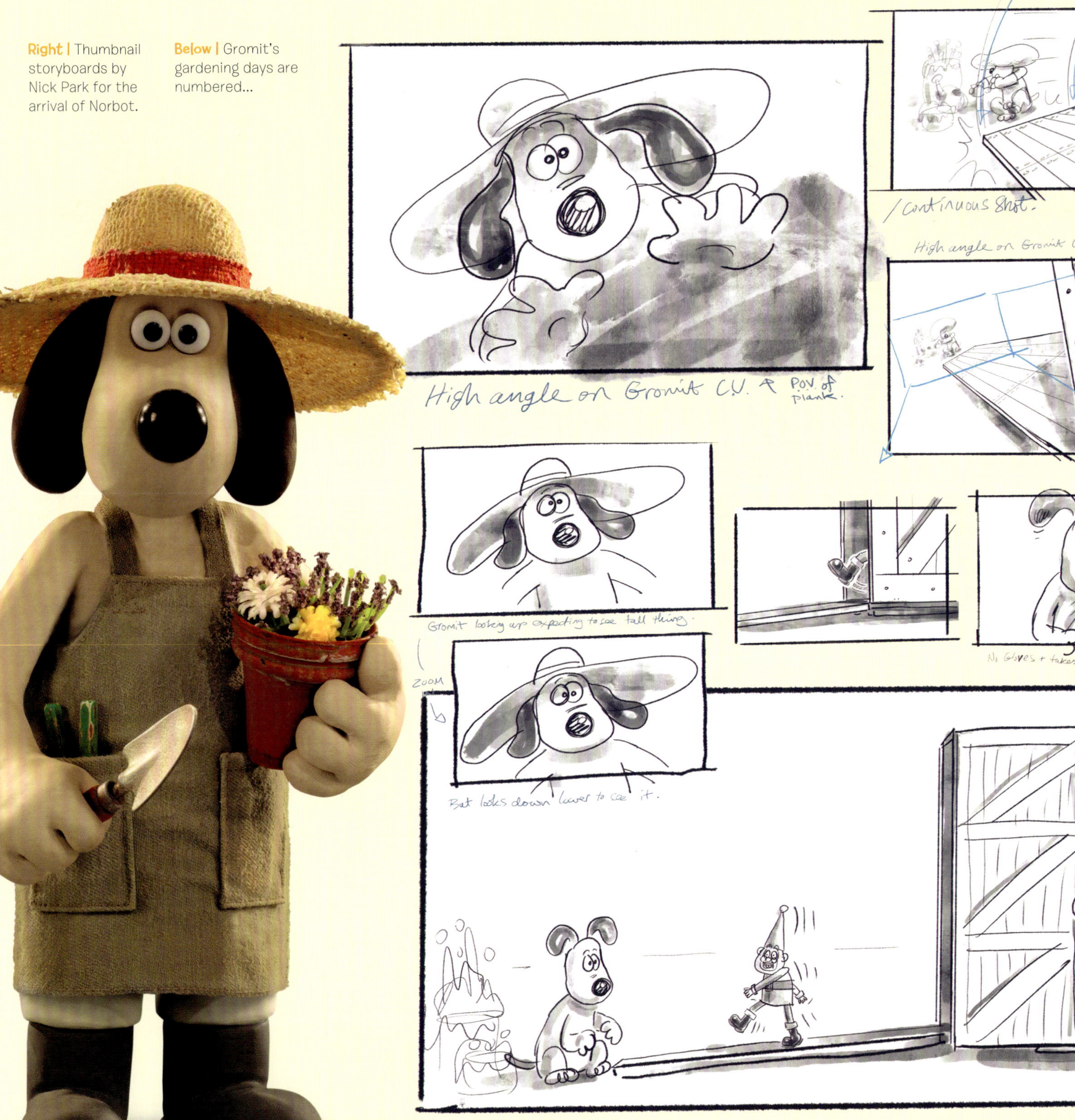
/ Continuous shot.
High angle on Gromit C.U. & P.O.V. of plank.
High angle on Gromit C.U. & P.O.V. of plank.
Gromit looking up expecting to see tall thing.
No Gloves & takes hat off.
ZOOM
But looks down lower to see it.

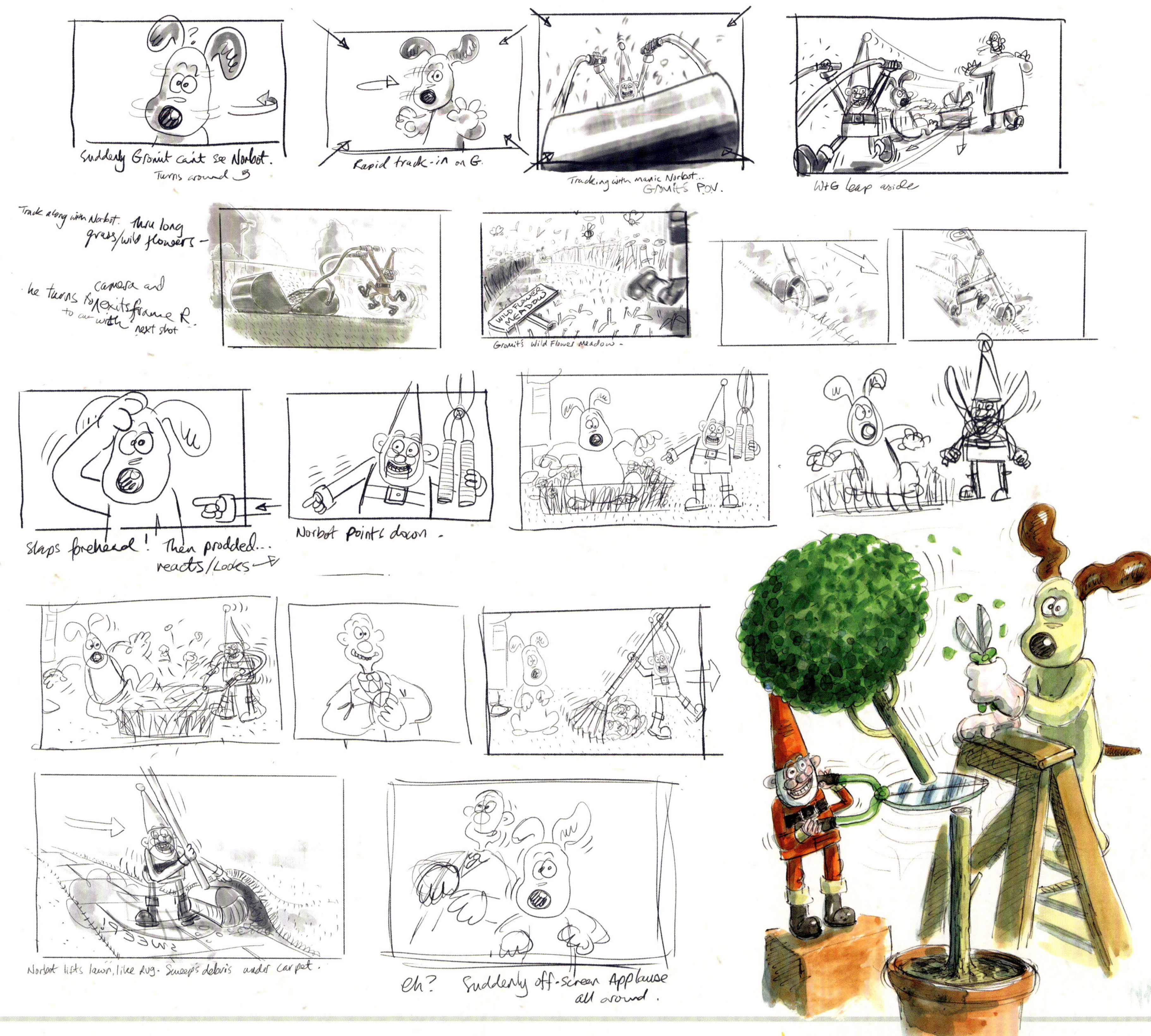
Suddenly Gromit can't see Norbot. Turns around
Rapid track-in on G.
Tracking with manic Norbot... GROMIT'S P.O.V.
W+G leap aside
Track along with Norbot. Thru long grass/wild flowers —
he turns to camera and exits frame R. to cut with next shot
WILD FLOWER MEADOW
Gromit's Wild Flower Meadow —
Slaps forehead! Then prodded... reacts/Looks
Norbot points down —
Norbot lifts lawn, like rug. Sweeps debris under carpet.
eh? Suddenly off-screen Applause all around.

Nick's process for designing the character of Norbot involved loose sketching in a variety of colours, proportions, poses and scenarios to find what 'clicked' in terms of capturing his vision. The finished version is a long way from the traditional jolly, chubby garden gnome. "It's more of a Wallace version," Nick reveals. "The traditional garden gnomes are cuddly and round, but for me that didn't quite translate into a Wallace-style robot. So that's where the design came from." Various members of the art team then help to develop these sketches through character drawings and model sculpts to explore how Norbot will work in both 2D and 3D.

Story artist Mike Salter has a long relationship with Nick, having been part of the team since *A Close Shave*, and the two share a shorthand that helps Mike firm up Nick's sketches into more finished designs. "I like to stay very hands-on with the drawing," says Nick, "but Mike and a group of story artists have been brilliant at helping to develop the whole thing. Mike is a great *Wallace & Gromit* artist."

In typical Aardman fashion, Mike is very modest about his contribution: "I mostly work on Nick's drawings and beef them up a bit, really," he explains. "He's thought about all the shots and angles. He'll give me a page of thumbnails, where he's working it out as he goes along.

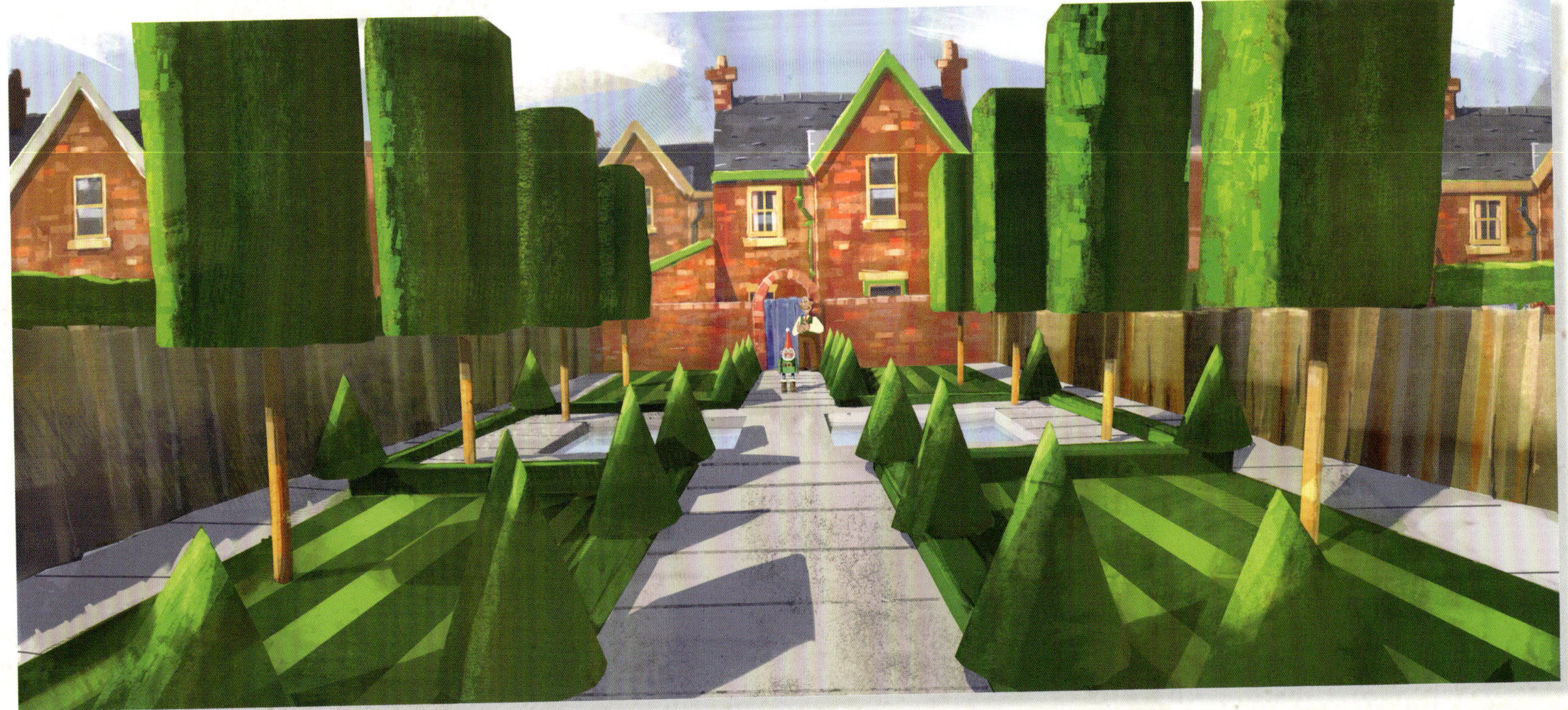

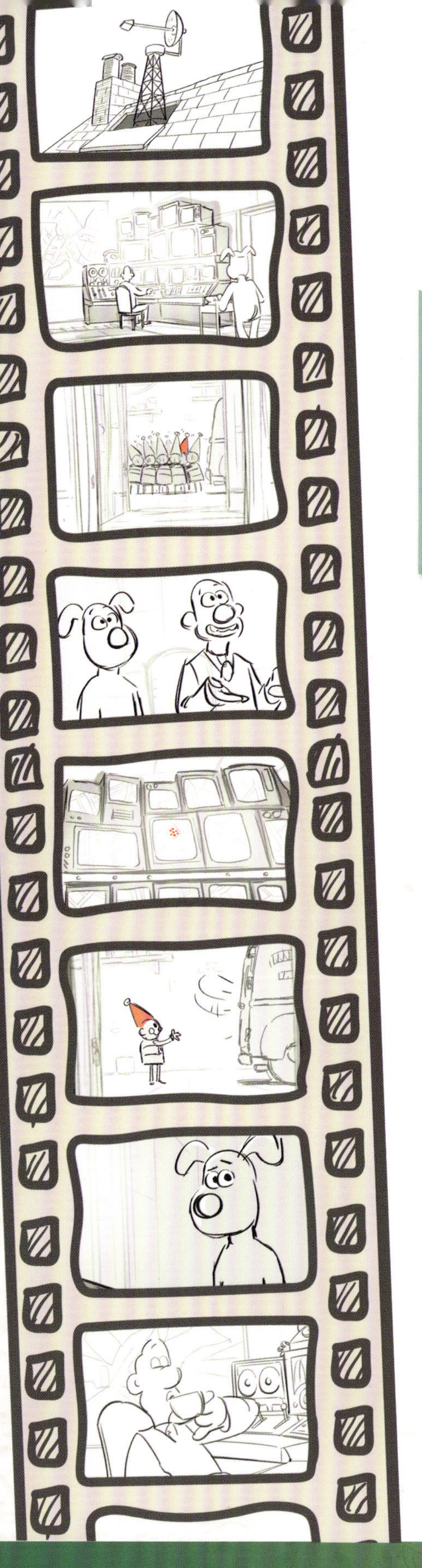

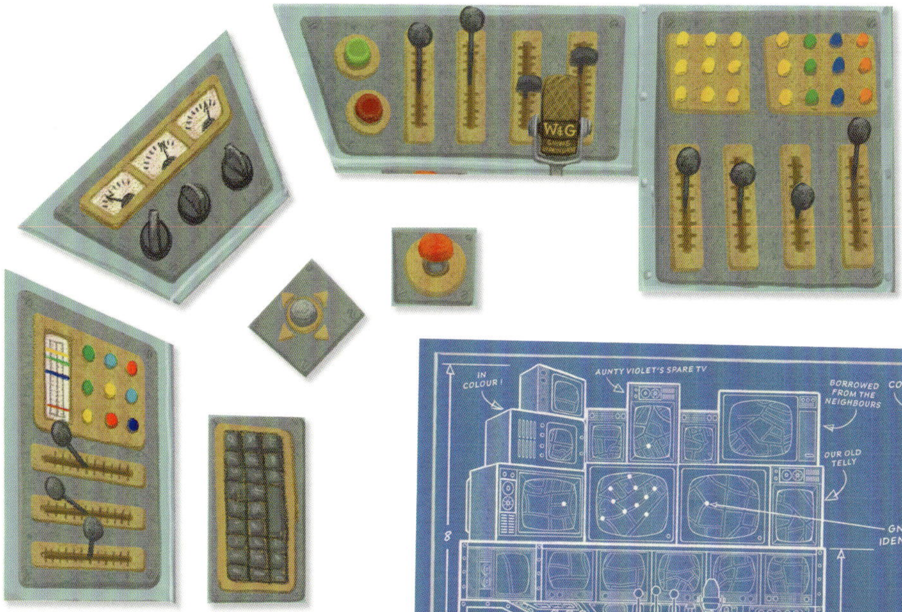

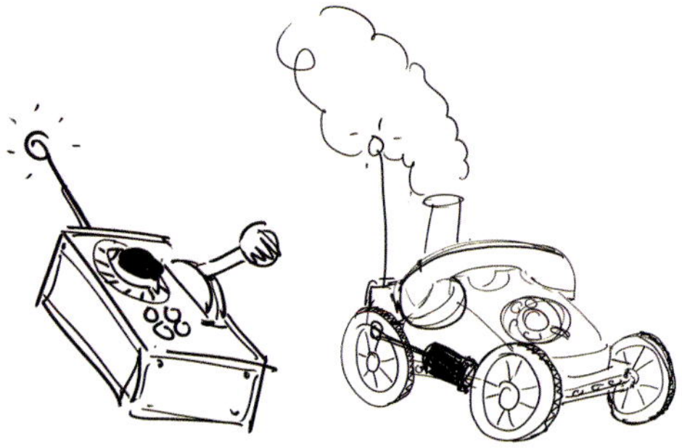

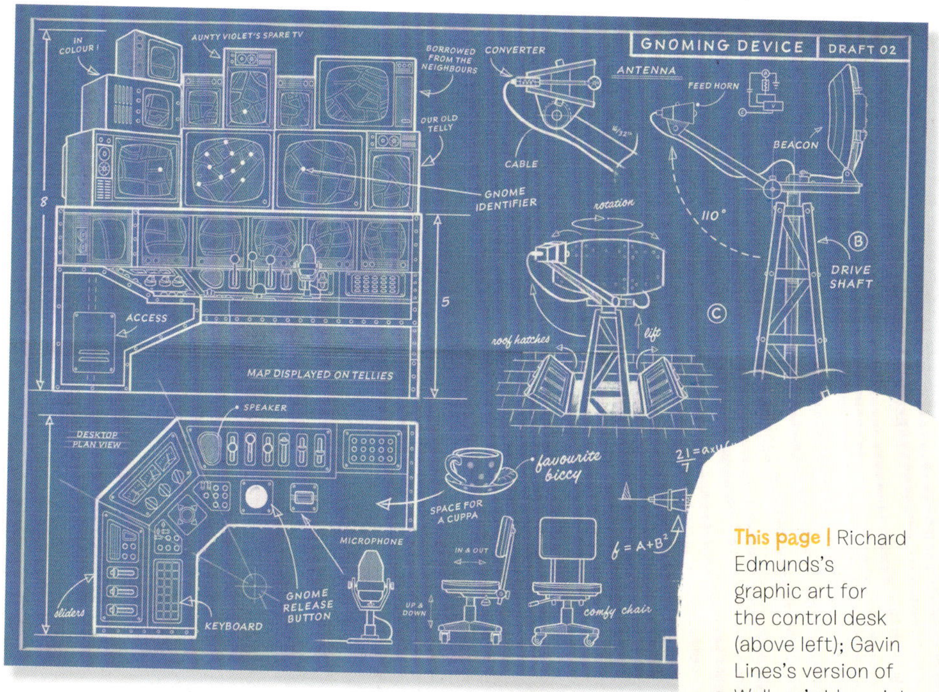

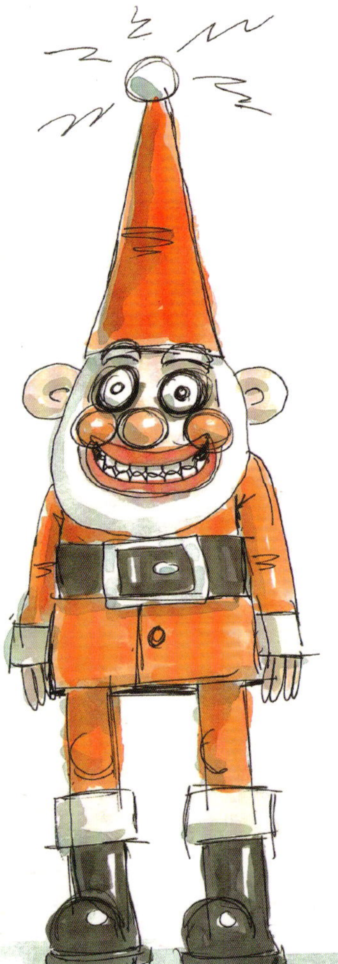

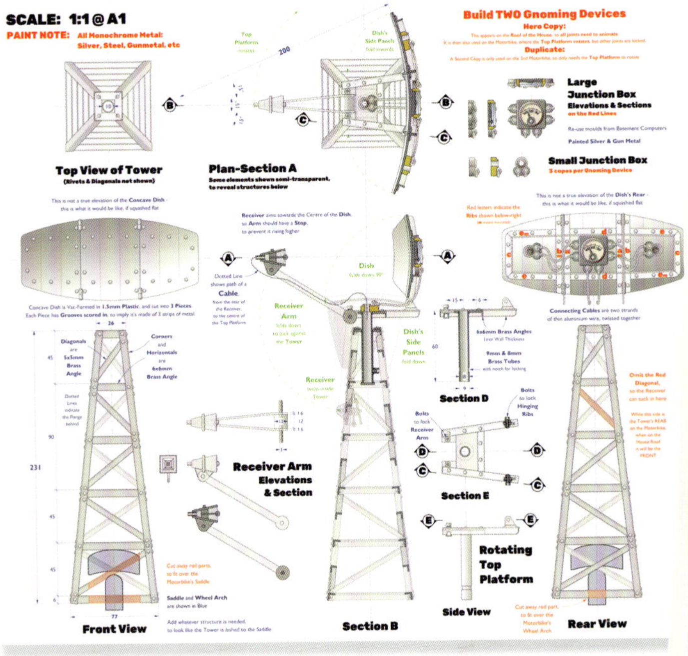

SCALE: 1:1 @ A1
PAINT NOTE: All Monochrome Metal: Silver, Steel, Gunmetal, etc

Build TWO Gnoming Devices
Here Copy:
This appears on the Roof of the House, so all joints need to animate.
It is then also used on the Motorbike, where the Top Platform rotates, but other joints are locked.
Duplicate:
A Second Copy is only used on the 2nd Motorbike, so only needs the Top Platform to rotate.

Top View of Tower
(Rivets & Diagonals not shown)

Plan-Section A
Some elements shown semi-transparent, to reveal structures below

Large Junction Box
Elevations & Sections

Small Junction Box

Receiver Arm Elevations & Section

Rotating Top Platform

Front View

Section B

Side View

Rear View

Section D

Section E

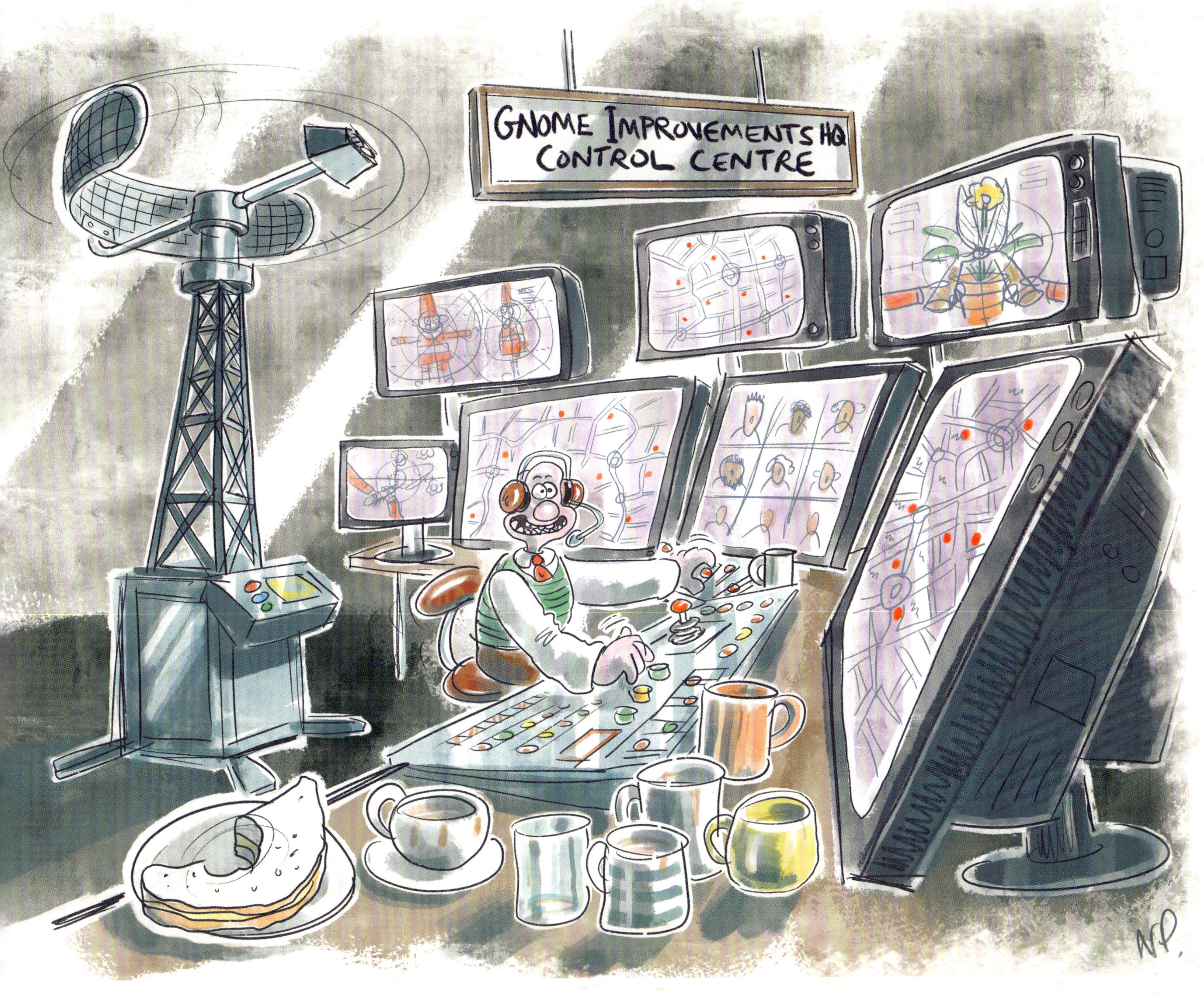

GNOME IMPROVEMENTS HQ
CONTROL CENTRE

I might get one frame and do three different positions of Wallace turning his head to Gromit and winking."

Mike digitally produces basic 2D animation from Nick's sketches, which he incorporates into his storyboards (frame-by-frame breakdowns of the action). He will add some 'comic-book'-style effects such as motion lines and eyebrows for Gromit to convey character and action: "It's done digitally, but it's old-school drawing, really. It won't be super-fantastic animation, it's pretty basic stuff." His approach to working with the two directors differs, given his long experience of translating Nick's ideas: "If I'm doing it for Nick I'll go straight for finished drawings; he's done the vast majority of it already. If I'm doing it for Merlin, I'll go for a much rougher thumbnail to begin with."

But for stop-motion animation, 2D images are only part of the story and it is essential to work out how the character is going to exist in three dimensions. This is where sculptor Andy Spradbury comes in. He develops models of all the main characters, working in the thoroughly low-tech medium of fingers and clay, going through various iterations until he finds one that fulfils the creative and technical requirements. Norbot was one of his biggest

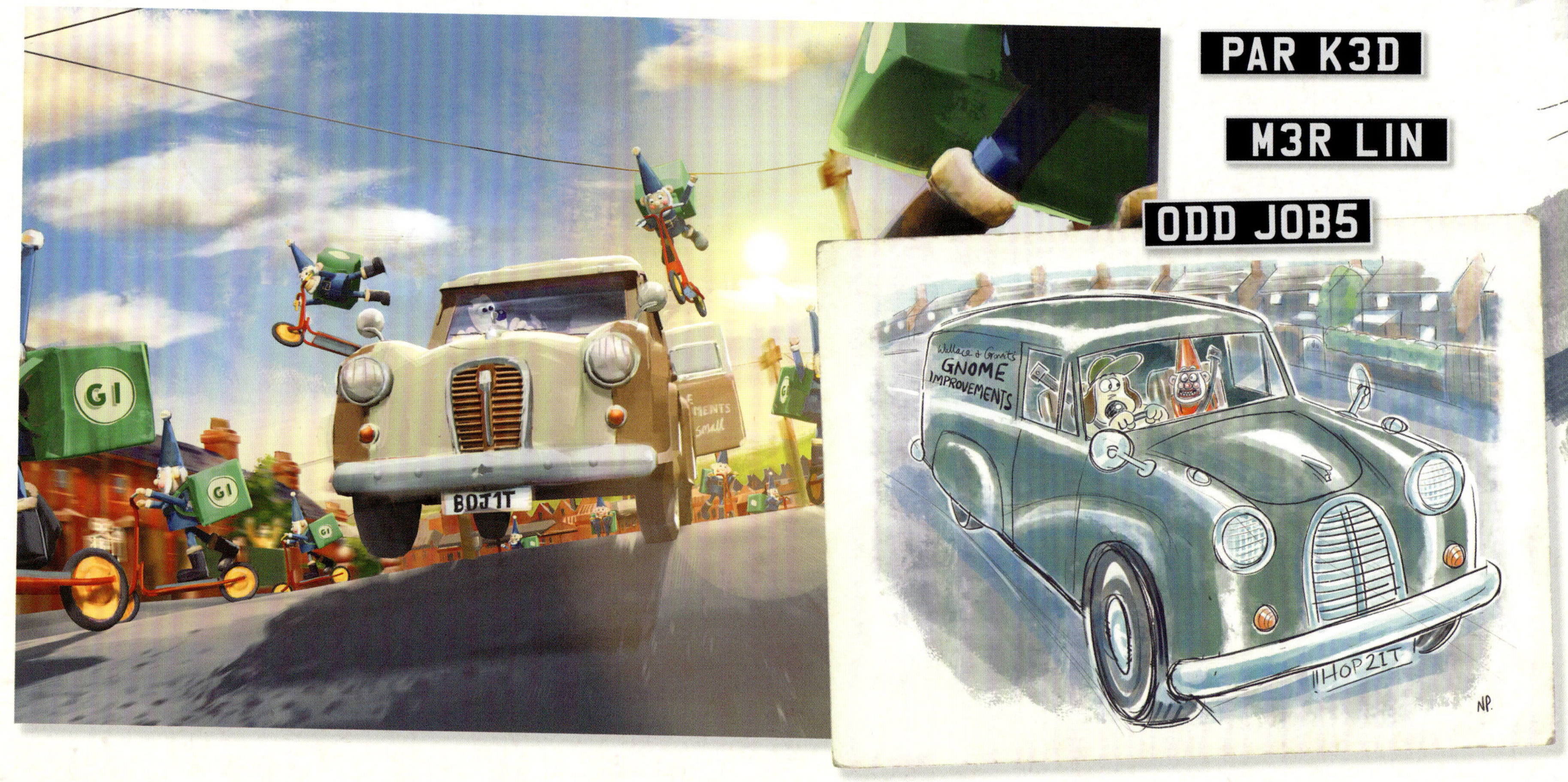

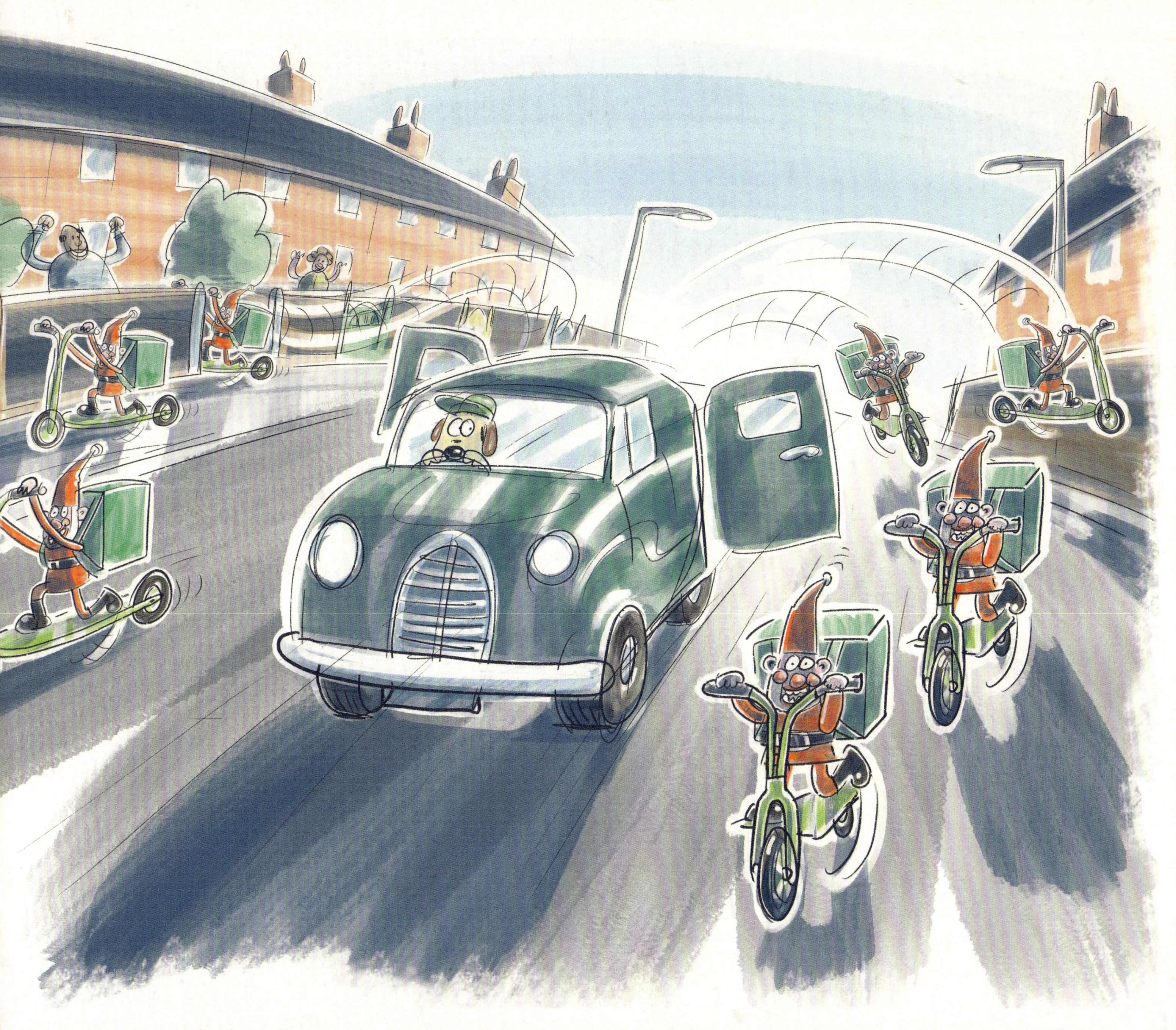

challenges: "He was a very long process," admits Andy, "mainly because I don't think Nick had an exact idea how he wanted him to look. He started off being made from panels of metal like a tin toy, then they wanted him quite round with cheeks stuck on and a jaw and lots of teeth like a ventriloquist's dummy. He's had a lot of different versions – different head sizes and body sizes: big head, small body, long legs, then the head a bit smaller, body a bit taller… You change the proportions until the directors are happy. Nick is the mastermind behind it all; we keep developing it until he works out what he wants to see."

Capturing the look is only part of Andy's job,

as he also needs to be aware how the puppet will be built and animated. "When you're sculpting," he says, "you realise that if they're saying it has to twist in the middle then his belt has to be completely round, otherwise it won't twist properly; and there has to be enough space to be able to fit some sort of turntable system in. There are practical considerations because that's part of the character. How it moves is as important as how it looks."

Once the final sculpt is agreed, it's off to the modelmaking department to develop a fully animatable puppet – or, in the case of Norbot, an army of fully animatable puppets. At this point, the simplicity of Andy's clay is replaced by a

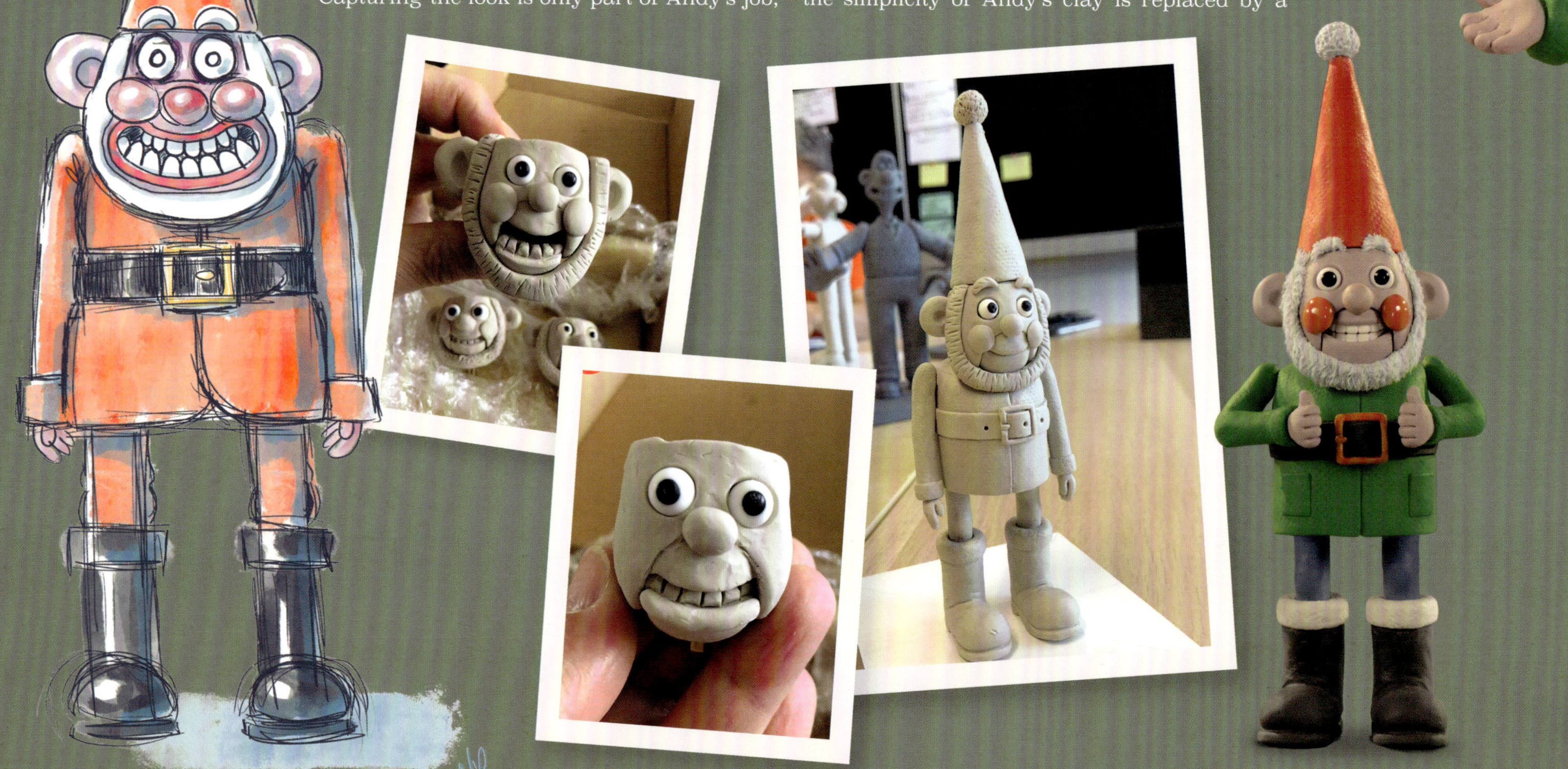

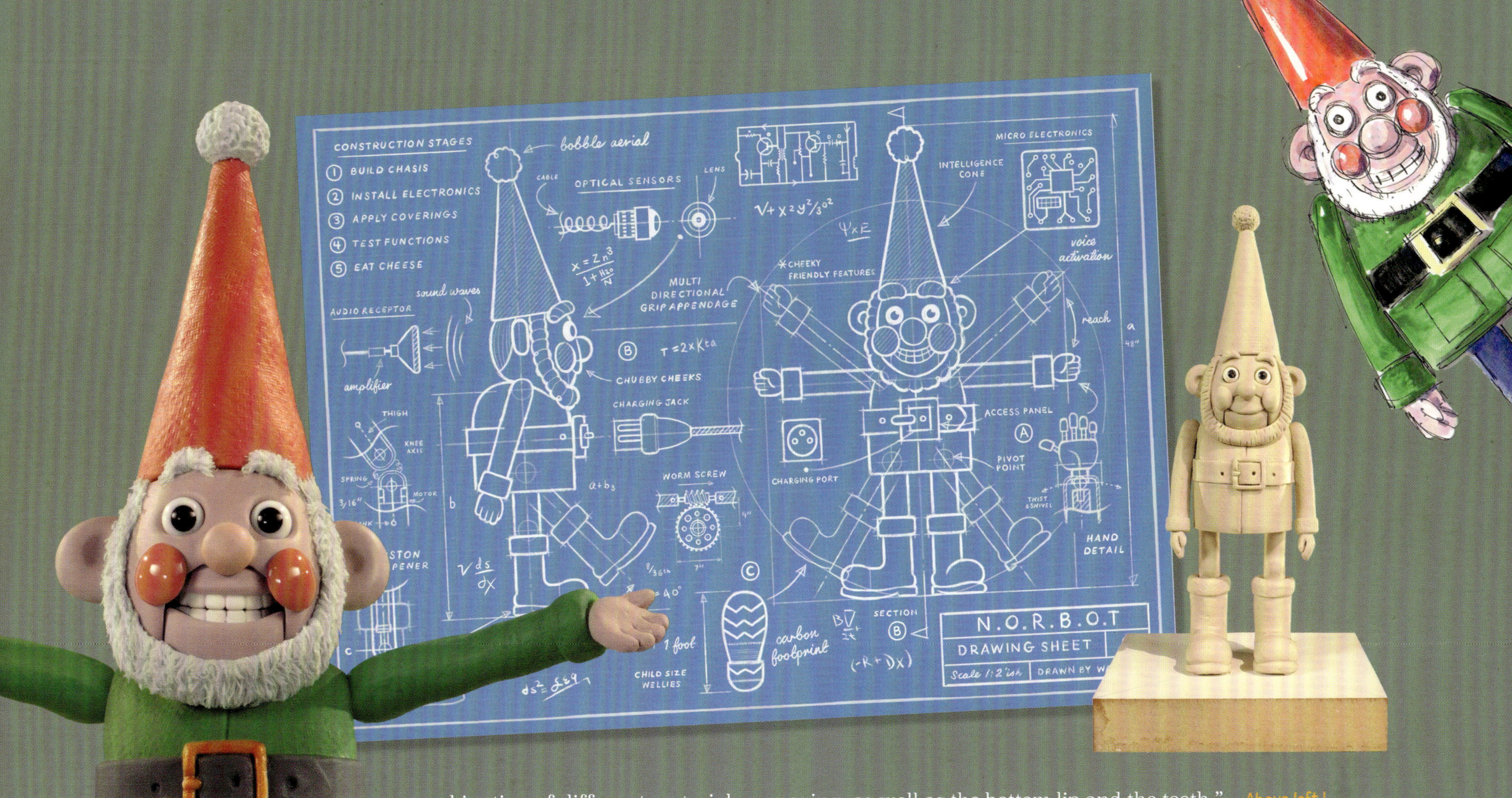

Above left | Wallace's original Norbot blueprints, as replicated by Gavin Lines.

Above | Andrew Spradbury's final production sculpt for Norbot.

Above right | Nick Park drawing of Norbot.

combination of different materials: "They are a mixture of silicon, resin and 3D printing," explains Head of Puppets Anne King. "They've got legs and arms that are silicon and plug-in arms that can be changed for different lengths, with little tiny ball joints. The heads are resin and are 3D-printed and painted. With the Evil Norbots, the skin colour is slightly different. These are the only puppets without any clay on them."

The complexity of the puppet's structure had to be adjusted to allow for the most efficient animation. "Originally, we had the top lip moving, as well as the bottom lip and the teeth," recalls Anne, "but then they decided to fix it to the teeth. Trying to manage it all became too much, so now we have just the bottom teeth going up and down." It was important that the multiple Norbots all looked identical and here recent developments in 3D printing were a boon. The heads could be mass-produced, with separate top lips, top teeth and cheeks to make the faces animatable and moulds for the resin elements like the hats were 3D-printed as well. The steel armatures were prototyped in-house, then sent out to other manufacturers for mass production. Another technological development with this film is the 3D scanning of practical models, which allows them to be reproduced

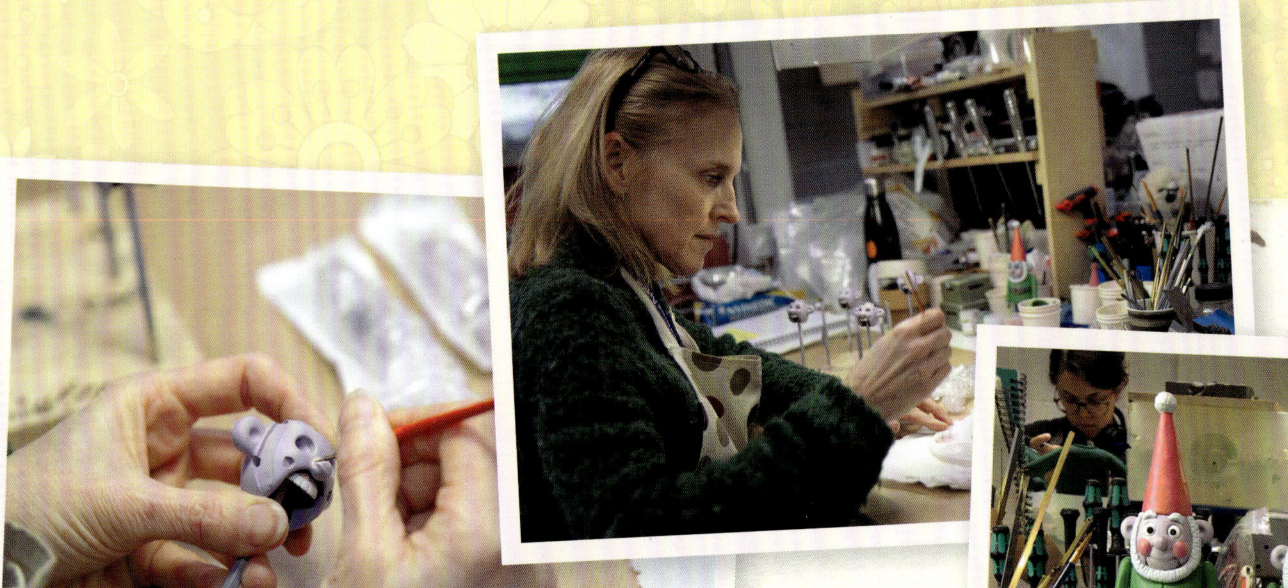

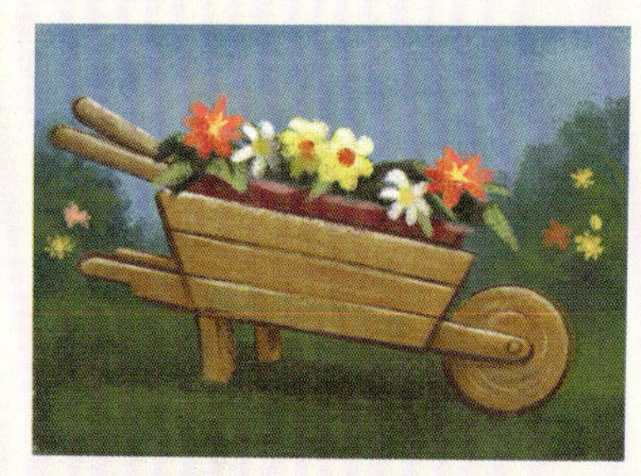

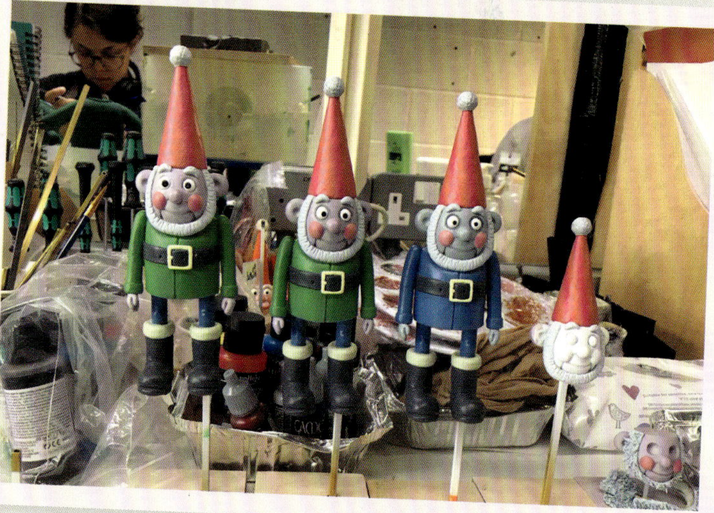

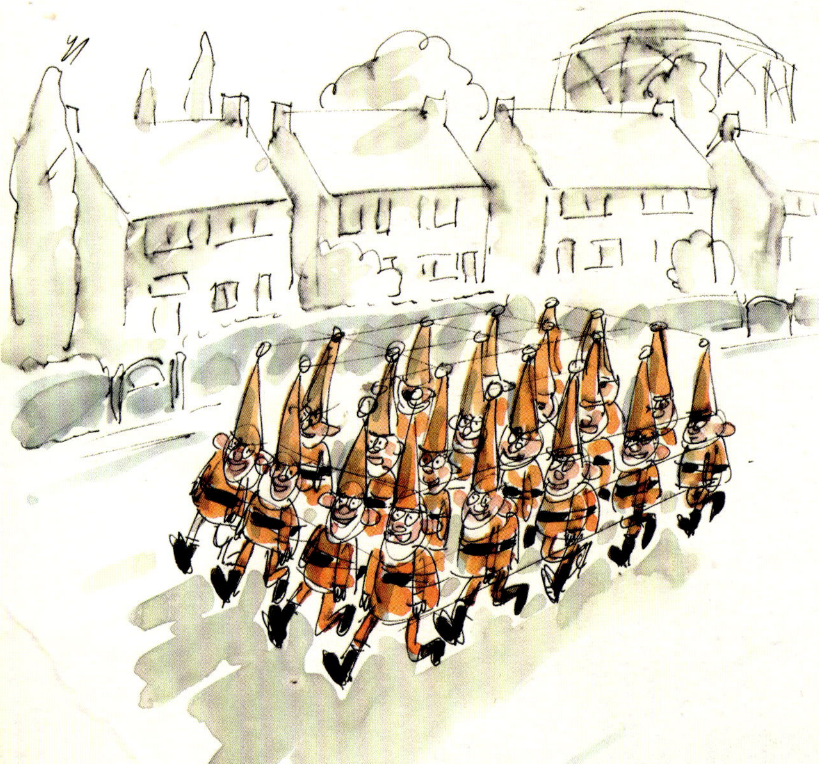

accurately for other areas such as gaming, licensing and archiving.

At the time of writing, 56 individual gnome puppets had been made, with the modelmaking department still working flat out on dozens more – a feat of mass production only rivalled by Norbot himself in his basement workshop.

All this sophisticated modelmaking would be in vain, however, without a team of highly skilled animators to bring the puppets to life. Once the prototype Norbot was built, Andy Symanowski and Laurie Sitzia were tasked with the initial testing. "They did dozens and dozens of walks and runs," recalls lead Norbot

Above | Adjusting the eyes on a 3D printed Norbot head (left); senior puppet maker Claire Drewitt painting a Norbot puppet (centre); colour-testing the army of Norbot puppets (right) (photos by Richard Davies).

Left | Nick Park's initial colour sketch for the army of Norbots.

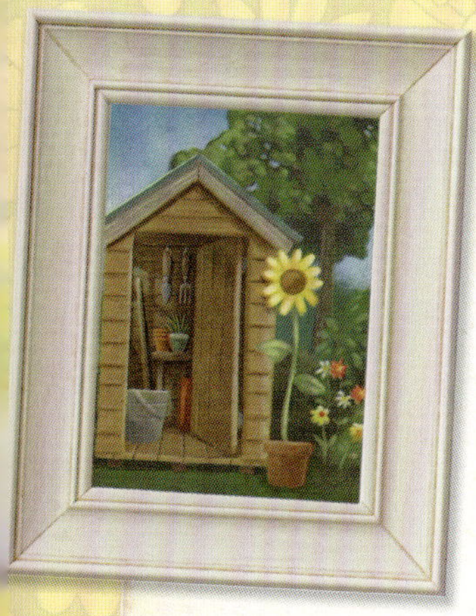

animator Rhodri Lovett. "You repeat those things at different speeds and with different variations, and oftentimes you don't know what it is you're looking for. It's a matter of showing it to directors and them saying 'Let's go with that.' In Norbot's case, Nick had really set ideas about lines. He wanted the legs and arms to be dead straight, so we'd spend a lot of time early on posing the puppet to get it looking robotic and stiff."

The style of movement for each character is then summarised in an Animation Bible, a list of Do's and Don'ts for how to approach each puppet compiled by supervising animator Will Becher. "With the animation team, everyone brings something," says Will. "There's always a bit of evolution, finding out the characteristics as we shoot. Wherever there's a characteristic that works, we'll feed that back to the rest of the team. We have a weekly meeting with the animators where we watch all the shots from that week, look at things that work, things that didn't quite work, how the characters blink, how they stand, the poses, all of that. I put together a working version of the Bibles with all of those details – this is how the mouth

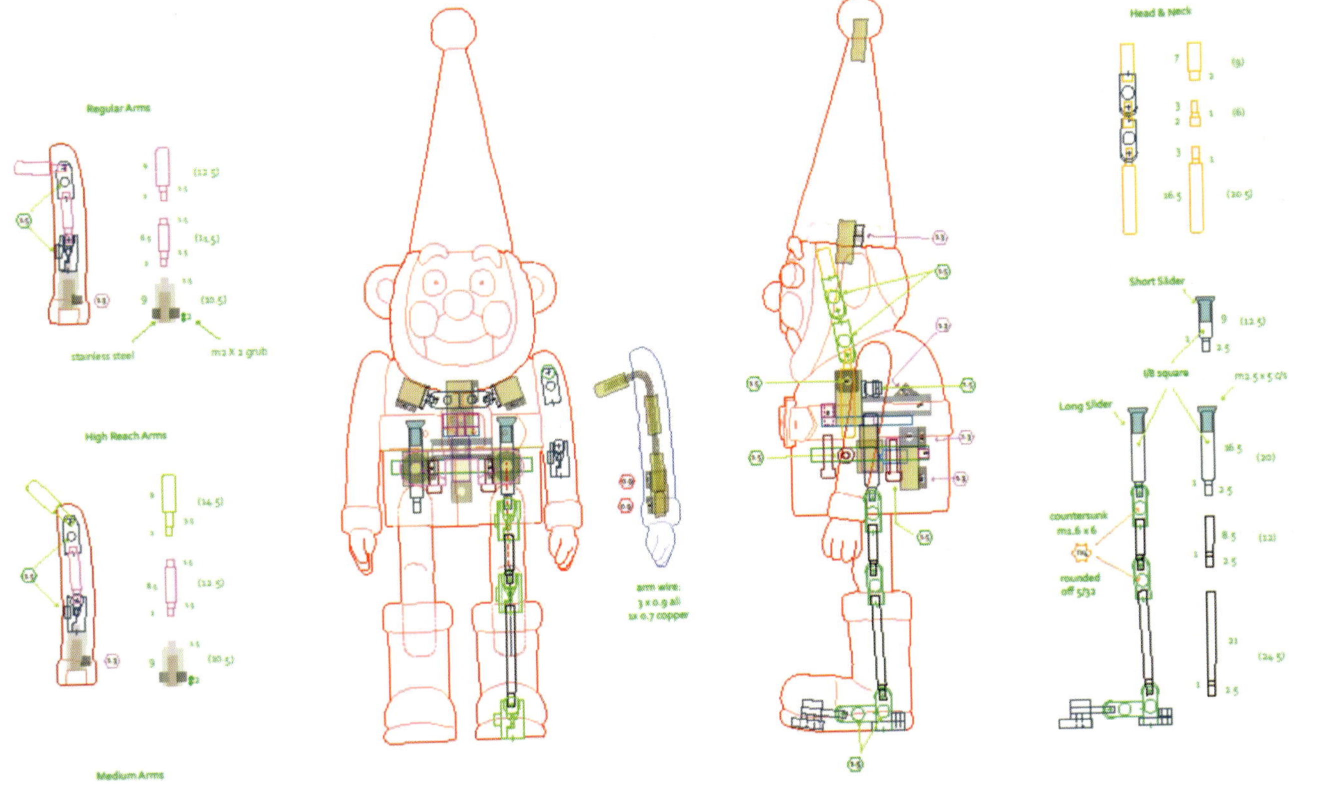

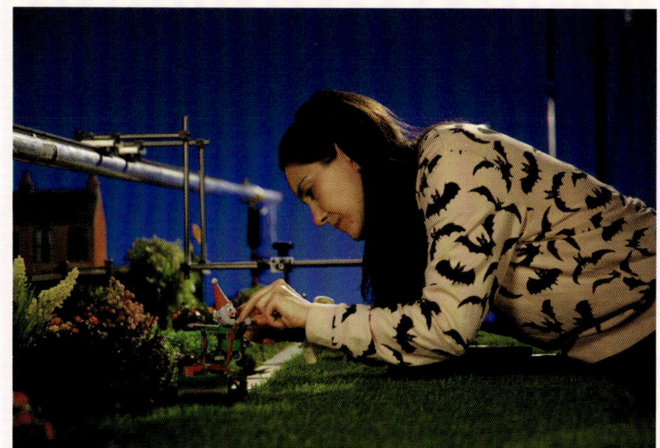

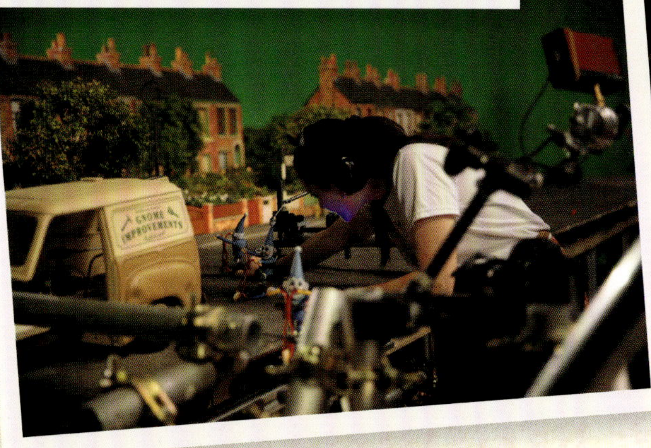

shape works, this is the colour of the lid, plus a bit about the personality of the characters."

With over 25 animators and seven or eight assistants, it is important that the way each character moves remains consistent whoever is doing the shot. There are several lead animators responsible for specific characters. "Rhodri did some of the first shots with Norbot," recalls Will, "and really seemed to click with how to make him work, how to make him funny, how to make him engaging. In the end, all the animators will have animated Norbot, but Rhod feels like he has a bit of ownership. I can send other animators to him and say, 'Talk to Rhod about finding that expression.'"

The overall approach to the character was set by directors Nick and Merlin. "They had certain basic ideas in their head," explains Rhodri. "How he would turn, for example; this sense of two barrels rotating to give him a mechanical element. A lot of it was making him robotic but readable in a human sense, so you can understand what's going on in his head."

So how would he define Norbot's character? "He's very innocent, very childlike, very dutiful, obviously, because that's what he's been made to do, and he's oblivious to the fact that he's treading on Gromit's toes. He'll take the most efficient route from A to B and if that means walking through something, he'll do it. So with tidying up a garden it means ripping up things that already look nice and replacing them with something that he thinks looks nice. But it's not

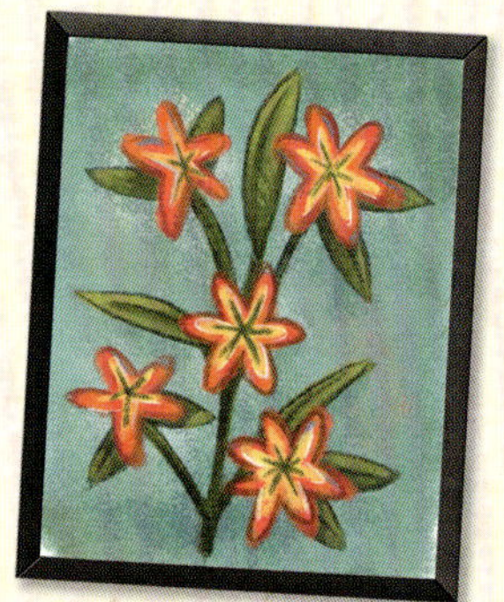

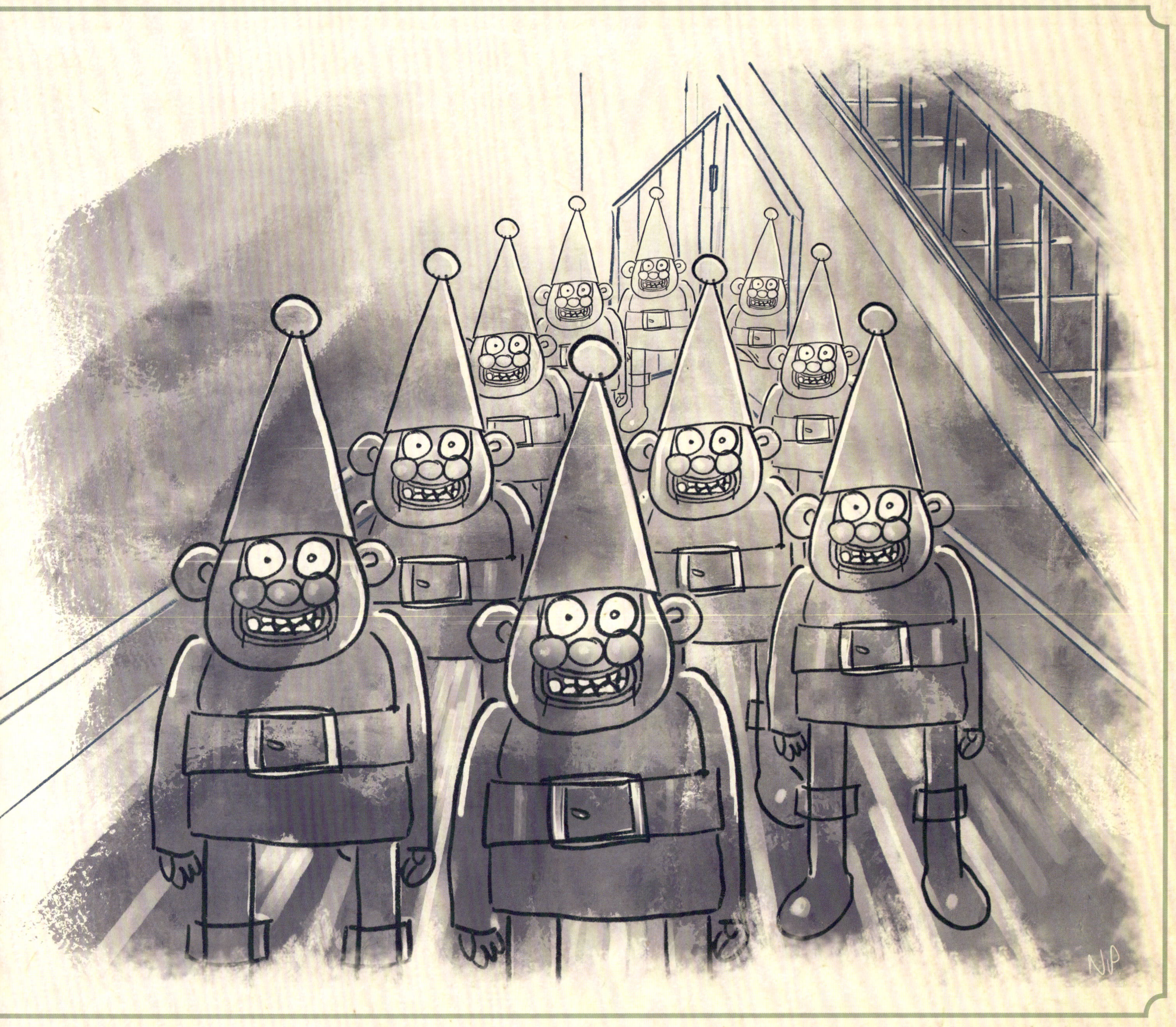

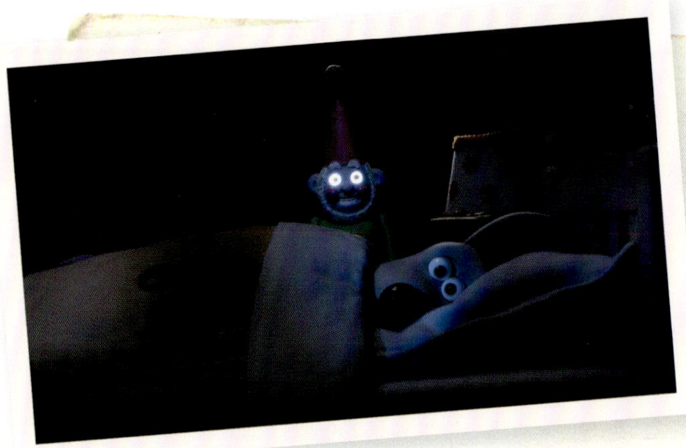

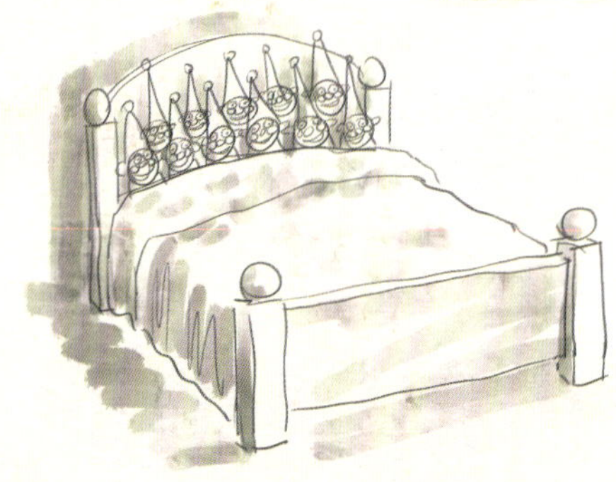

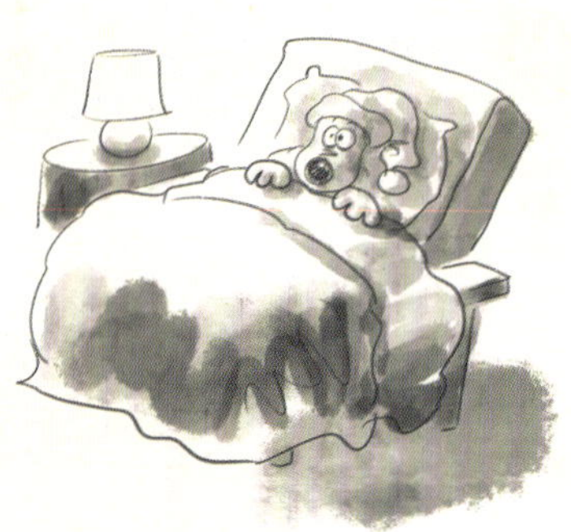

out of malice, it's just what his programming has told him to do."

One of the trademarks of Aardman's design style is that characters tend to be a little cross-eyed, giving them a rather goofy look. But for Norbot, Merlin and Nick found that having him look straight out was a little more discomforting. "That's something I've played with," says Rhodri. "Early on, I did a lot of shots where they're straight out or even further than straight out to give a sense that he has just been cobbled together in a shed. But then for some of the comedy moments like the recharging scene it made more sense to have him slightly cross-eyed, which seemed sillier in the moment."

And, of course, once Norbot is hacked, the innocent gnome has to turn evil. "That switch of character has been interesting," Rhodri admits. "He's got a slightly different look, his eyes change, and the way he moves is a little more cold and slow. Because he's been hacked by Feathers, we were trying to inject a bit of Feathers's character into him. Feathers is quite economical in the way he moves and

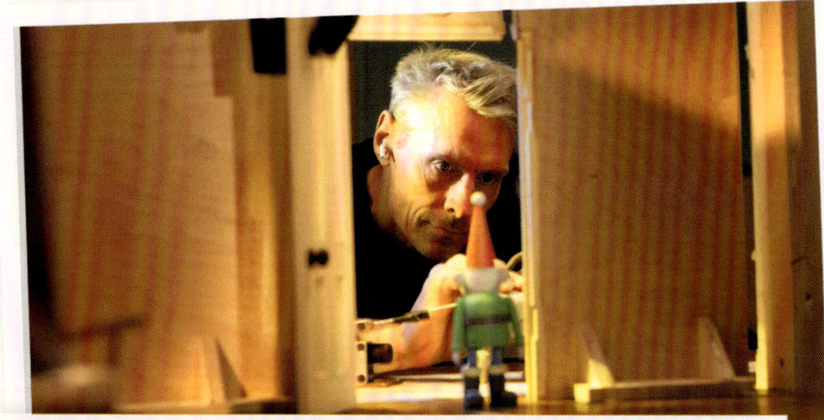

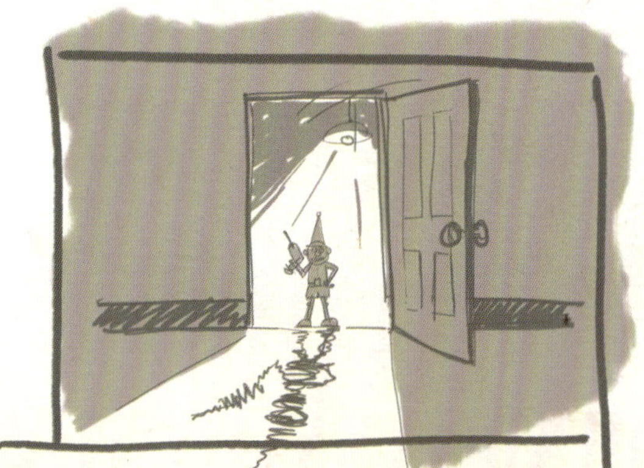

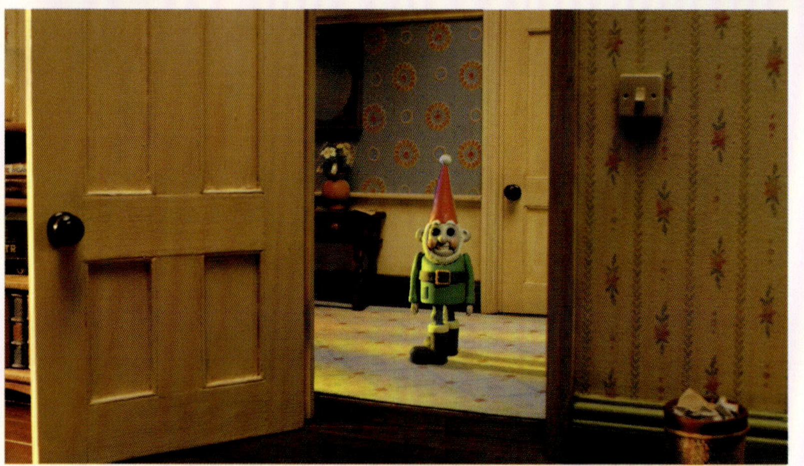

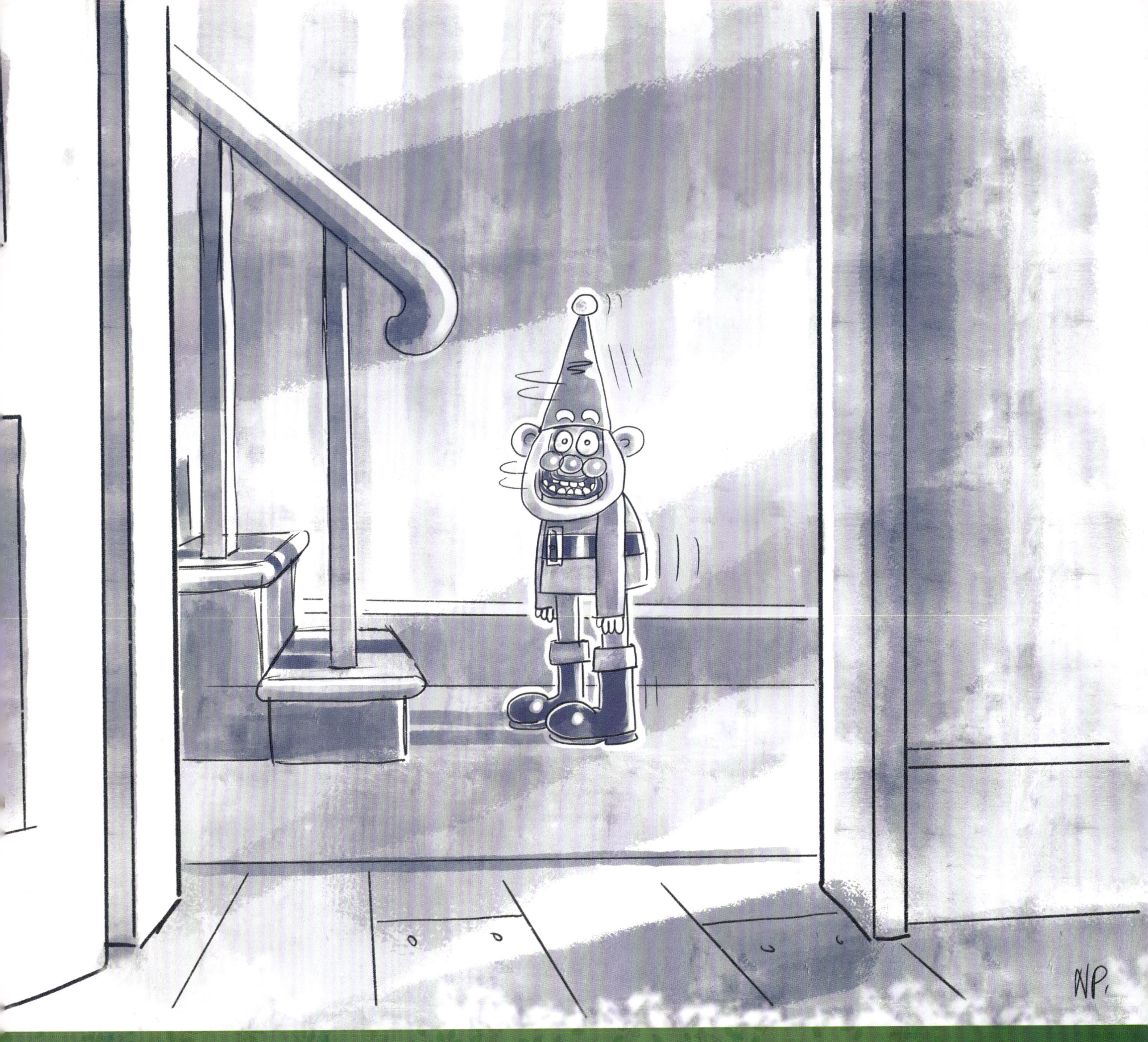

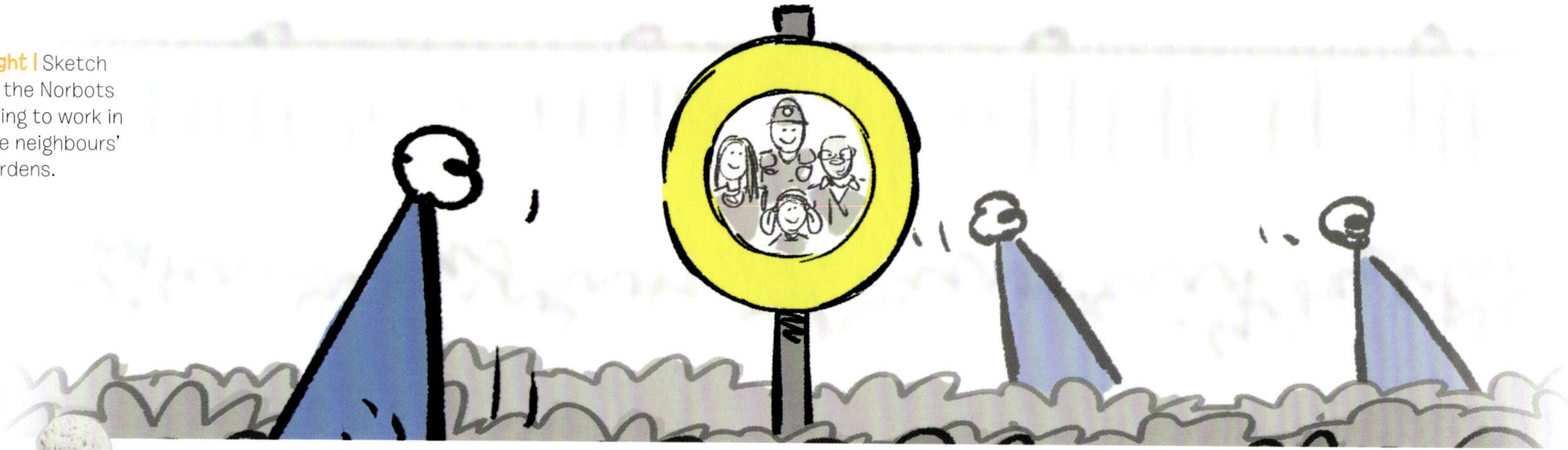

everything is very deliberate, so in the scene where you first see Evil Norbot in the corridor, he stops in the doorway and turns slowly, just how Feathers would do it – a very cold, clinical turn towards Gromit."

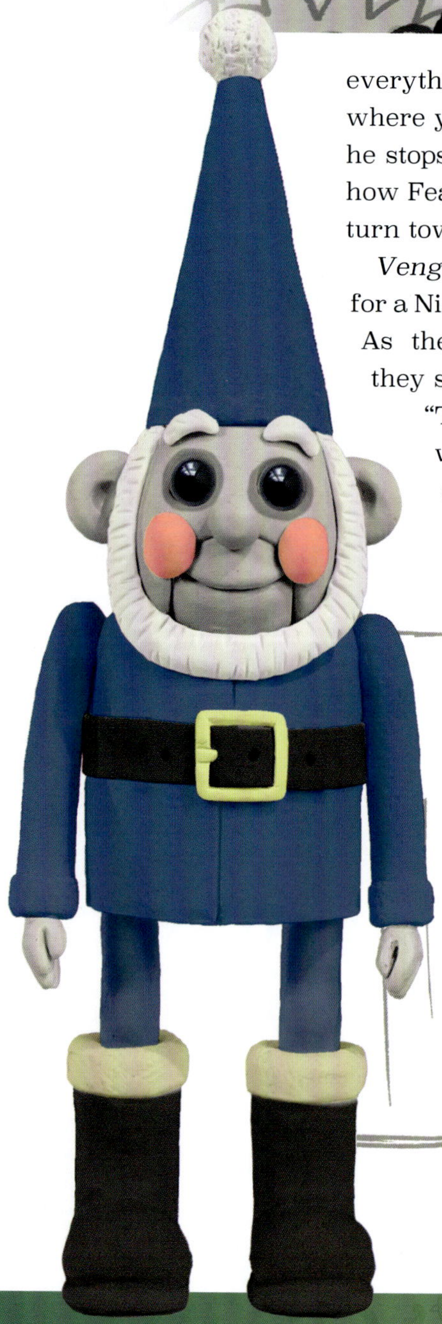

Vengeance Most Fowl contains another first for a Nick Park film – a song and dance routine! As the Norbots go about their gardening, they sing the jaunty 'Gnome Working Song'.

"The idea came from Mark [Burton, co-writer]," recalls Nick. "It started off as a homage to another song from a popular dwarf-based movie, but then we thought 'we can't be too close'. Mark wrote the lyrics and Julian [Nott, long-time *Wallace & Gromit* composer] came up with the music."

This sequence in particular went through a series of extensive revisions, recalls storyboard artist Richard Phelan: "It was a very open brief; [Nick and Merlin] didn't pin down exactly what type of musical they wanted. And I didn't have any lyrics at that stage either! So I watched a lot of musicals from different periods and genres – *Oliver!*, *Fiddler on the Roof*, the Golden Age 1950s/1960s, and then *Gold Diggers of Nineteen Thirty-*

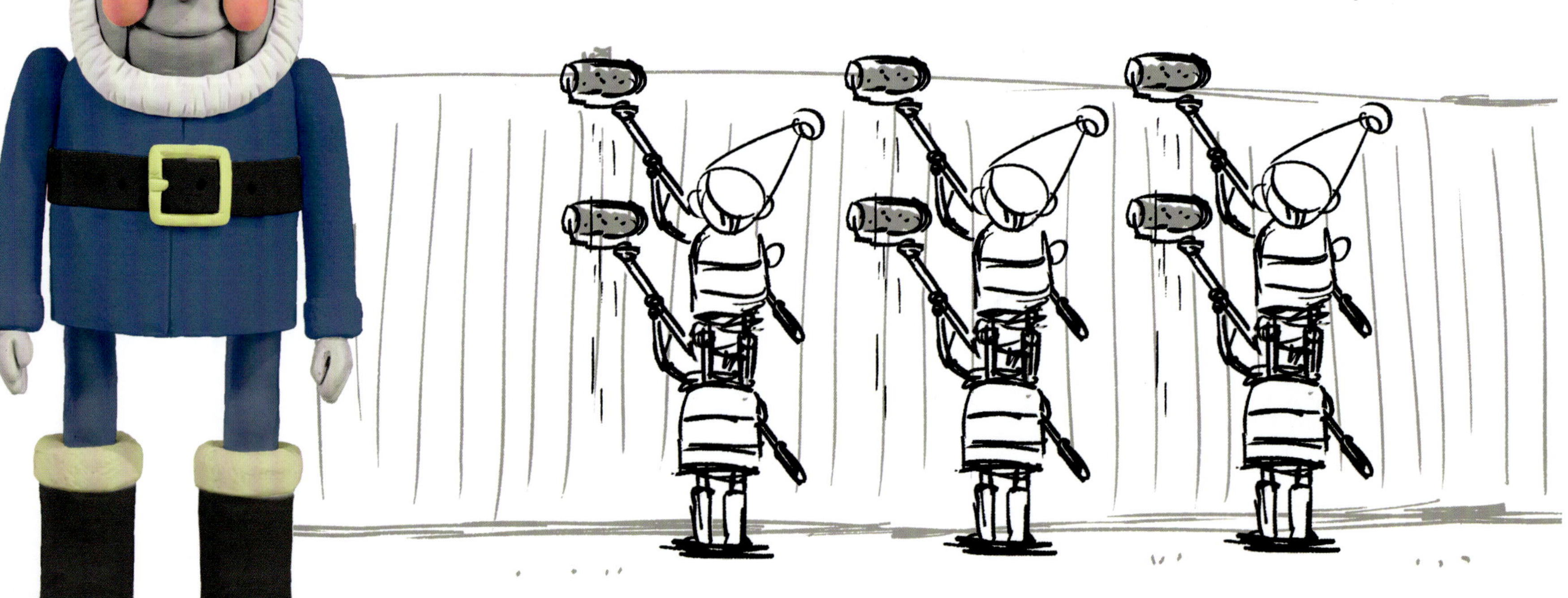

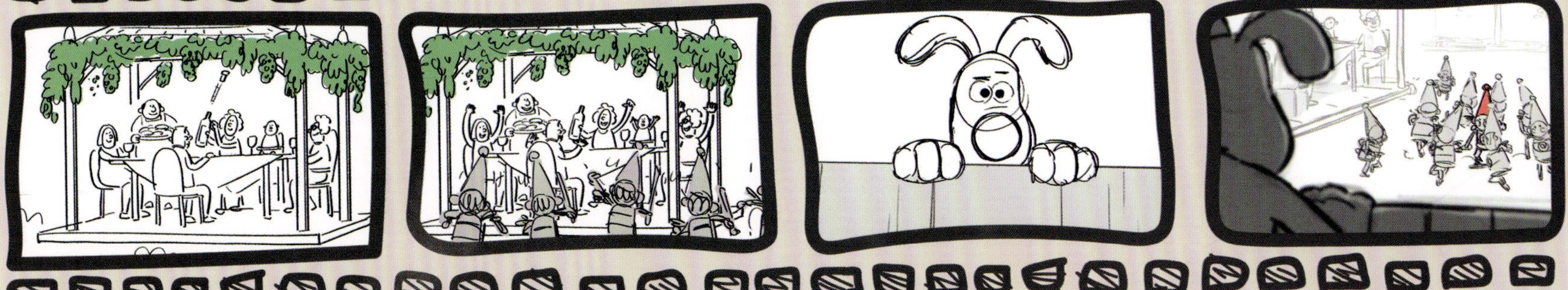

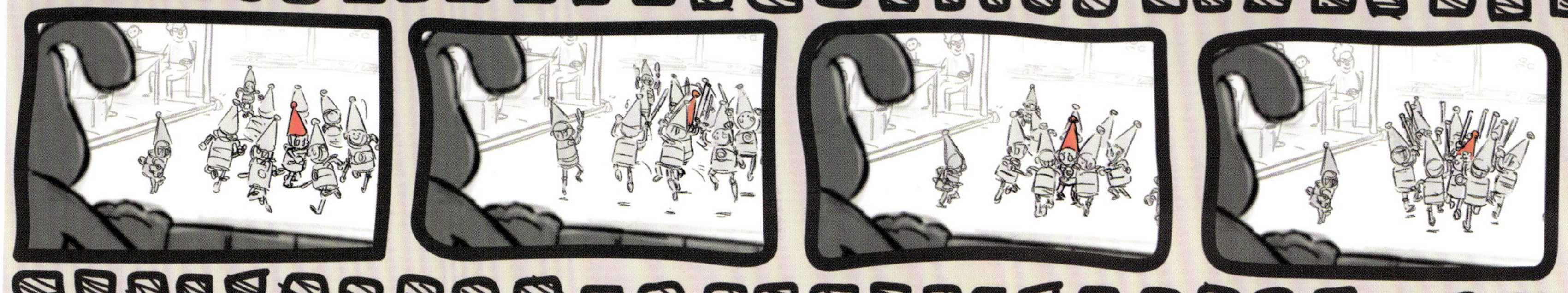

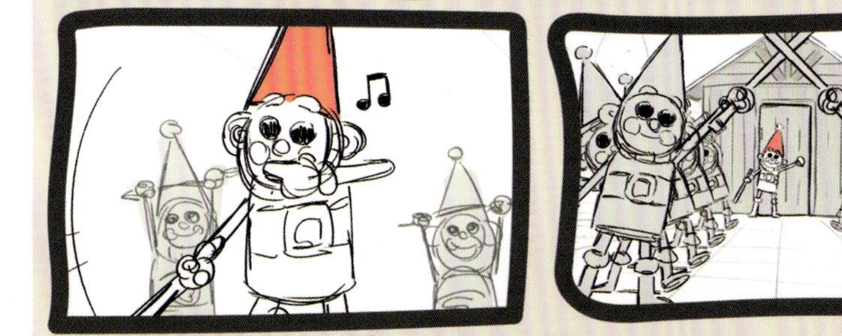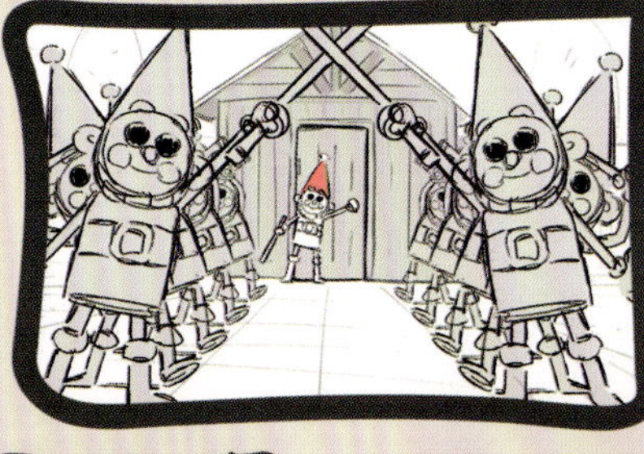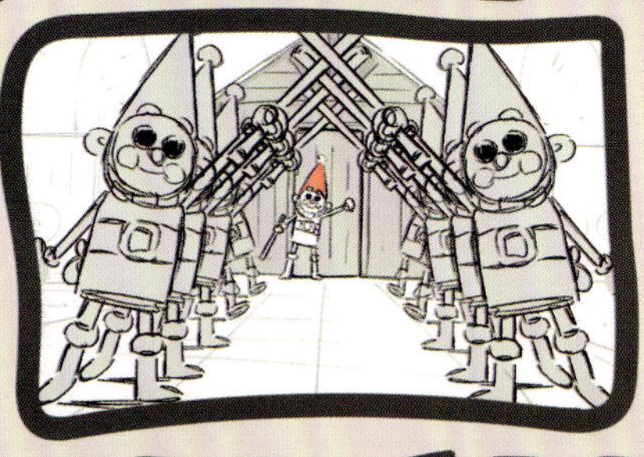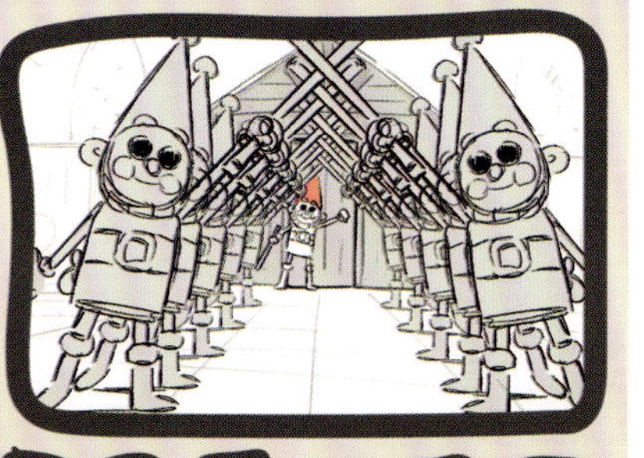

something with Busby Berkeley's huge choreographed numbers.

"The first version was very dream-like, with this elaborate ladder dance. The camera got really high up so you could see the choreography, which is very Busby Berkeley, and I don't think Nick liked that at all. He liked the comedy of things like Gromit's near-misses, Gromit being beaten up, so then it became more like *Seven Brides for Seven Brothers*, where a family of brothers build a barn and another family is trying to hit them with hammers. Every action towards Gromit had to look like an accident – 'Ooh, I swung this ladder and it hit you', or 'This wheelbarrow ran over your toes because you're in the way'.

"The point is that the gnomes are stealing things, but you don't want anyone to notice them doing

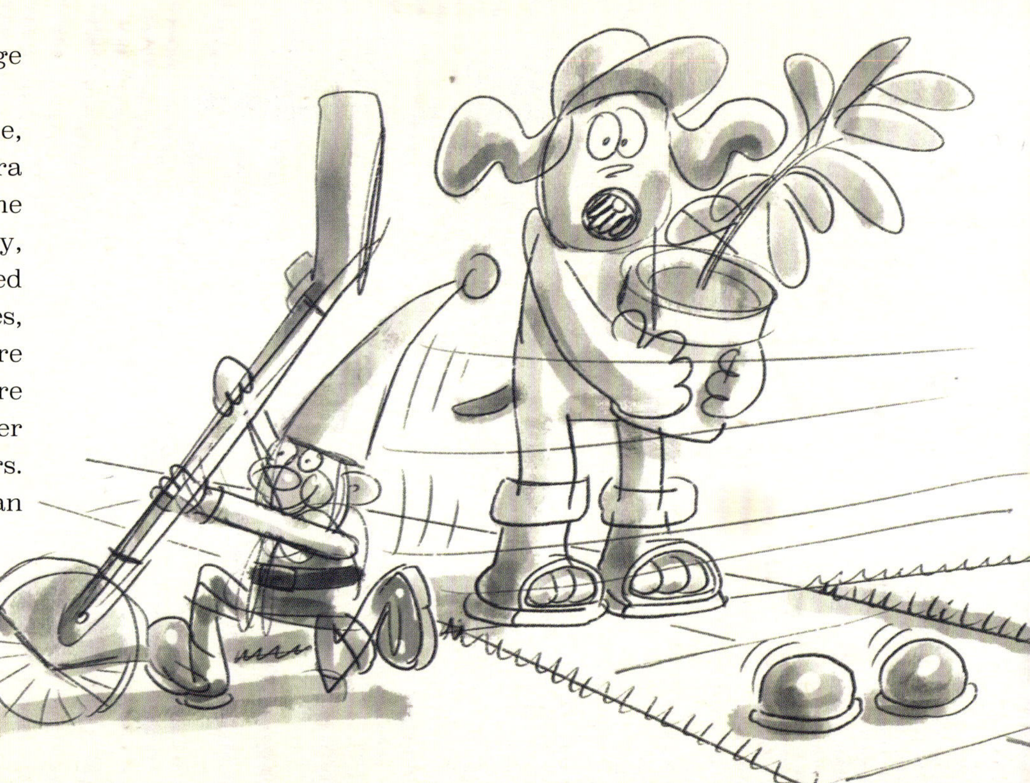

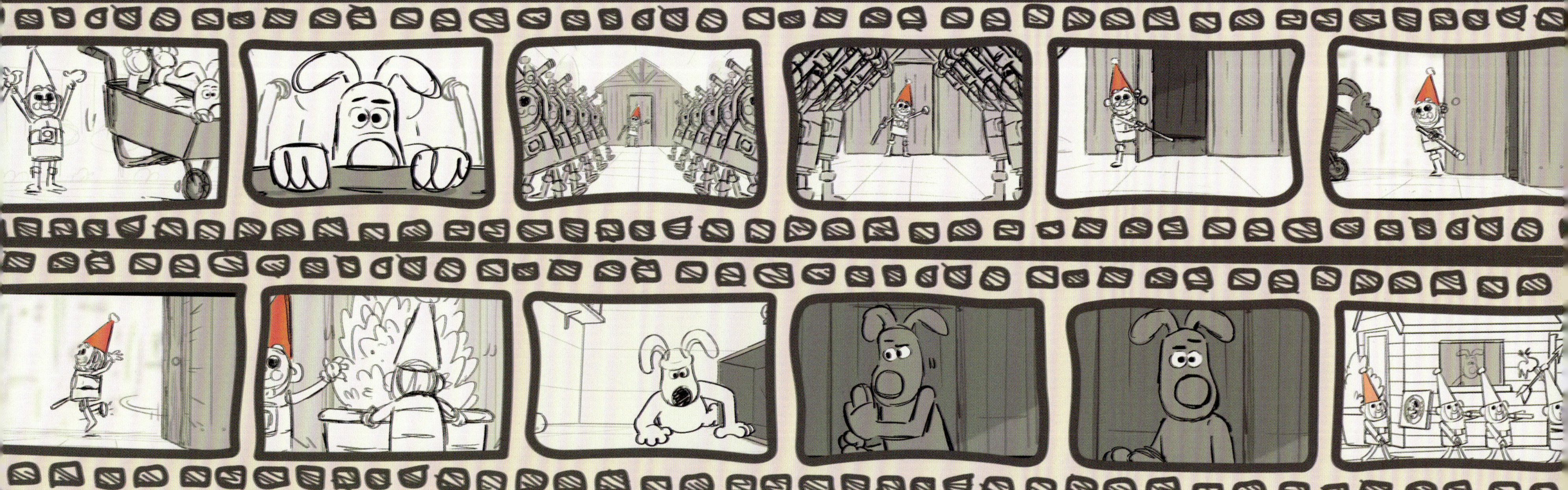

Right | An early
concept sketch
by Nick Park of
Gromit playing
gnome chess.

Below | Various
storyboard artists'
versions of the
Norbots trapping
Gromit in the shed.

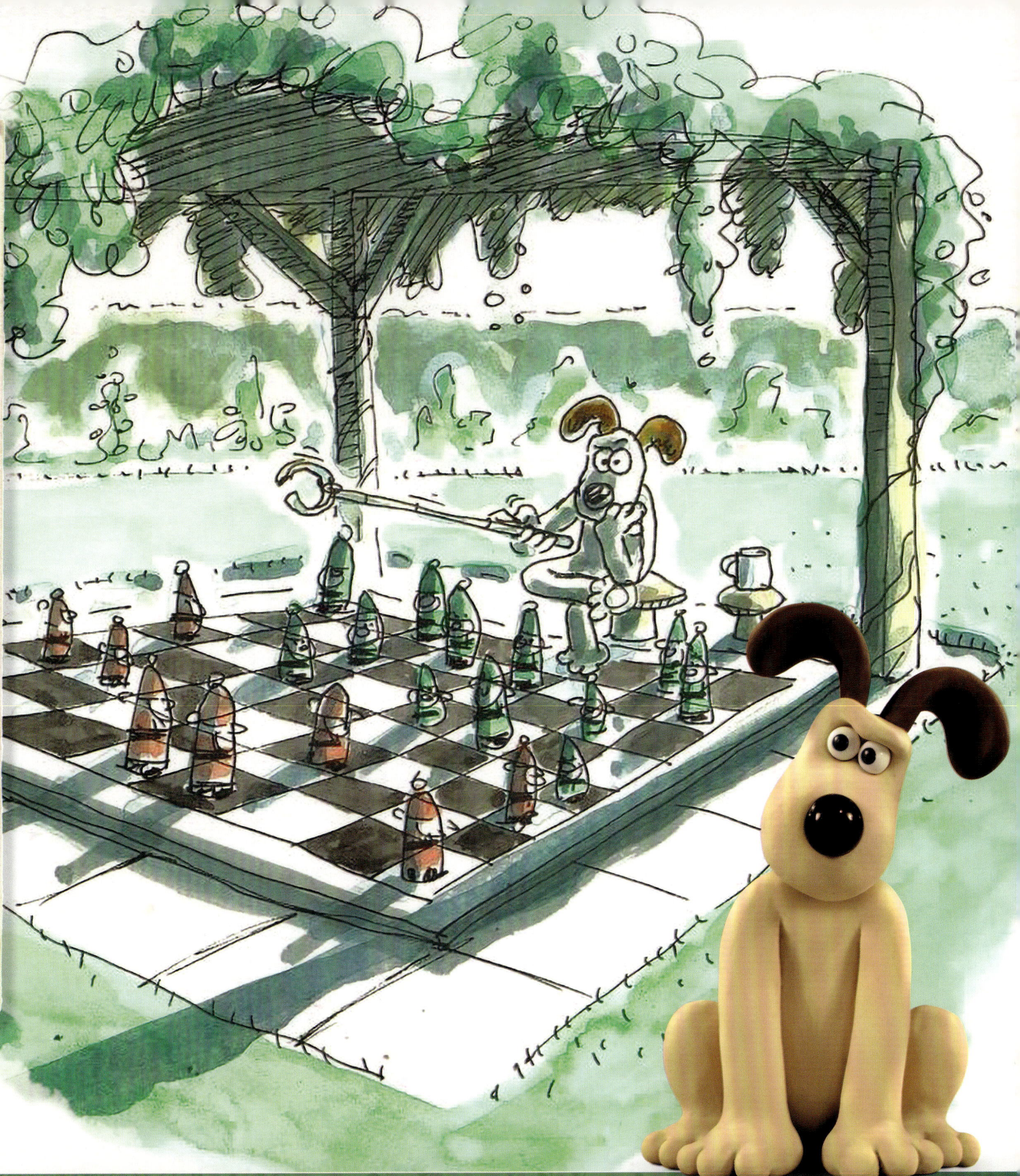

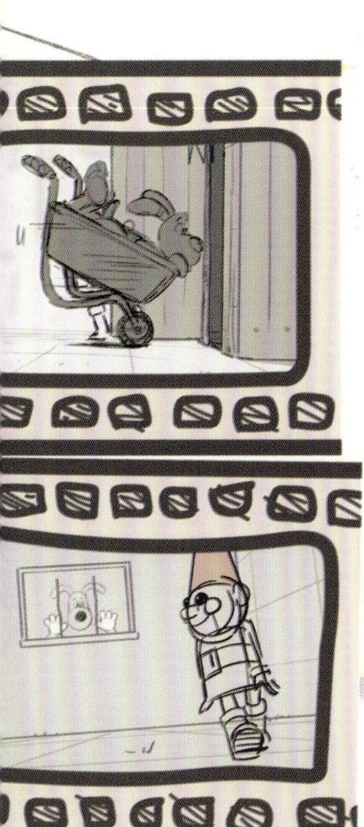

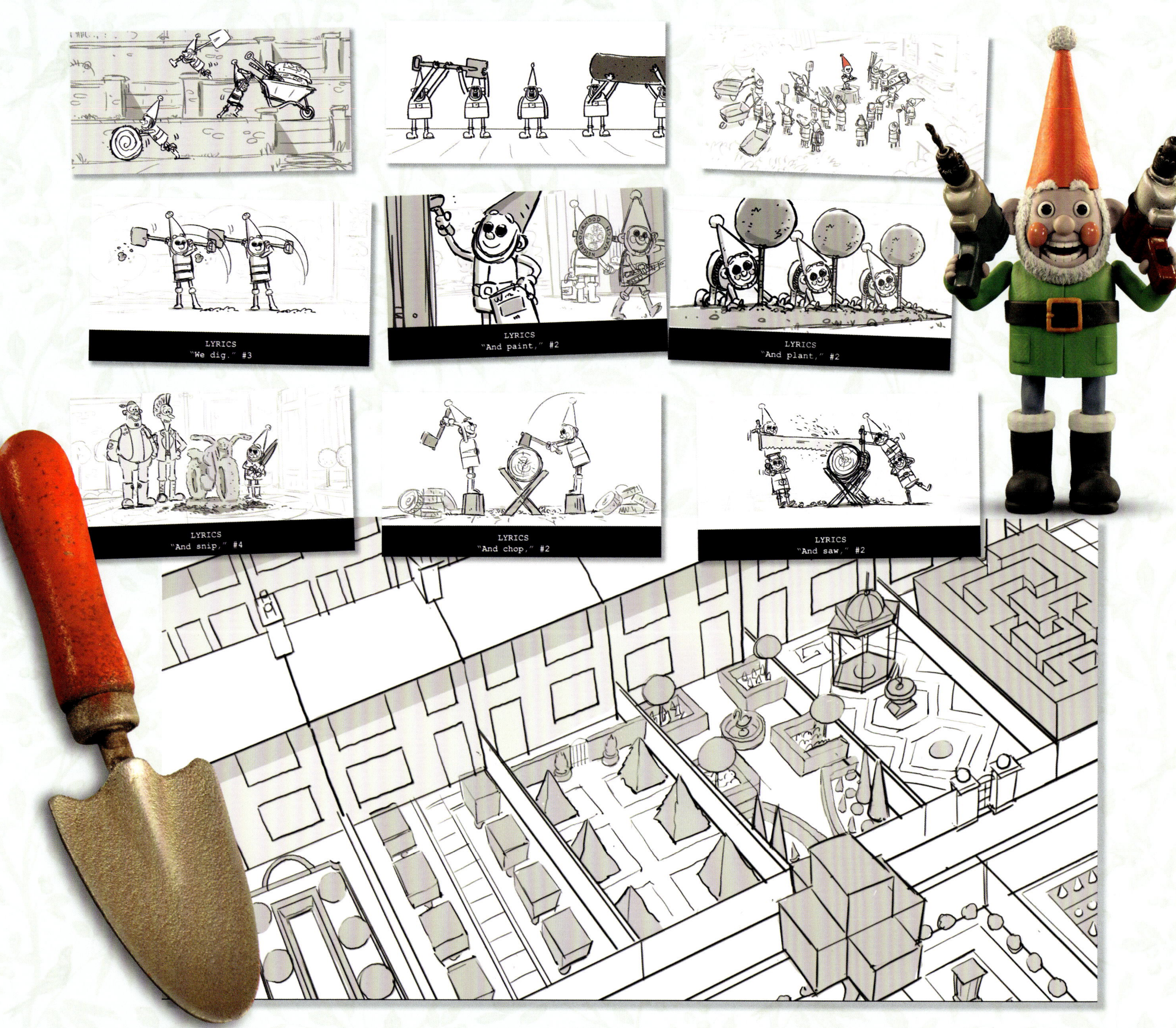

LYRICS
"We dig." #3

LYRICS
"And paint," #2

LYRICS
"And plant," #2

LYRICS
"And snip," #4

LYRICS
"And chop," #2

LYRICS
"And saw," #2

it: the impossible task of showing them stealing while not stealing, so that was a real challenge. First, I had gnomes as background dancers walking away with objects while your eyes focused on other things. Then the lyrics started to arrive and Nick wanted this very rhythmic cutting pattern as they sing 'We dig, and chop, and plant, and snip'. The first time they say it they're building, the second time they're actually stealing. Because it's all in extreme close-ups you don't actually know what they're doing. And this had to tie in with the eventual design of the submarine, so I had to ask the art department what the gnomes would need to steal to build a submarine."

Another version of the number was based on traditional folk dance, and in fact a morris-dancing sequence remained until almost the final cut, when it was decided that global audiences might be somewhat bemused by all the handkerchief-waving. "You just throw these ideas out to see what sticks and what doesn't," reflects Richard. "It's always a very long-winded, iterative process. It's part of the job when the morris dancing or the elaborate ladder dance sequence gets cut: it all whittles down to the strongest version." But one thing's for sure – the rigging department will be eternally grateful that the ladder dance didn't make it into the final version!

Given the challenge of animating multiple puppets in stop-motion, the portrayal of an

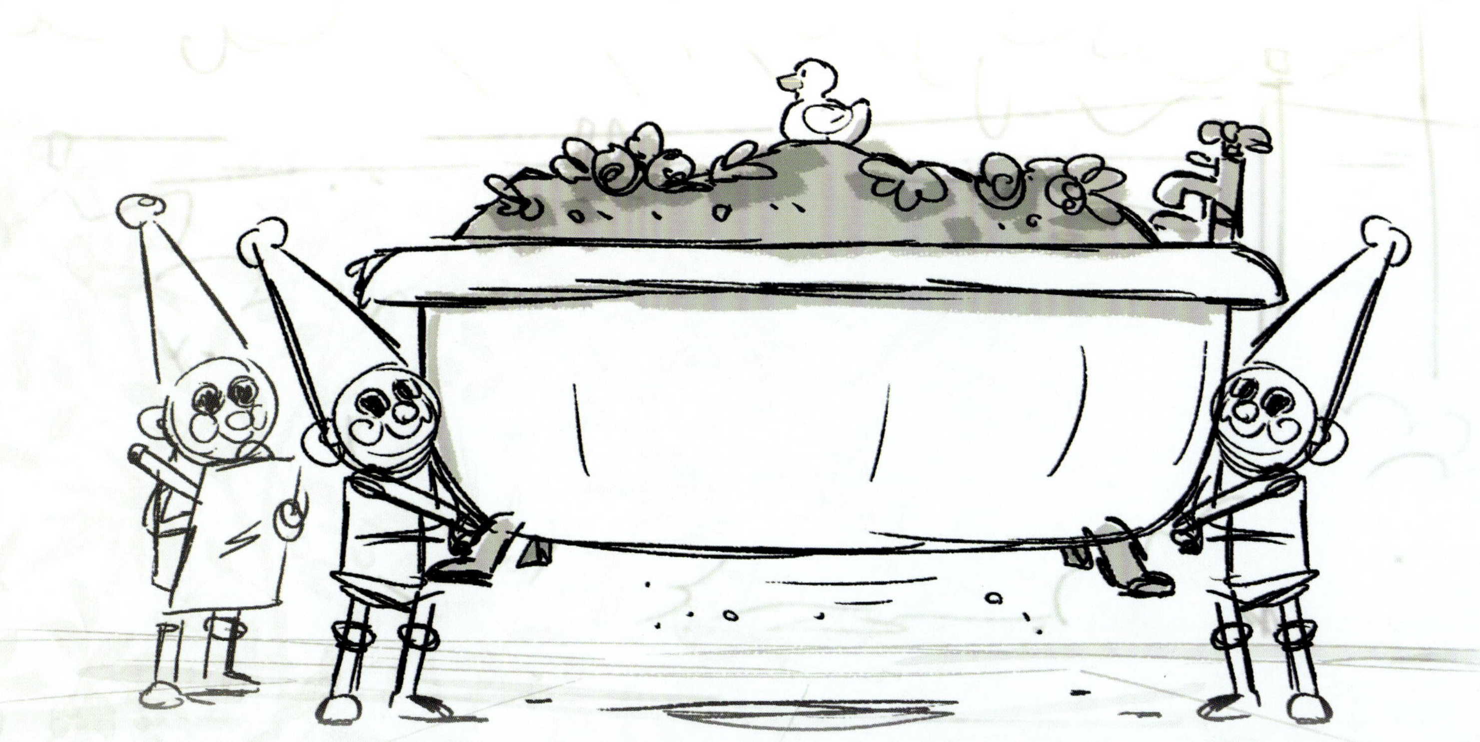

army of identical Norbots required some lateral thinking. It wasn't an idea that could have been attempted without advances in technology. "In the past we would have restricted ourselves from doing something that would be too much to animate," admits Nick. "So we would edit ourselves. We certainly did in *The Wrong Trousers*; there were no secondary characters in it, for example. With the Norbots, it was always the idea that they would replicate that would be the escalation of their threat. But the fact that they're all the same did help a lot because they are literally copies of each other. We just changed the paintwork really."

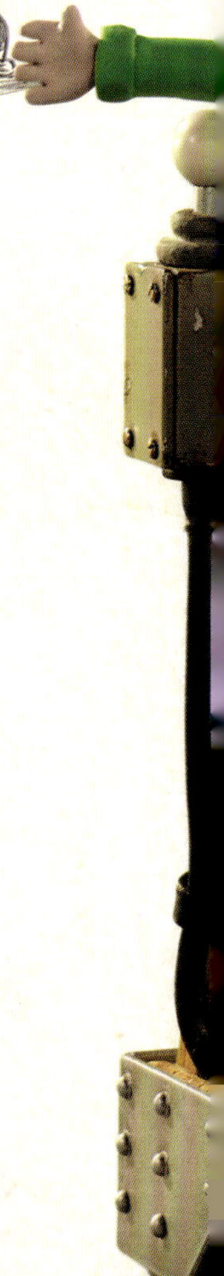

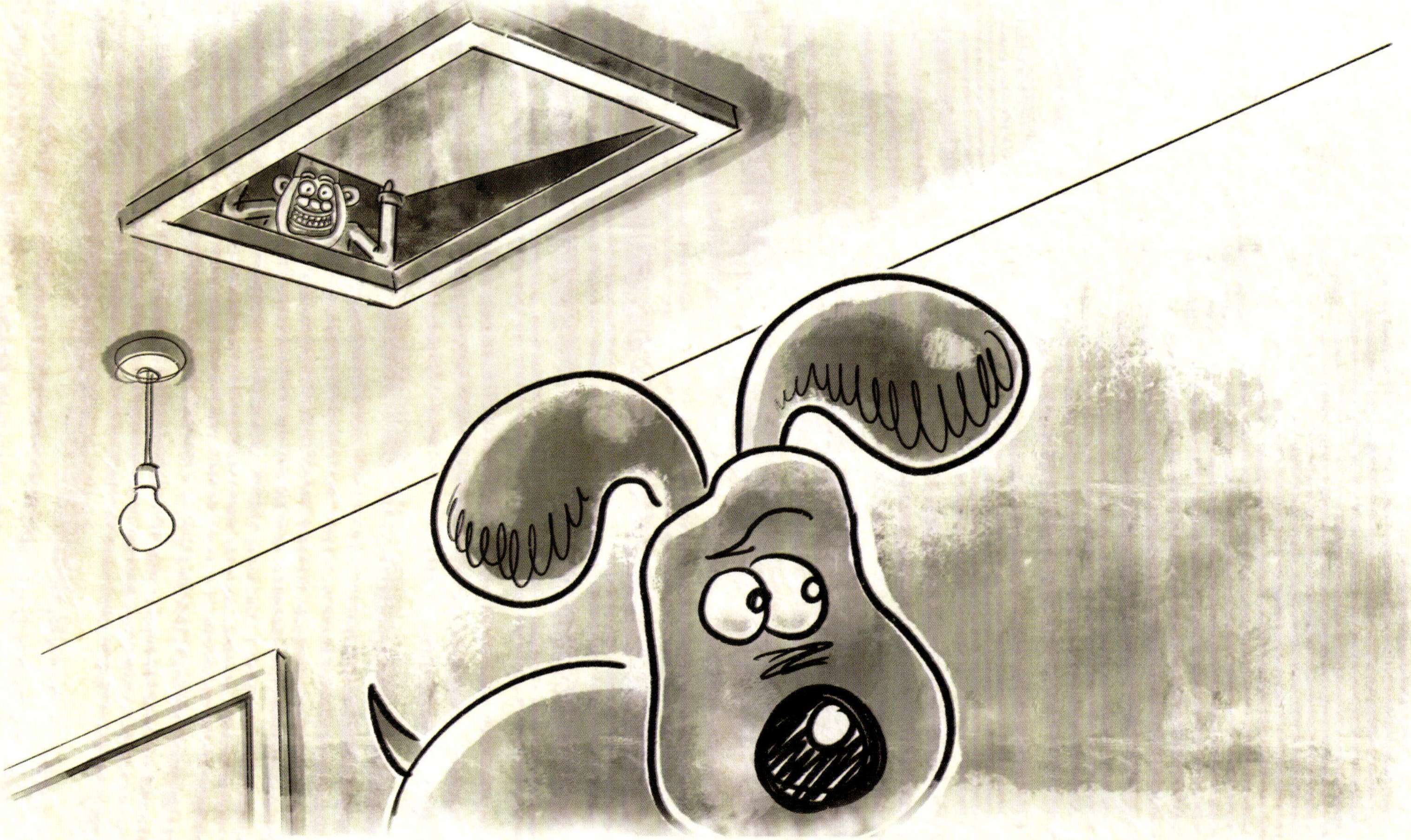

It would have been simple to use 'digi-doubles' – computer-generated copies of the physical puppets – but the unique quality of texture and lighting in stop-motion animation would have been lost, so director Merlin Crossingham and VFX supervisor Howard Jones came up with an original approach: "We needed to make a whole Norbot army walk towards camera, and I had an idea which I think has never been done in stop-motion before." A row of four puppets was

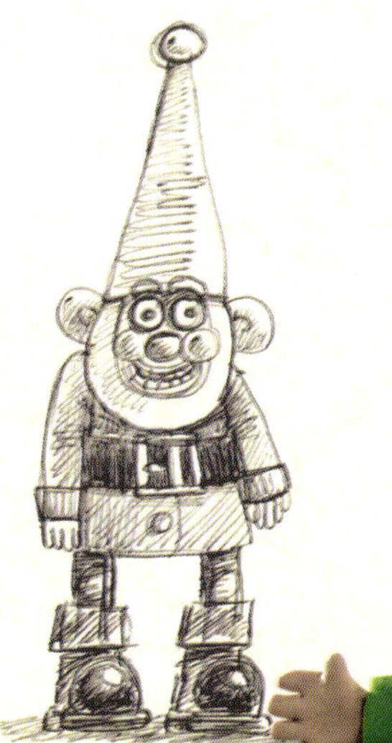

attached to a motorised rig, and animator Jay Grace moved them incrementally a frame at a time, shooting them using motion control. After each move, the rig is moved back to second-row position, then to the third row and so on, each row being shot on a separate 'plate' (a digital image that can be composited with other shots to create the final image). Then the rig is brought all the way to the front, the puppets are moved fractionally for the next shot, and the process is repeated. "So all of them move in exactly the same way," explains Merlin. "You can cut and paste in CG, but we couldn't do that because they were all moving through light – the stained glass of the front door throws different-coloured light. If it was just plain light we could have animated it once with a green screen, then cut and pasted it. We think this may never have been done before – in this day and age, who [would've] thought there was a stop-motion animation process that hadn't been done before!"

But Norbot's skills go beyond gardening, submarine-building and synchronised marching to include a surprising aptitude for knitting, as the nifty gnome produces what is destined to

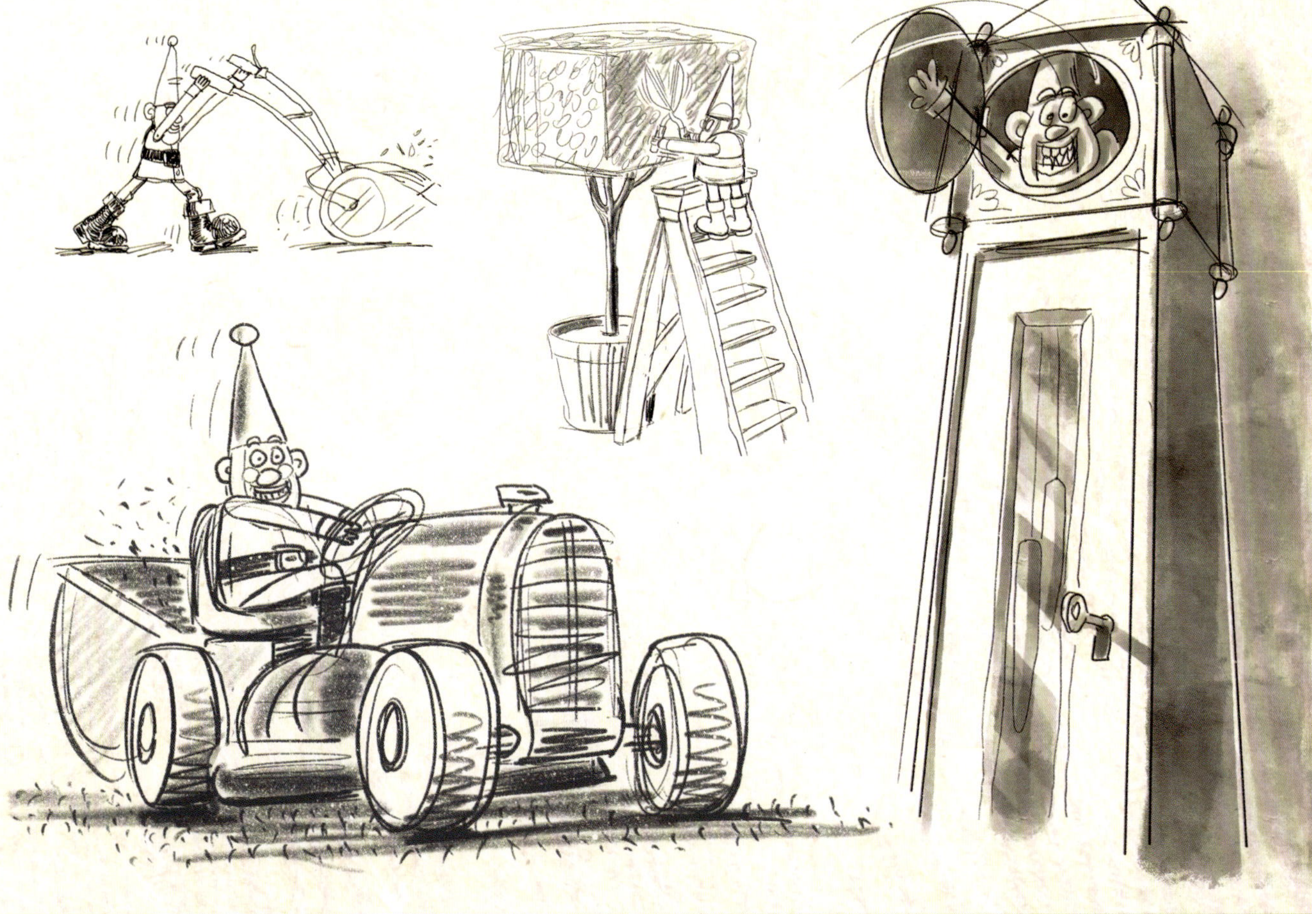

be the most iconic piece of merchandising since the Shaun the Sheep backpack – the Wallace Onesie! Creating this miniaturised knitwear presented a novel challenge for modelmaker Mel Tague: "Being asked to knit for work was pretty awesome because I do it as a hobby – it was such a weird request and I really loved how strange it was. The design meetings were great because Nick and Merlin were throwing out all of these ideas, but in the end they pared it down. At one point they mentioned the idea of having a 'bum flap' at the back, but I'm thankful they didn't go ahead with that – it would have been a whole other level!"

The onesie had to practically fit a nine-inch-high Wallace puppet, so the level of detail was incredibly intricate, involving a combination of several different knitting techniques. "Under the onesie there's a mesh leotard with some pinky flesh-coloured stuff to make it easier to get on and off," reveals Mel. "And there are hidden wires so you can animate it. The collar insert – or 'dickie' as they're called in the US – is really awkward, it's so tiny. I had to knit it in the round and then in the flat, there's a lot of shaping going on. The onesie itself is made from acrylic TK [triple knit]-weight wool, knitting with 4 or 5 DPNs [double-pointed needles], tiny pointy needles arranged in a circle, which is so fiddly. It's such a small scale that if you don't do

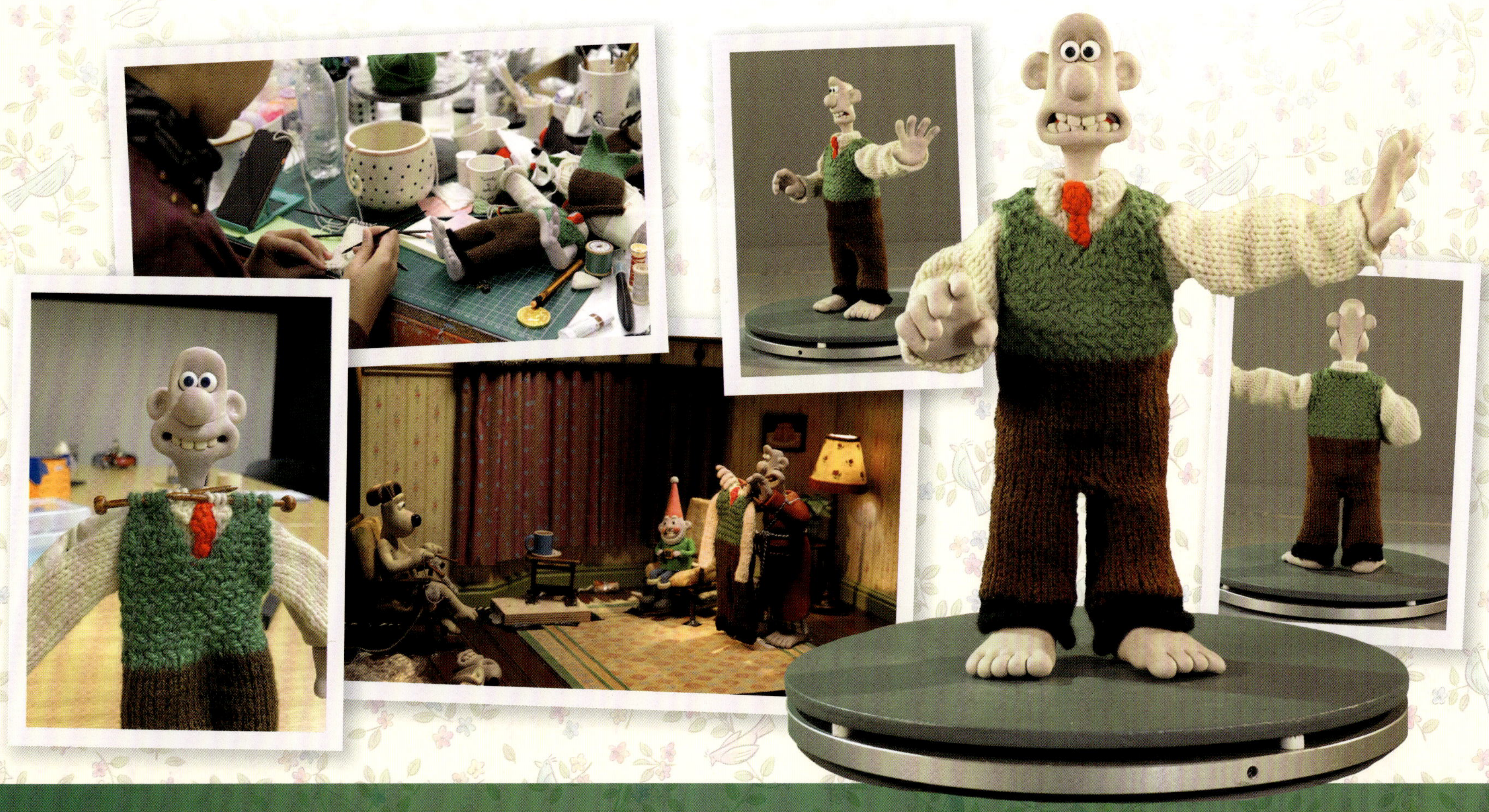

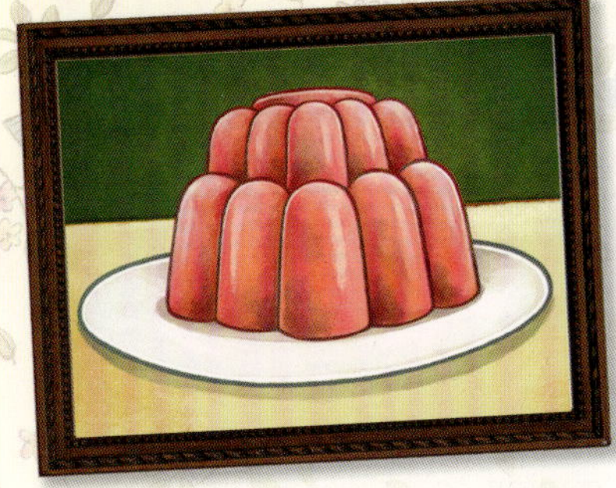

it just right you lose your tension and it gets gappy and you have to do it again. It takes a whole day to knit all the parts together, and then there's several days of prepping it – sewing, the wires have to be put in, it has to be assembled, you have to stain-proof it, you've got to stiffen up the collar with some PVA mix, and finally it has to be stitched onto the puppet. So it's like a week to get one done."

Mel has written down her knitting pattern so the model-making team can duplicate it if they need to. "Any knitter who can read the instructions should be able to recreate it," she says. So who knows? Soon we may be seeing the more dedicated Aardman fans out and about in their very own Wallace Onesies!

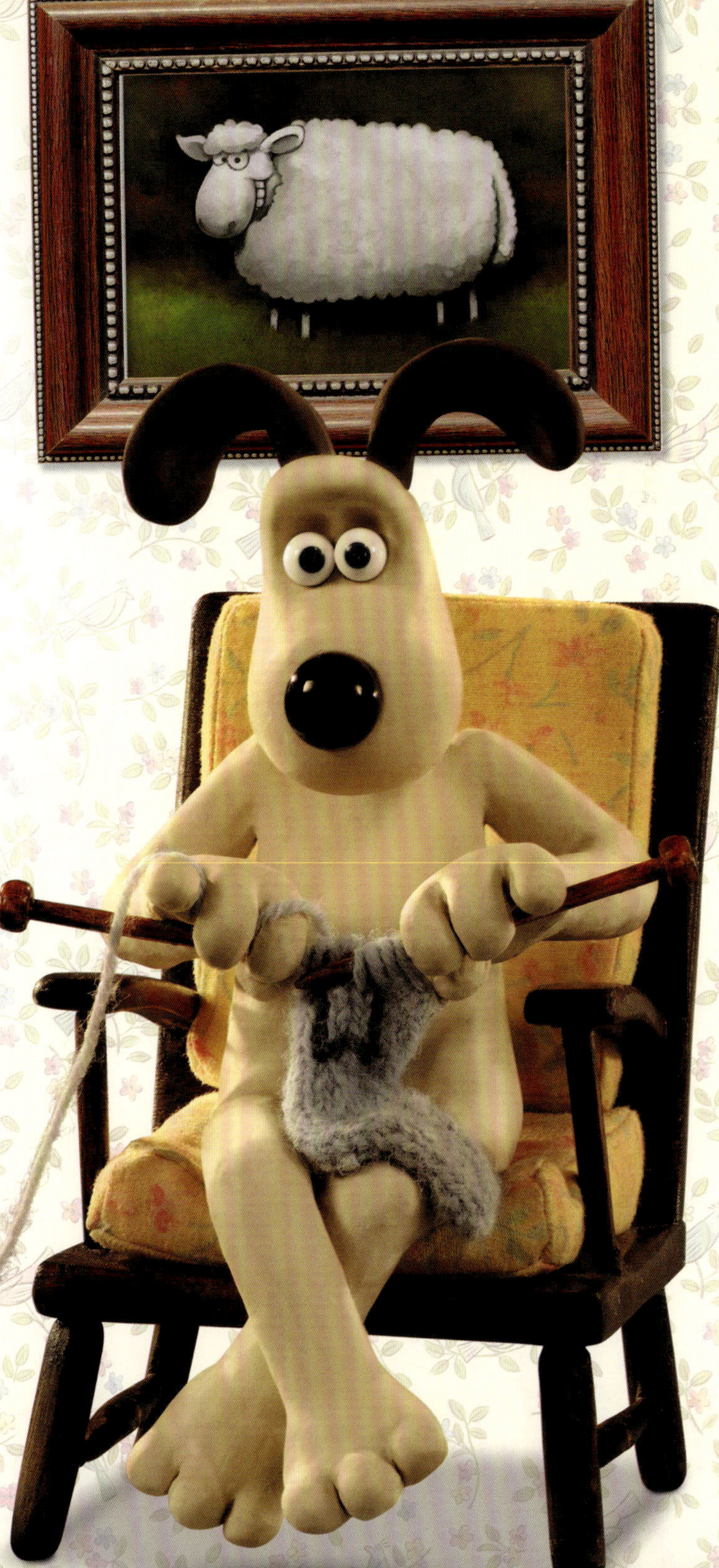

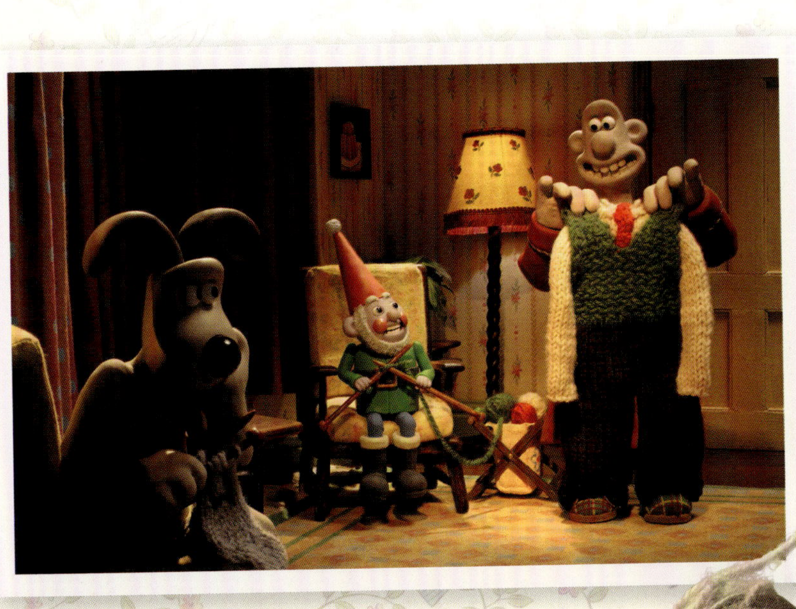

CHAPTER FOUR

West Wallaby Street, We Have a Problem...

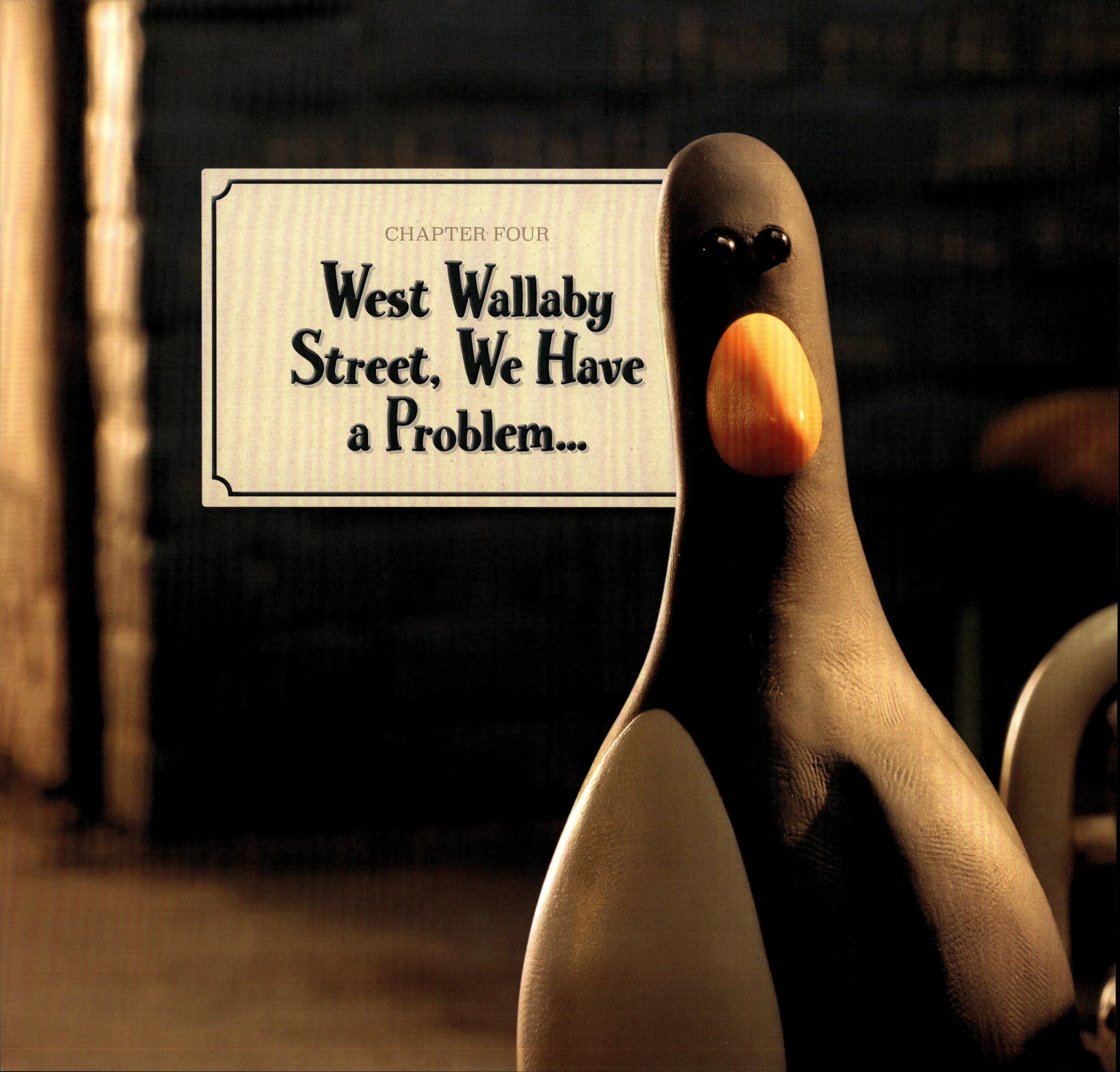

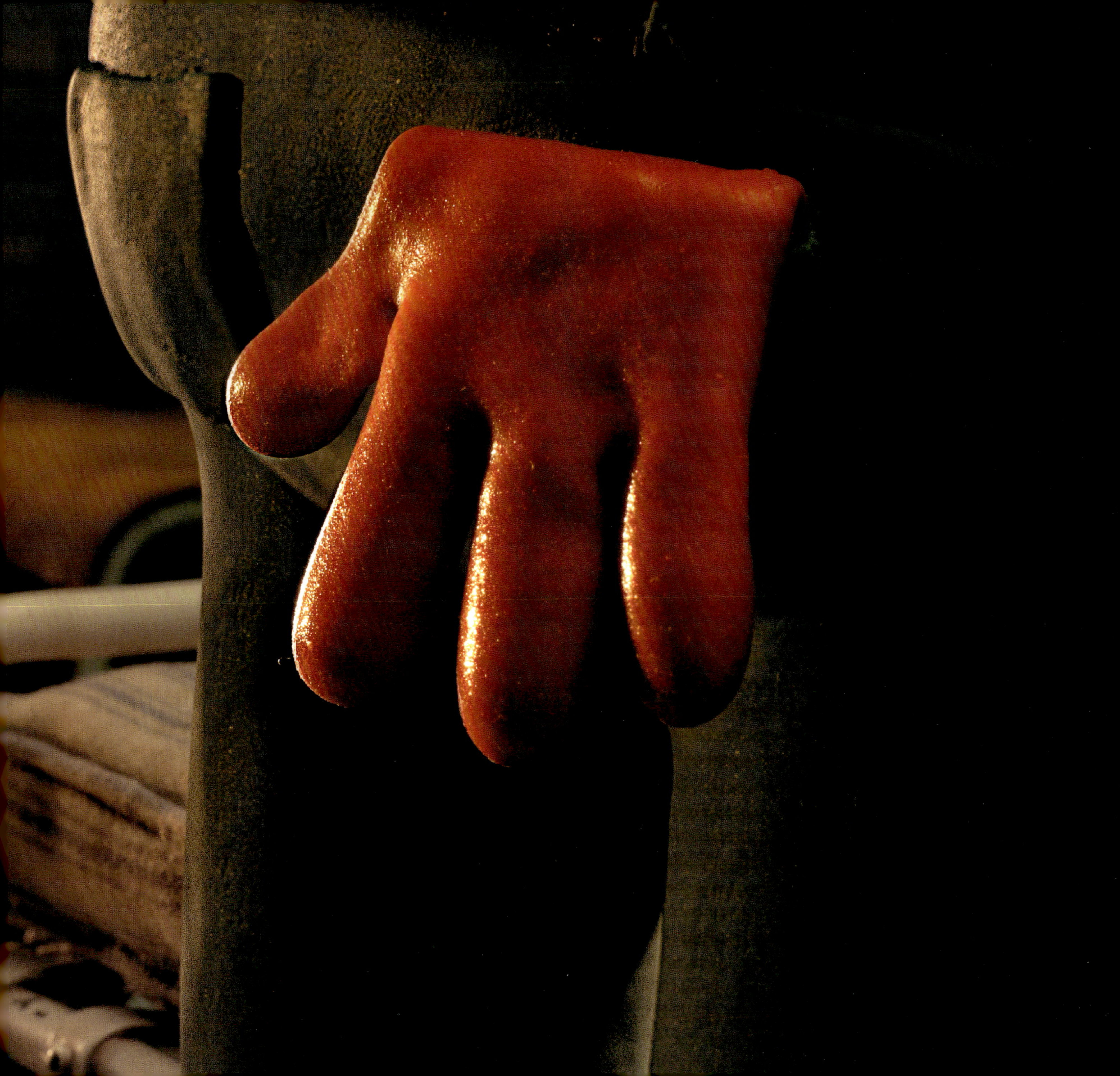

West Wallaby Street, We Have a Problem...

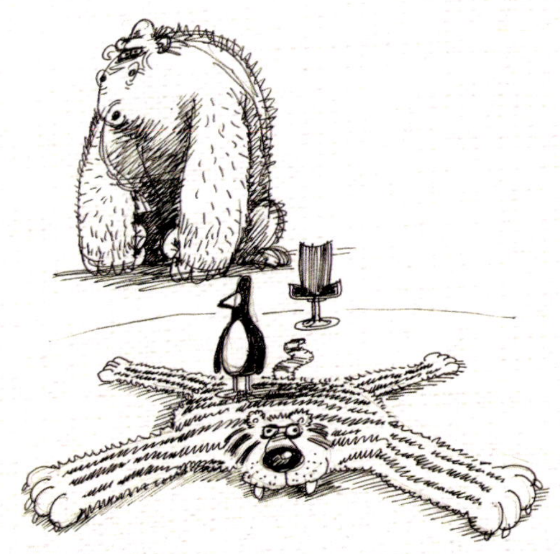

ANOTHER MILESTONE FOR *VENGEANCE MOST Fowl* is that, as the title suggests, it sees the first returning villain for *Wallace & Gromit* – and who could be more villainous than the sinister Feathers McGraw? Feathers became a legend in *The Wrong Trousers*, famed for his cold-eyed stare, his rubber-glove chicken disguise and his dastardly diamond theft, into which he inveigled a sleeping Wallace in his NASA-designed Techno-Trousers. The ending saw the flightless fiend carted off to jail, but, as we discover in this adventure, Feathers was down but not out, and spent his time plotting rather than rotting in jail. Vengeance, of course, being a dish best served cold…

Above | Feathers doodle by Nick Park.

Below left | Mugshots of jailbird Feathers McGraw.

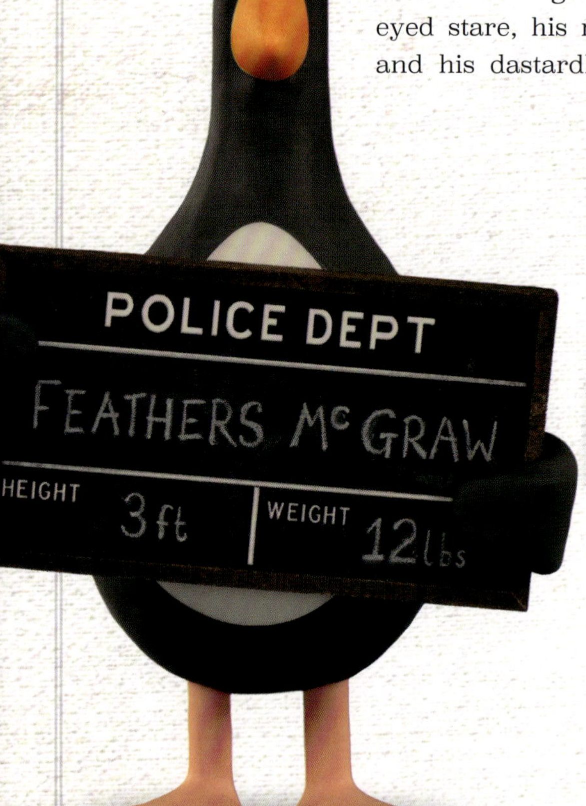

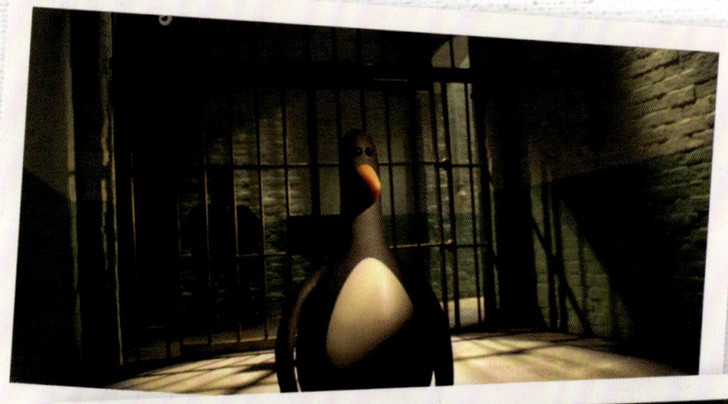

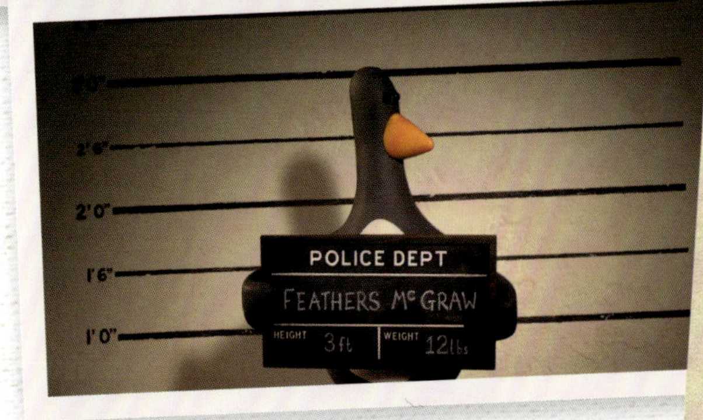

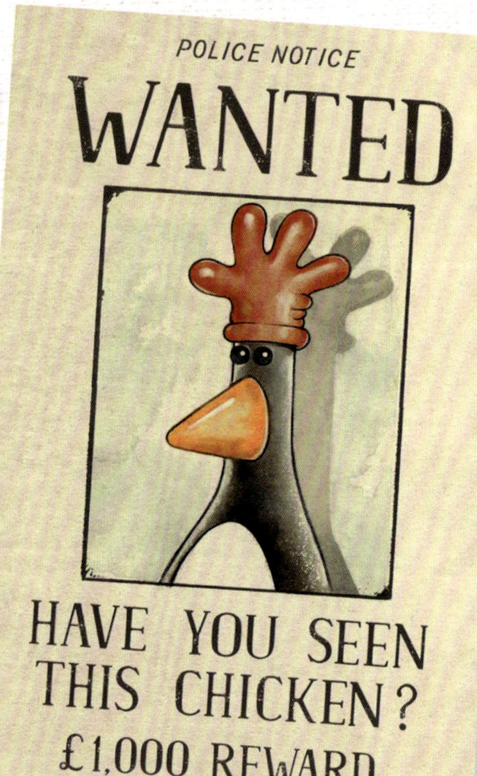

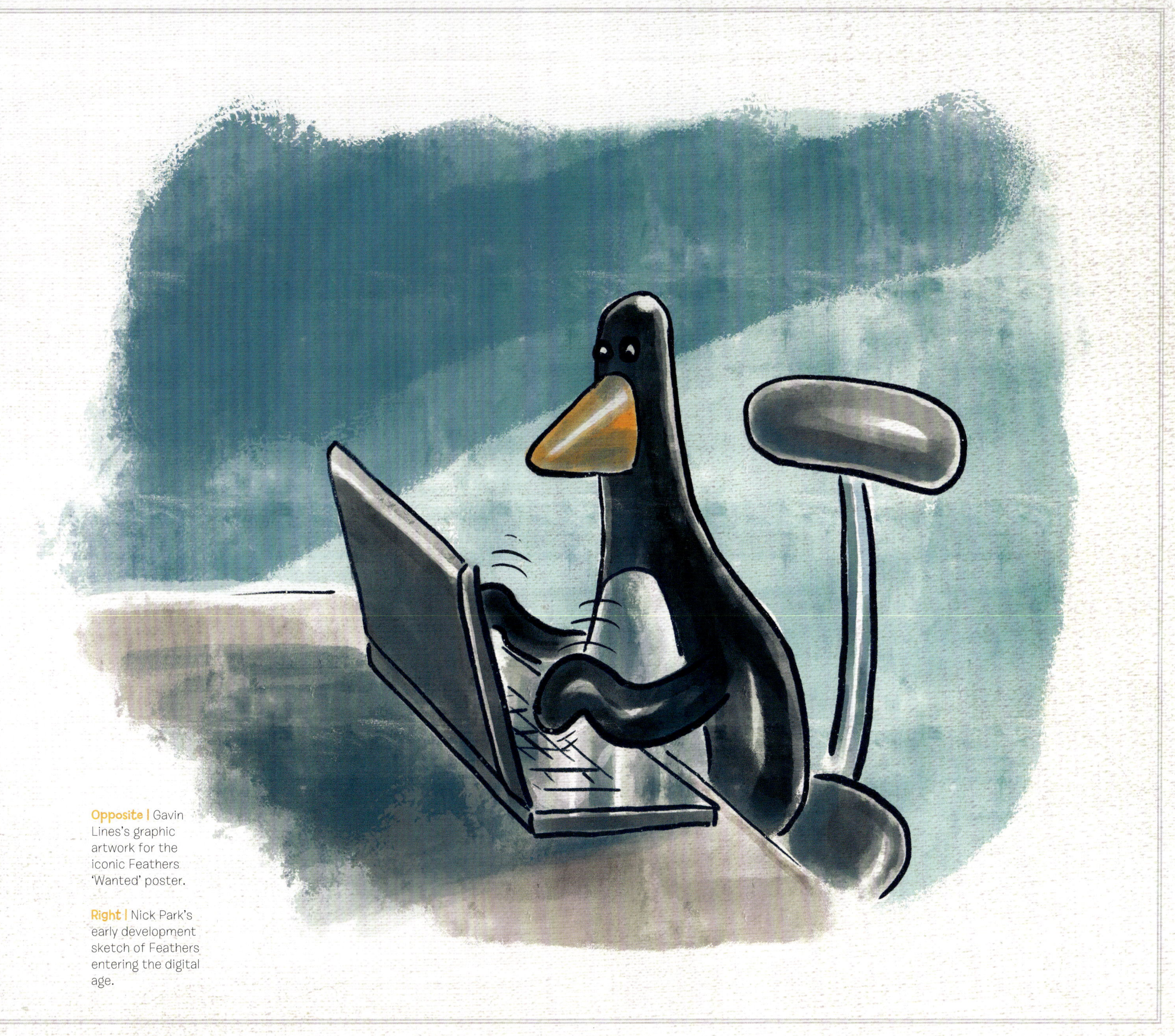

Opposite | Gavin
Lines's graphic
artwork for the
iconic Feathers
'Wanted' poster.

Right | Nick Park's
early development
sketch of Feathers
entering the digital
age.

Originally, the script just focused on Norbot and his gnomes, although Nick couldn't find a convincing reason for them to turn evil. Separate to that, one of the most frequent questions he was asked by fans was whether Feathers would ever return, but he could never justify why he should. "I can't remember how it came about, but suddenly I had a brainwave – what if Feathers was revealed to be the person behind all this, and he's using the gnomes to get something he wants? I pitched it to Mark [Burton] and he was very inspired by this idea of who controls the technology controlling us, and it all started to spin around like that.

"That's how it developed for a while, but we were still a bit unsure what he wanted, what his whole motivation was. And then it hit us – we thought, 'What if the diamond was still at Wallace and Gromit's house and he needed to get back in to get it, and that's why he's using the Norbots?' All the pieces of the jigsaw seemed to come together. And once Merlin came on board, we were prompted by the Creative Council to lean more into the revenge idea – he's not just trying to get something back, it's personal. Wallace and Gromit locked him away."

Aardman's Creative Council is "a collective of creative brains," as executive producer Carla Shelley puts it. "There's a core group that is chaired by Pete Lord and Sarah Cox as our two creative directors, and then myself and some development brains – James Higginson and Nat McKay – and director Tom Parkinson, who's so good on comedy. We provide creative

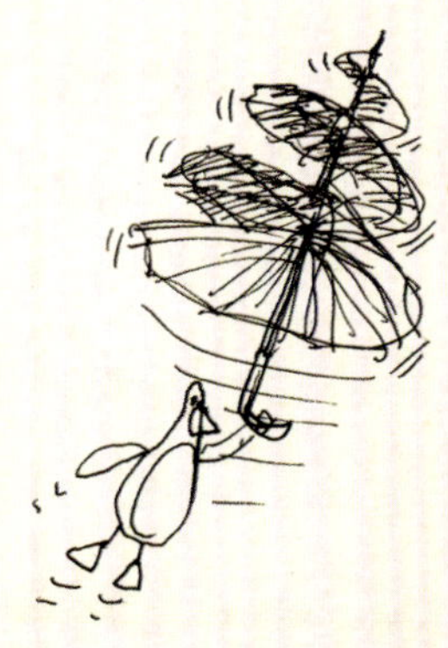

Opposite | Graphic art by Gavin Lines for the front page news of Feathers's capture.

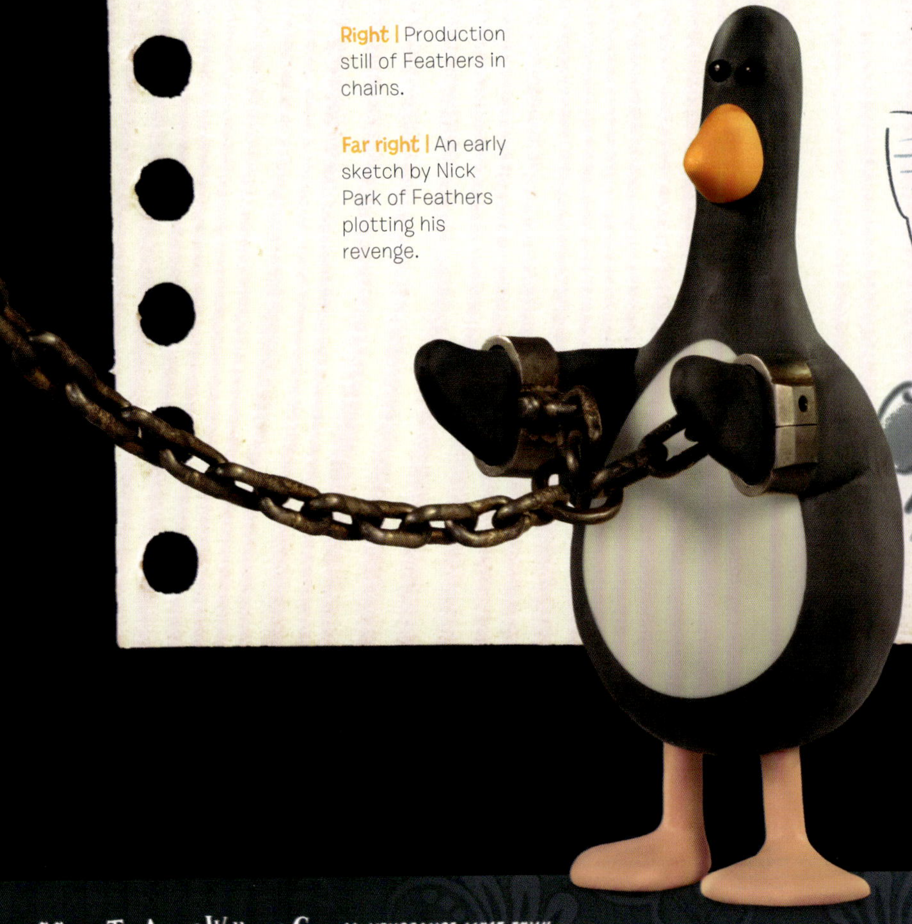

Right | Production still of Feathers in chains.

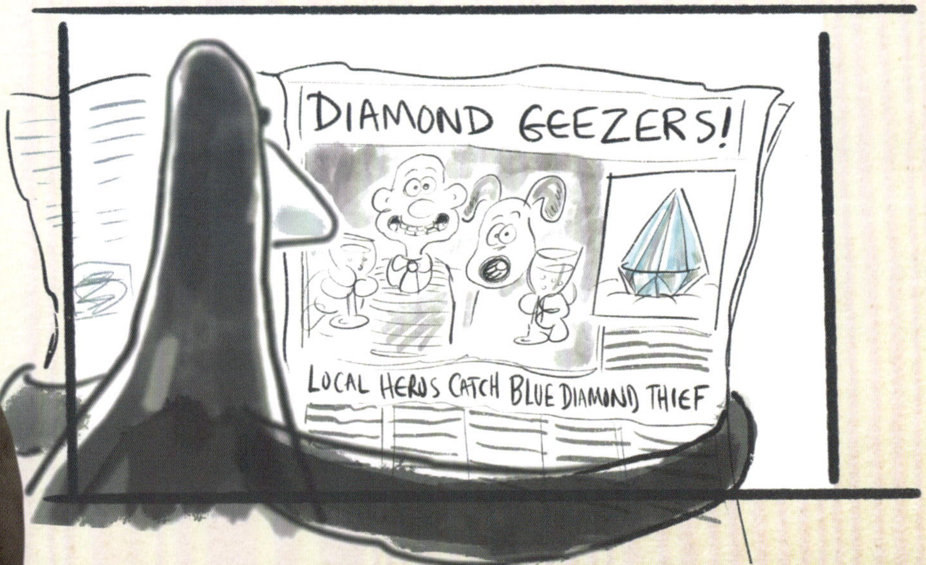

Far right | An early sketch by Nick Park of Feathers plotting his revenge.

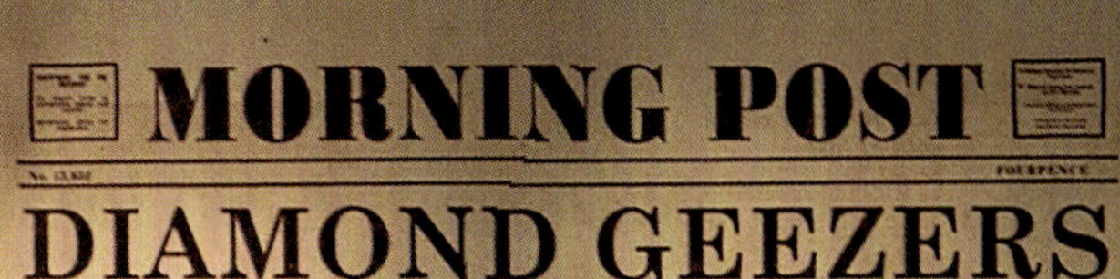
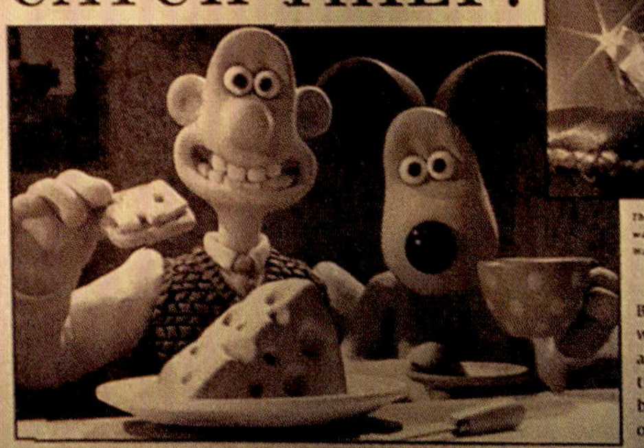

MORNING POST

No. 13,856   FOURPENCE

DIAMOND GEEZERS CATCH THIEF!

The stunning Blue Diamond which was recovered by local inventor Wallace and his faithful hound (left)

LAST NIGHT THE BLUE DIAMOND gem was secure in the safe after being handed back to it's rightful owners by local hero Wallace, of West Wallaby Street.

Police praise hero pair

FULL STORY PAGE 2

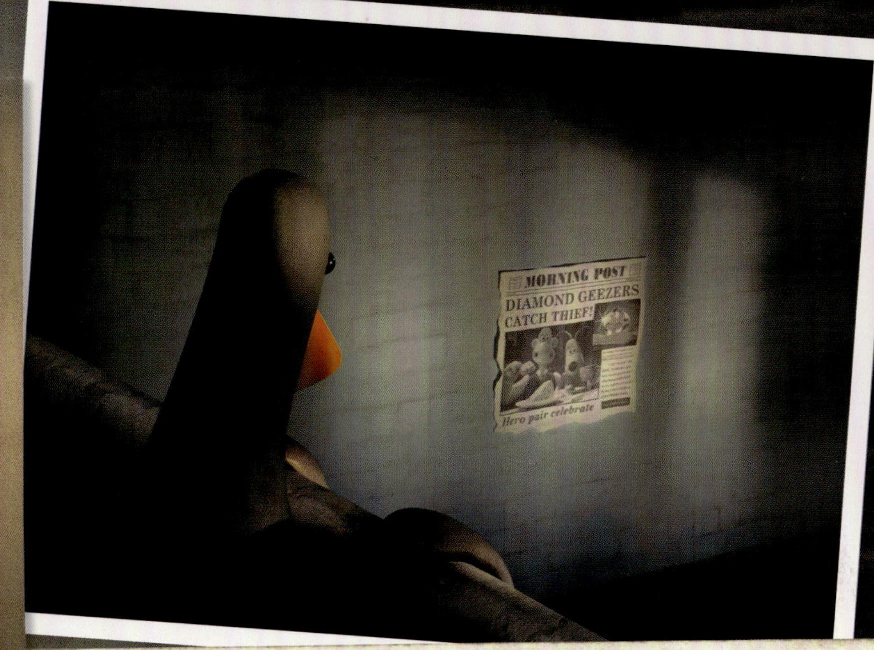

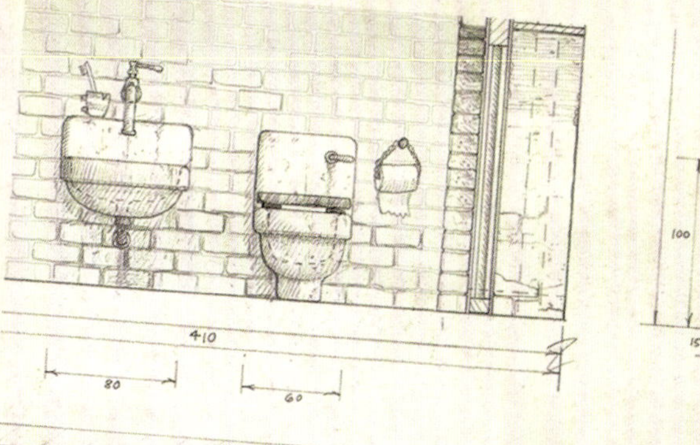

FEATHERS' CELL SINK + TOILET

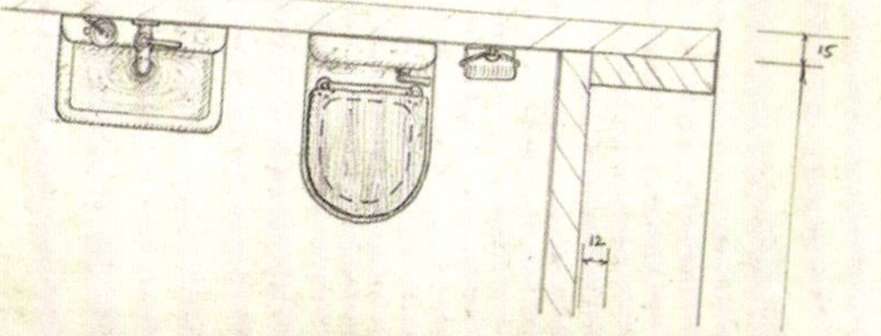

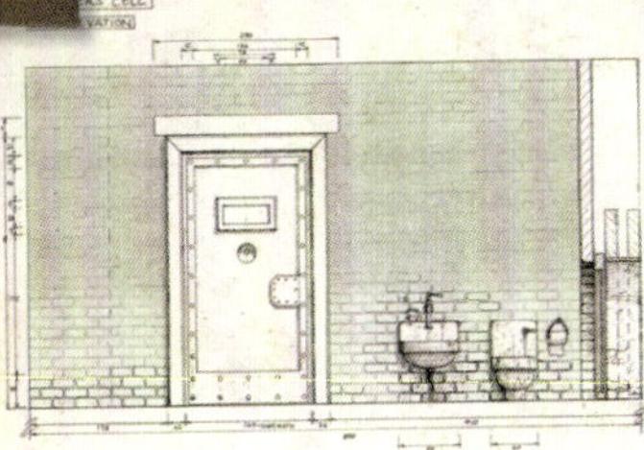
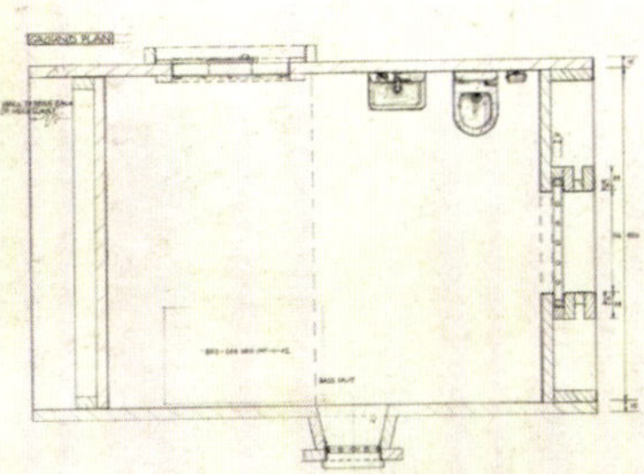
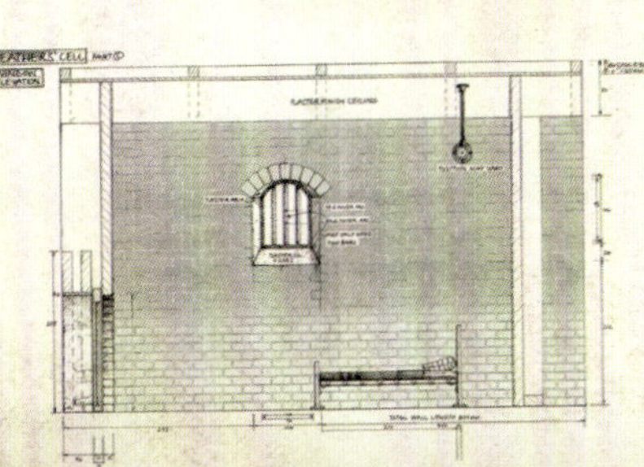
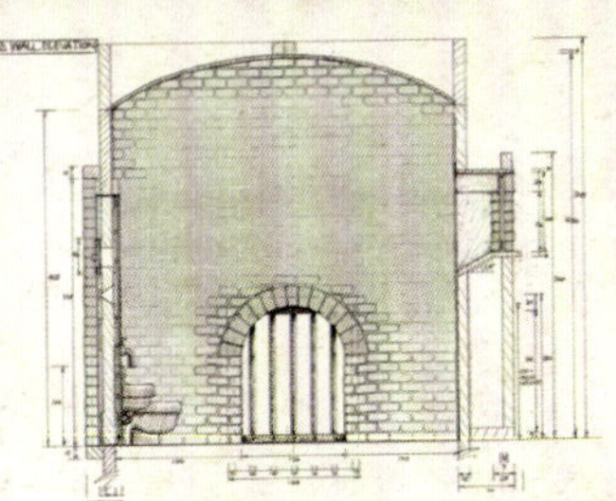
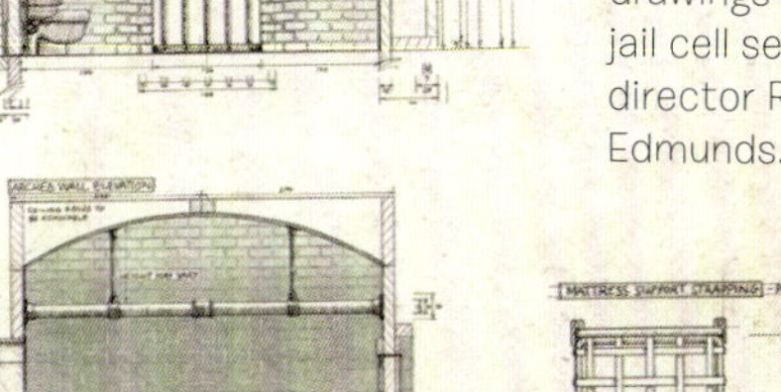
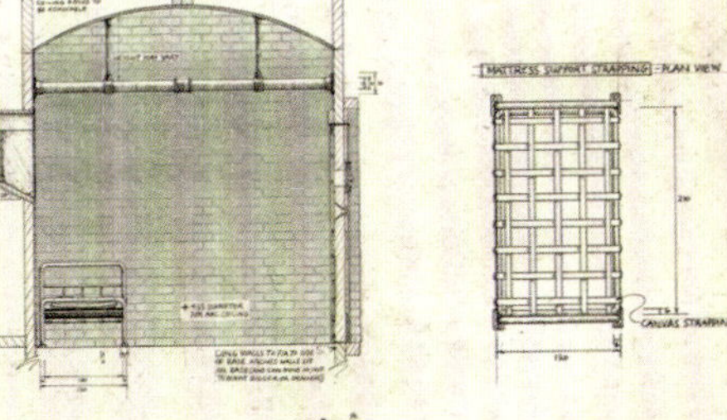
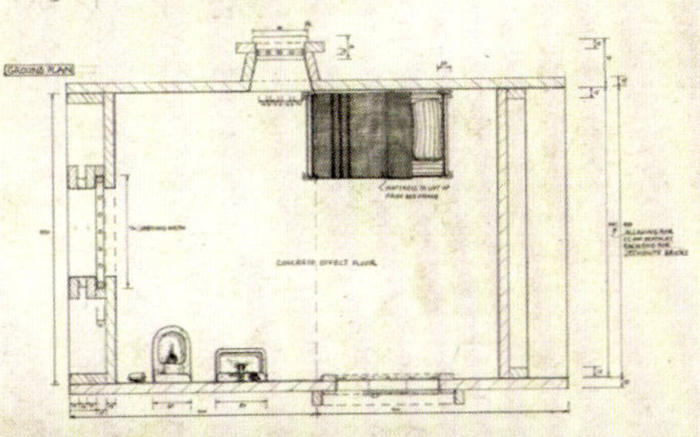

Above | Feathers silently contemplates the fellows who put him away.

Left | Technical drawings for the jail cell set by art director Richard Edmunds.

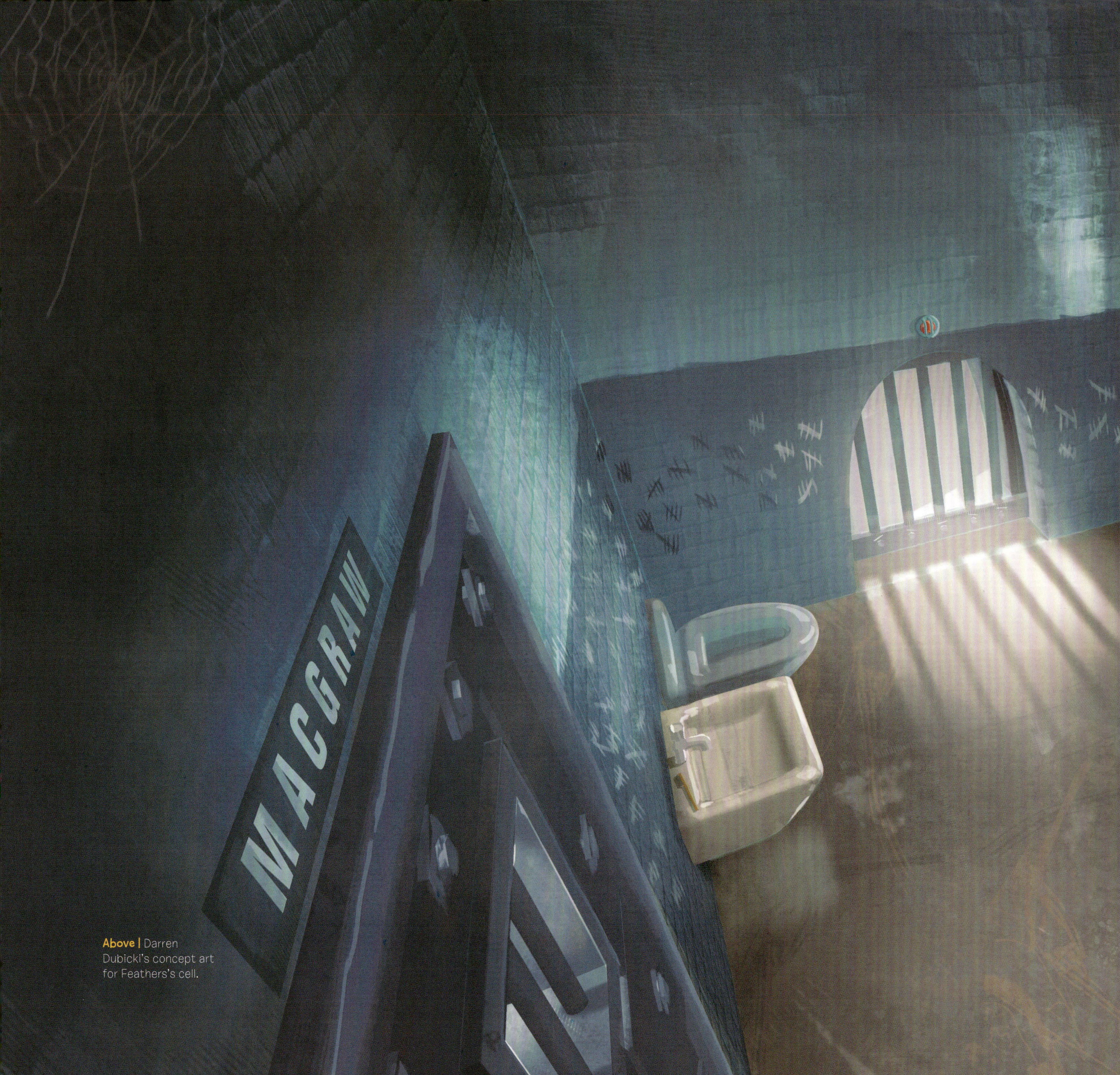

MACGRAW

Above | Darren
Dubicki's concept art
for Feathers's cell.

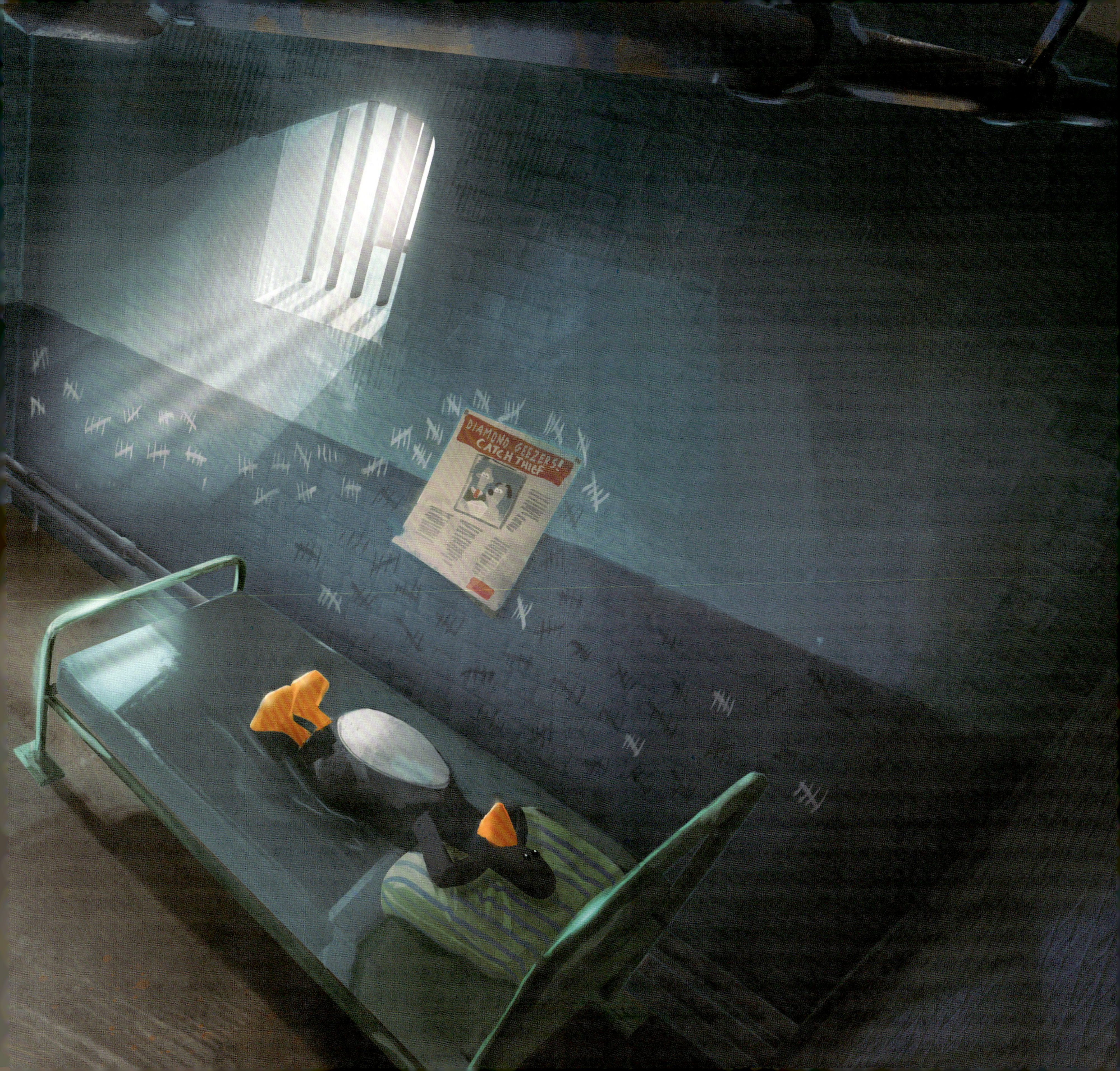

DIAMOND GEEZERS!
CATCH THIEF

support and a fresh eye at certain key stages. We tend to assign a couple of people who would regularly review a project, rather than having the bigger team constantly looking at it, and on this film that's been Sarah and Pete along with James. With Nick, he's so confident in his role as director he absolutely welcomes input from elsewhere. With a less experienced director they can find it slightly trickier trying to navigate a wide set of notes, but for a director who knows where they're heading, they can pick and choose what supports their vision and what doesn't."

What distinguishes Feathers as a character is his ability to project maximum menace with minimal movement, and this provides a unique challenge for the animators. "Because he hasn't got an expression, it all has to be in the body language," explains Head of Puppets Anne King. For *The Wrong Trousers,* Feathers was predominantly animated by Steve Box (who later co-directed with Nick on *Curse of the Were-Rabbit*) and this provided a fly-on-the-wall opportunity for then propmaker Ian Whitlock to watch his work. Now one of Aardman's key animators, Ian has an unparalleled level of familiarity with the character. "Ian seemed like a really useful person to have," says supervising animator Will Becher. "He was the only animator touching Feathers for the first three months." This gave him the chance to establish an approach for the rest of the animation team to follow. When he moved on to other projects, upcoming talent Sean Gregory took over as lead animator on Feathers.

So what is the key to conveying his personality? "Less is more, definitely," says Sean. "The design is so strong and so funny, yet also so scary, that he almost animates himself. When he's directing us, Nick always says, 'He can do that, but not too much'. He compares him to a bottom-heavy milk-bottle; he glides. Another genius bit of direction I had from Nick was, 'He's got to stroke his chin, like that'. And I said 'He hasn't got a thumb… or a chin! So how can I do that?' So Nick just said, 'Believe that he's got it'. I laughed at first, but then I thought, 'That's exactly what I needed.'"

"It's always a bit of a challenge," Ian concurs, "because you don't have what all the other characters have. You don't have brows, which are super-expressive, you haven't got eyelids or proper arms and legs. He's like a bowling pin with feet, just tottering around. But if you play it right, you do get a lot back from him."

"He's a tricky character," agrees animator Raul Eguia. "Everything you do with the puppet dictates his personality, whether he's leaning backwards or forwards, or moving his head from side to side, or even just blinking. It's a simple puppet, but it's one of the most difficult characters to bring to life. He's a perfect villain." In fact, the Animation Bible reveals that Feathers's

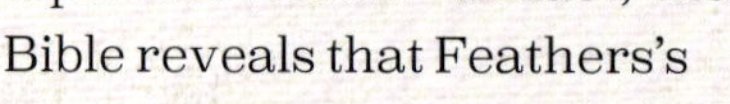

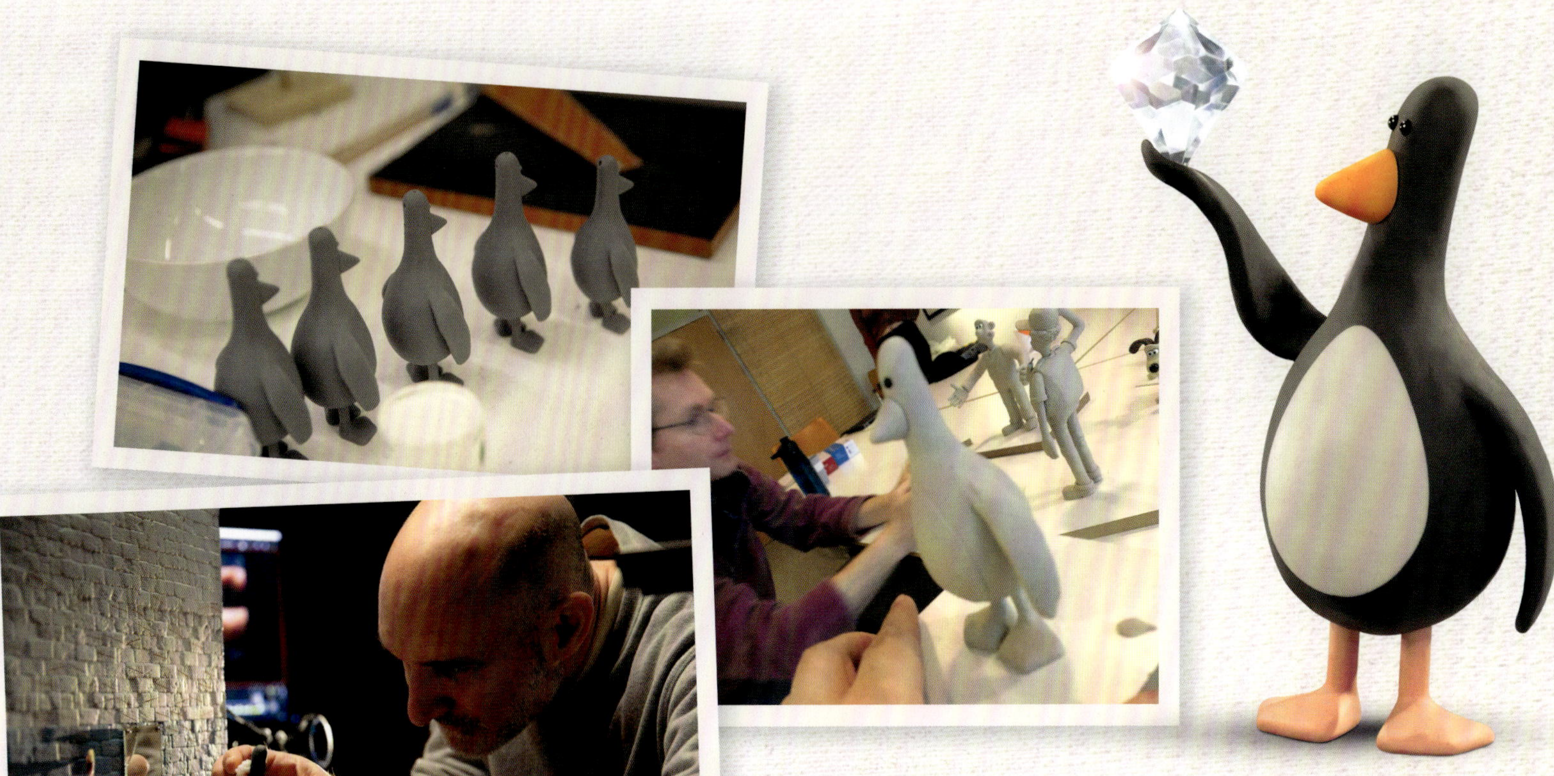

sinister stillness, icy stares and gliding gait all have their roots in another classic British movie villain: Mrs Danvers from Hitchcock's *Rebecca* was a big inspiration for Nick. Even down to the slope of his shoulders and monochrome look, the echoes of Judith Anderson's menacing performance are unmistakable.

As a puppet, Feathers is one of the only characters still largely made of clay. Attempts to re-work the model in silicon proved unsuccessful, as the material tended to 'pull' when the head or the arms were twisted, so it was still necessary to blend and smooth clay to keep his appearance consistent. But nothing is ever wasted at Aardman: the silicon version does make one appearance, when Feathers is disguised as a nun and his flippers are hidden under his habit! Usually, all the black parts of Feathers's body are clay – not that they are black, though, as pure black and white tend to lose colour under camera. "He's slightly off-black, between black and grey," reveals marketing production manager Blair Brown. "We have a similar issue with Shaun the Sheep – he's not totally black and white; he's dark grey and cream."

Under the clay there is a much more sophisticated armature than was used for Feathers's first appearance. "He used to be just a lump of something with the legs plugged in," Anne recalls. "The accuracy that is desired now is of a much higher level of sophistication. In

Top left | March of the penguins... multiple 3D printed models of Feathers.

Left | Lead animator Ian Whitlock poses Feathers while he shaves.

Above centre | Director Merlin Crossingham reviews a Feathers sculpt.

Above | Feathers reviews the Blue Diamond in a production shot.

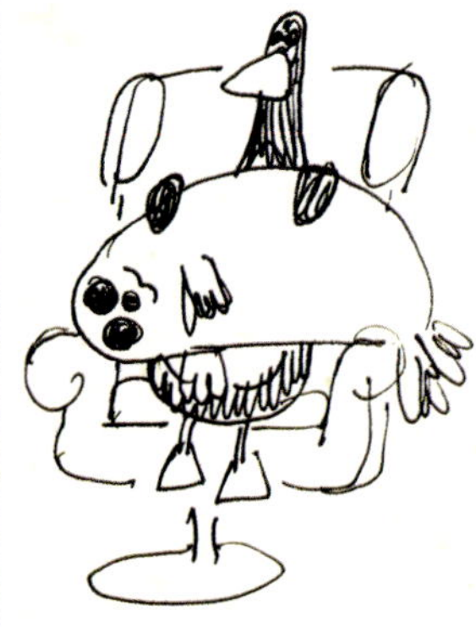

The Wrong Trousers, Feathers changes from one shot to another and nobody seems to mind – his legs changed length and width as they were just pinned in. Now we have armatures with legs that can be plugged in and out, and proper joints and wide feet. We make head cores where the eyes pin into place, so they're always the right distance apart and the relationship to the beak is always exactly the same. If you get a shift in any of that it can change the expression of the whole head. That was something that took a long time to get right."

Even recreating Feathers's eyes created an unanticipated problem. In *The Wrong Trousers* they were simply shop-bought pins with black glass beads as pinheads, which were stuck into the clay. But now that multiple models are required, allowing the animators to shoot various Feathers scenes on different sets at the same time, it is vital that the puppets remain 100% identical. "We had to buy masses and masses of pins to get the right size," says Anne. "Some of them were ever so slightly big. We couldn't cast them ourselves because they're glass beads, so we had to buy pots of 50 then get the Vernier gauge and measure them all and pick out all the ones that were the right size!"

Like any world-class villain, Feathers deserves a world-class lair, and we discover he has secretly adapted the local zoo's penguin enclosure for his own nefarious purposes. The set is reminiscent of the modernist style of London Zoo's celebrated Penguin Pool, designed by architect Berthold Lubetkin. However, concept artist Darren Dubicki describes how Feathers's lair plays against the usual hi-tech slickness of a typical villain's HQ: "It was taking that level of

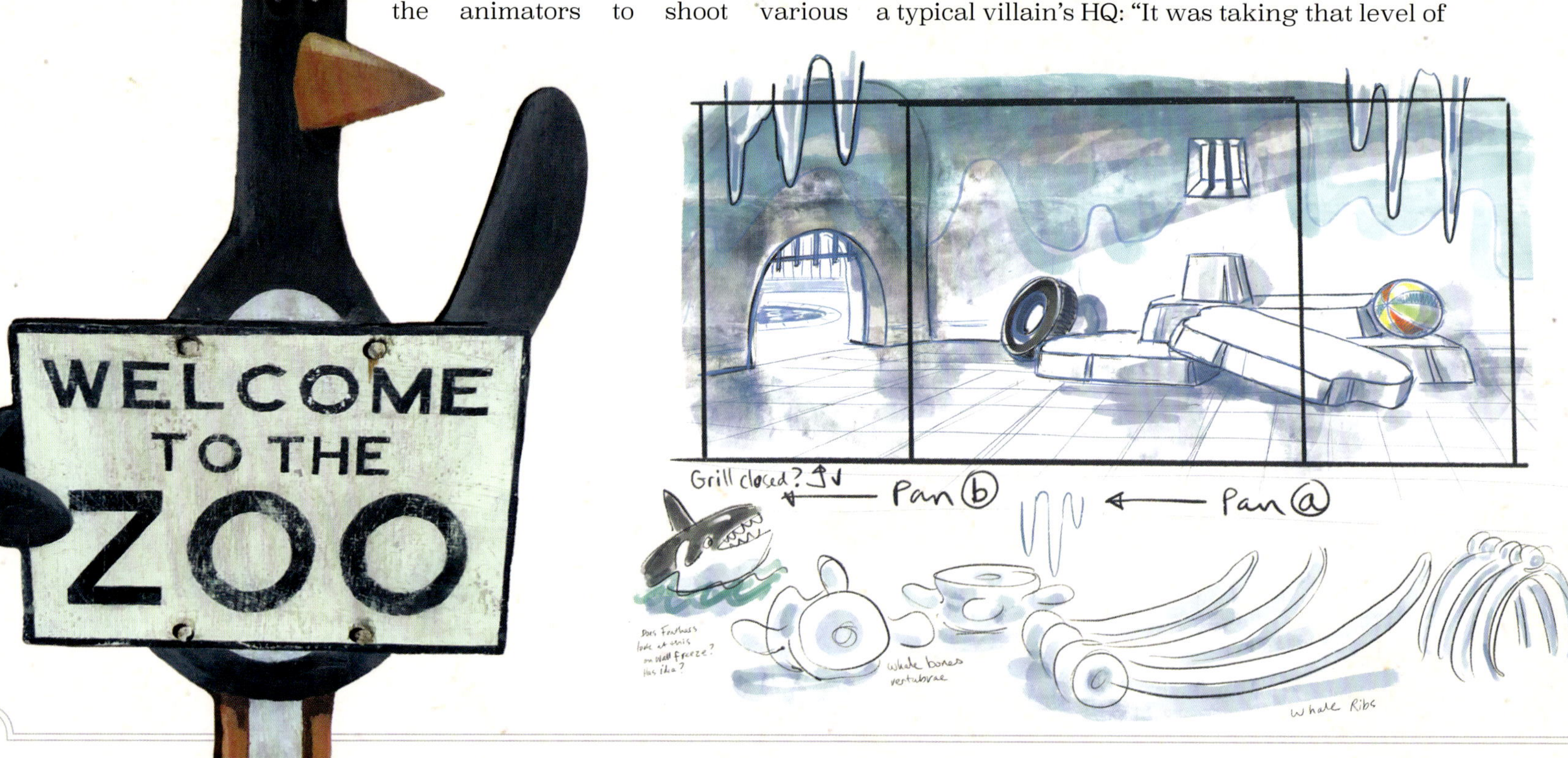

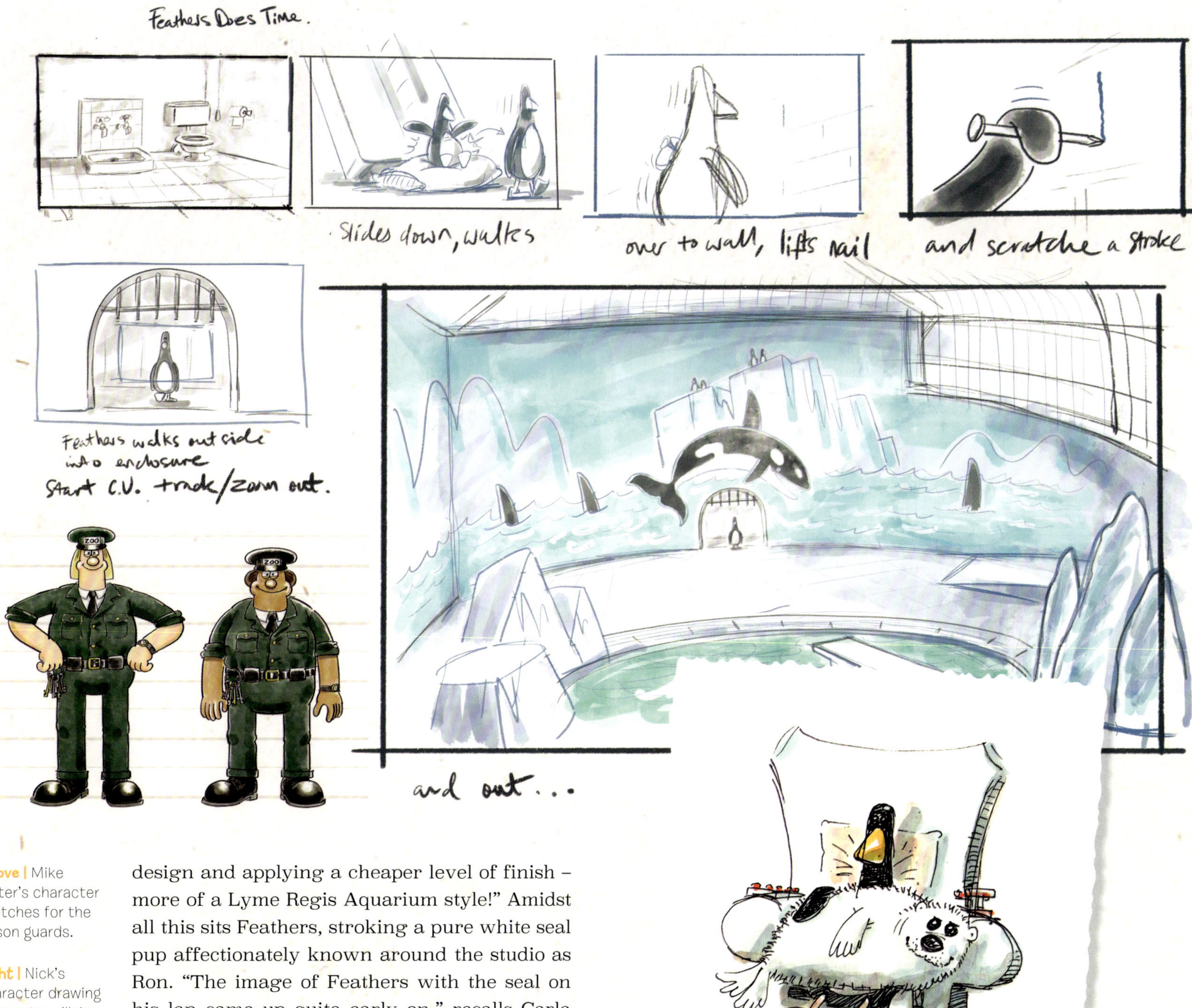

design and applying a cheaper level of finish – more of a Lyme Regis Aquarium style!" Amidst all this sits Feathers, stroking a pure white seal pup affectionately known around the studio as Ron. "The image of Feathers with the seal on his lap came up quite early on," recalls Carla Shelley. "Just seeing that image of Feathers reminded us how long it had been since we've seen him and what a fantastic villain he is."

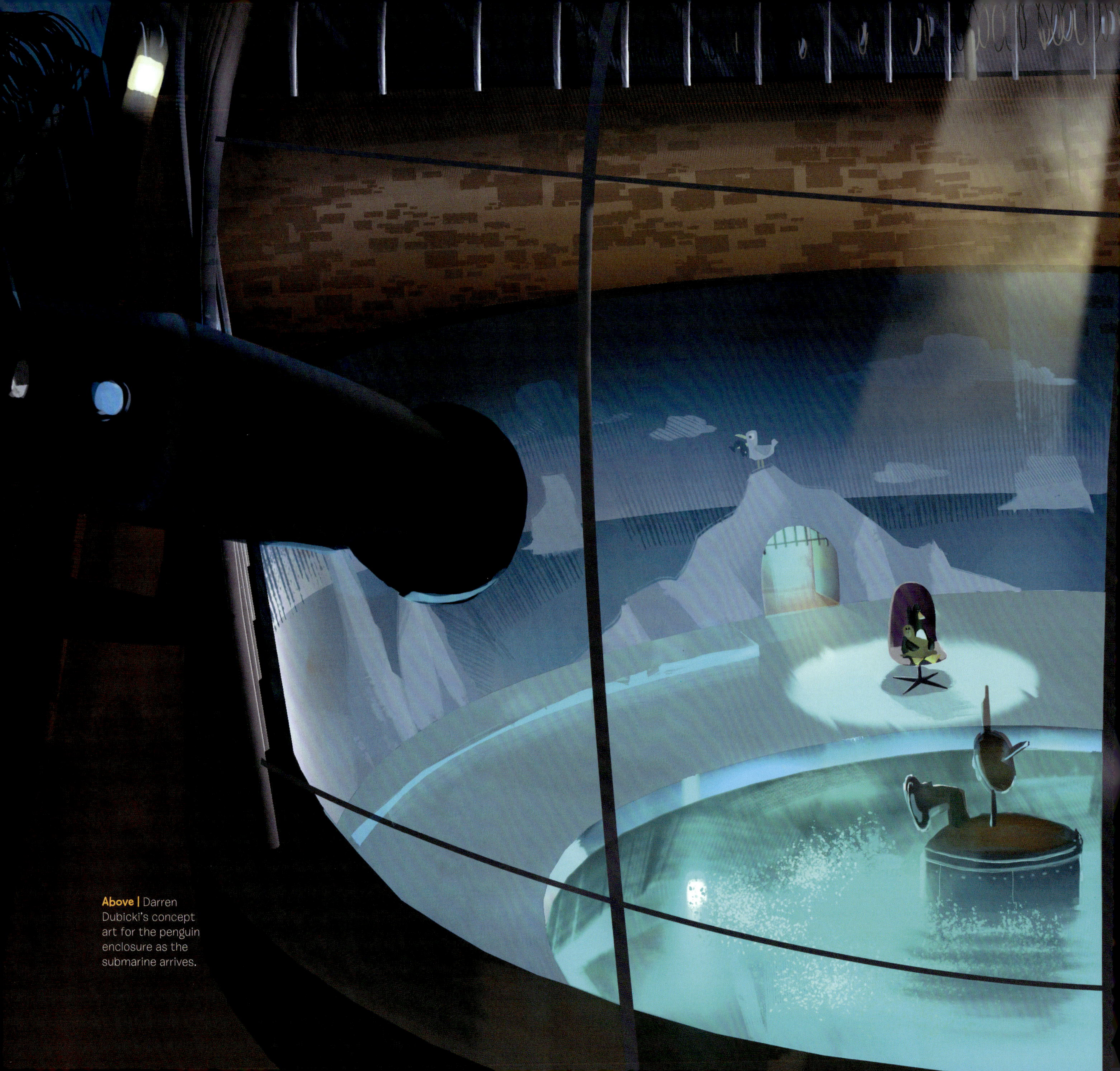

Above | Darren Dubicki's concept art for the penguin enclosure as the submarine arrives.

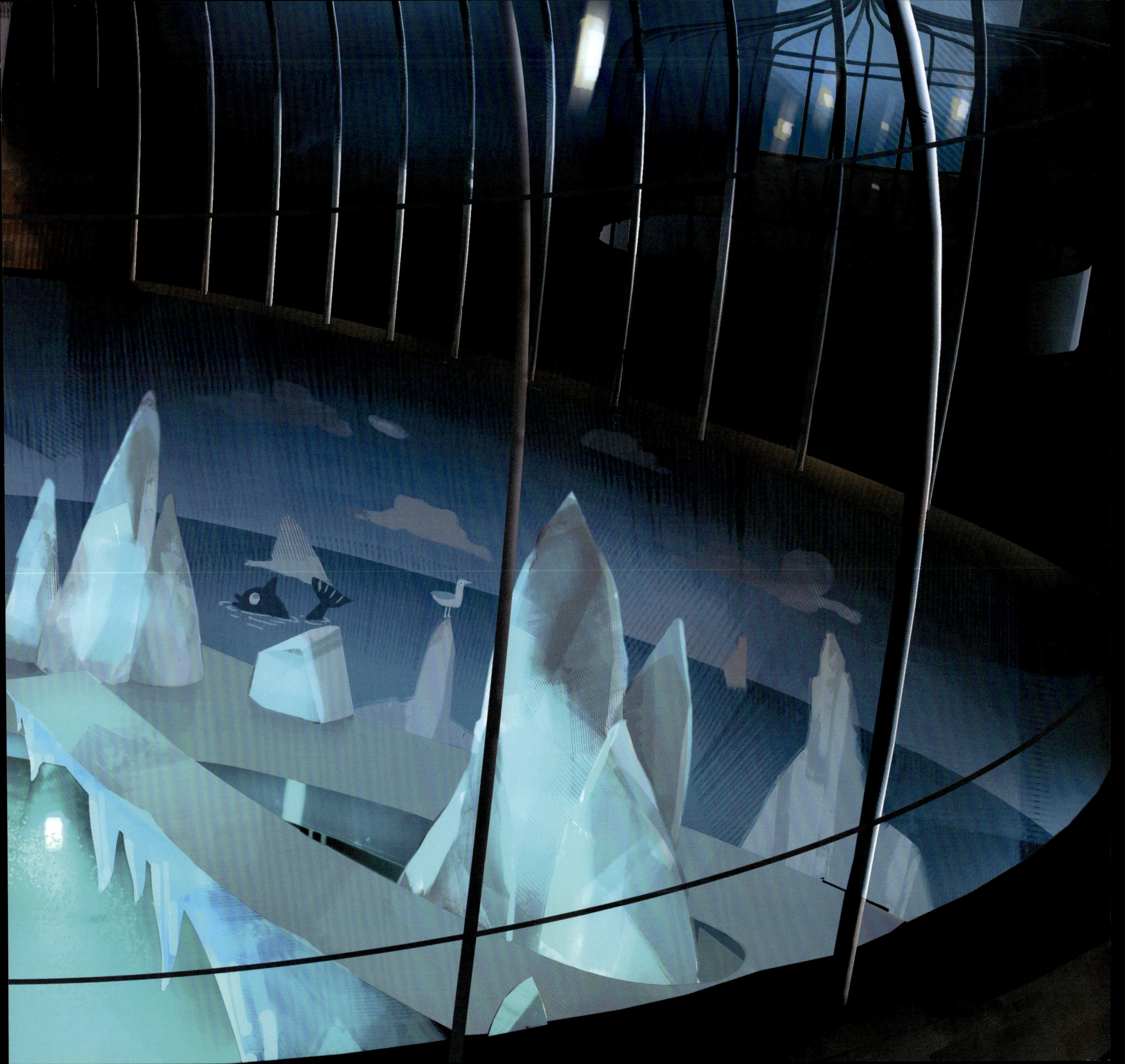

It is from his cell behind the Penguin Pool that Feathers hatches his master plan. This sequence is directed by Merlin, so storyboard artist Mike Salter had more scope to bring his own perspective to the action, rather than working to the detailed thumbnails typically provided by Nick. Merlin might produce perhaps a single key image for the scene, but tends to give more of a verbal brief, which Mike then works up into some initial rough sketches. This can save a lot of time and heartache for the production team before the scene reaches the studio floor, as the feasibility of various shots can be examined at the animatic stage.

For example, Mike provided alternatives for Feathers spying on the prison guards' television. Within an overall layout of the set produced by Nick, the initial idea was to use a mirror made from ice-lolly sticks and a foil wrapper, litter Feathers found lying round the zoo. A camera move was planned from the TV screen, over the guards' heads and round to Feathers in his cell. However, when the team looked at the thumbnails, this was deemed to be too complicated, so a simple cut from the television to the cell was instituted instead. Similarly, the makeshift mirror felt too close to the contraption he later uses to hack into the computer system. "Then we came up with him just having a mirror," recalls Mike, "but they thought that was a bit boring. So then someone will think of something clever, something that's hidden in his cell but we don't know is there until he brings it out. Feathers is making this matchstick galleon with a sardine tin base, so now he just sticks out the tin, which is reflective."

With potential problems de-bugged, Mike then proceeds to a version of the storyboard with more finished drawings. Here he will establish camera angles and the composition of certain shots. "Merlin will give you an idea of what needs to be there, but after a bit you know what's going to look good. A low angle is going to be dramatic, that's hard-wired into your brain, so you just follow your instincts." Does he feel that storyboard artists get enough recognition for their contribution? He recalls a conversation with Sarah Smith, director

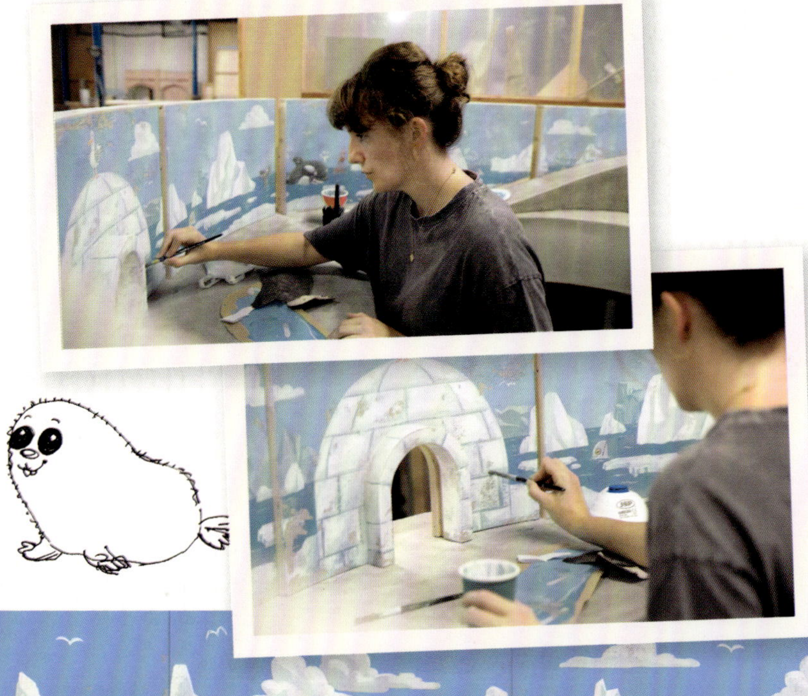

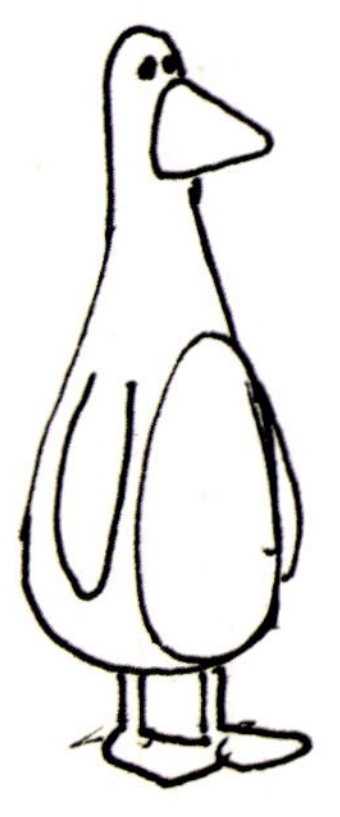

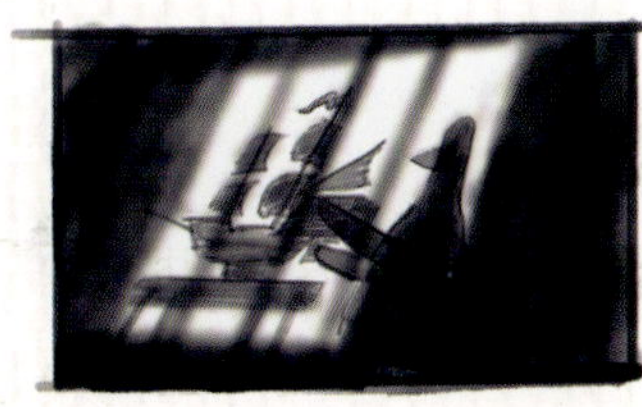
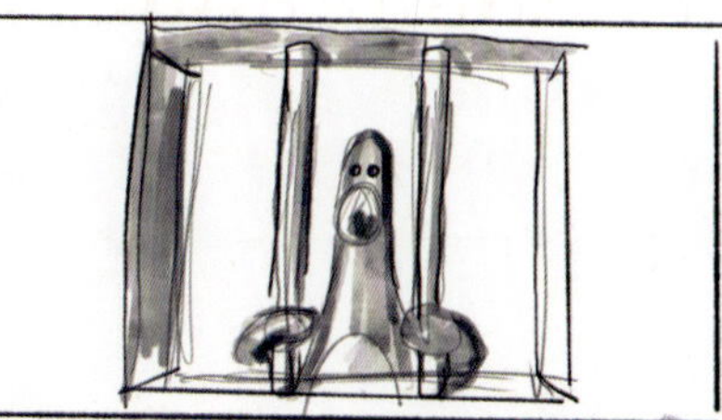

Lightning flashes
Camera tracks IN on window FM Turns around

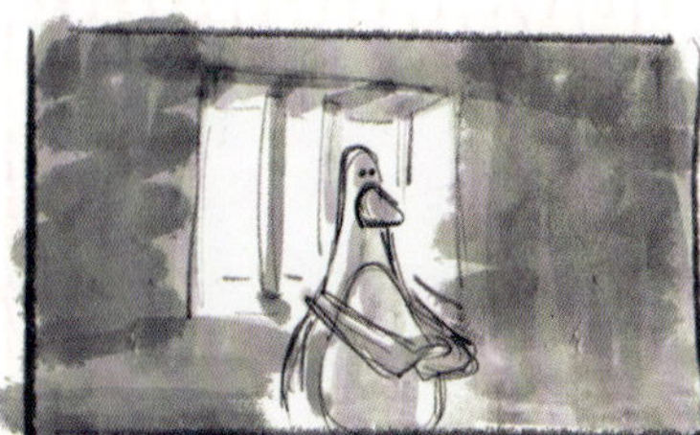

FM turns, stretches hands in readiness. Crinks neck.

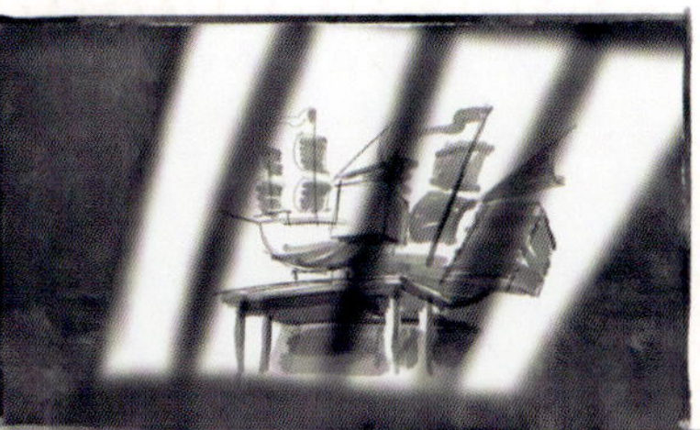
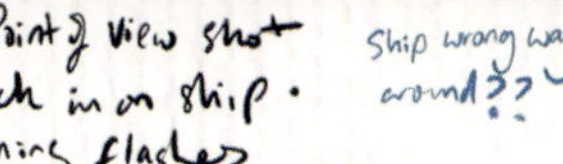

FM Point of view shot track in on ship. Lightning flashes.
Ship wrong way around ??

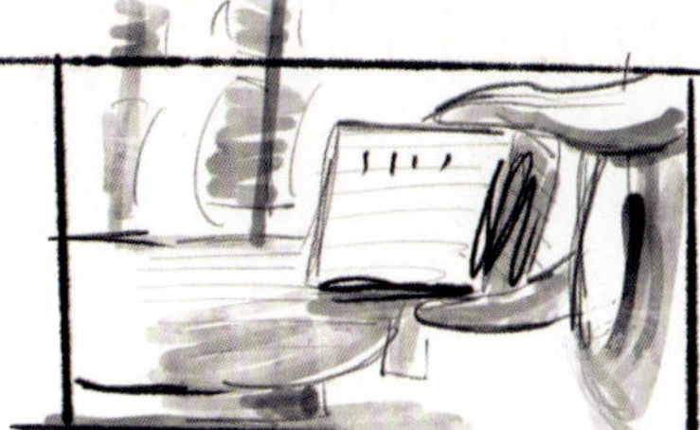

Then FM Pushes crate upto wall and removes Newspaper clip of W+G. + reveal brick hole.
FM Breaks box off stern of ship.
Flop this shot ??

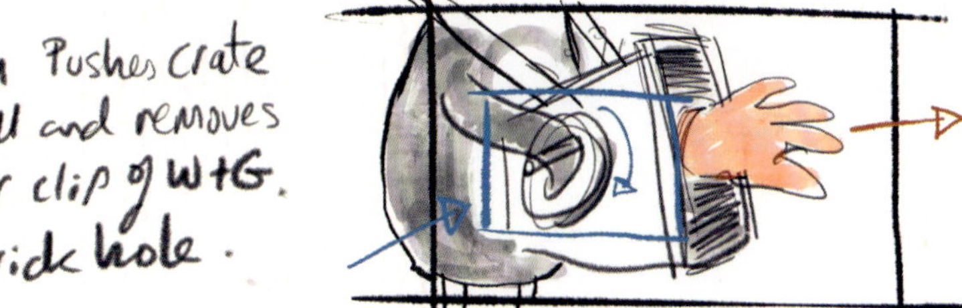
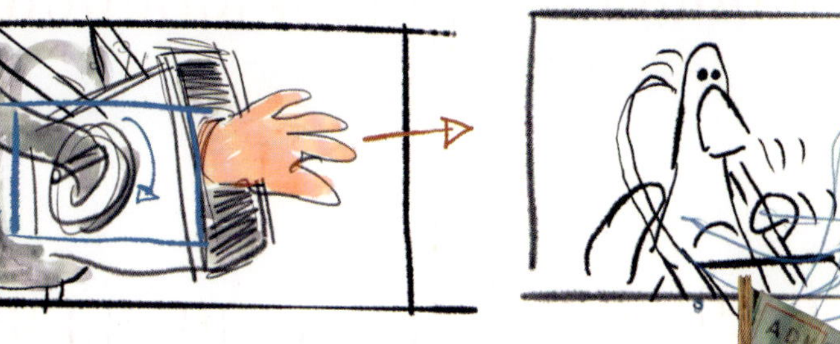

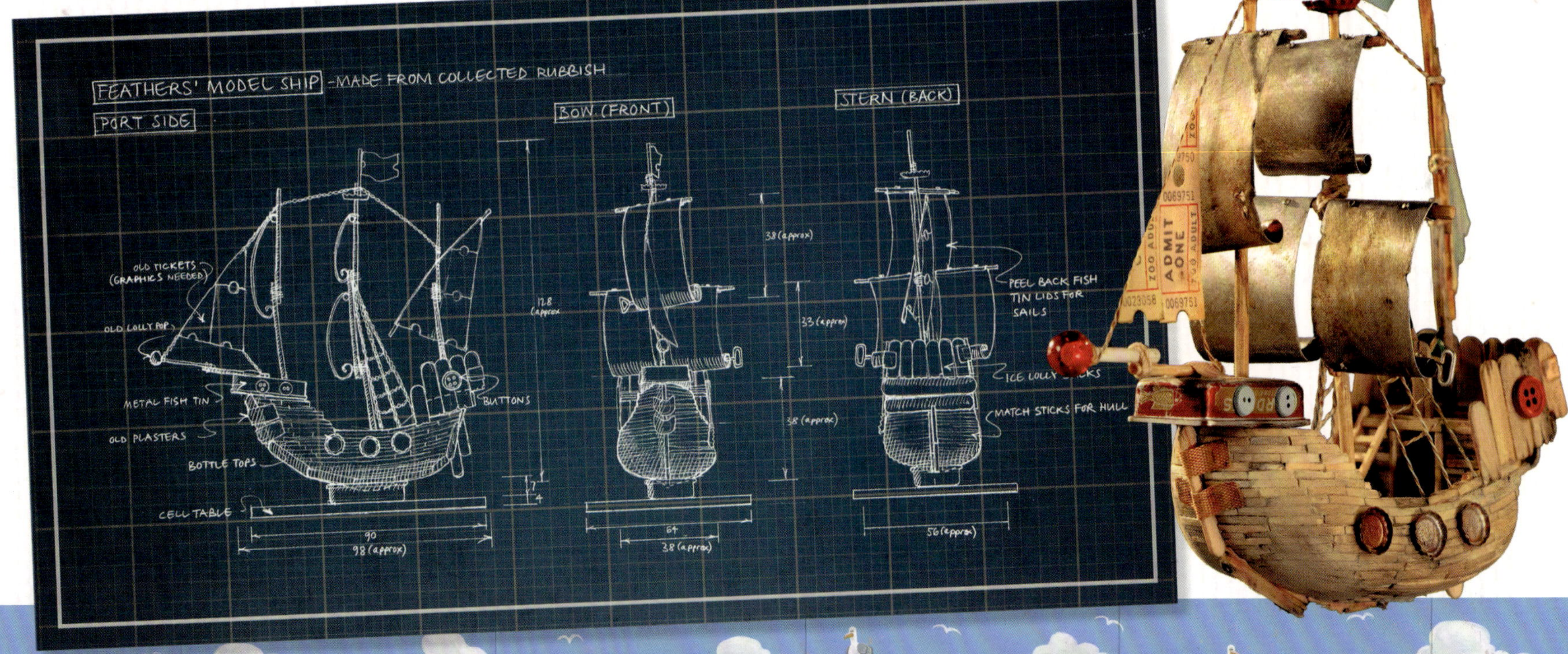

FEATHERS' MODEL SHIP —MADE FROM COLLECTED RUBBISH
PORT SIDE
BOW (FRONT)
STERN (BACK)
OLD TICKETS (GRAPHICS NEEDED)
OLD LOLLY POP
METAL FISH TIN
OLD PLASTERS
BOTTLE TOPS
CELL TABLE
BUTTONS
128 (approx)
90
98 (approx)
64
38 (approx)
38 (approx)
33 (approx)
38 (approx)
56 (approx)
PEEL BACK FISH TIN LIDS FOR SAILS
ICE LOLLY STICKS
MATCH STICKS FOR HULL

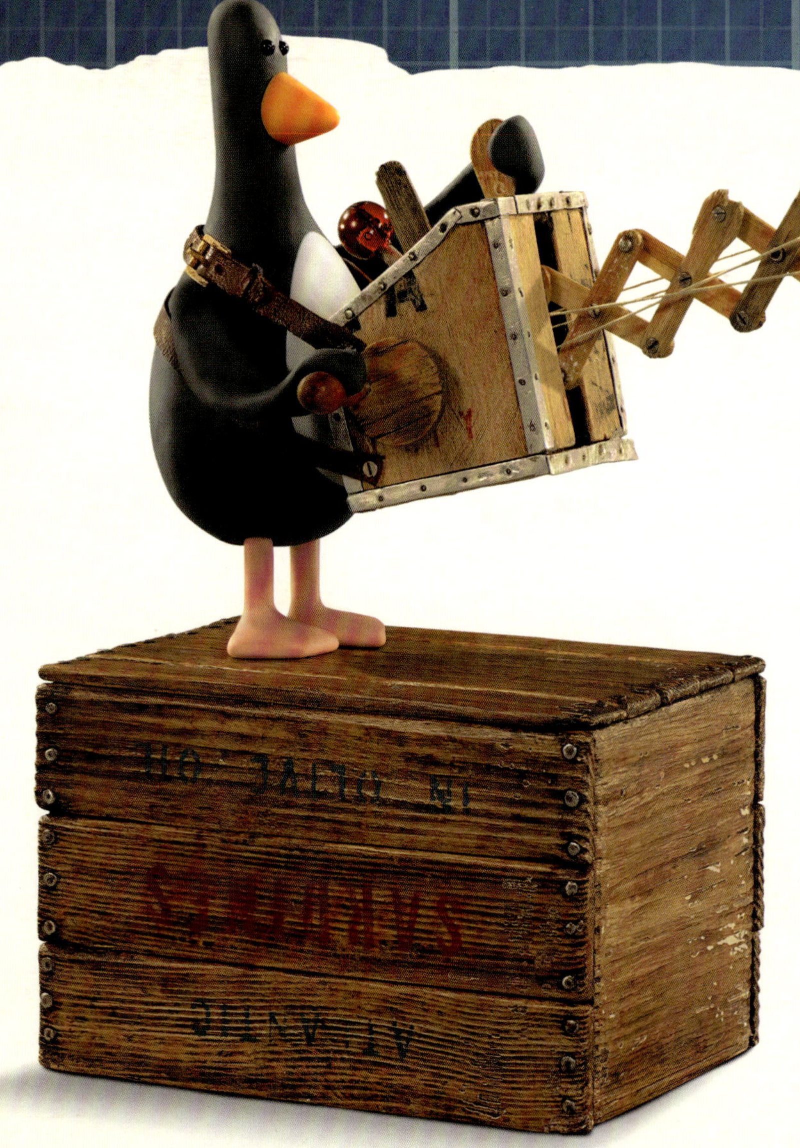

character animation. Using his iconic rubber glove on a concertina arm made from lollipop sticks and bits of plastic, he stretches past the sleeping guards to reach their computer keyboard. The level of personality and comedy invested into this inanimate object is a perfect illustration of the unique qualities stop-motion can bring. The physicality of a real object creates an indefinable magic to its movement, which wouldn't be the same in CGI. "The rubber glove on the end of the arm, that's pure clay all the way through," explains Anne. "We had to make it so that it can be taken off easily and the animator can sculpt it and put it back on, so it's got this little pin in there to fix it to the arm. It's amazing what Raul did there."

Animator Raul Eguia originally approached the glove as an extension of Feathers's personality. "I tried to think how Feathers would do it, but Nick wanted something a bit different with the hand, more cartoony I guess, more expressive than Feathers. It's very theatrical, a completely different character that works on its own. The arm is so mechanical when it starts coming into the shot, and suddenly you realise it's another character."

One of the most amazing aspects of Aardman's style of animation is the perfect timing, which flows so naturally when you watch the film – for example, when the glove stifles the sleeping guard's sneeze. But how does the animator approach the process of mechanically breaking the action down into 12 frames per second to

of *Arthur Christmas*: "She was asking what storyboard artists actually did, so I said we get the script and we work out the shots and all the rest of it. And she asked 'What's the difference between you and a director?', so I explained we're mini-directors, that's how I described it. If you're doing thumbnails from the script and working it right up to finished boards, you're being a guided director, I'd say."

Feathers's hacking of the Norbot computer system is a particularly striking example of

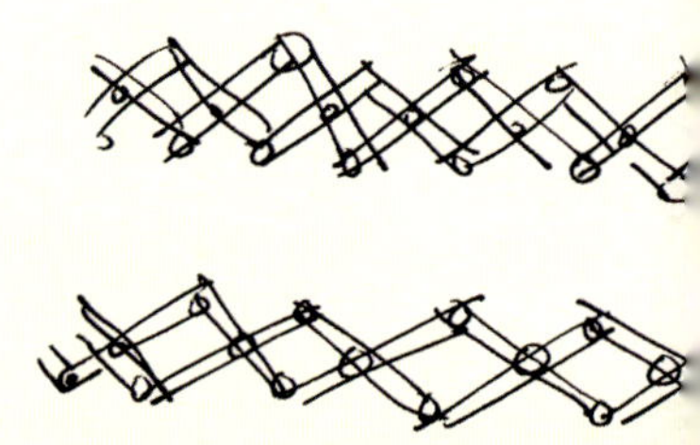

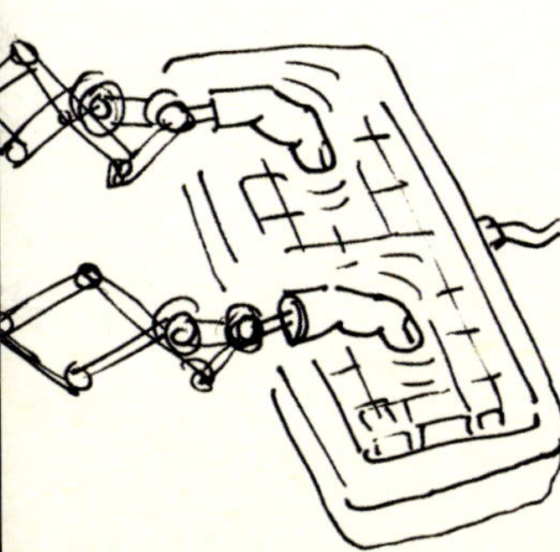

such great comic effect? "For me, the most important thing is the timing," explains Raul. "You have to think about what the audience is seeing, and you have to be very clear about where you are going to wait, or where you do something quite slow and then a lot faster to get the laugh. Sometimes in comedy you have to go with extremes to get a strong reaction from the audience. You've got a character sleeping; the hand doesn't want to wake him up, so it has to be very careful and slow and gentle, but suddenly something happens and everything moves so quick. It makes you react and that makes it funny."

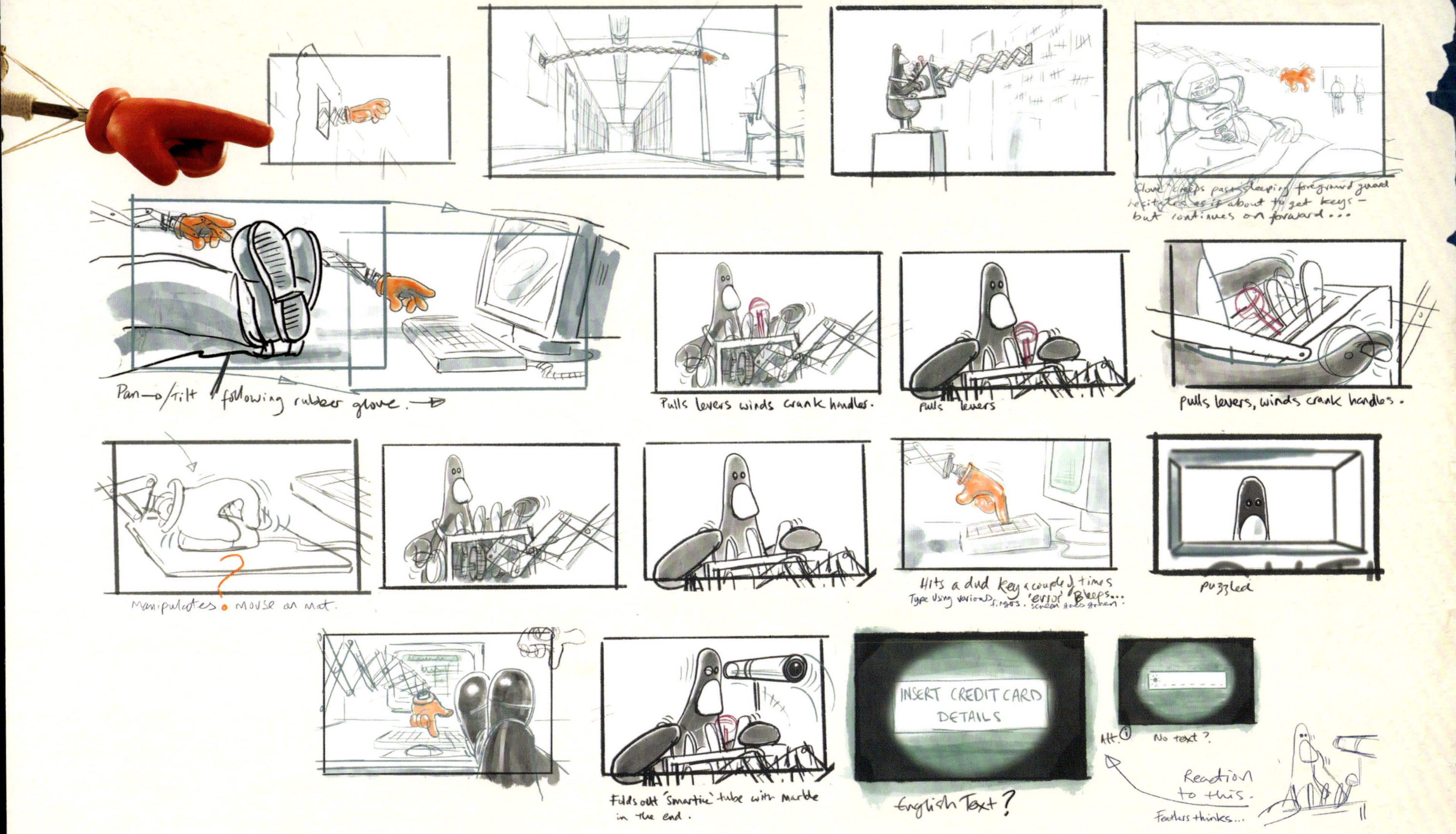

With typically creative modesty, Raul refuses to take credit for the comedy. "It's part of the script, part of the storyboard, so it's something that I didn't come up with." But Nick believes in

Above | Nick Park's early thumbnail storyboards for the hacking sequence.

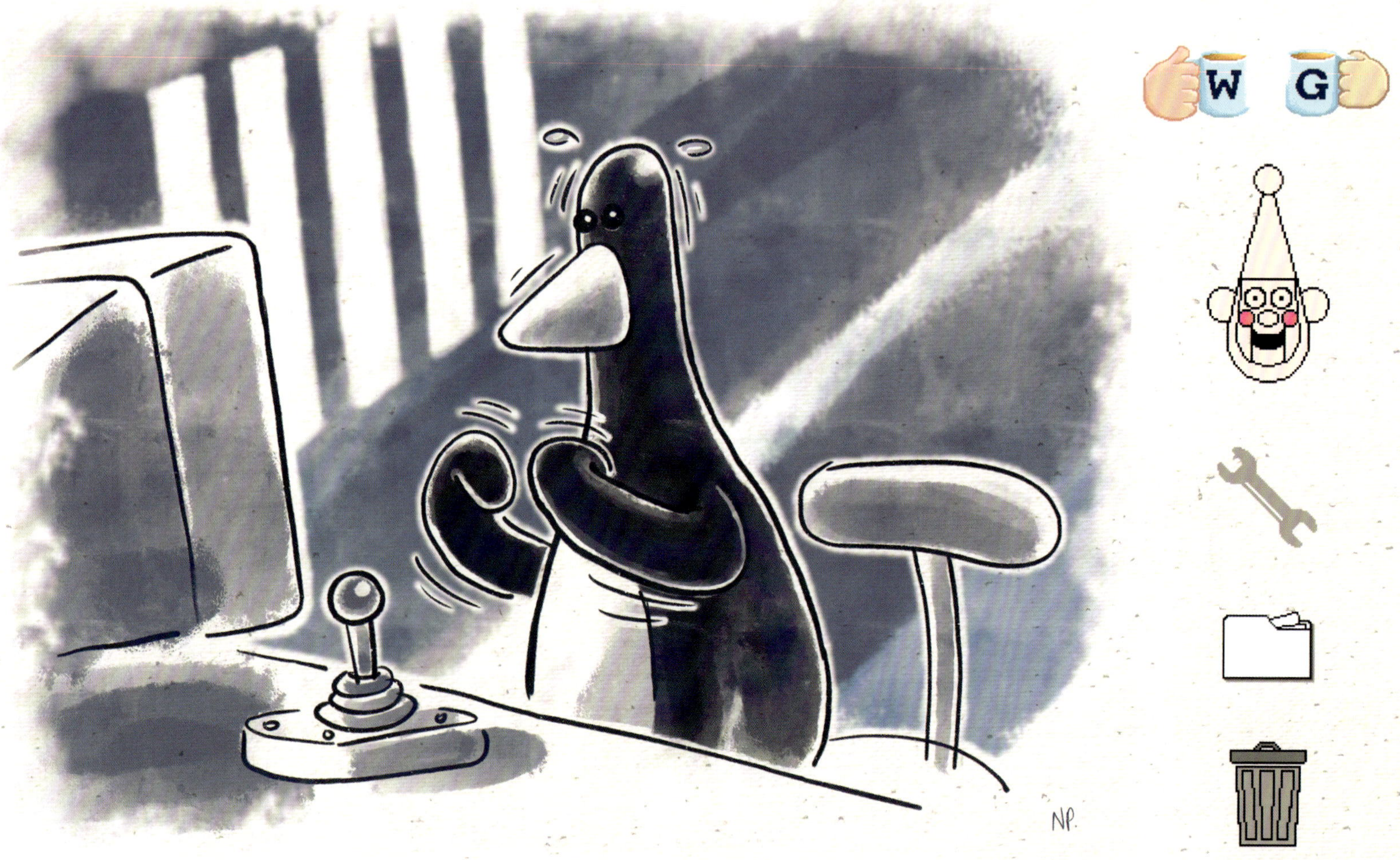

giving the animators the latitude to bring their own touch to the scenes. "With Nick I feel I've got the freedom to interpret what he wants. He talks more about feelings than the number of frames or the speed. He doesn't want to know how long the shot is, he just wants to have that reaction. And we use animation 'blocks', of course, which is the shot with just the key frames so you get an idea of the speed and the poses. It's very useful for him to see that and talk about it, to help him find what he wants to get the perfect performance."

Perhaps one of the biggest departures from the previous *Wallace & Gromit* films is that *Vengeance Most Fowl* sees our intrepid inventor enter the computer age – in a fashion, at least. The 1950s period ambiance of the series is one of its most striking features, but here the challenge was to portray the Artificial Intelligence aspects of the story without losing its old-fashioned charm. "We're still trying to keep that really nostalgic English feel," explains production designer Matt Perry, "but we sneak into the 1970s with answerphones and things like that. We try and stop at the 70s, but we've gone into the 80s with the very earliest computers as our

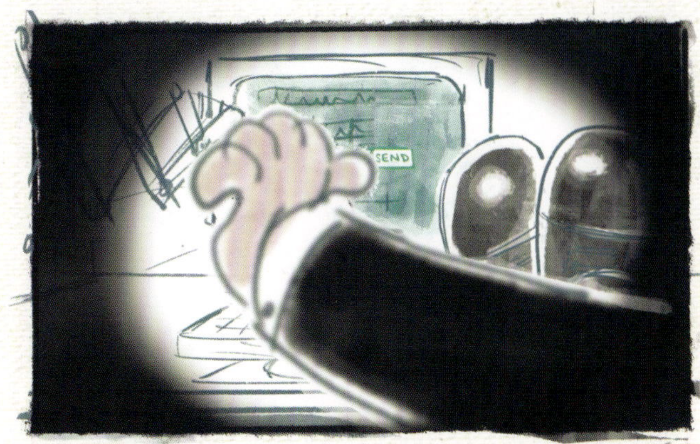

Guard's arm lifts up in foreground –
shot continued

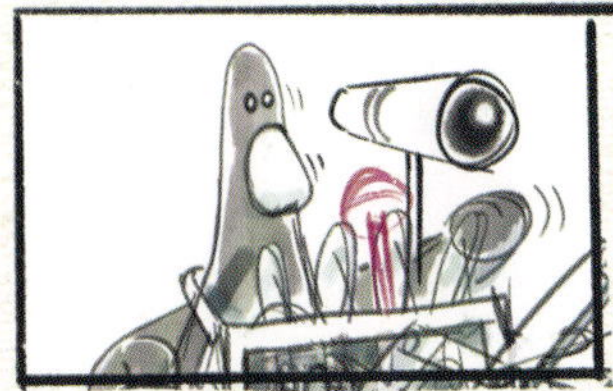

Feathers halts everything!

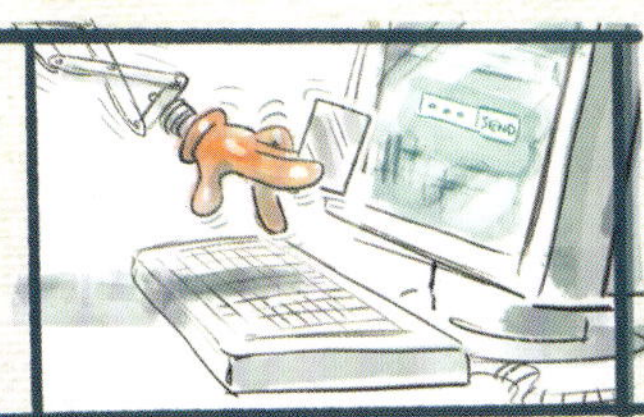

Hand halts in space... whips out left

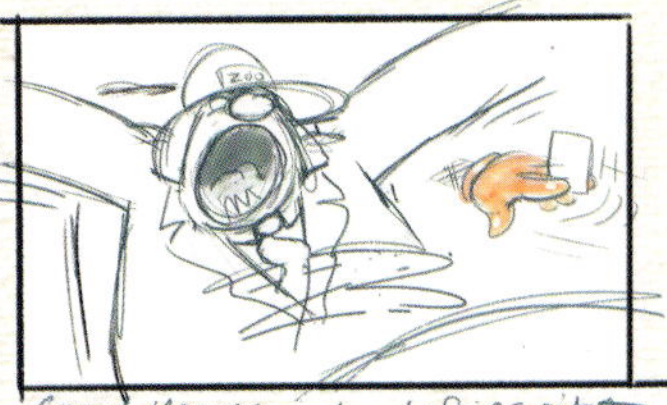

Guard yawns – hand whips out unseen.

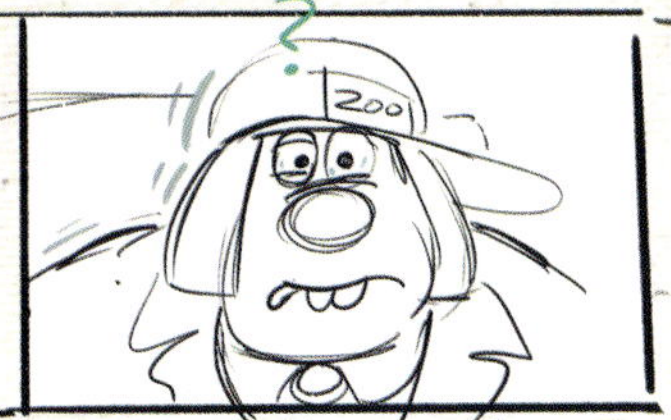

Still dazed – leans in noticing something

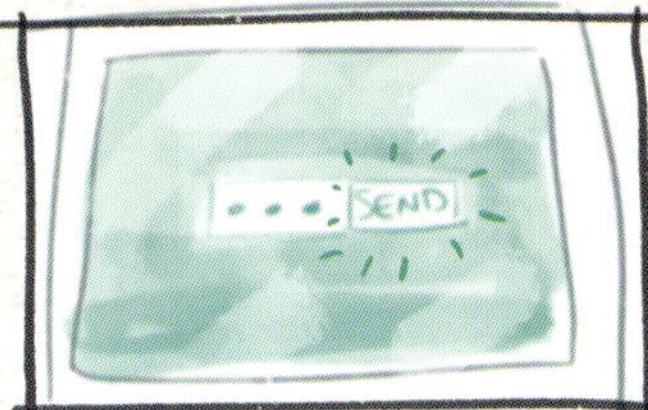

not quite focuses yet.

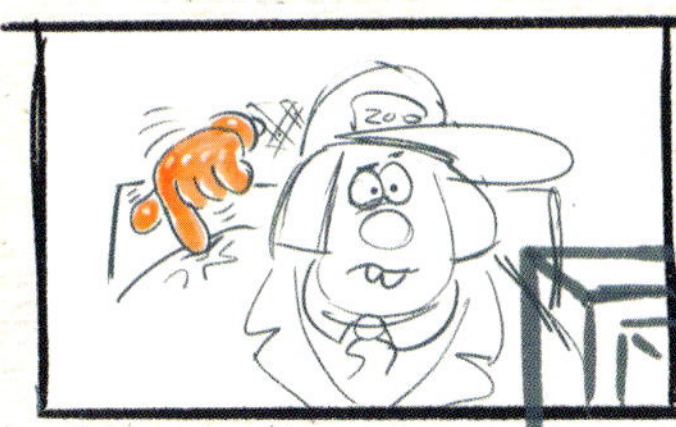

Tap on shoulder distracts her

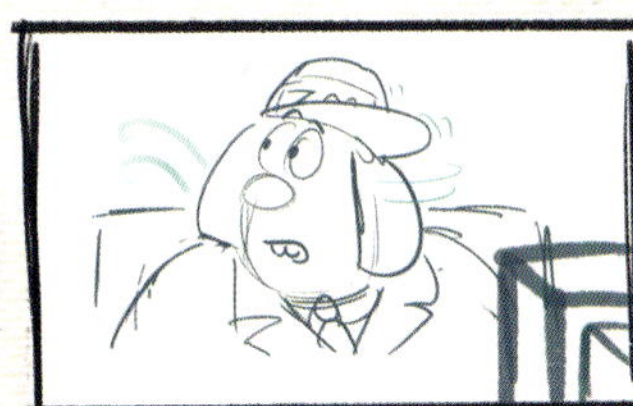

Looks around as hand whips away.

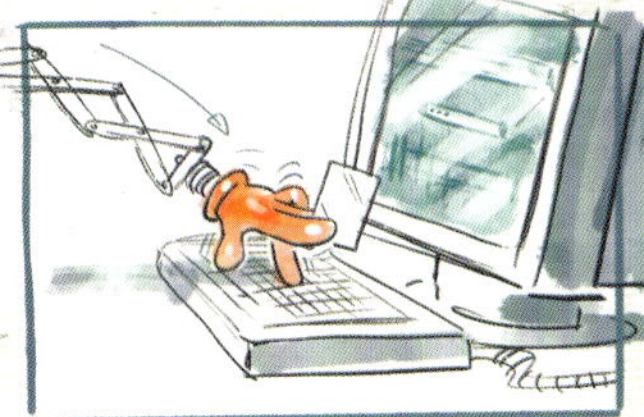

Hit once for 'send!'

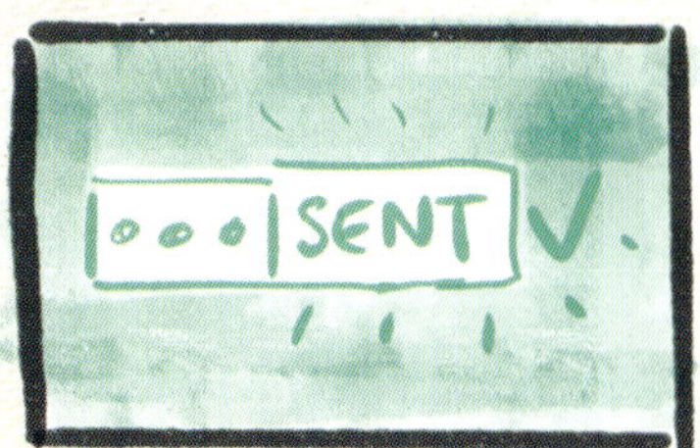

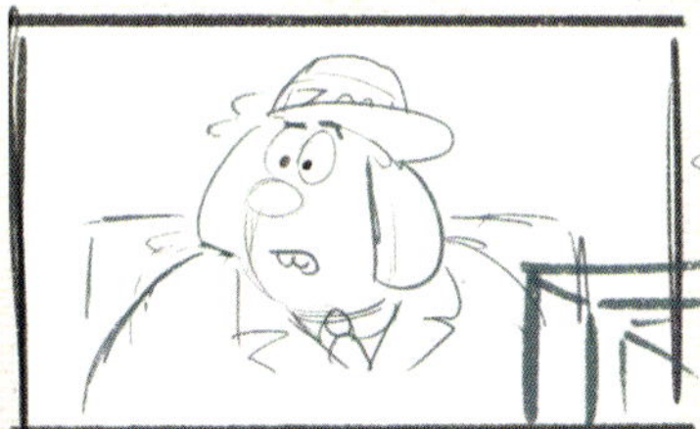

She gets suspicious hears something –

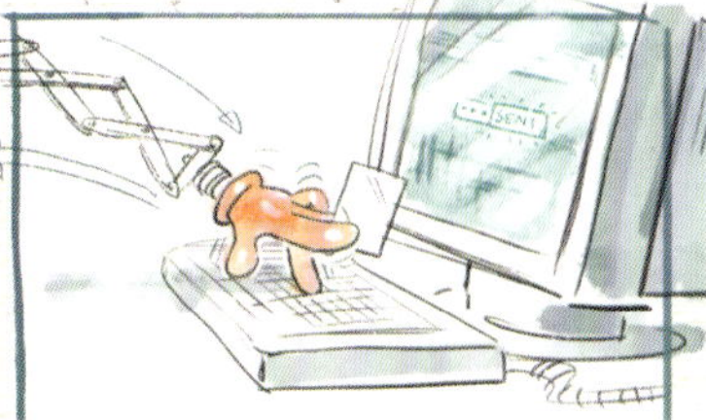

Hits another couple of keys
Screen goes to a transition and whips out

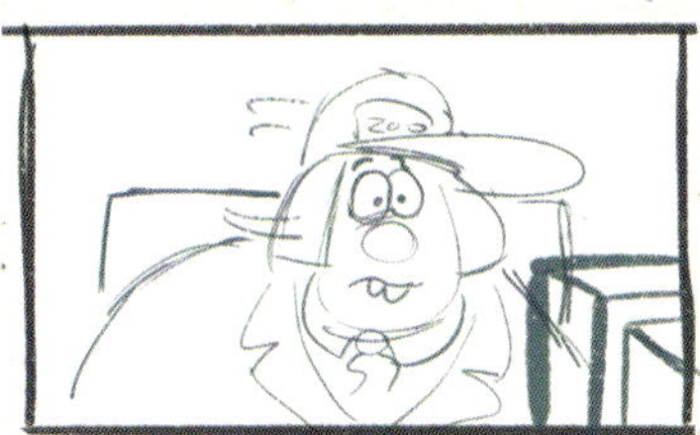

Then turns + glances

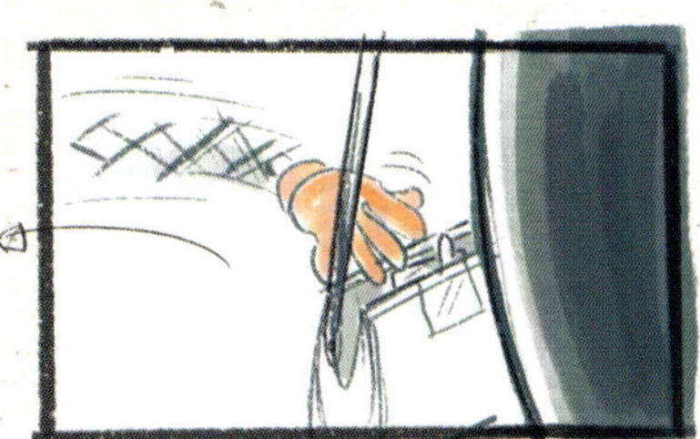

Throws credit card in handbag and snaps it shut. then walks off.

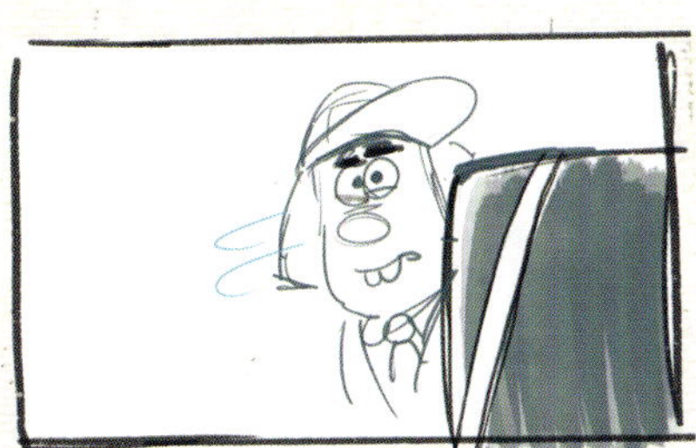

'Look' brick slides into place. Updated roster?

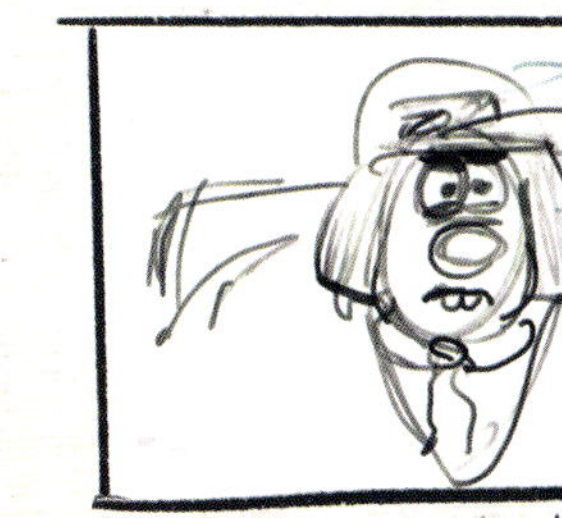

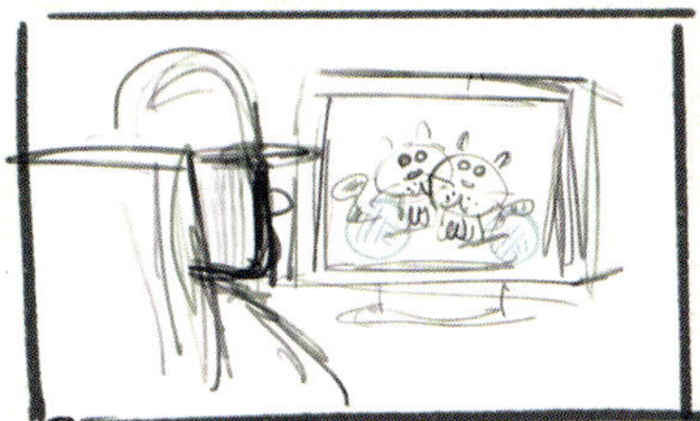

She turns back dumbfounded –

But oh there's kittens...

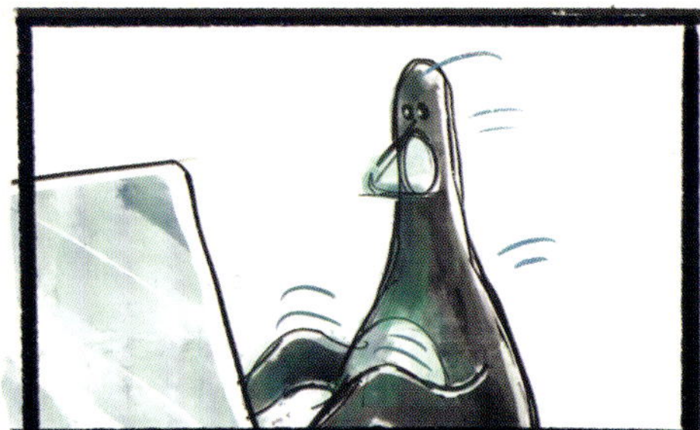

He enters one letter at a time...

Then 'Ping' we're in!

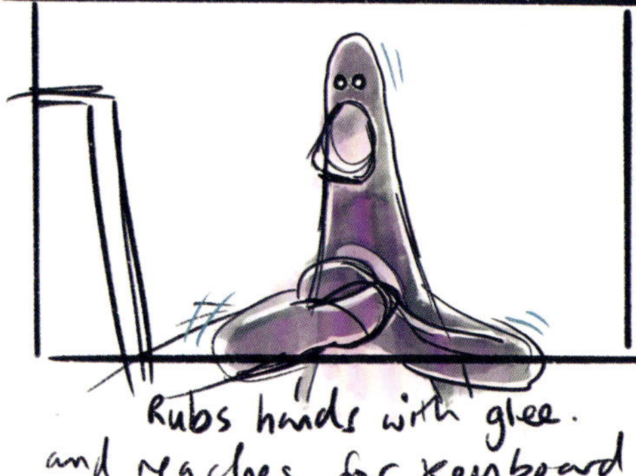

Rubs hands with glee.
and reaches for keyboard

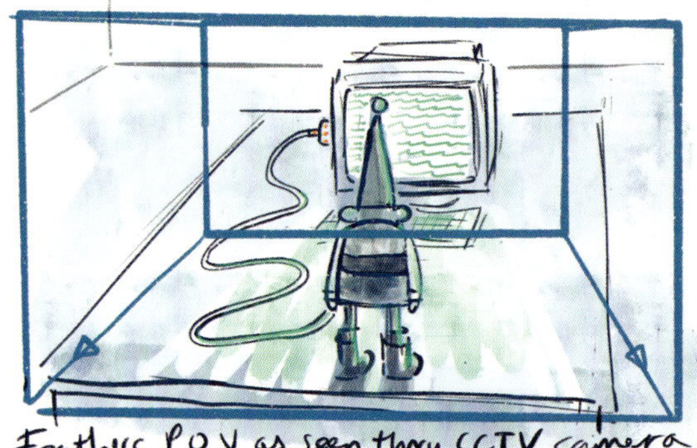
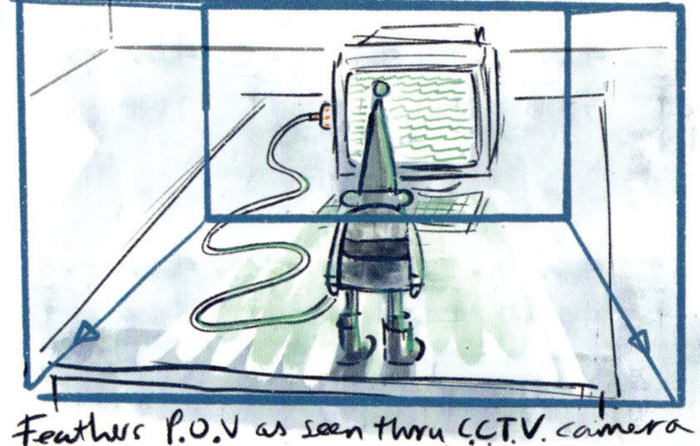

Feathers P.O.V as seen thru C.C.T.V. camera.
Code flows into Wallace's computer screen —
ZOOM OUT To Reveal Cable going to Norbot.

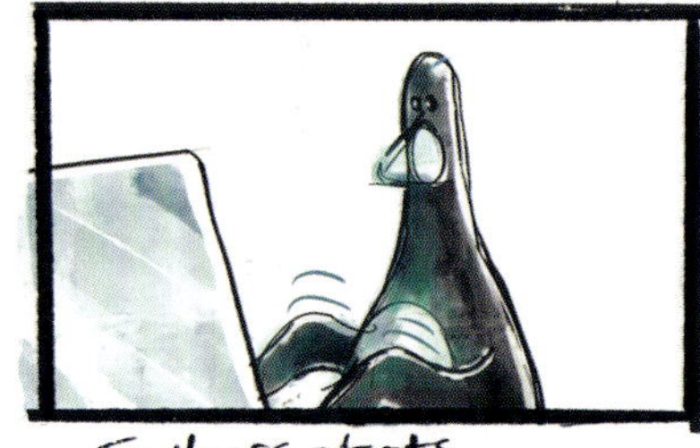

Feathers starts
controlling Norbot -
Then cut to previous seq
of Norbot contortions.

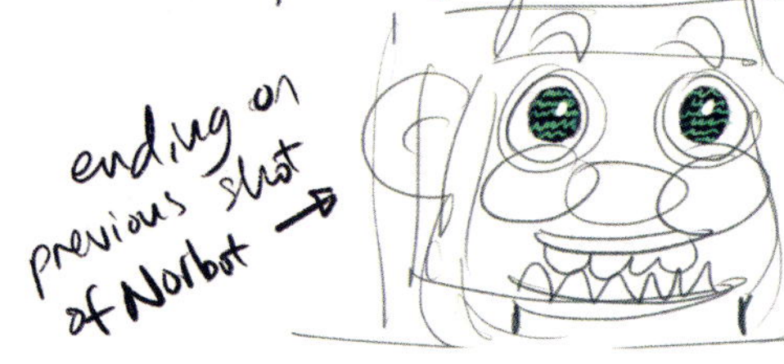

ending on
previous shot
of Norbot

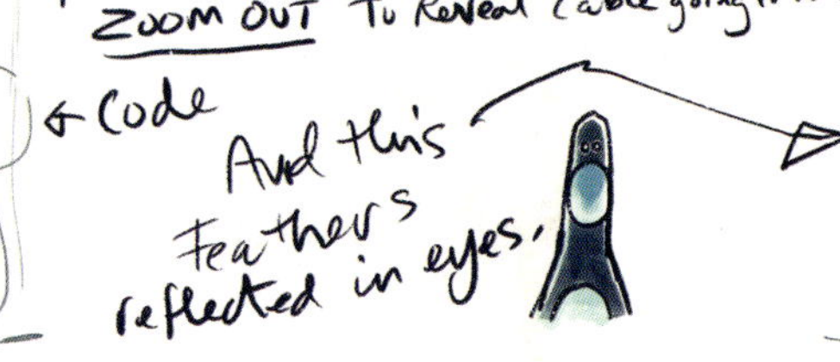

Code
And this
Feathers
reflected in eyes.

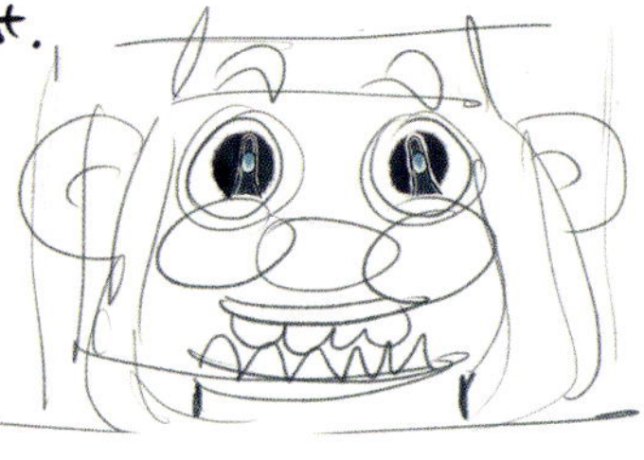

reference for Wallace's technology."

"It can't feel too modern," agrees supervising animator Will Becher. "The whole world is a retro one that's blended with slightly modern elements. You don't want to question it because it's really confusing when you've got radars and cathode ray TVs and walkie talkies. You've got lots of different eras."

Matt sums the look of the film up concisely: "It's just *Wallace & Gromit*".

The retro look of the technology was a gift for Gav Strange, who designed the computer graphics and online environments. "I'm a big fan of that era of computers and tech; it's nostalgic for word processors – all you had was black and green, black and green… We're connected to the internet in this movie and we have AI, but nothing is smooth and homogenous in terms of the look of the technology. In the hacking sequence the screen is 4:3, but the operating system is more 90s. When Feathers double clicks the Norbot Operating System,

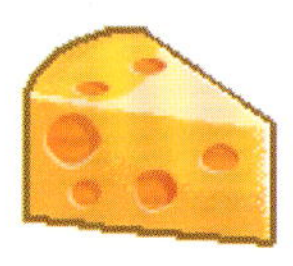
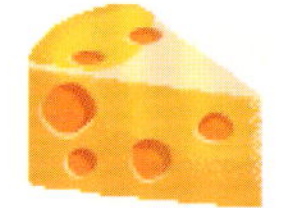

Above | Thumbnail storyboards by Nick Park as Feathers gains access to Wallace's Norbot files.

Opposite | Mike Salter's storyboards for the hacking sequence, with fully developed artwork.

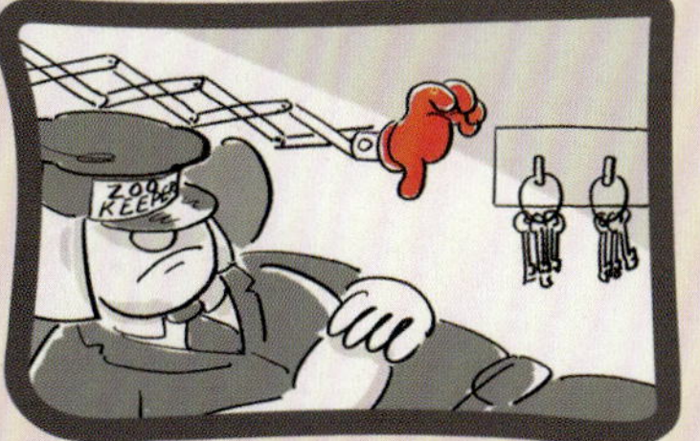
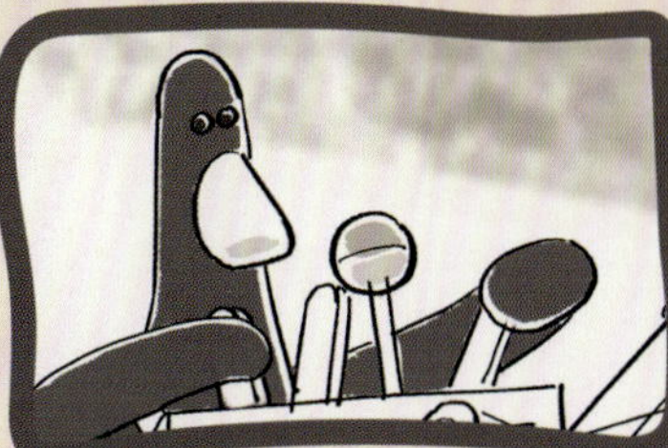
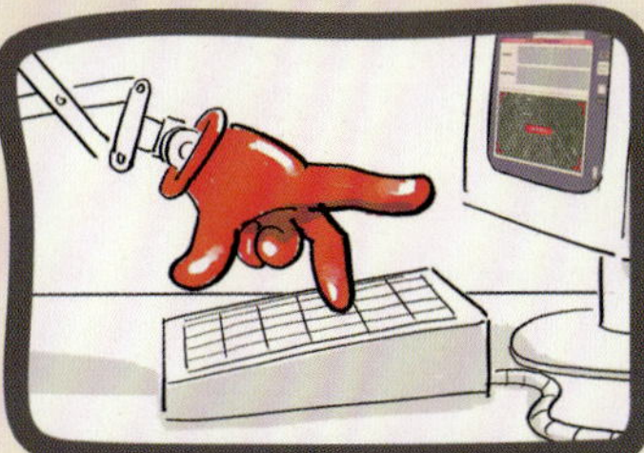

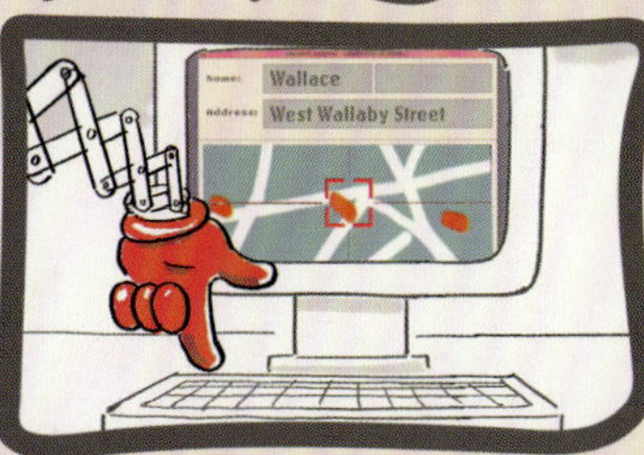

Wallace
West Wallaby Street

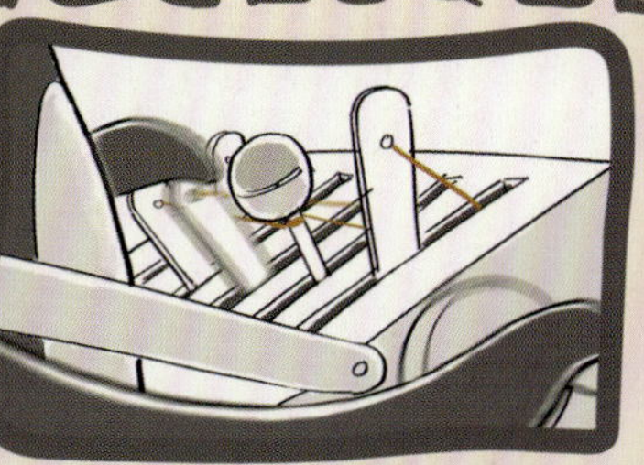

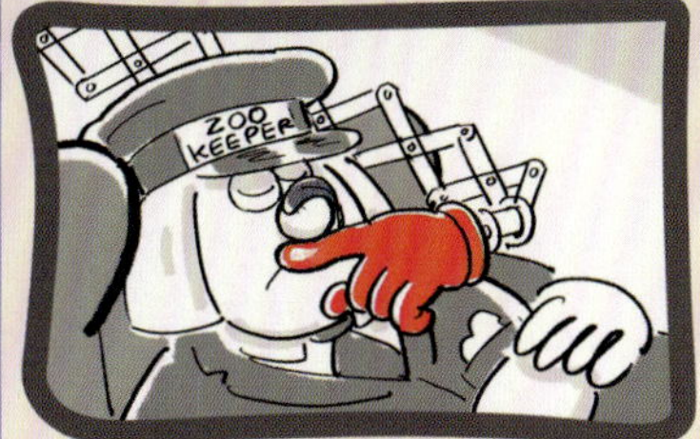

ZOO KEEPER

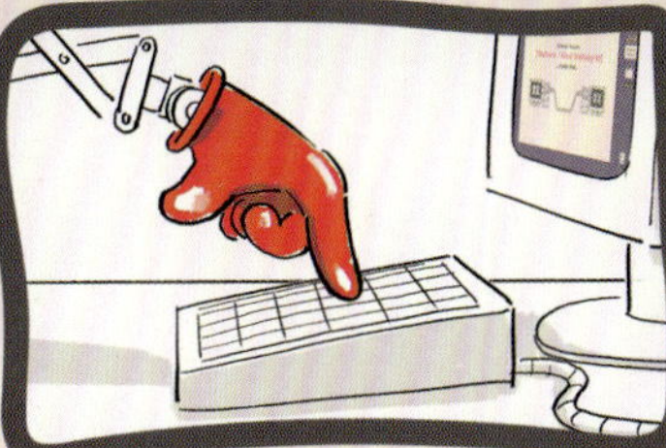

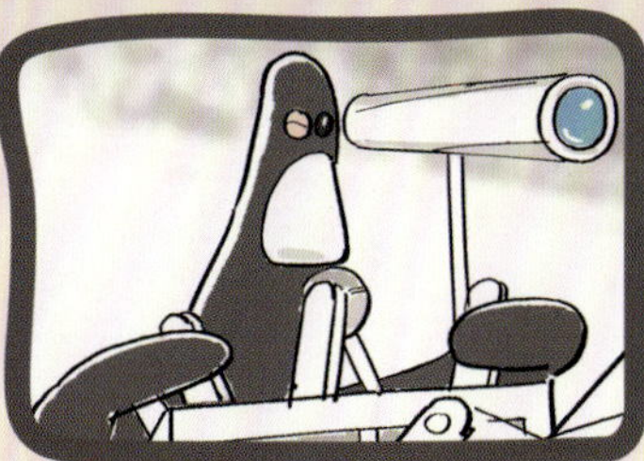

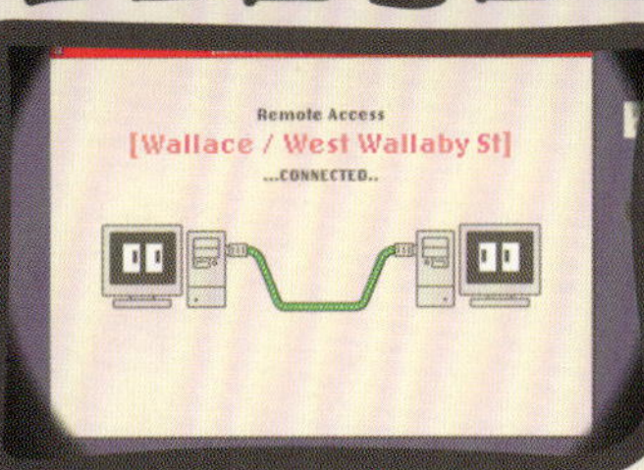

Remote Access
[Wallace / West Wallaby St]
...CONNECTED..

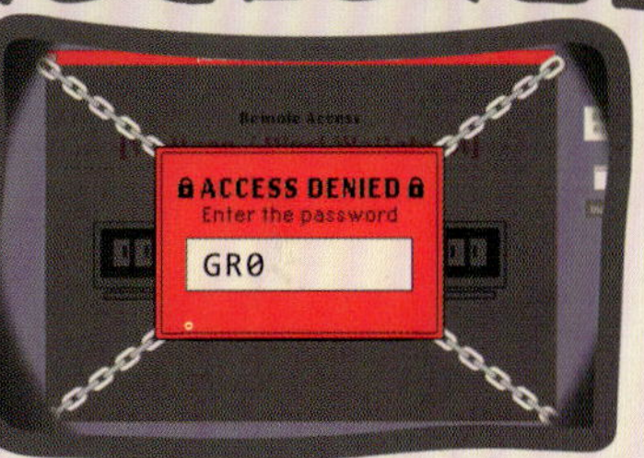

ACCESS DENIED
Enter the password
GR0

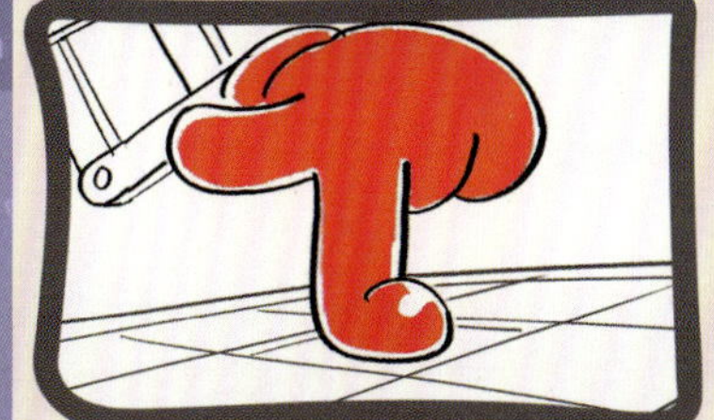

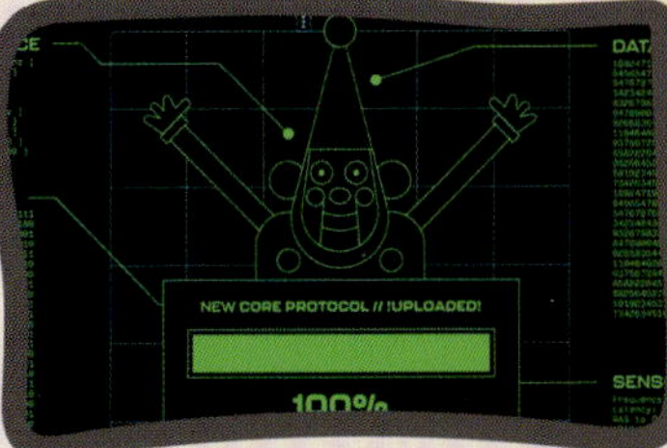

ACCESS GRANTED
Password correct
CHEESE

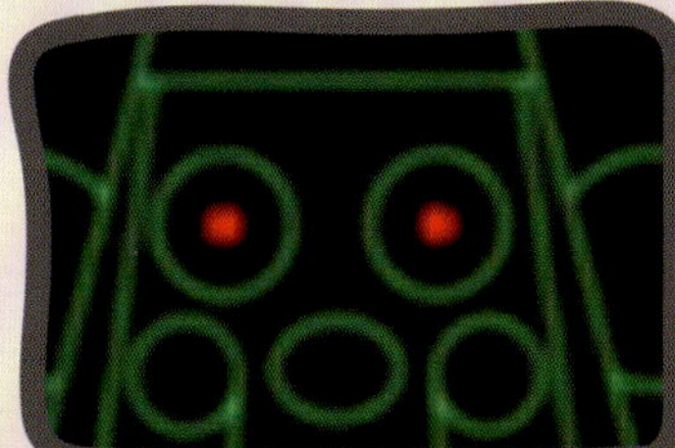

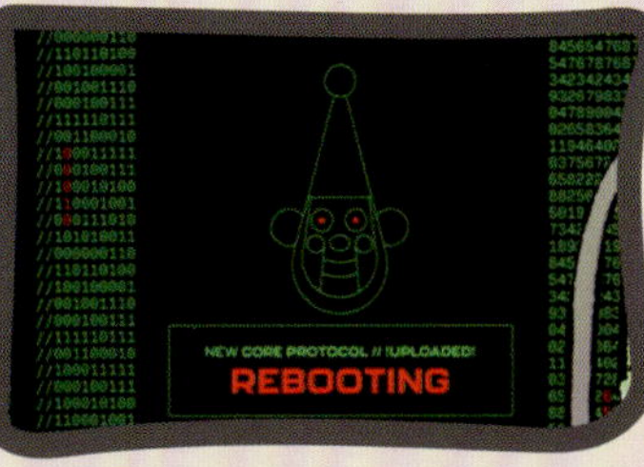

BE EVIL

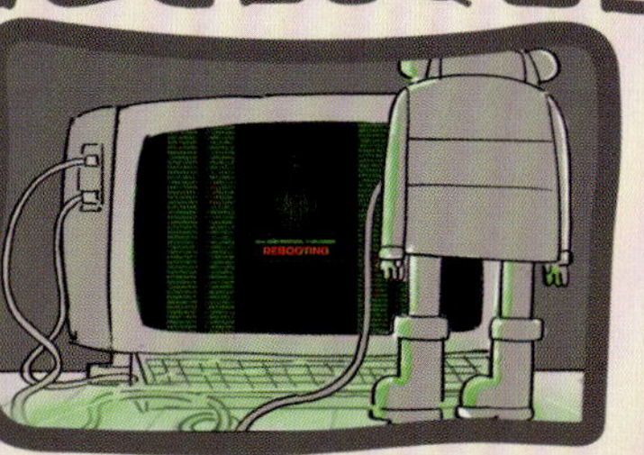

NEW CORE PROTOCOL // !UPLOADED!
100%
REBOOTING

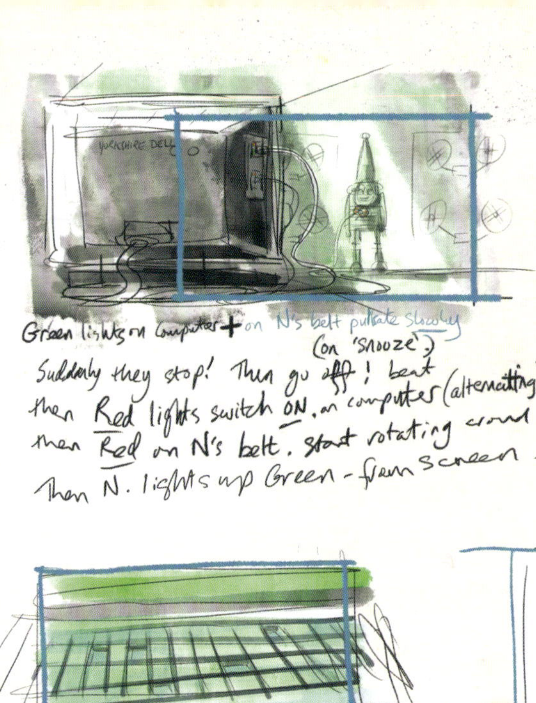
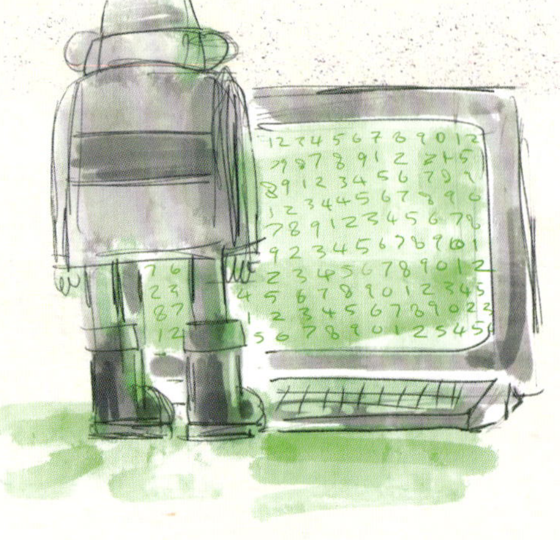
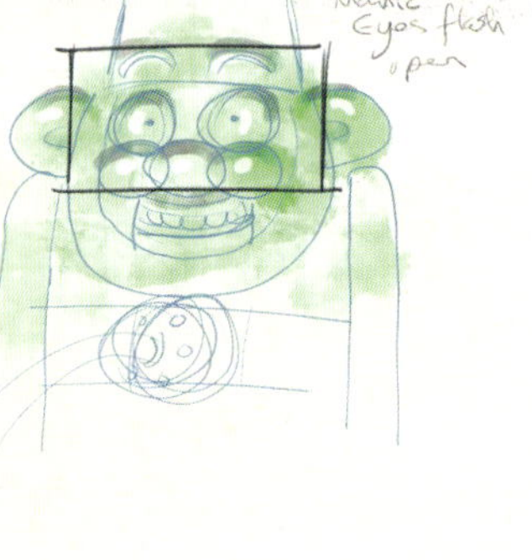

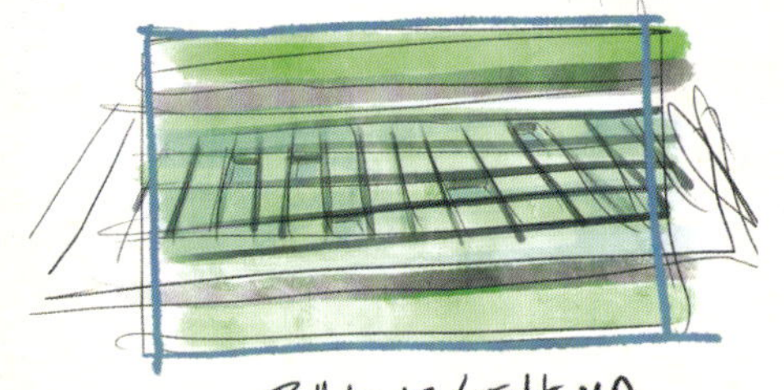
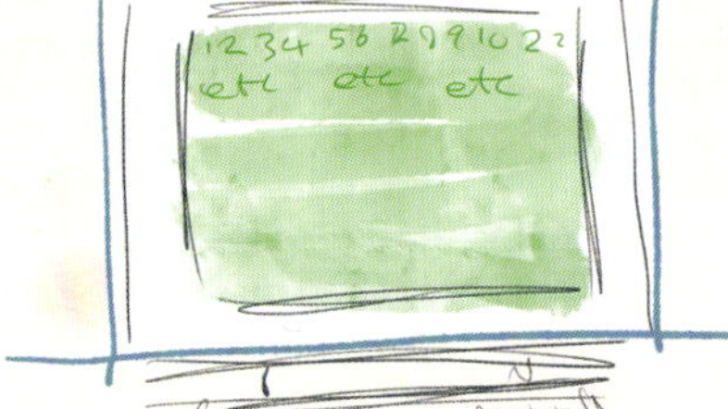
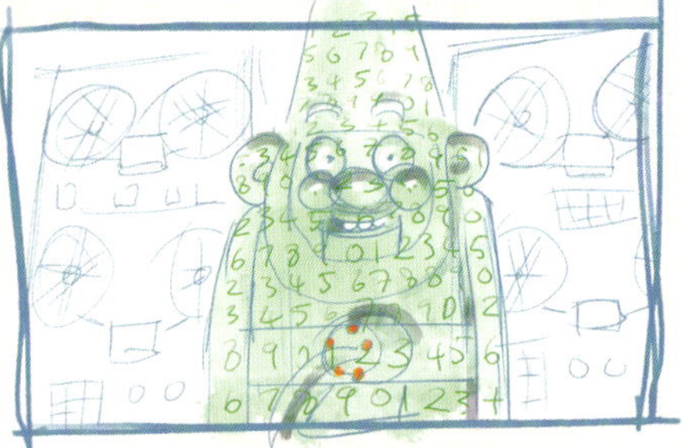

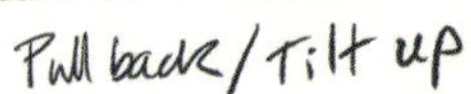
Pull back / Tilt up

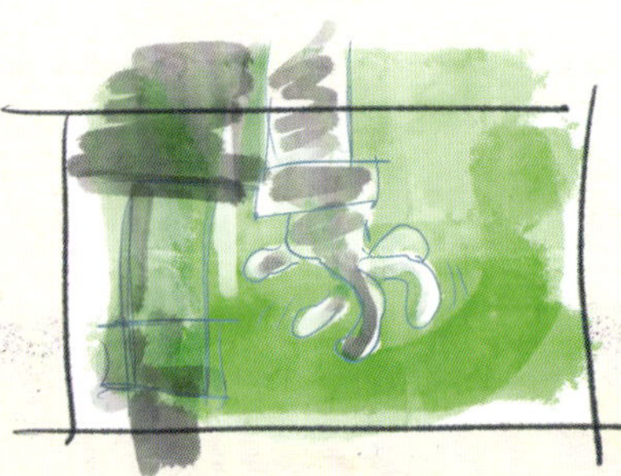
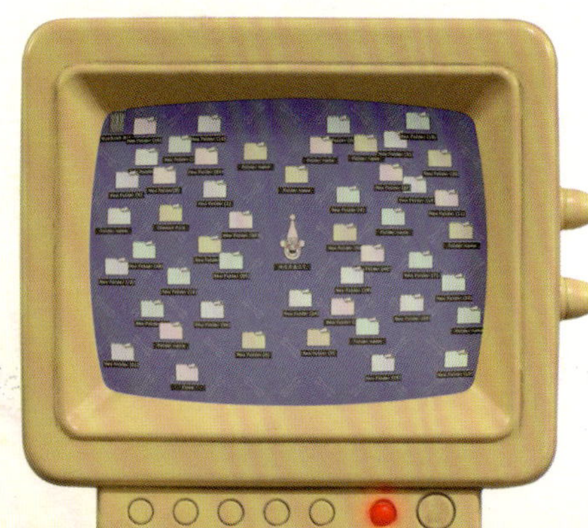

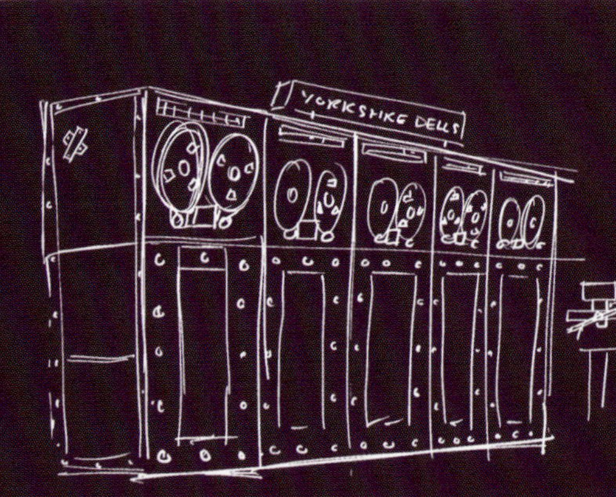
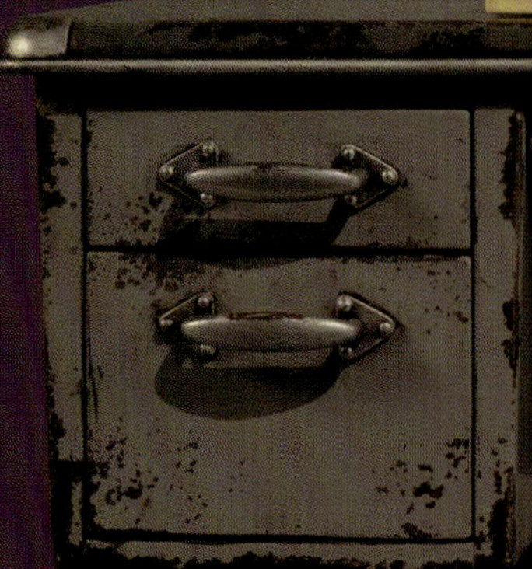
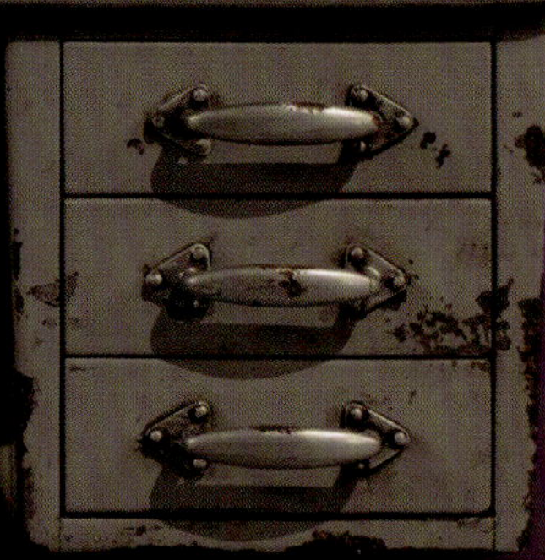

WELCOME TO WALLACE'S FILES!

it's a custom-made software that Wallace has written, which has its own look but still serves the story."

Although the model-making department now creates 3D scans of the puppets, Gav decided not to use these when designing the wireframe of Norbot. "It was so hi-res it would have taken more work to simplify it, so in the end I digitally modelled it myself. In the era of the film, to have that 3D sophistication would have been mind-blowing, so I used open-source 3D software to build it from primitive models – that really low polygon look is the correct aesthetic."

Feathers's hacking of Norbot sets up one of the most atmospheric shots in the whole movie as the nifty gnome is rebooted in the cellar of 62 West Wallaby Street, bathed in lines of cascading green code. Director of photography Dave Alex Riddett outlines how this reflects the ambition to shoot as much of the film 'in camera'

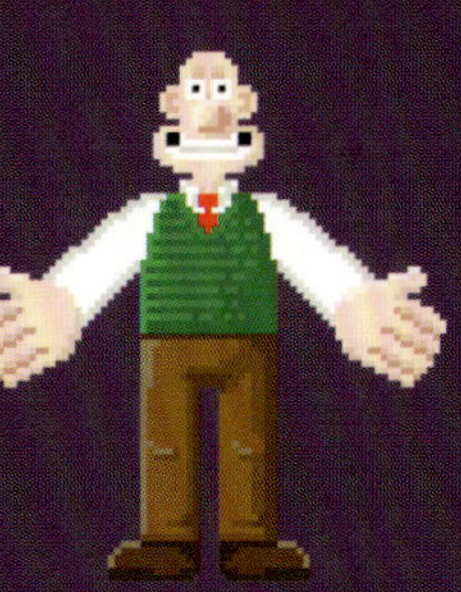

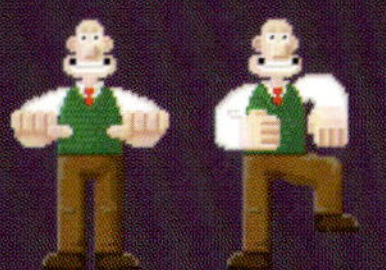

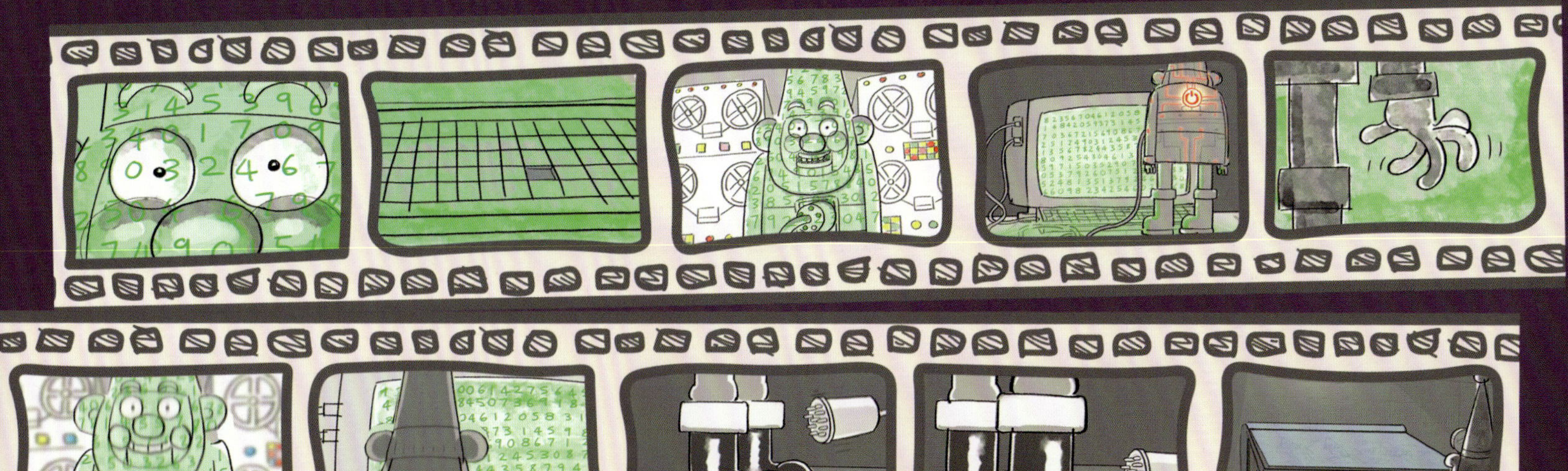

as possible without the use of digital effects. "That is going back to the basics, like with *The Wrong Trousers*," he explains. "How do you do something with what you've got – the simplest thing possible? Quite often that's what people would miss out. So with the numbers, people were saying, 'Well, you're obviously going to use CG for that', but I thought, 'No, why not simply project them onto the puppet?'. For the animator it's so much more exciting that it's actually happening in front of you, you're not looking at a blue screen."

Initially he explored using a regular video projector, but that proved too cumbersome so he searched the internet for a tiny one that was just the right scale. This was used to project a file of the 2D code graphics directly onto the Norbot puppet, feeding it through one frame at a time so it could be coordinated with the animation. Gav provided the code, and was amazed when he saw the results. "That was really cool! To see the integration of a computer and stop-motion was so magical. That's real light hitting a real puppet – you've got that bleed, and that blue. The combination looks really, really good. It's a great reflection of Aardman in 2024 – the hybrid approach with everyone pulling in the same direction. There's a home-made ethic reflecting the home-made look."

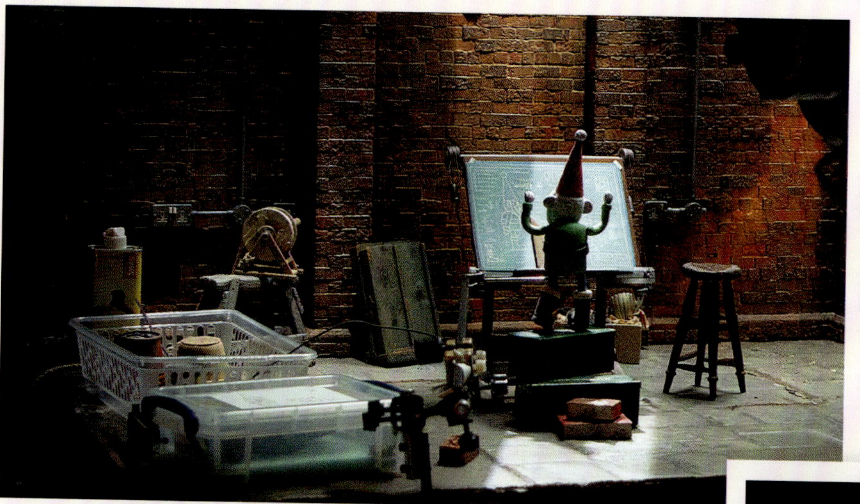

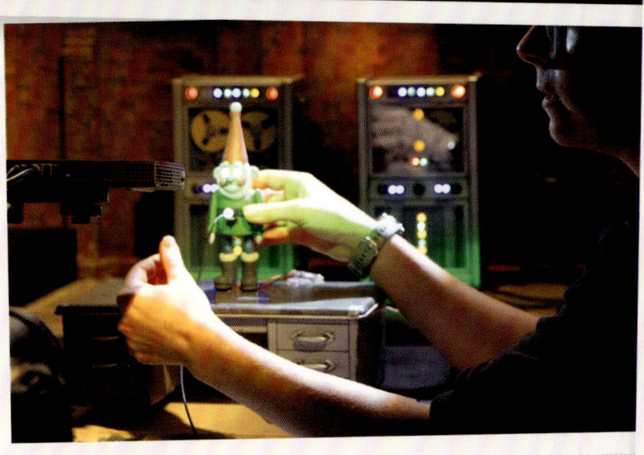

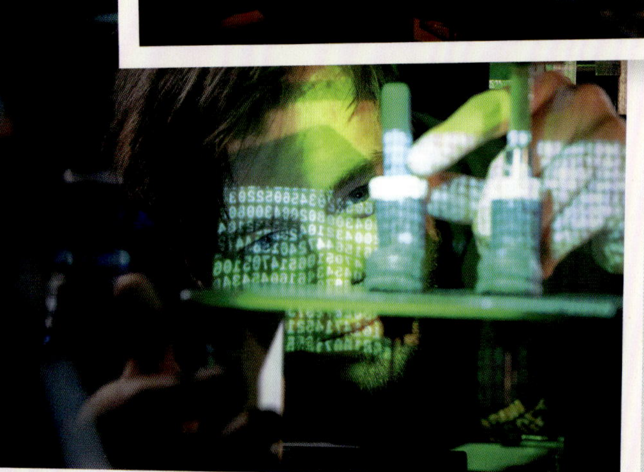

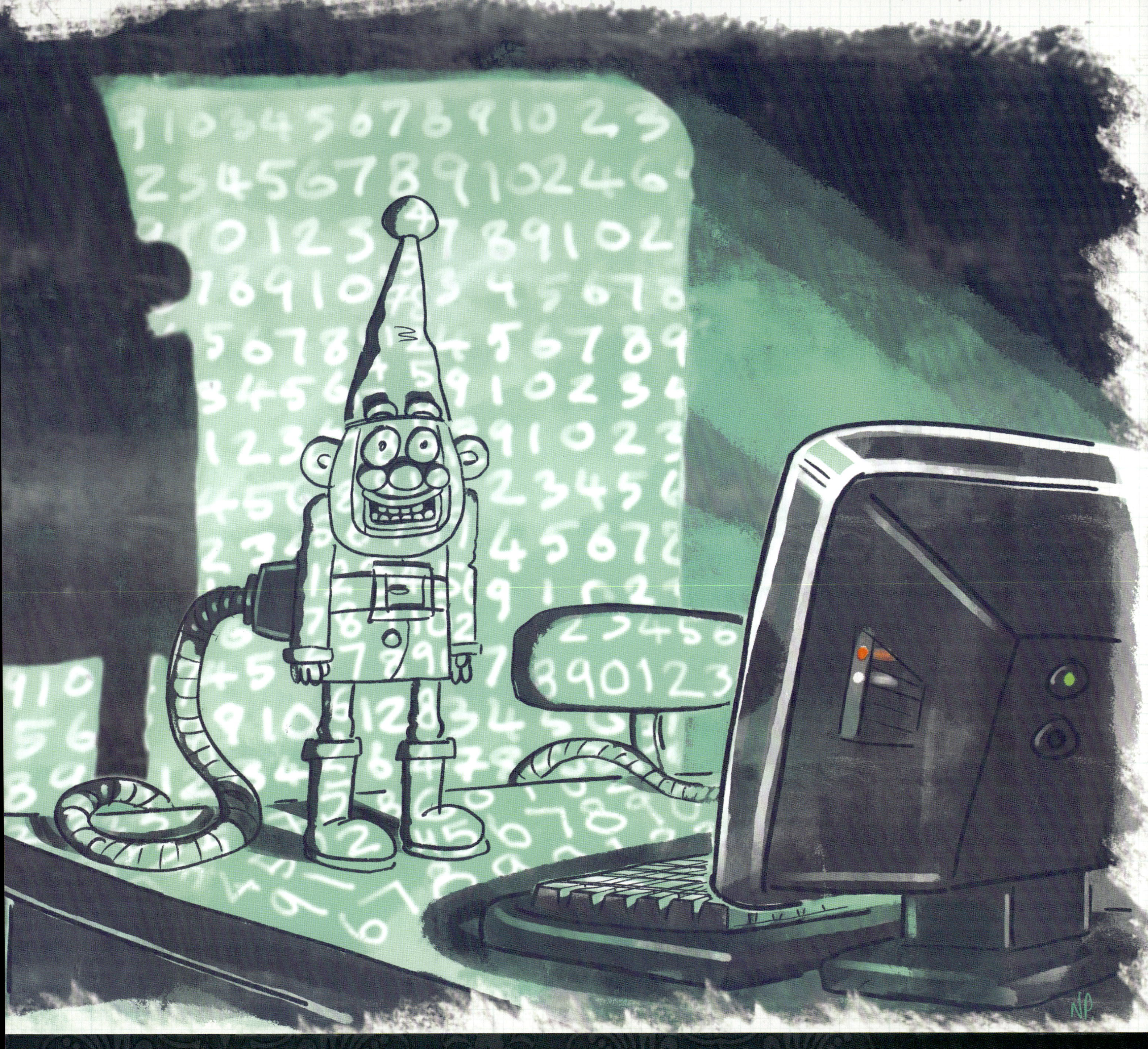

CHAPTER FIVE

There's Something Going on in the Basement...

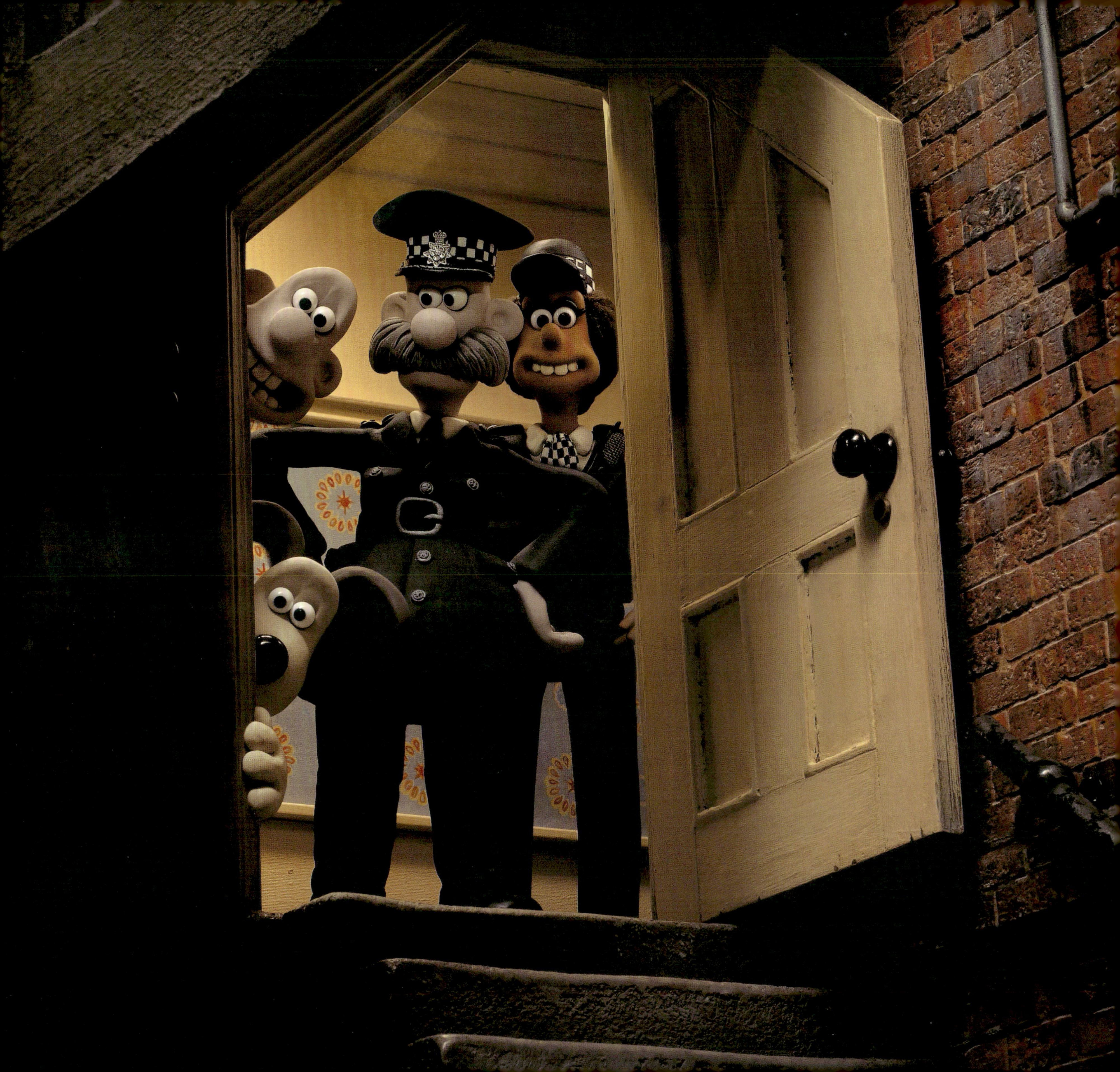

There's Something Going on in the Basement...

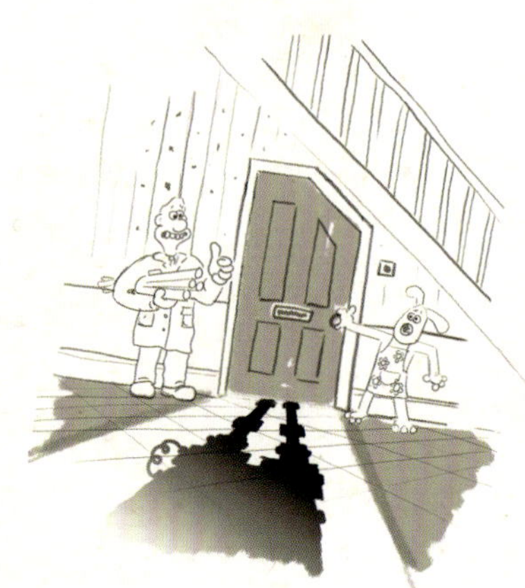

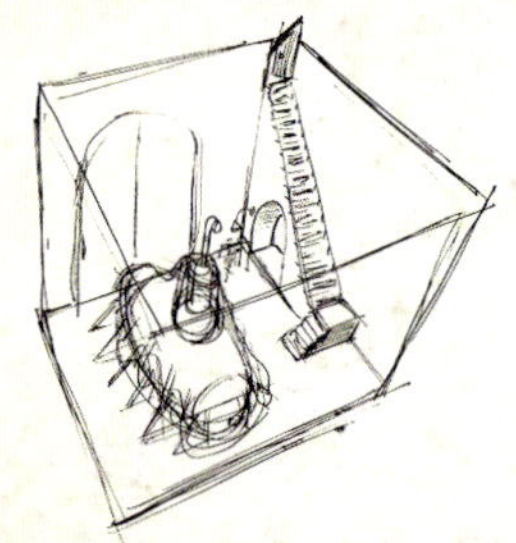

THE BASEMENT OF 62 WEST WALLABY STREET has been host to many strange goings-on over the years, from Wallace's first attempt to build a space rocket in *A Grand Day Out* to being turned into a full-blown TV studio for *Wallace & Gromit's World of Inventions*. But *Vengeance Most Fowl* sees it commandeered by Evil Norbot and his army of gnomes for more sinister purposes, as Gromit discovers them hard at work on a colossal contraption. This provides one of the most striking visual sequences in the film as the gnomes transform the cellar into a miniature steel foundry with smelting, arc-welding and other industrial activities, utilising the gardening implements they've stolen during their odd-jobbing.

Concept artist Darren Dubicki remembers the original brief from Nick and Merlin for this scene: they wanted the Ring Forge from *Lord of the Rings*, but created by garden gnomes. "We needed to make it feel like there was lots of industry going on within the confines of their cellar. They wanted this thing to become really expansive, to give it a grandiose scale. I did worry that it would start to feel like a

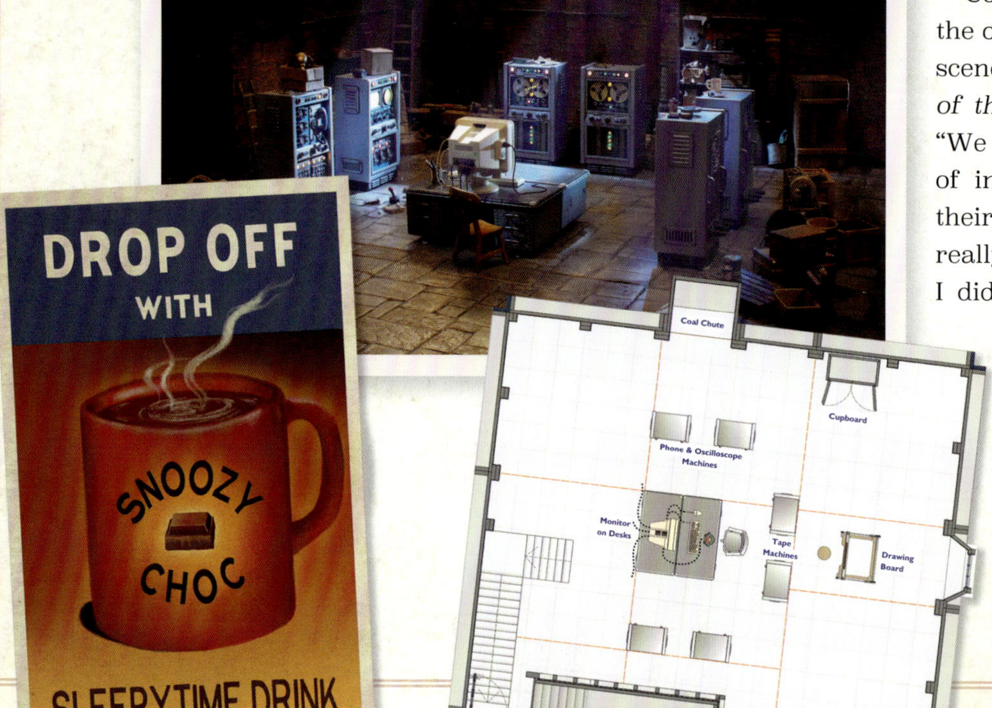

Above | Early sketch by Merlin of Evil Norbot emerging from the basement.

Top left | Nick's initial thumbnail of the submarine being built in the basement.

Middle left | Gavin Lines's recreation of the Snoozy Choc poster from *The Wrong Trousers*, which makes a reappearance.

Bottom far left | The basement of 62 West Wallaby Street turned into a hi-tech haven (photo by Richard Davies).

Left | Art director Matt Sanders's plan for the revamped basement.

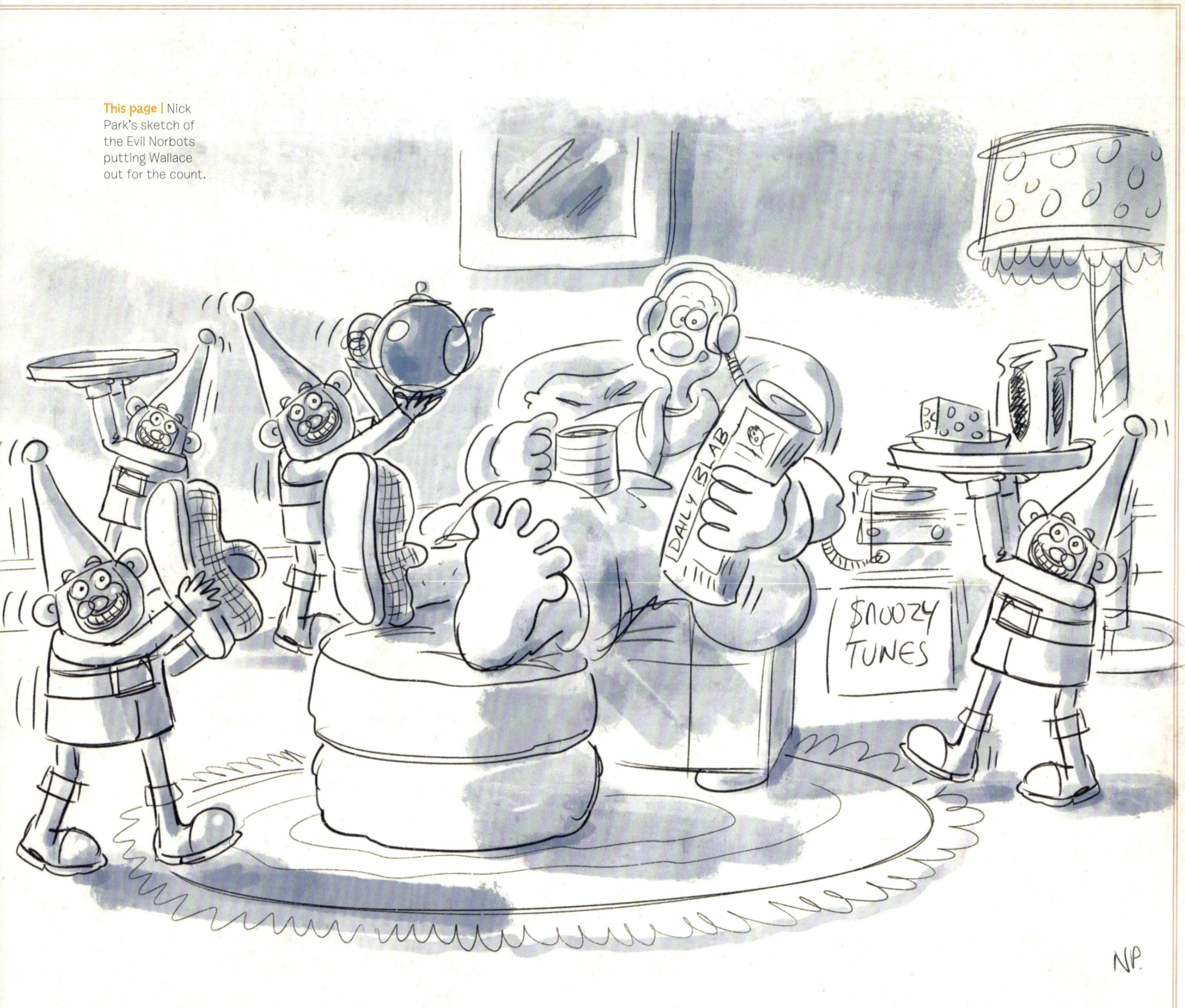

This page | Nick Park's sketch of the Evil Norbots putting Wallace out for the count.

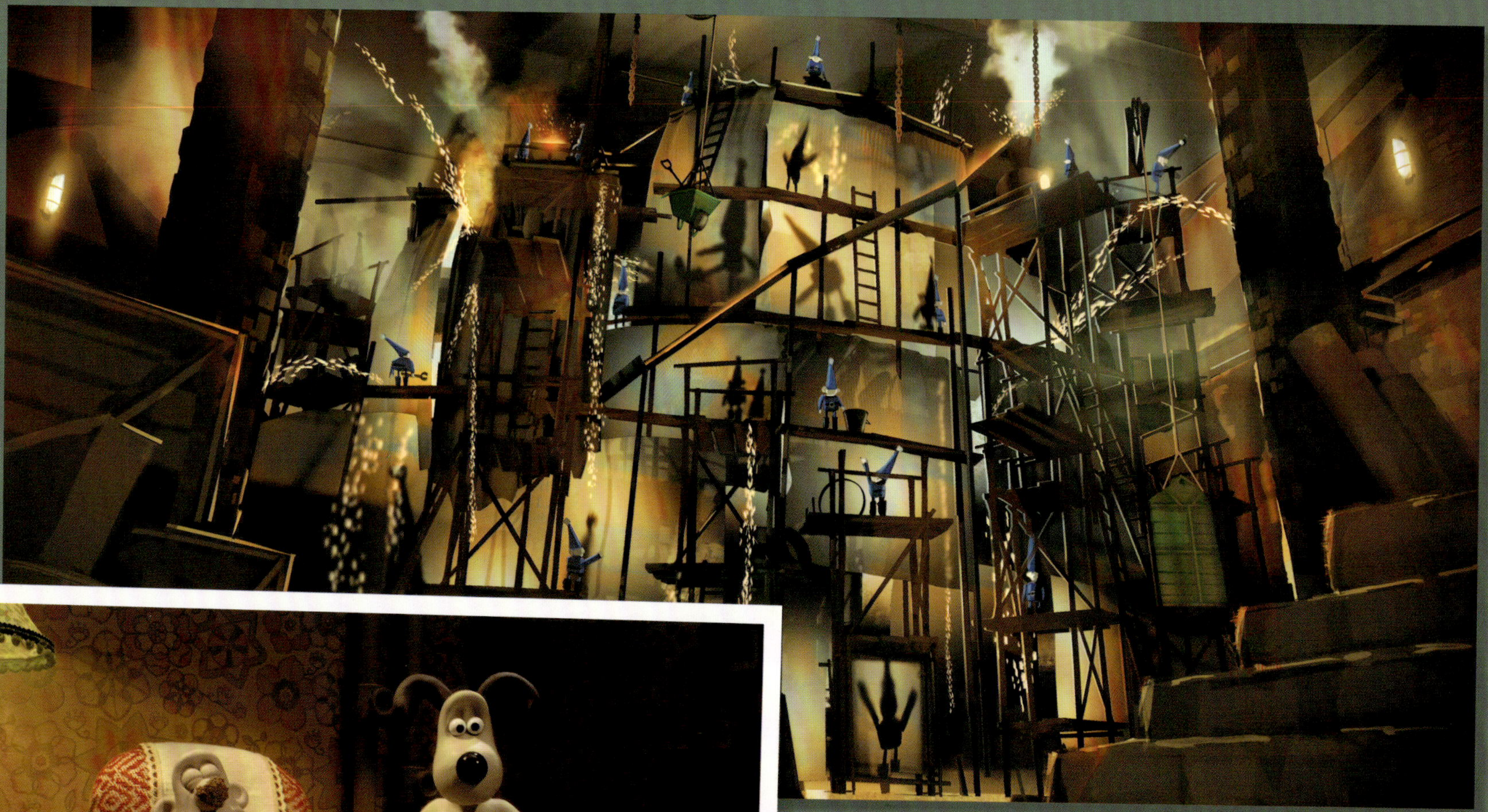

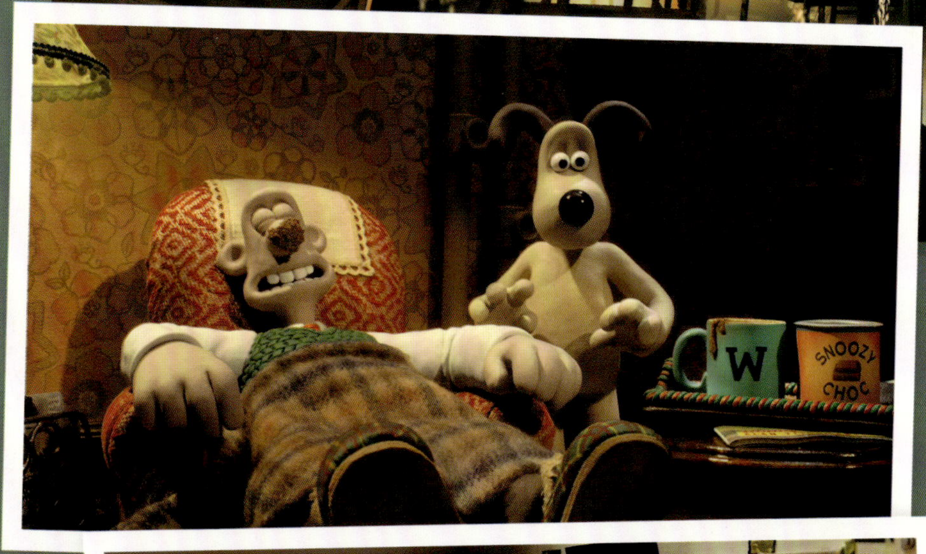

completely different environment, but the idea is to hide everything, giving the sense that they're creating something, but we have no idea what it is. The tone and atmosphere will build from the lighting, the flashing, the sparks, the shadows, the movement of the characters – it all feels like impending doom."

The concept art has echoes of many cinematic influences, not just Middle Earth. Some might see shades of the factory scene from silent sci-fi epic *Metropolis*, or even Blofeld's volcano HQ from *You Only Live Twice* – especially when the floor opens up. But Darren was more focused on the practicalities and the mood of the scene. Working from a couple of Nick's original sketches, he explains. "I wanted to

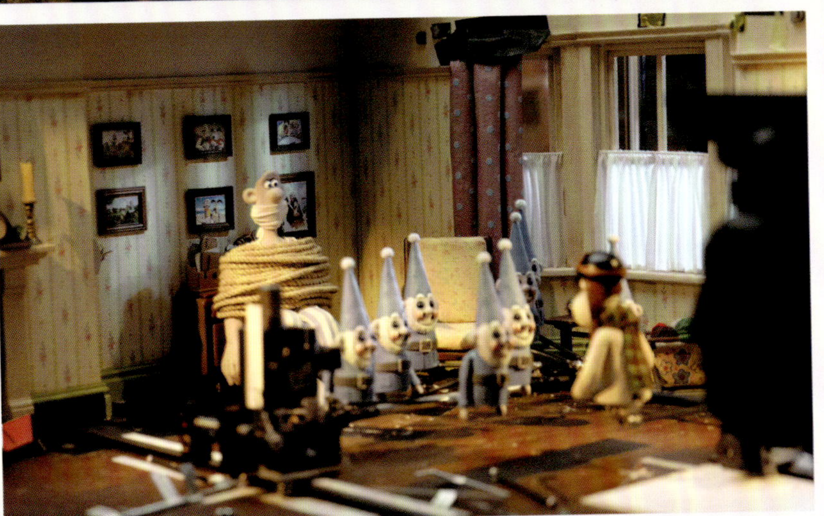

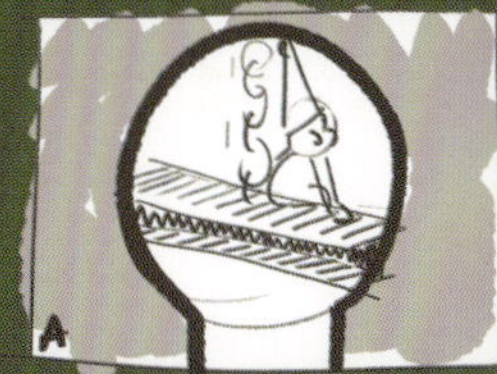

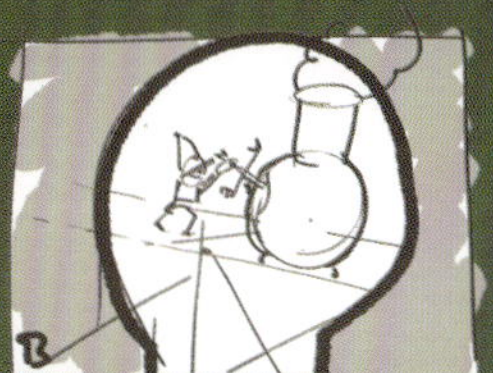

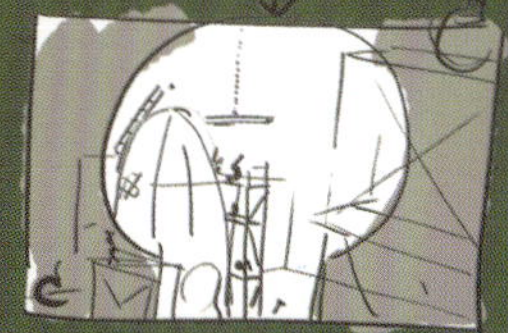

think about how they find the materials to make this thing, in a very Aardman way. I was keen to push the atmosphere and the lighting tonally to get that film noir feel, which is a key theme of the movie."

Darren initially produced a mood board of different inspirations, a hybrid of sci-fi and film noir classics that drew on a wide range of visual reference. But the specifics weren't as important as the overall sense of style, which synthesised the various influences. "With a mood board there are often 20 things that are conflicting and contradicting each other," explains Matt Sanders, art director for this sequence, "and you think, 'Well, which one is it, then?' But once we've got what Darren's drawn, it has its own style to it. Concept art is often broad strokes to show the mood and the lighting and the colours, but the details are quite vague at that stage, so there's a lot to resolve practically."

Whatever incredible designs were produced for this scene, they had to fit within the pre-existing geography of the West Wallaby Street basement, familiar from previous films. So it was an advantage for Darren to be based at Aardman's Aztec West studios where the set archive is stored. "I could actually go down and get a feel from those, then speak to Matt [Perry, production designer] about how we could make them more expansive. We had a lot of conversations about how much we could push this, but at least we had a starting point."

Having the physical sets available lent itself to Darren's unique way of working, as he was able to rebuild them in Virtual Reality and then create the entire environment digitally, an approach he developed for *Chicken Run: Dawn of the Nugget*. "What this allows me to do is create a virtual studio to scale, so I was able to walk around a virtual version of what

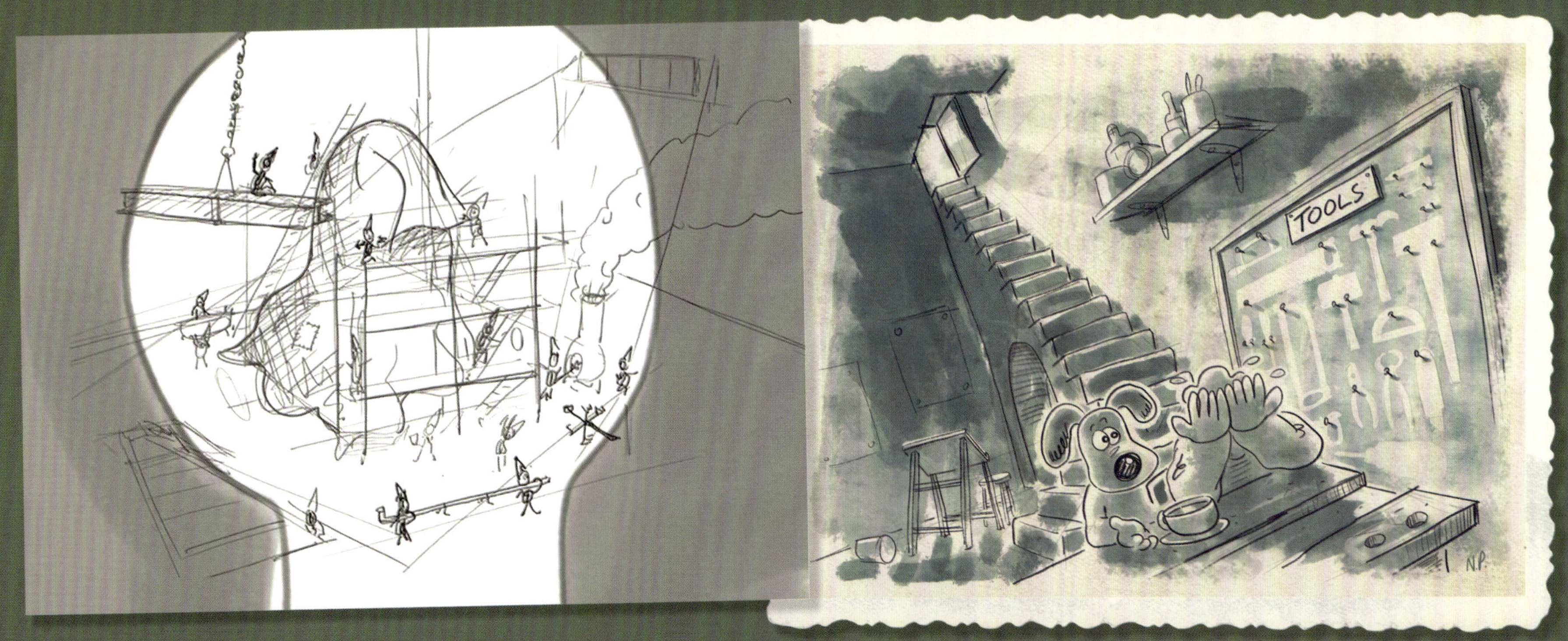

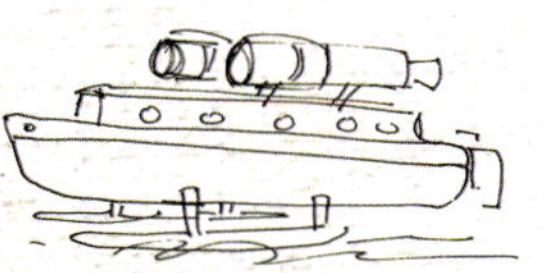
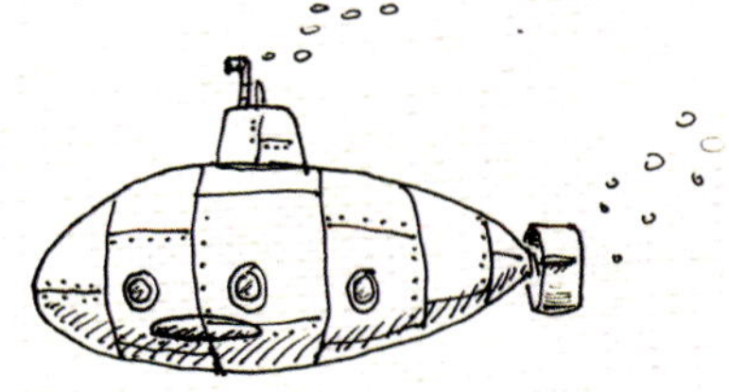
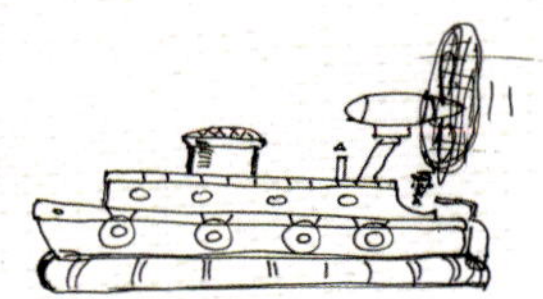

would be in the studio space. And that gives us 3D information that can be fed to the rest of the art department.

"My general process in VR would be sketching, colour concepting, finding reference, getting all of that reference into the virtual world, and starting to build. Then I talk to Matt about the studio space and what we can fit. We know full well that this is a much bigger film in Nick and Merlin's heads, but can it be achieved? So here we can build it, flesh it out and then make decisions about scaling down certain elements, or forcing perspective and background, that kind of thing. And we can do this before it gets to the process of actual set design and construction. It's much quicker in 3D and it feels like a physical object in front of me."

Using Virtual Reality technology allowed Darren to give the directors a much clearer vision of his designs as they developed. "When Nick and Merlin come to see me, I can sit with them and let them see how it's developing through the eye of a camera. I find a point where we're happy, and then I'd take a screen grab, and that would become the basis for me to work on the finished concept art." Through his use of the wide array of colouring tools available in the 3D software, Darren is able to bring a range of techniques to the artwork, and looking at the final painterly images it's hard to imagine the complex technology that lies behind the process.

The concept art for the various sets is then given to one of three art directors by Matt Perry,

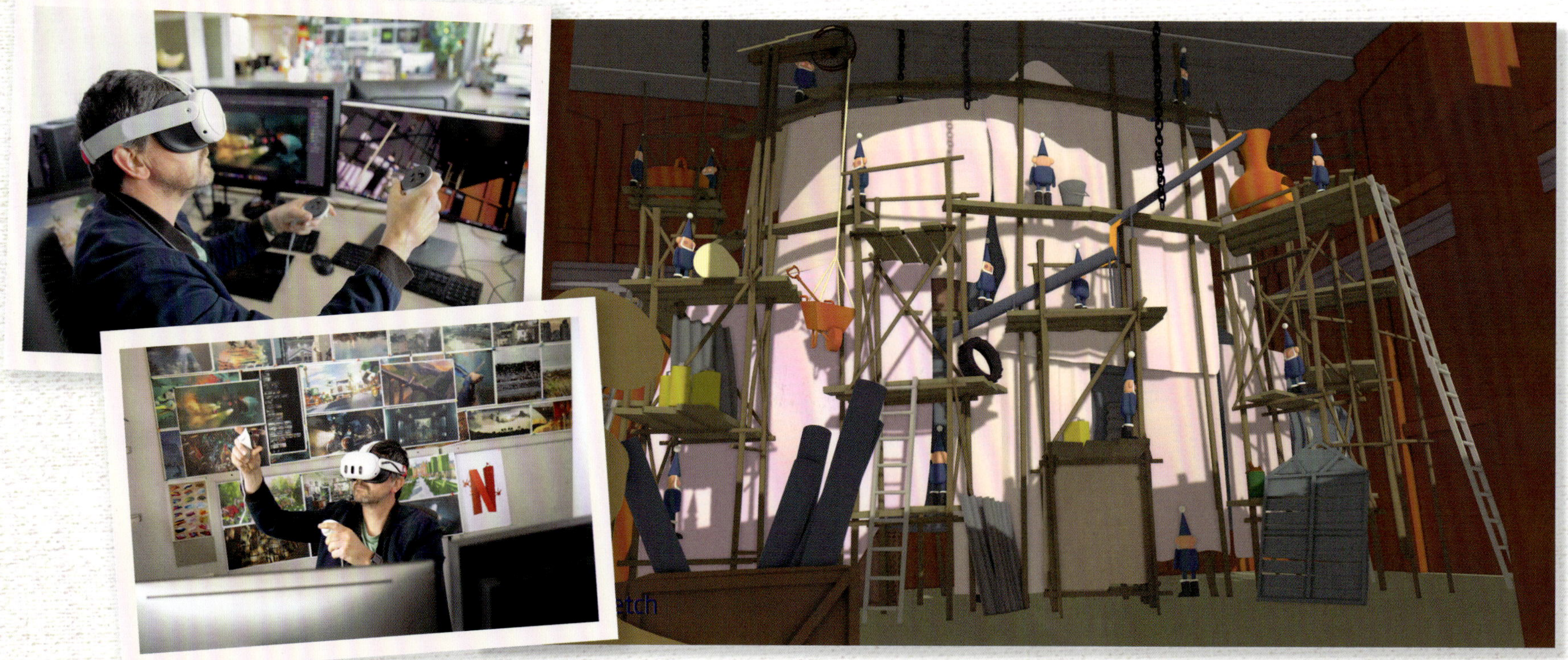

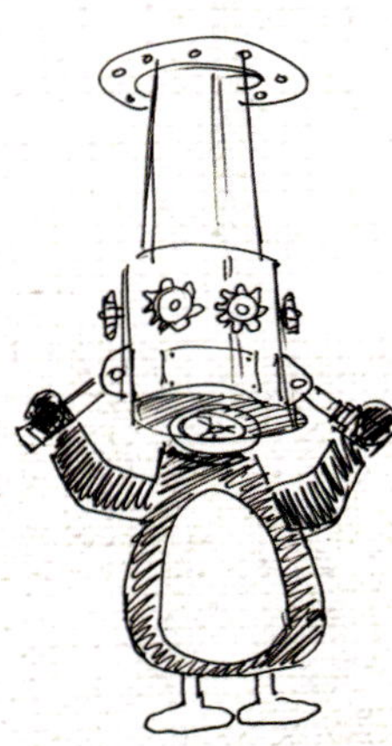

who allocates the scenes depending on the particular skill set of the individual, a process somewhat akin to casting the right actor in a role. Their job is to flesh out Darren's ideas into detailed technical drawings for the set-builders and prop-makers. So after the hi-tech VR-created concept art, the next step, counter-intuitively enough, is a little working model made out of old-fashioned cardboard and wire. "That's very Aardman, isn't it?" observes Darren. "They're still using software to generate the drawings for construction, but it's a double-checking system to have the physical thing there before it goes out to be made."

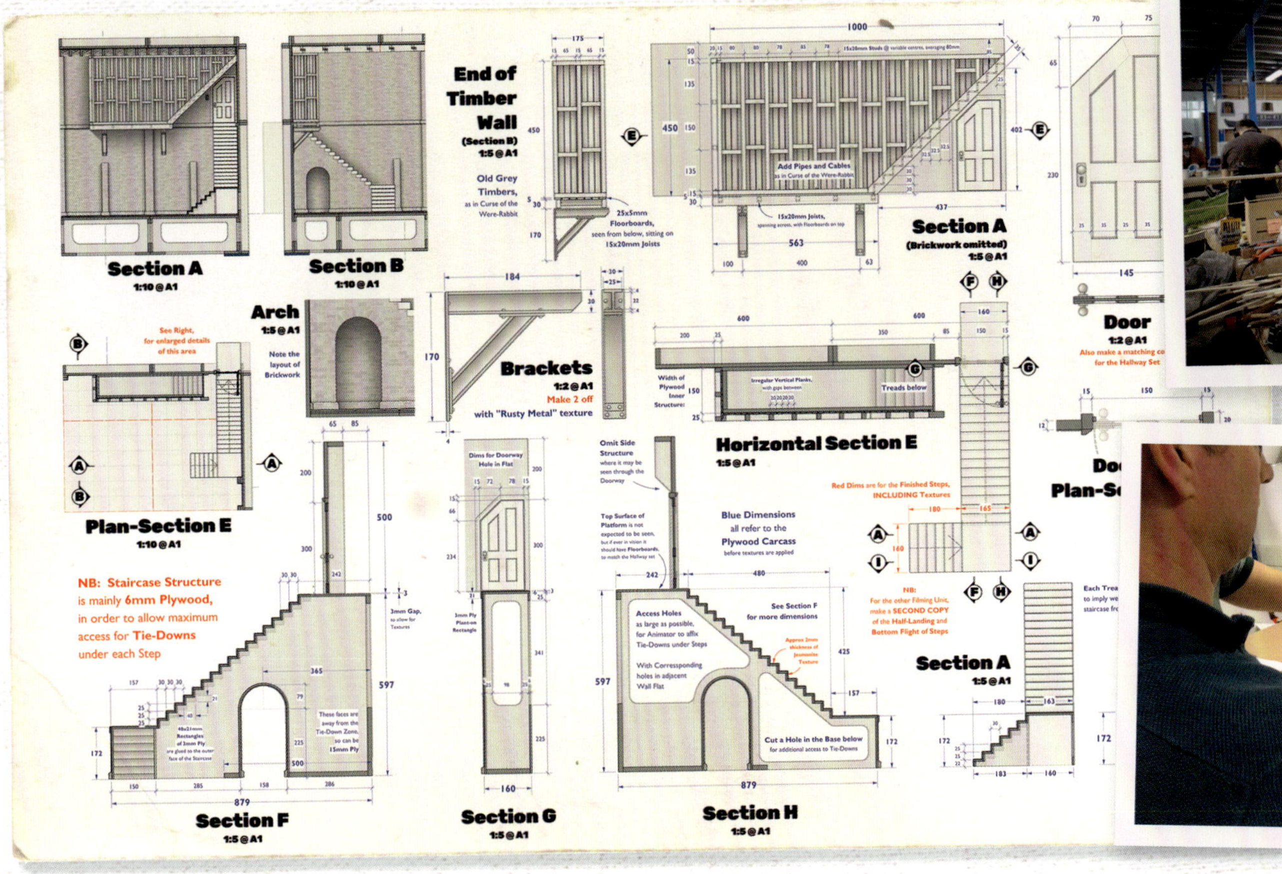

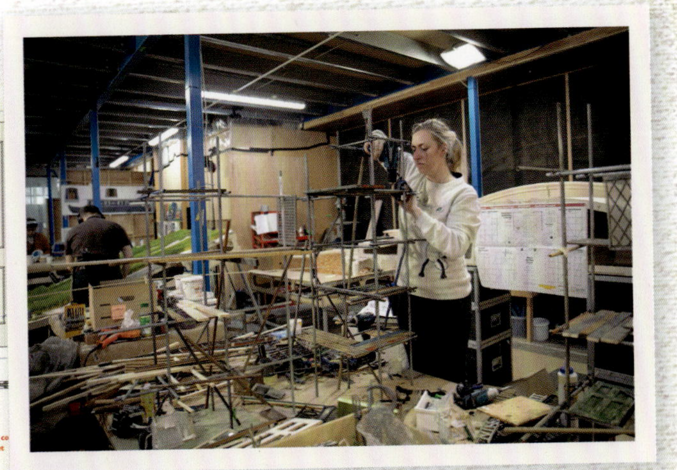

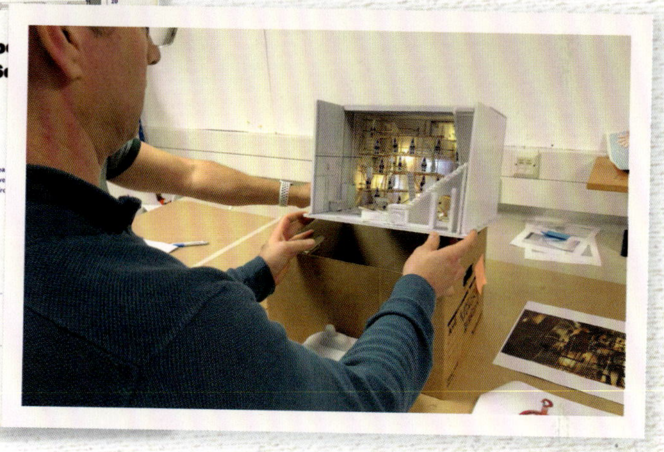

Art director for the cellar scene, Matt Sanders, has to pin down the dimensions of the final set. "Our normal basement is a certain size, but we actually made this a bit bigger than usual. We've raised the walls up 20cm, so we'll either put more brick at the bottom or we'll pile things around the side. And the whole room is wider than usual. But then you've got the size of the gnomes, so we need to have a set that's based on the scale of the puppets. From that you work out that it's 20cm from one level to the next, so on the main set we can have four or five levels before we hit the ceiling. Then it's a case of saying to the directors, 'Is that enough or do

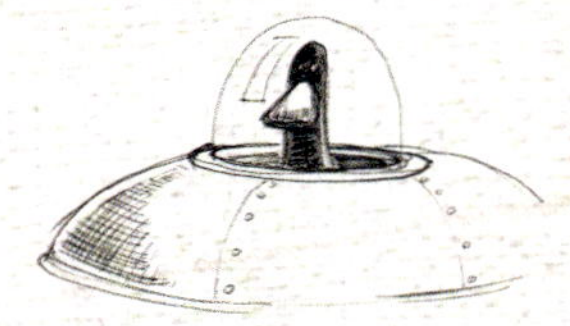

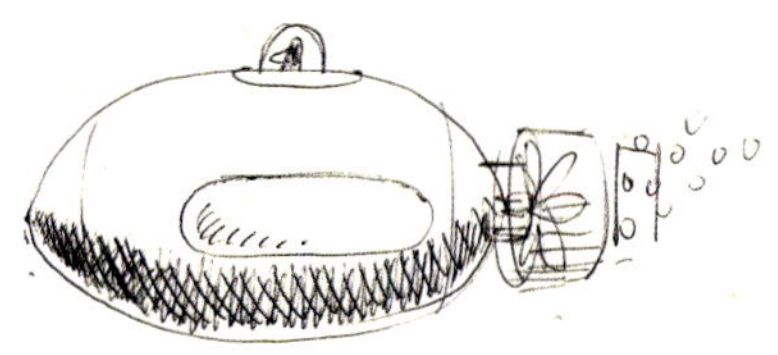

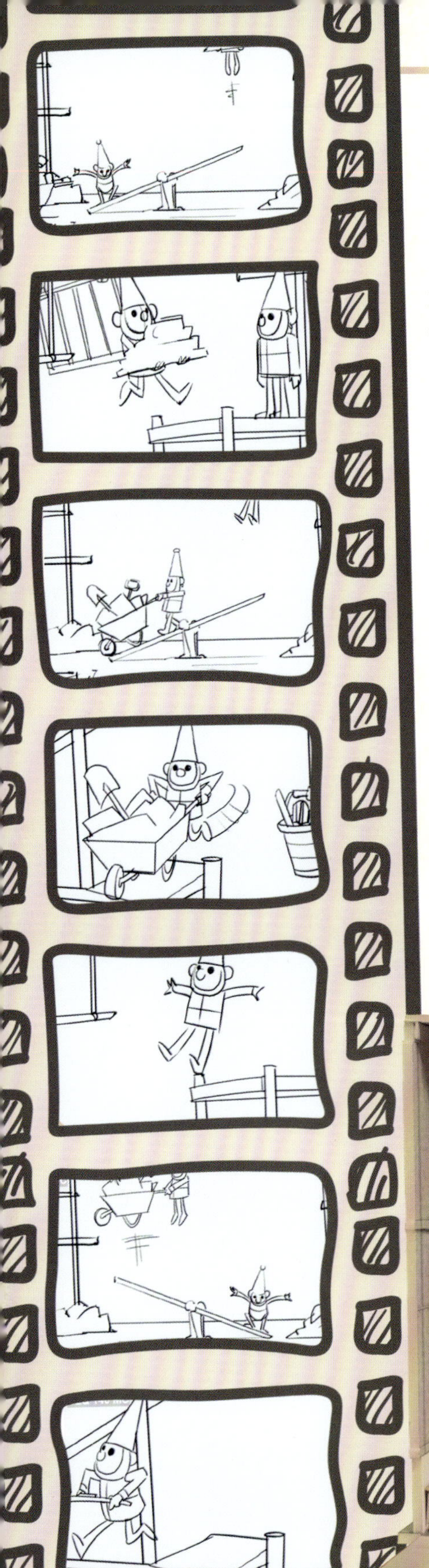

you want to go bigger?' and here they said, 'It's enough, because it still gives us quite a lot of gnomes.'"

These dimensions are then incorporated into the cardboard scale model, which gives a sense of how the set will work in dramatic terms. Matt's first version of the scaffolding towers was rejected in favour of a more 'splayed out' version so that the gnomes staring down at Gromit could have a scarier impact. The model will include versions of the key props: in the storyboards for the basement sequence, the see-saw was drawn in the style of a children's playground. "But they wanted it to look more as if the gnomes have just made it, so now it's like a plank and a sawhorse," explains Matt. "We often do these mock-ups to see the size

alongside the characters, and they might say, 'Oh yes, we like the style, but we want it three inches longer.'"

To give more of a sense of the atmosphere of the scene, Matt incorporated some illumination into the cardboard towers. "Because the lighting is so important here – they're doing welding and stuff so there will be a lot of flashing going on – some of the electricians from downstairs have wired up half a dozen LEDs for me in a couple of different colours. That helps because the scene is set in a dark space and it becomes more about the silhouettes of the gnomes rather than their faces."

Even the smallest visual detail of each scene is discussed with the directors and the production team at regular art department meetings. This gives Nick and Merlin a chance to communicate their vision more fully, for example their idea of using bits of bamboo and other found material

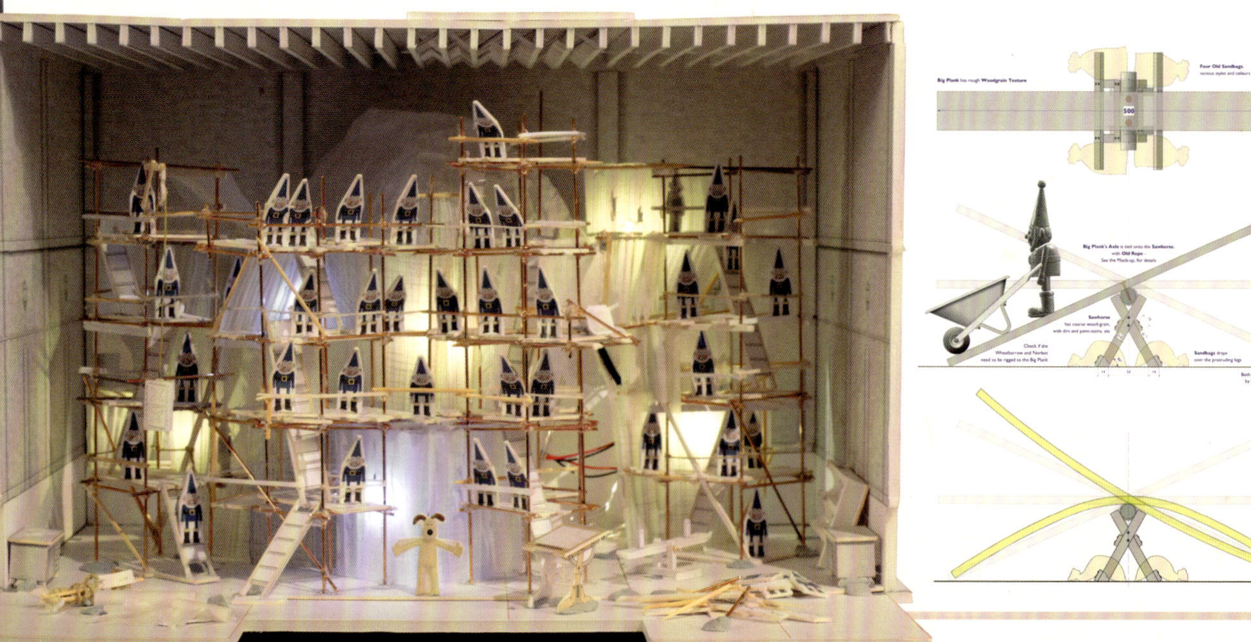

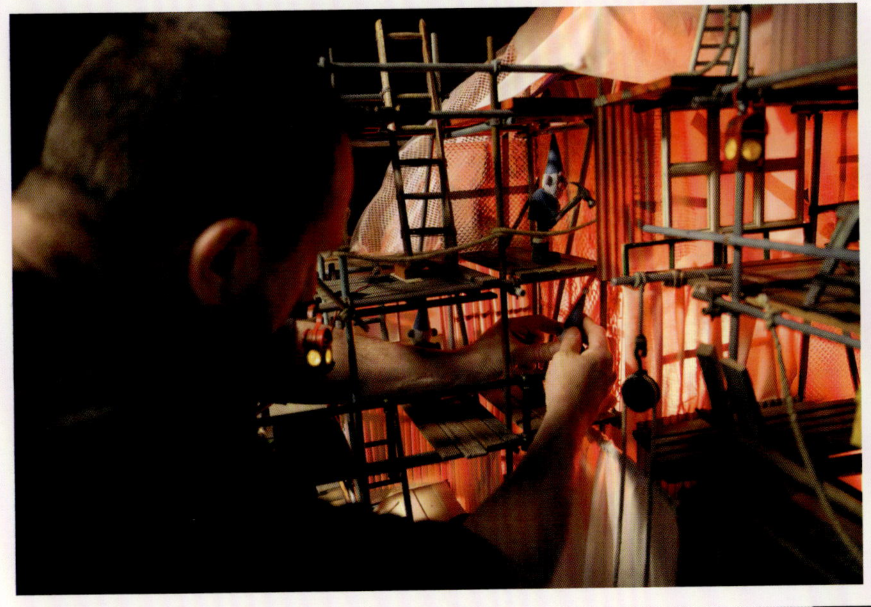

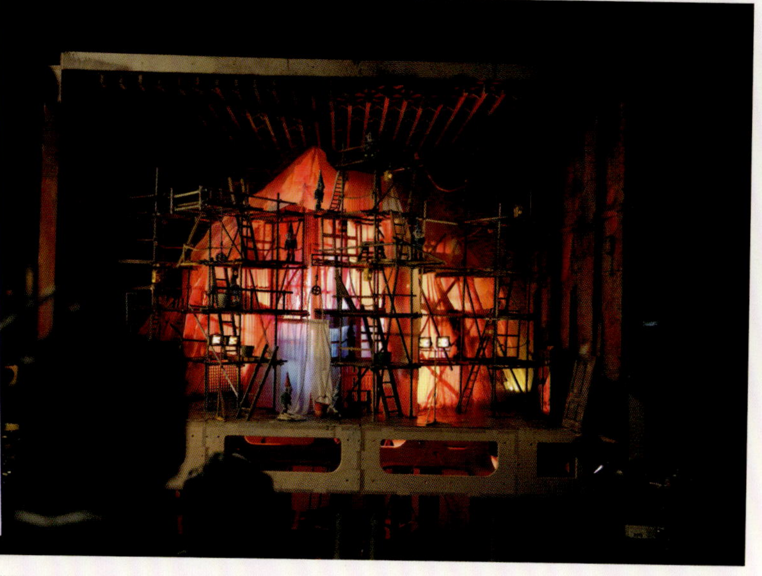

to make the scaffolding frame rather than traditional metal bars. These meetings can often get sidetracked into surreal discussions such as whether it would be physically possible to smelt a metal road-sign inside a metal cauldron, or whether a stone birdbath or ceramic plant pot would be more believable. "I'm always ribbing the guys a little bit in these meetings," says Matt Perry, "because logic only applies in certain circumstances!"

From cardboard and wire, it's back to the computer screen for the art directors as they produce final technical drawings. "Most of my drawing is done digitally," says Matt Sanders. "We have a file with the basement set, which shows the floor plan and the elevations with the stairs going up. It's quite handy when you're doing brick walls because the computer can just keep repeating them so you don't need to draw the bricks every time." The assistant art directors then allocate the work to the set builders and model-makers and keep an eye on construction. "I put as much detail as possible onto the drawings and communicate everything I've got to say at the beginning because I can't really go round saying, 'Left a bit, right a bit' all day long or I wouldn't get anything done for the next set. It's handy having been a model-maker myself because you know what questions someone is going to ask. And, on the whole, they do what you're expecting."

For director of photography Dave Alex Riddett, the basement scene was an opportunity too good to miss. While he controls the overall look of the lighting and interpreting what the directors want, he delegates many scenes to senior lighting camera people Laura Howie and Charles Copping, who are experienced DOPs in their own right, working with a team of other lighting camera operators, camera assistants, electricians and the motion-control crew. But this was one scene he was determined to

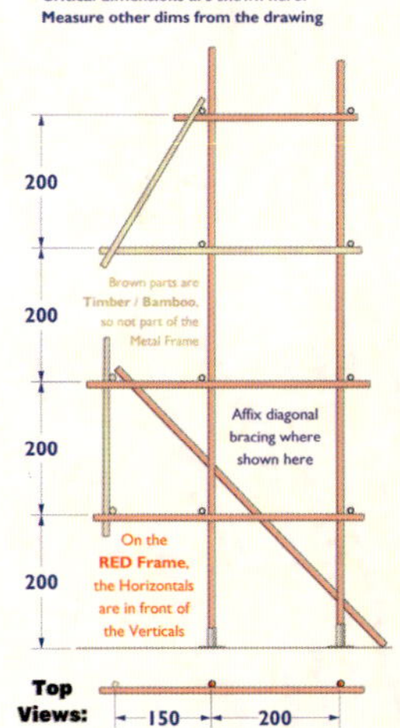

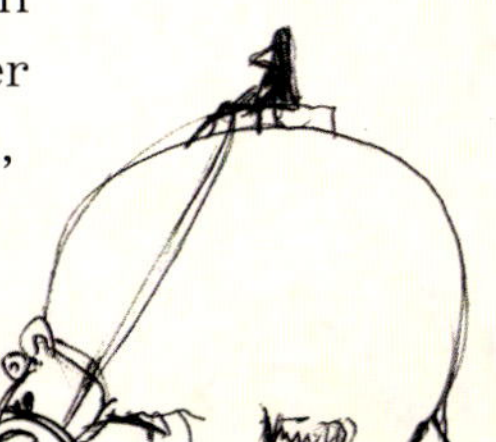

keep for himself. "This is what I call the Sheffield Steelworks sequence, which I'm very excited about, where they turn the basement into a foundry. When I went to art college in Leeds, the train passed through Sheffield and would always go right by the old steel works. There would be flames coming out of it and sparks, and the idea of having that in your basement…! So I put together a collection of pictures of old foundries, silhouettes of people welding. I don't know what sort of genre you would call that – it's a scene of Hades!"

Given how *Vengeance Most Fowl* harks back to *The Wrong Trousers*, he felt it was appropriate to try and create the scene on the studio floor, just as they would have done back in the 1990s. "Nowadays, there's so much more that you can do with post-effects and things, but on this project the mentality is, 'Get as much of it in camera as you can, on the floor, as economically and simply as possible'. But

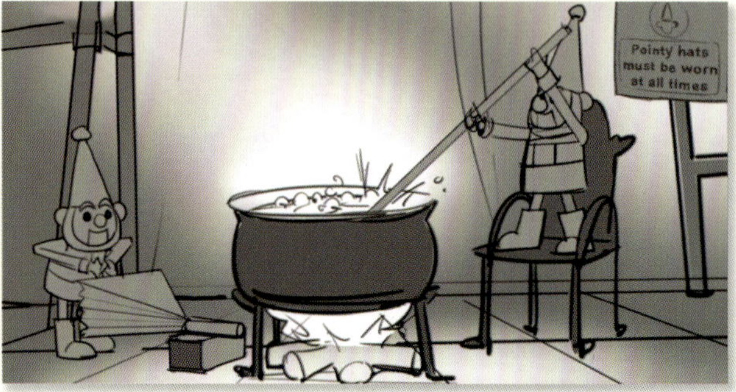

we also have all the advantages of the other techniques… the 'cutting-hedge' technology, so to speak."

As with the hacking of Norbot, the aim was to create the visual effects for the scene without relying entirely on CGI. "We can do most of that 'in camera'. Again, with the projectors I can back-project some of the effects onto the scaffolding and drapery. I'm using some of the Norbots themselves to make big shadows in the background. Then I put a baby projector at the back so I can project stylised effects, lights shining through stencils, that sort of thing. So you've got a structure there, like a big stage set, and

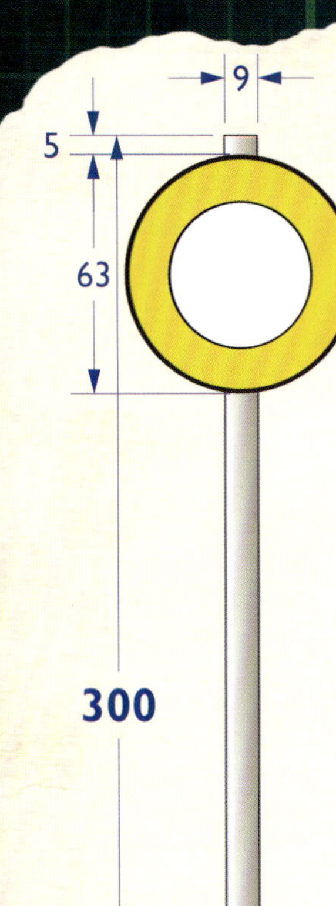

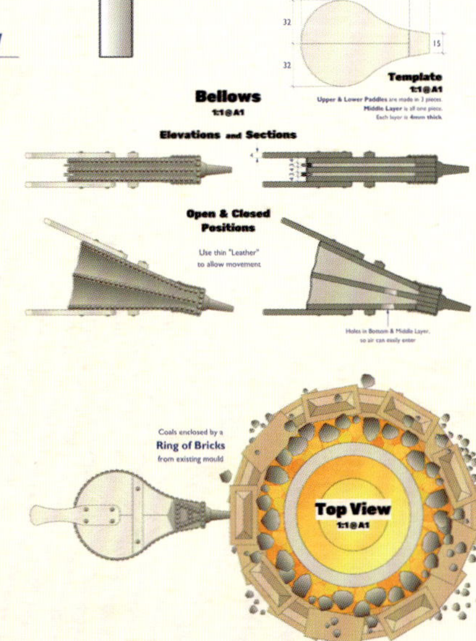

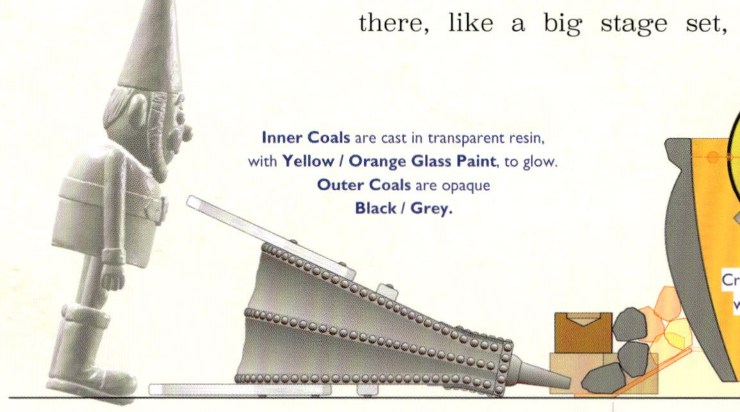

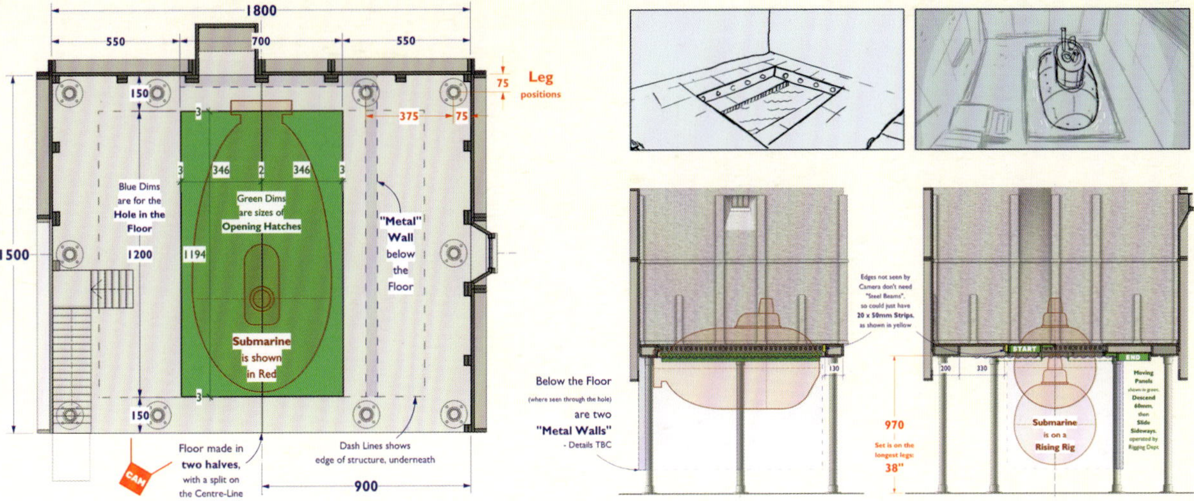

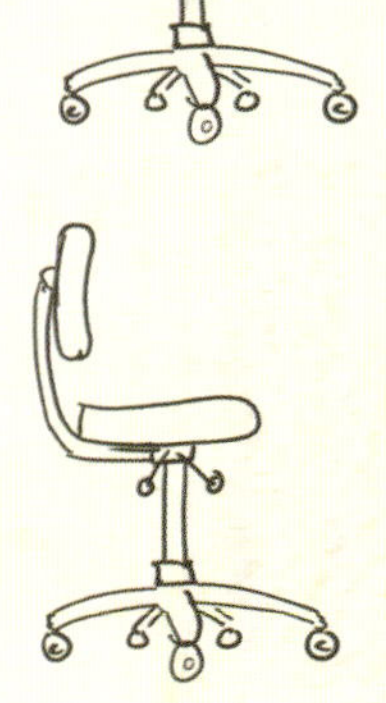

a red key light with lots of blue lights for the electric side of things – that suggested industry to me. With my senior gaffer Sally Wattiaux we went through the 140 frames of the first shot, programming where lights would flash, where lights would fade up and down, so you had a whole scenario of light changes – you want your lighting to be absolutely repeatable. We wanted sparks dropping down and bouncing off the floor when a Norbot is using an arc welder – those will be posted in – so we had special lights installed in the set that would light that Norbot up a little bit. Also, we shot the whole thing in stereo so you can produce a 3D version of the scene, which allows you to insert effects behind objects, putting depth into the scene without having to rotoscope around all the shapes to put smoke behind them."

For Dave Alex, working on a *Wallace & Gromit* film is a cinematographer's dream. "In terms of cinematography, it's all in there. You've got your Hitchcock, you've got your film noir, you've got your Hammer Horror, you've got Ealing Comedy. I've always loved the lighting on those old British films, that's all been absorbed. The great thing with Nick's scripts is the genre hopping. He likes camera moves – there's a lot of Hitchcockian camera moves in and out, a lot of Dutch angles from the old expressionist films [where the shot is filmed on a tilt to create a sense of unease]. It's all

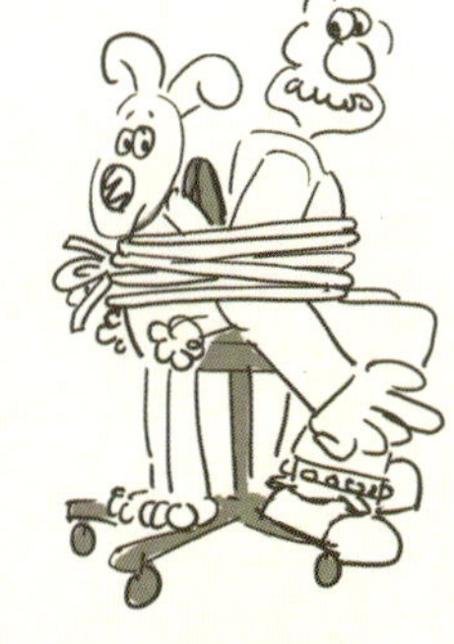

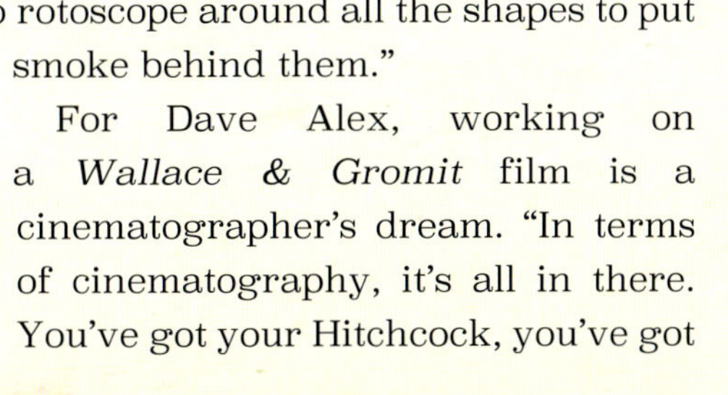

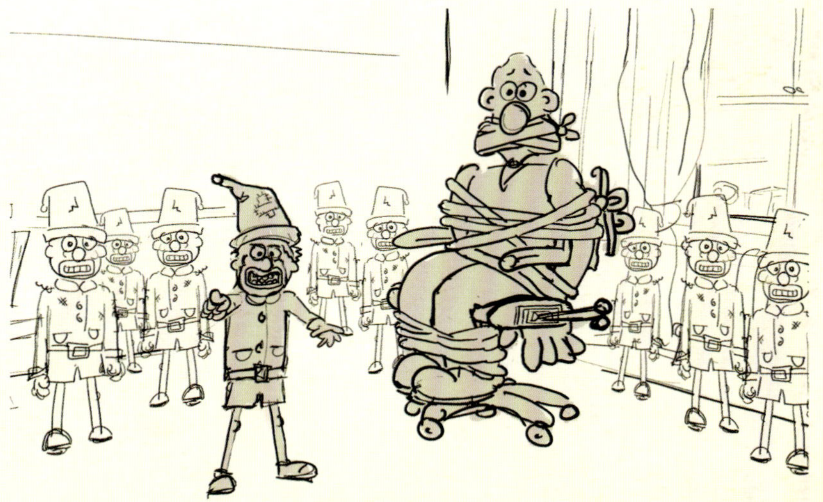

the things that Nick's generation grew up with – the shared memories of what you saw on television. There are bits of *Thunderbirds* in there, there's *Tom and Jerry*, there's the old British films that you watched on a Sunday afternoon, all that stuff is in Nick's head. It's your chance to indulge yourself, and you're allowed to because you've created that little world."

"That's the thing with *Wallace & Gromit*," agrees Matt Sanders. "Often, it's spoofing something, but it isn't always a specific film. It's a genre, like the train chase in *The Wrong Trousers*. There have been loads of train chases with people going along the roof of the train, but there's only one where it's a little miniature train."

So where are we in terms of genre with *Vengeance Most Fowl*? Nick has coined his own term to describe it, which will no doubt be the subject of many a film student's thesis for years to come: Gnome Noir. "That was my phrase," reveals Nick. "On every film there's been a phrase: on *Loaf and Death* it was 'A bread-based murder mystery' and *Were-Rabbit* was 'The first vegetarian horror movie'. And this is definitely a film for fans of 'Gnome Noir', as if it's a sub-genre. Kids are going to be scared

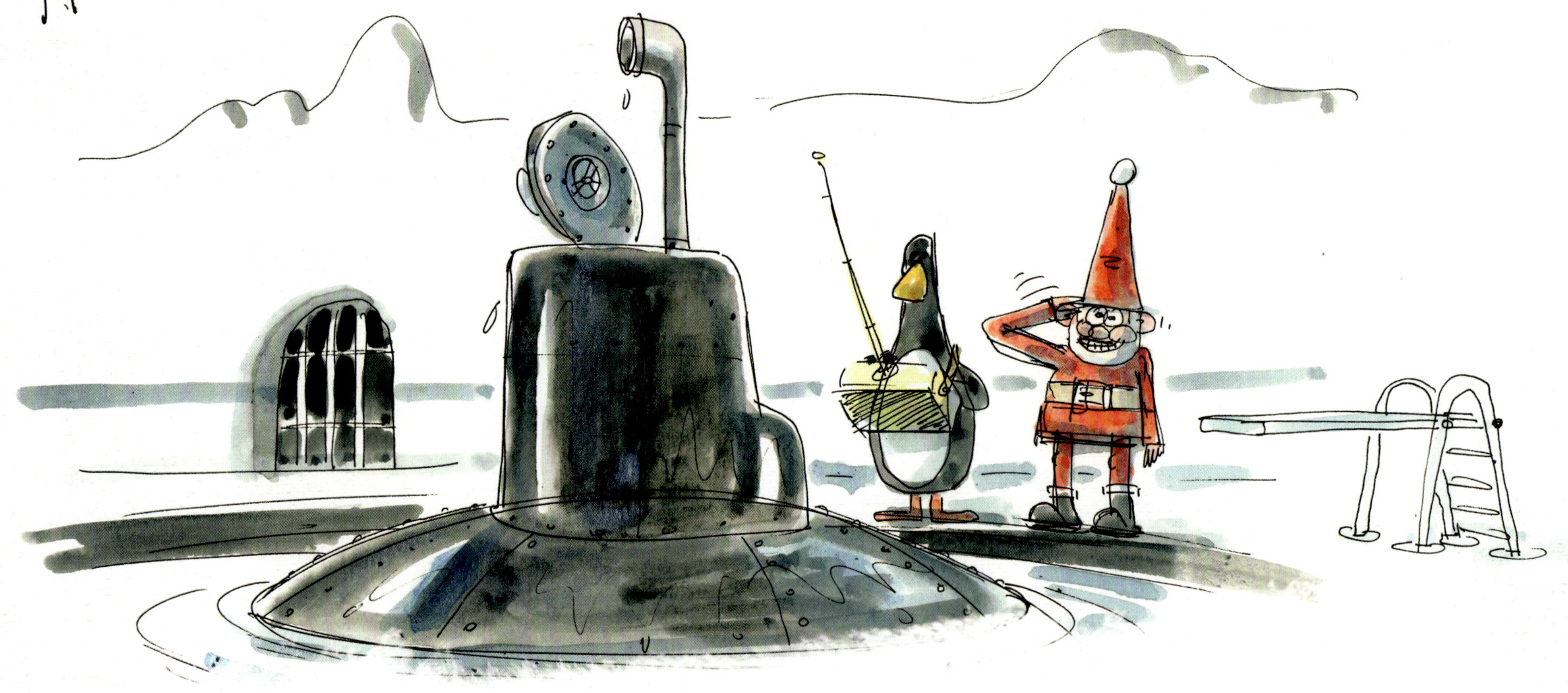

out of their wits on Christmas Day! But it's that sort of enjoyable horror when you were a kid – *Doctor Who* and hiding behind the sofa."

This spoof genre allows the story to move from broad comedy to expressionistic horror without the tone jarring. "It has an amazing variety of looks, which I think all gel together," says Dave Alex. "It's about crossing lines, keeping that cosiness when it's really essential, then throwing lots of Dutch angles in when you're being attacked by a giant pair of mechanical trousers or whatever. The stylisation knits it all together; wherever you go you've still got this goofy guy with big teeth."

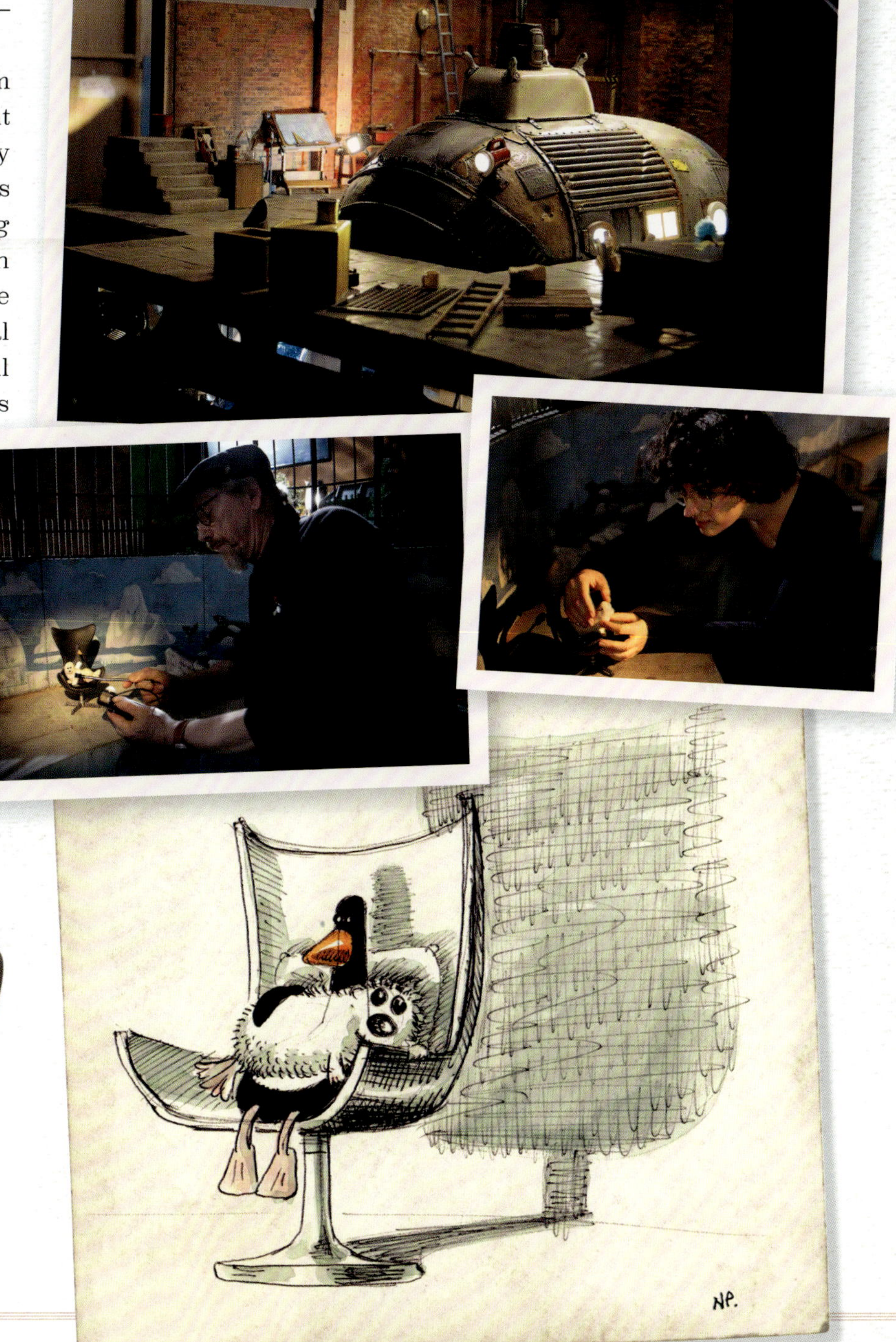

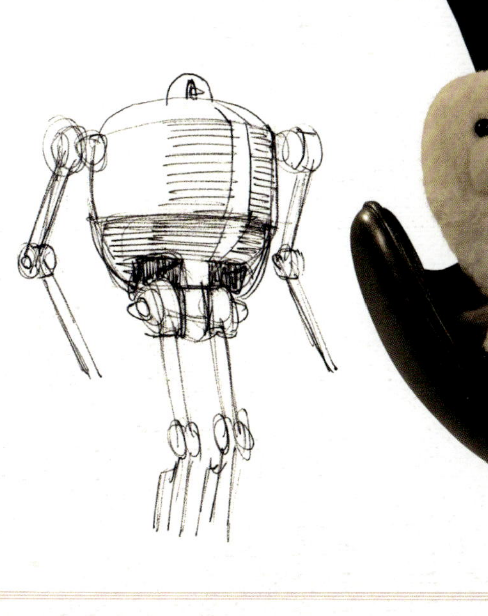

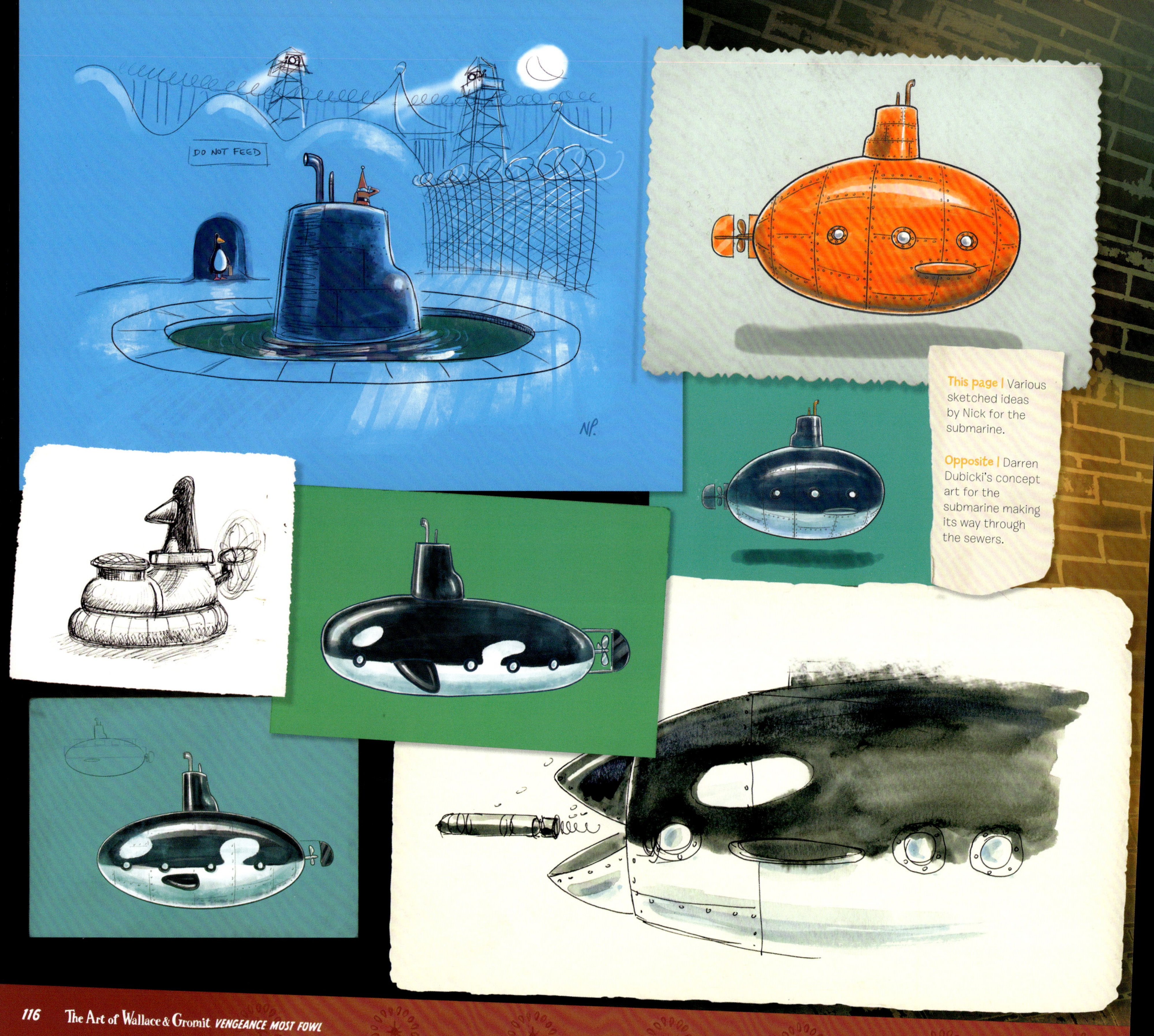

This page | Various sketched ideas by Nick for the submarine.

Opposite | Darren Dubicki's concept art for the submarine making its way through the sewers.

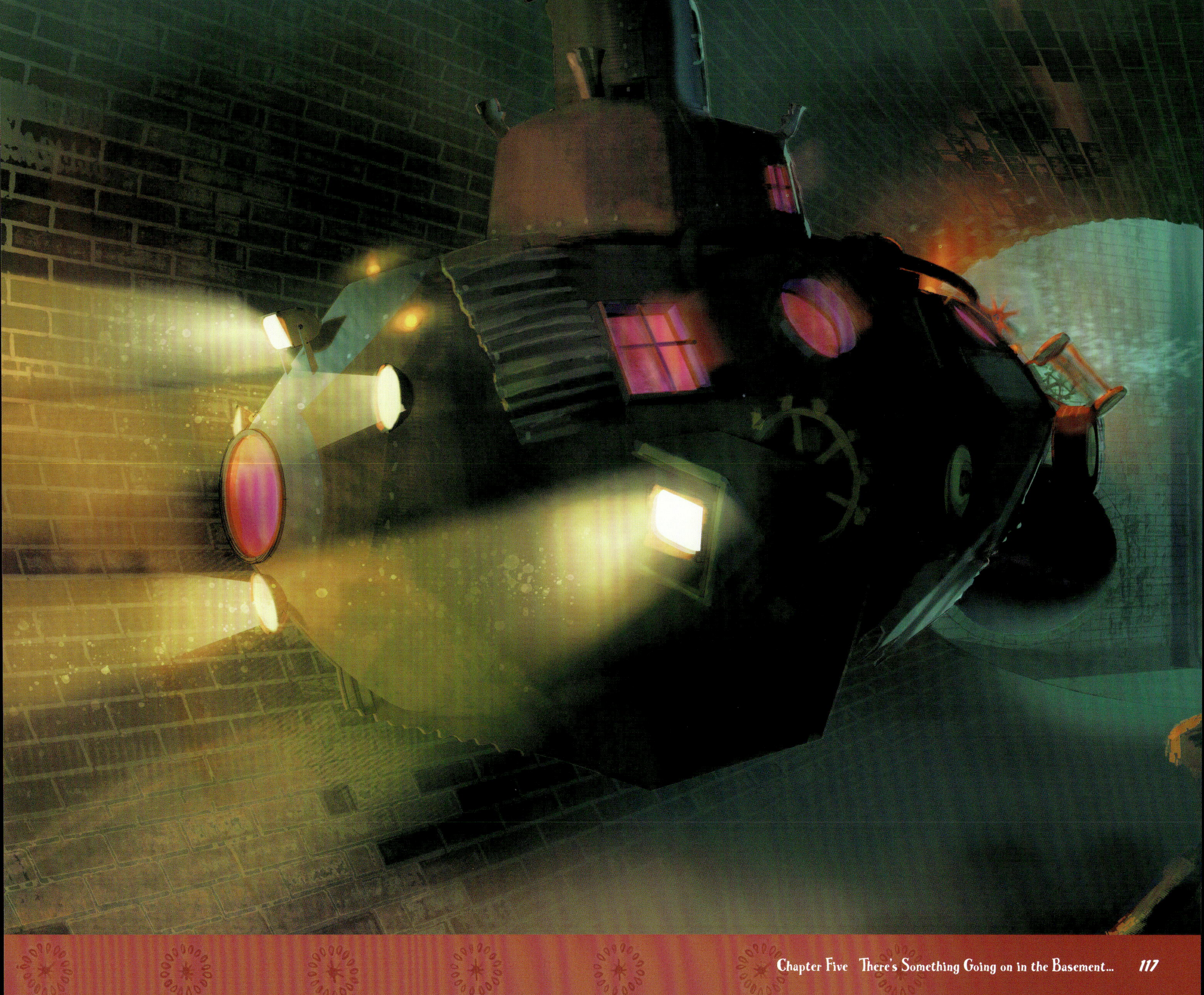

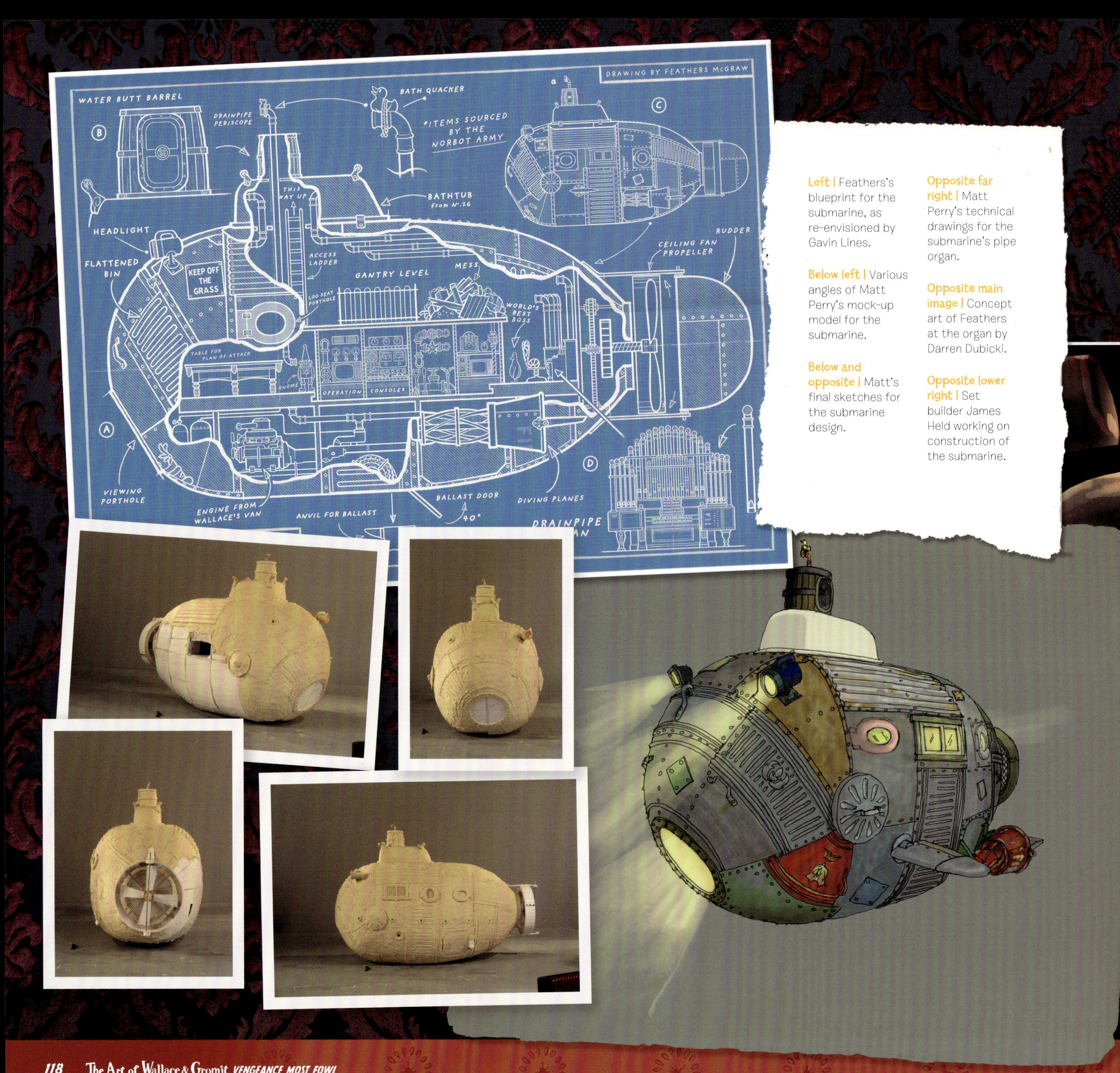

Left | Feathers's blueprint for the submarine, as re-envisioned by Gavin Lines.

Below left | Various angles of Matt Perry's mock-up model for the submarine.

Below and opposite | Matt's final sketches for the submarine design.

Opposite far right | Matt Perry's technical drawings for the submarine's pipe organ.

Opposite main image | Concept art of Feathers at the organ by Darren Dubicki.

Opposite lower right | Set builder James Held working on construction of the submarine.

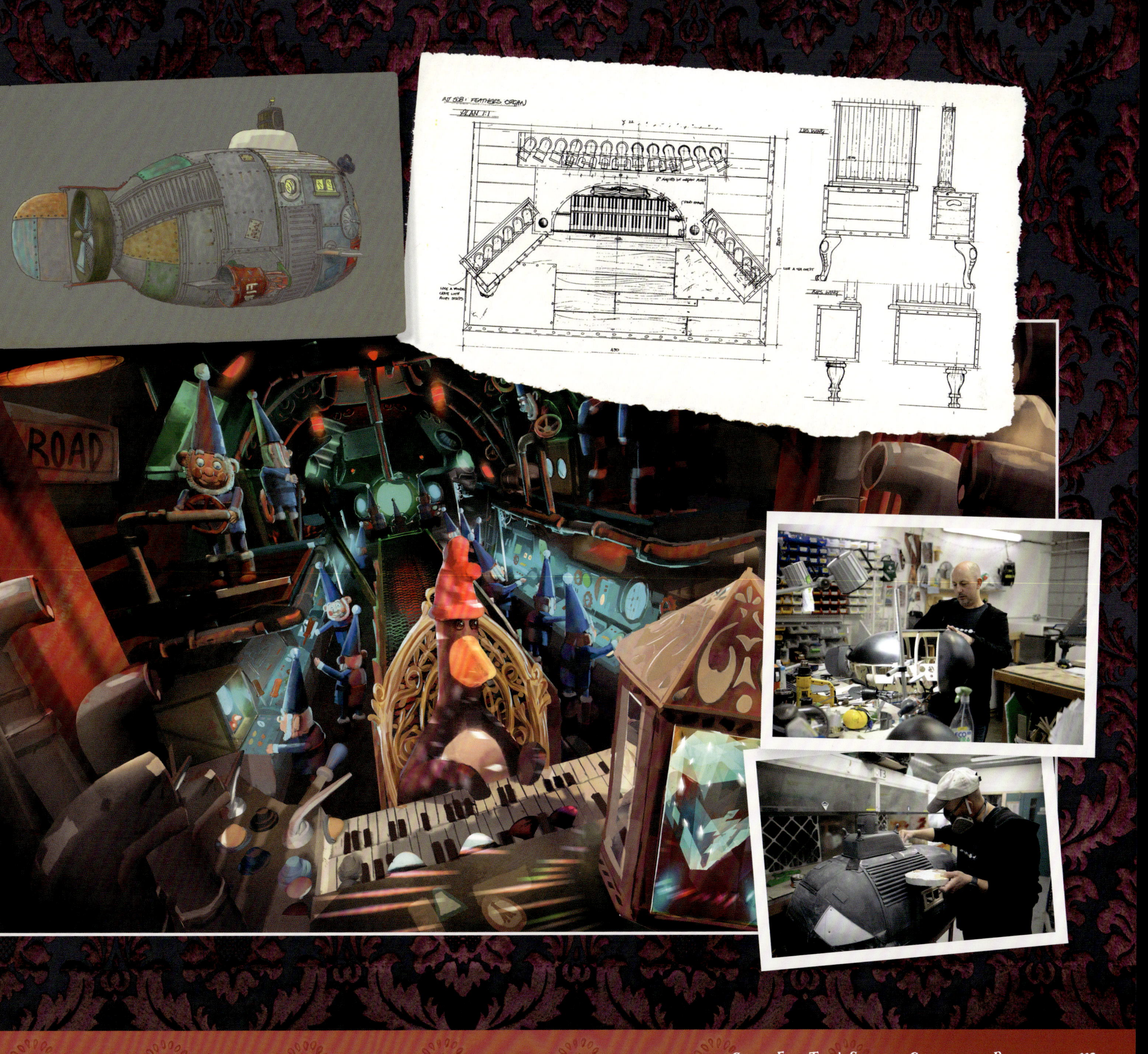

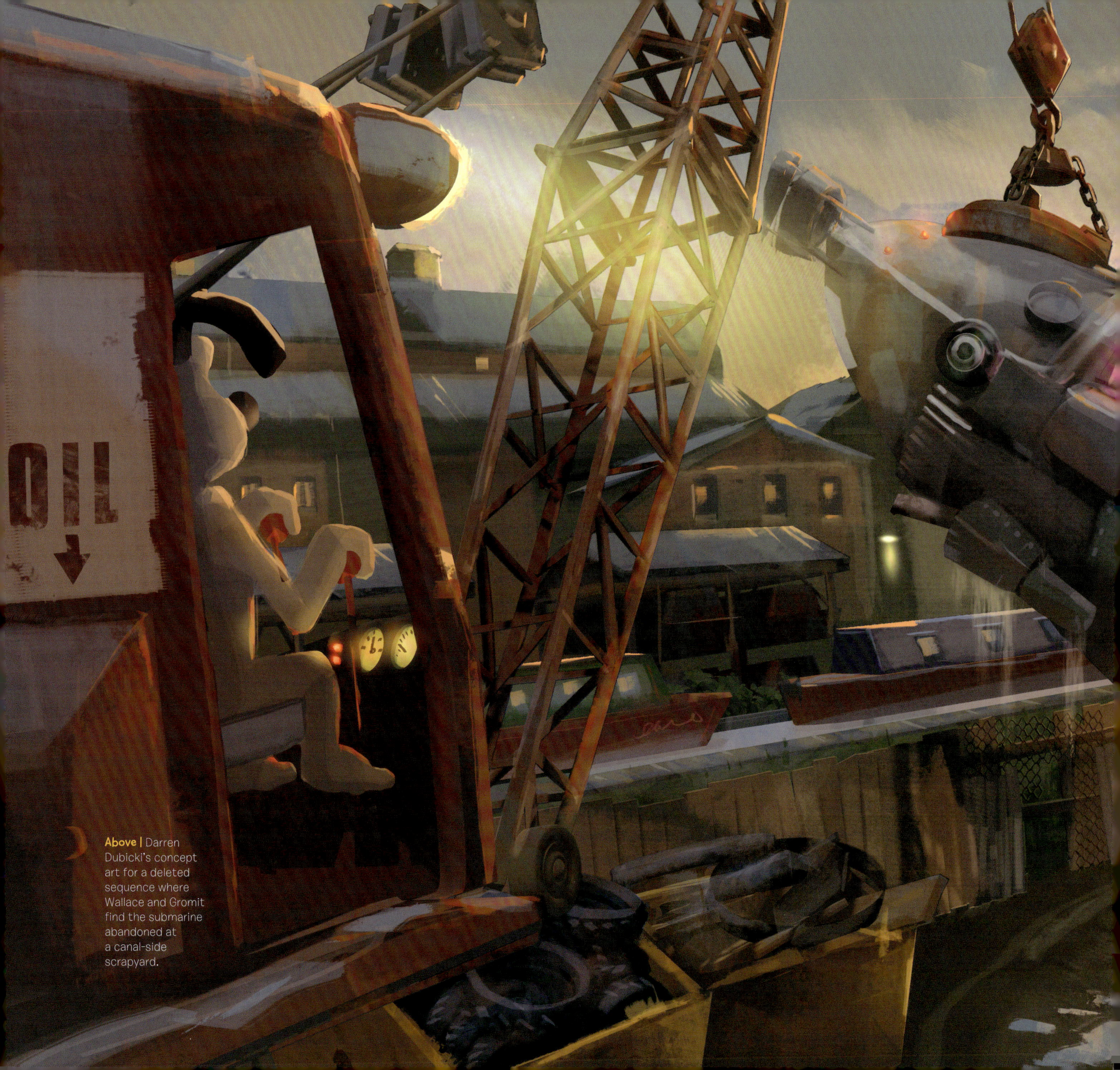

Above | Darren Dubicki's concept art for a deleted sequence where Wallace and Gromit find the submarine abandoned at a canal-side scrapyard.

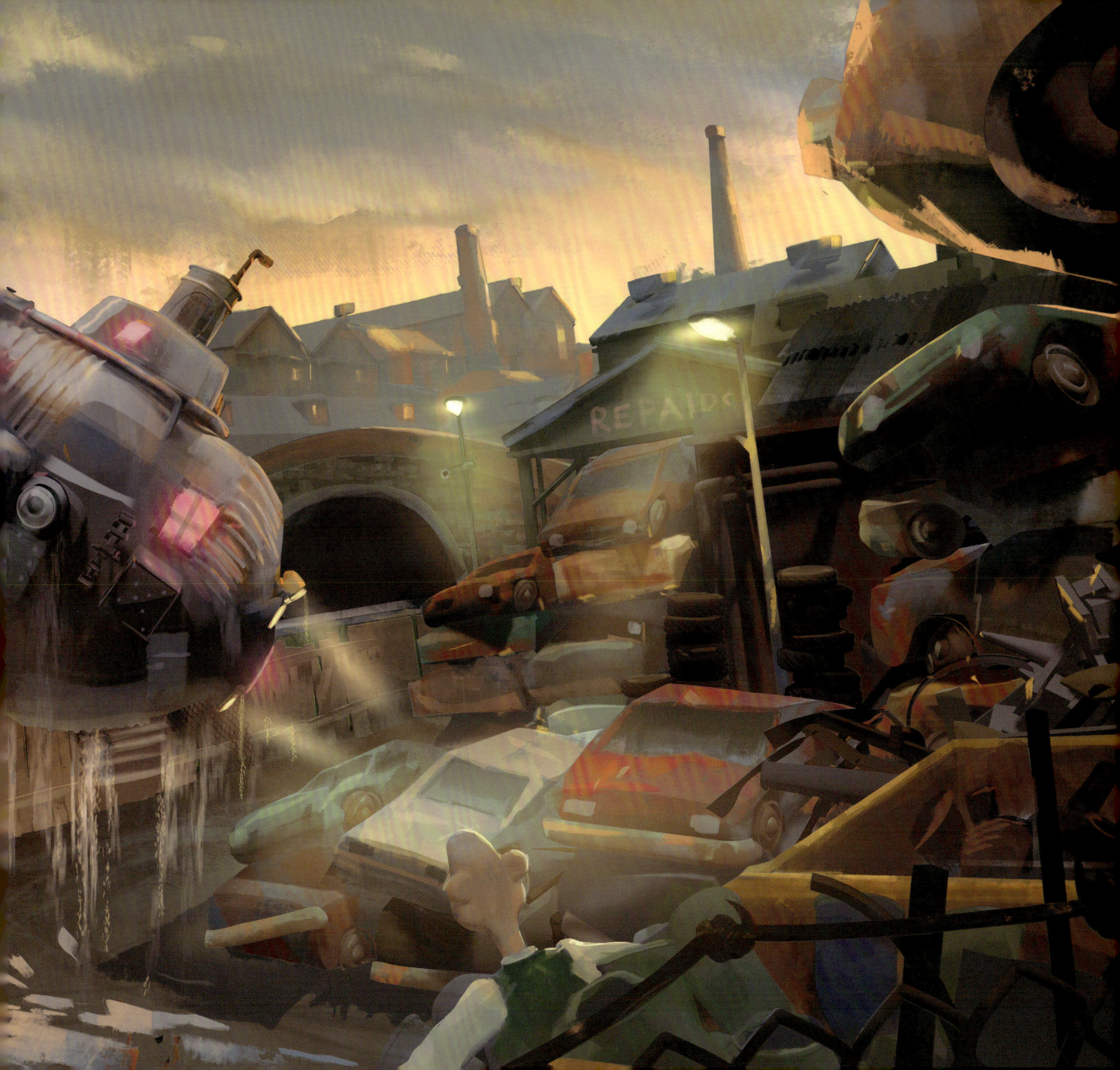
REPAIRS

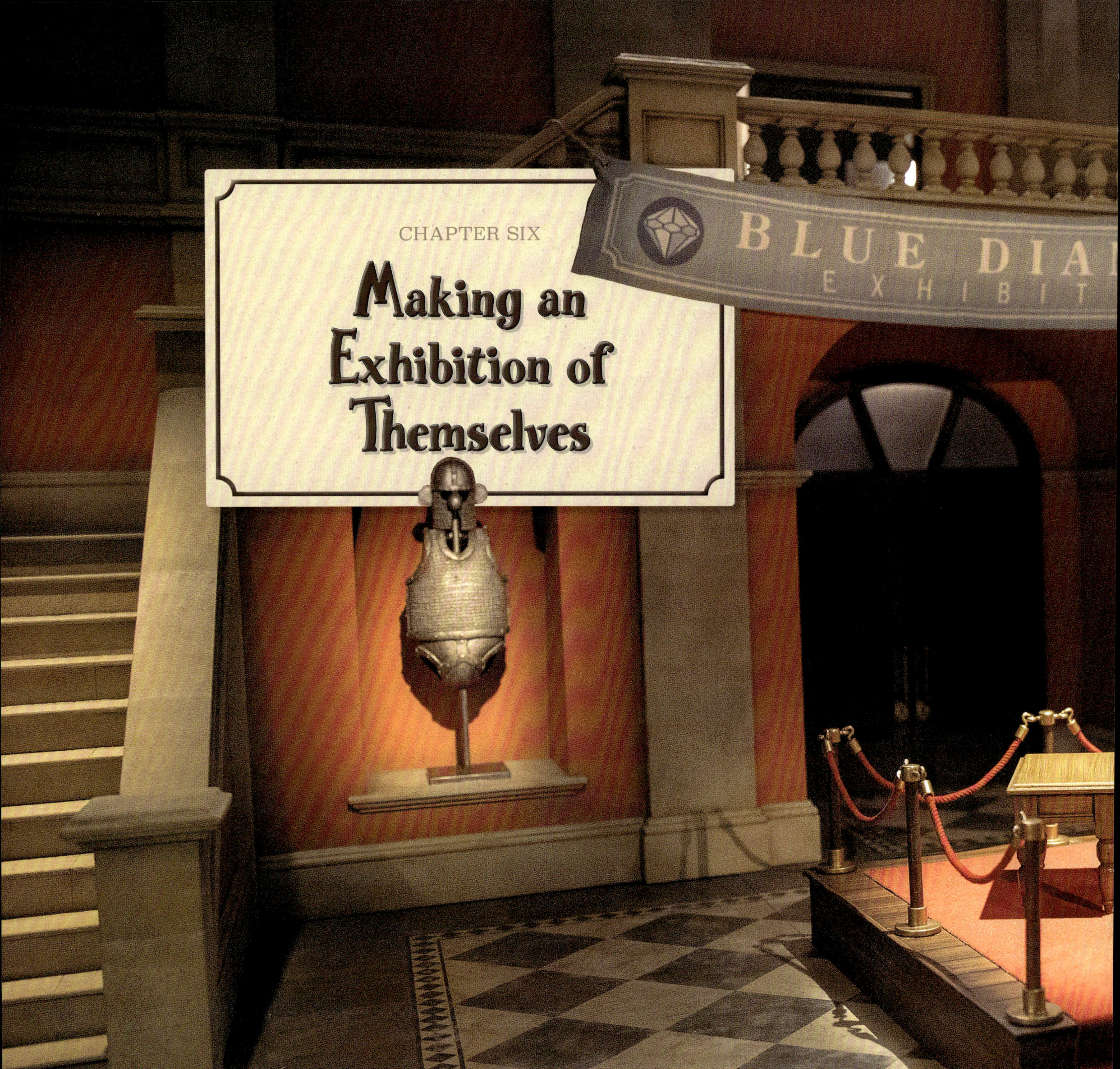

CHAPTER SIX
Making an Exhibition of Themselves
BLUE DIA
EXHIBIT

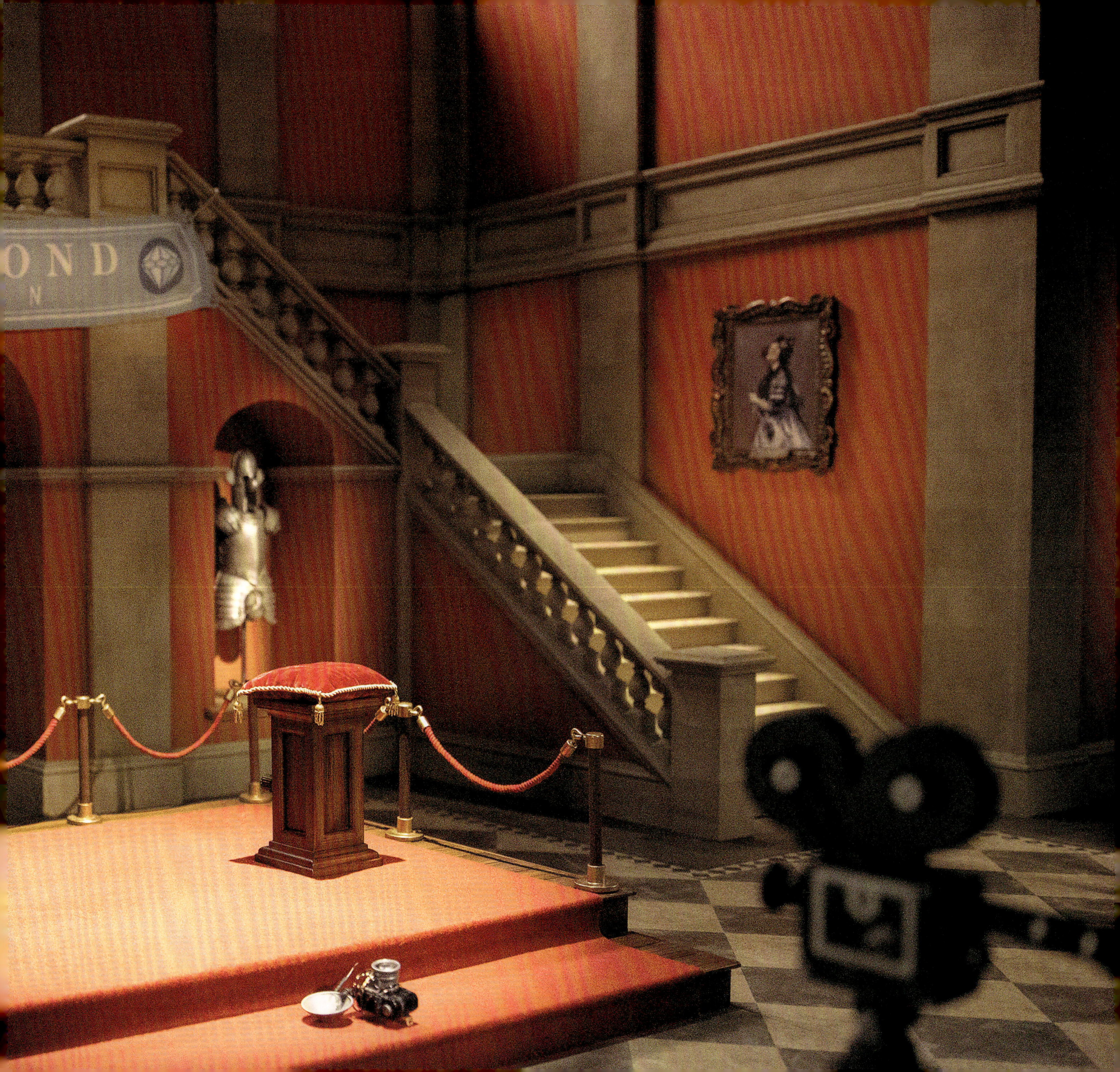
OND
N

Making an Exhibition of Themselves

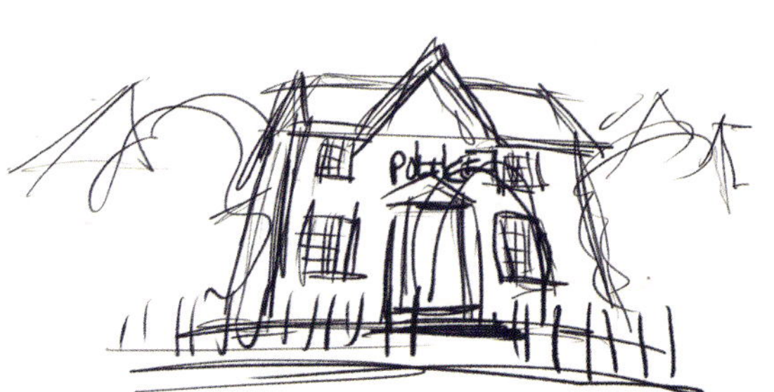

THEY SAY A VILLAIN ALWAYS RETURNS TO THE scene of his crime, and that looks like exactly what Feathers McGraw is up to as Wallace and Gromit's local museum plans to exhibit the precious Blue Diamond, the first time it has been on display since they rescued it from the clutches of the pernicious penguin's flippers. It's going to be a proud day for the soon-to-retire Chief Inspector Mackintosh (who was promoted from his position as PC Mackintosh in *Curse of the Were-Rabbit*) and a chance for his new assistant, PC Mukherjee, to show her true colours.

Vengeance Most Fowl presents the location on a far grander scale than its first appearance in *The Wrong Trousers*, where Feathers only had to break into the upstairs Diamond Room from a side street. But now the Town Museum can be seen in all its porticoed glory, with a formidable vault, beefed-up security and cavernous main

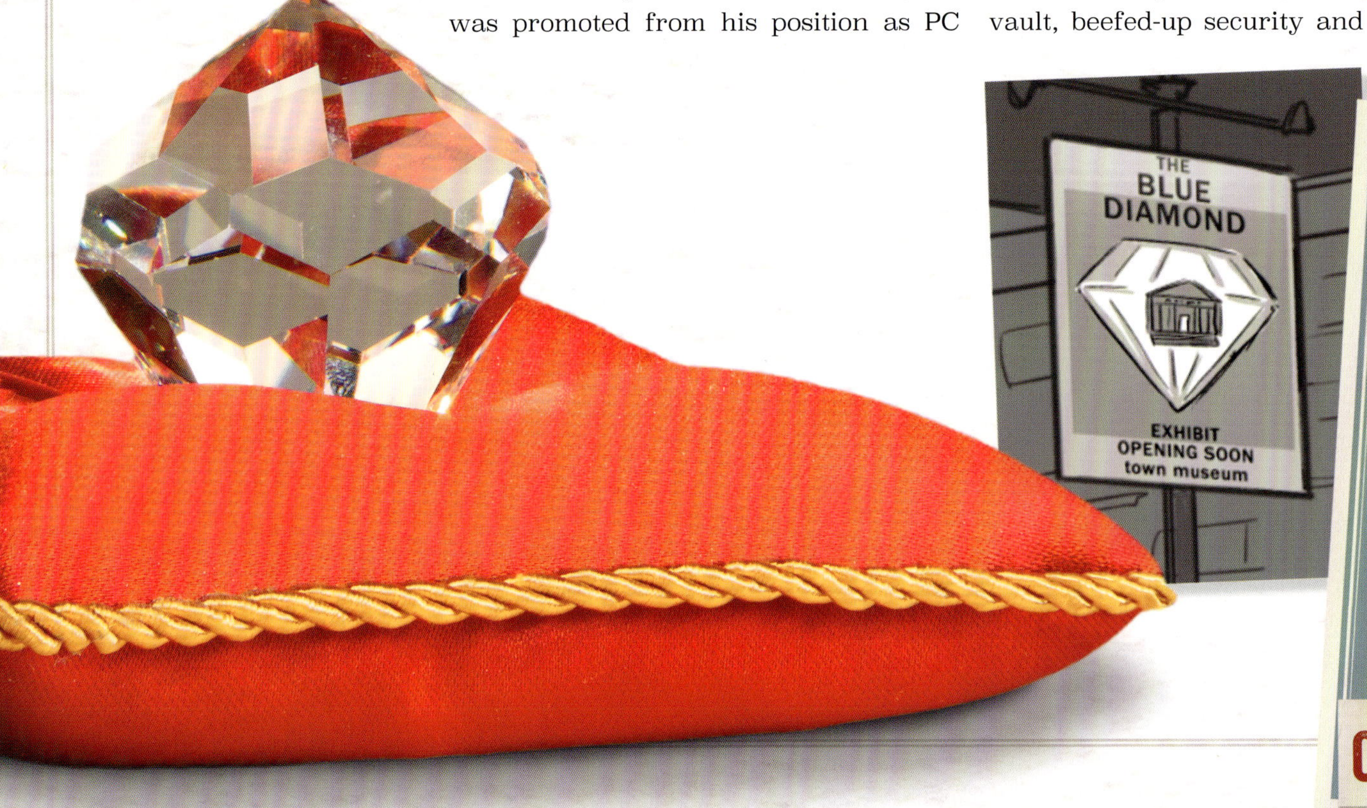

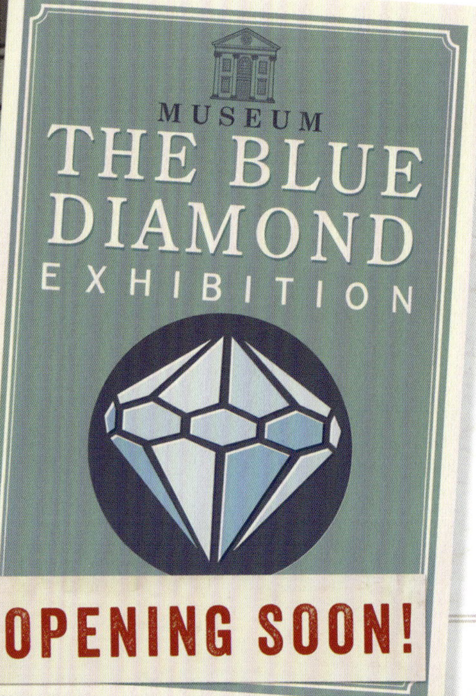

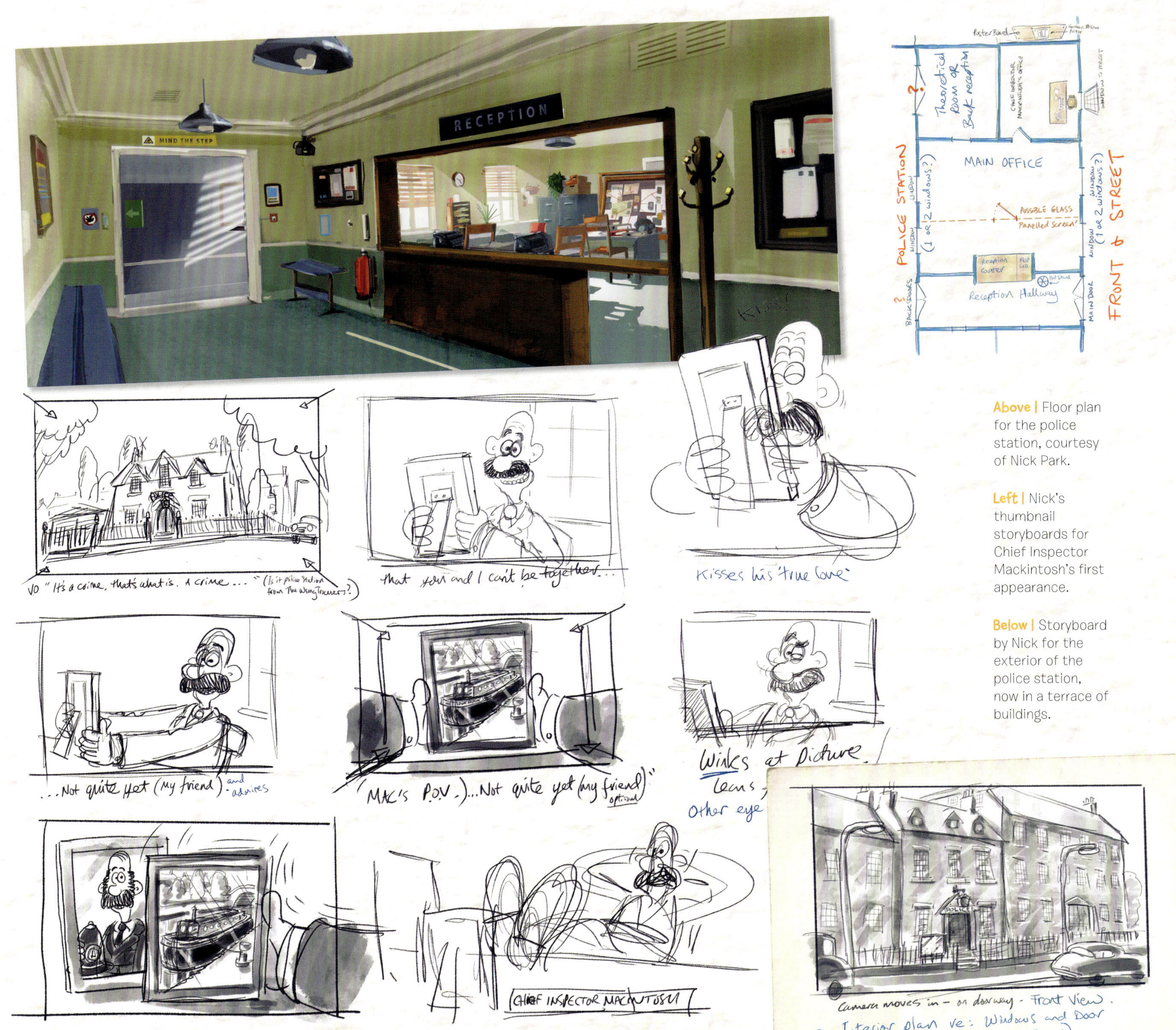

Above | Floor plan for the police station, courtesy of Nick Park.

Left | Nick's thumbnail storyboards for Chief Inspector Mackintosh's first appearance.

Below | Storyboard by Nick for the exterior of the police station, now in a terrace of buildings.

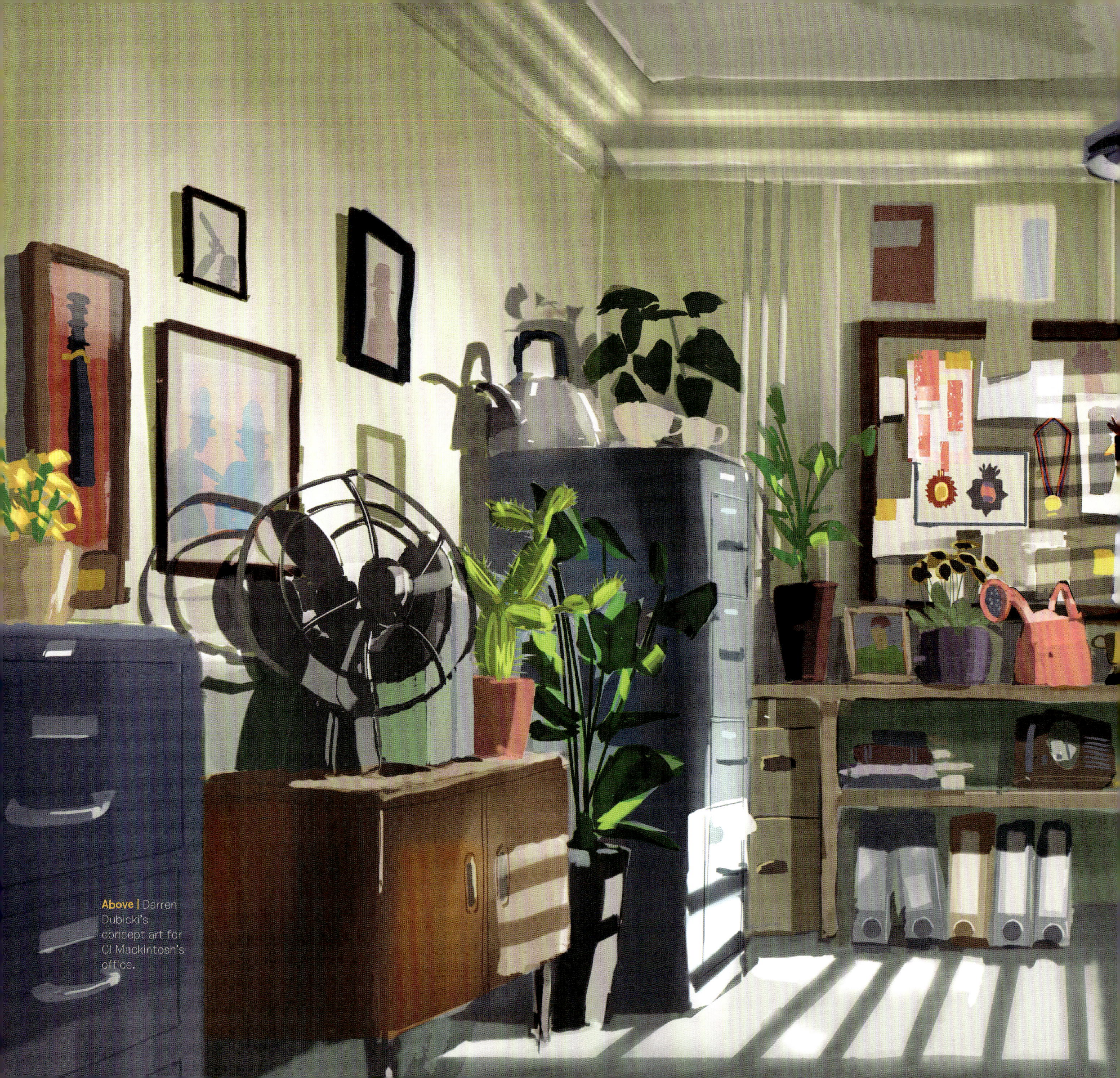

Above | Darren
Dubicki's
concept art for
CI Mackintosh's
office.

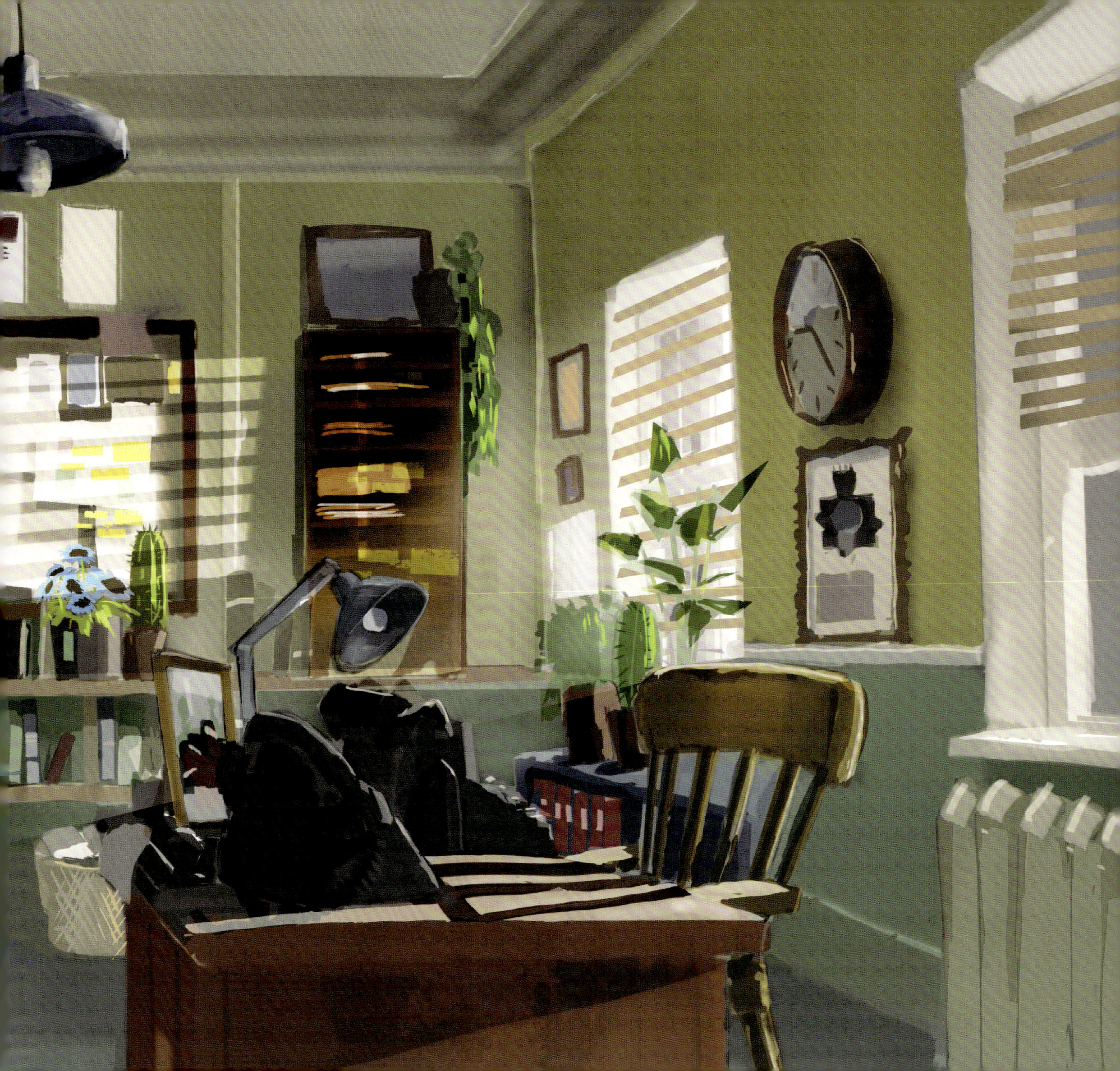

hall where the exhibition is to have its grand opening in front of a crowd of local dignitaries. The set is constructed in a modular style, so the portico can be detached from the main building, allowing the animators easier access when handling scenes in the doorway.

Nick was delighted to have Peter Kay return in the role of the bumbling copper. "I didn't dare suggest it because I didn't think we could use the character again," he recalls. "But then we found out that was OK and we thought that it would be excellent to bring him back. It was

Mark Burton's idea to give him an assistant, a trainee, so he suggested Mukherjee as a character early on, and Lauren Patel has been brilliant in the role, as has Reece Shearsmith as Norbot."

Nick sketched numerous versions of what Mukherjee might look like before he hit on the one that perfectly captured her personality and naive enthusiasm. This was worked up into a full-colour drawing, assisted by Mike Salter. "I did some character design on Mukherjee," recalls Mike, "working out what sort of

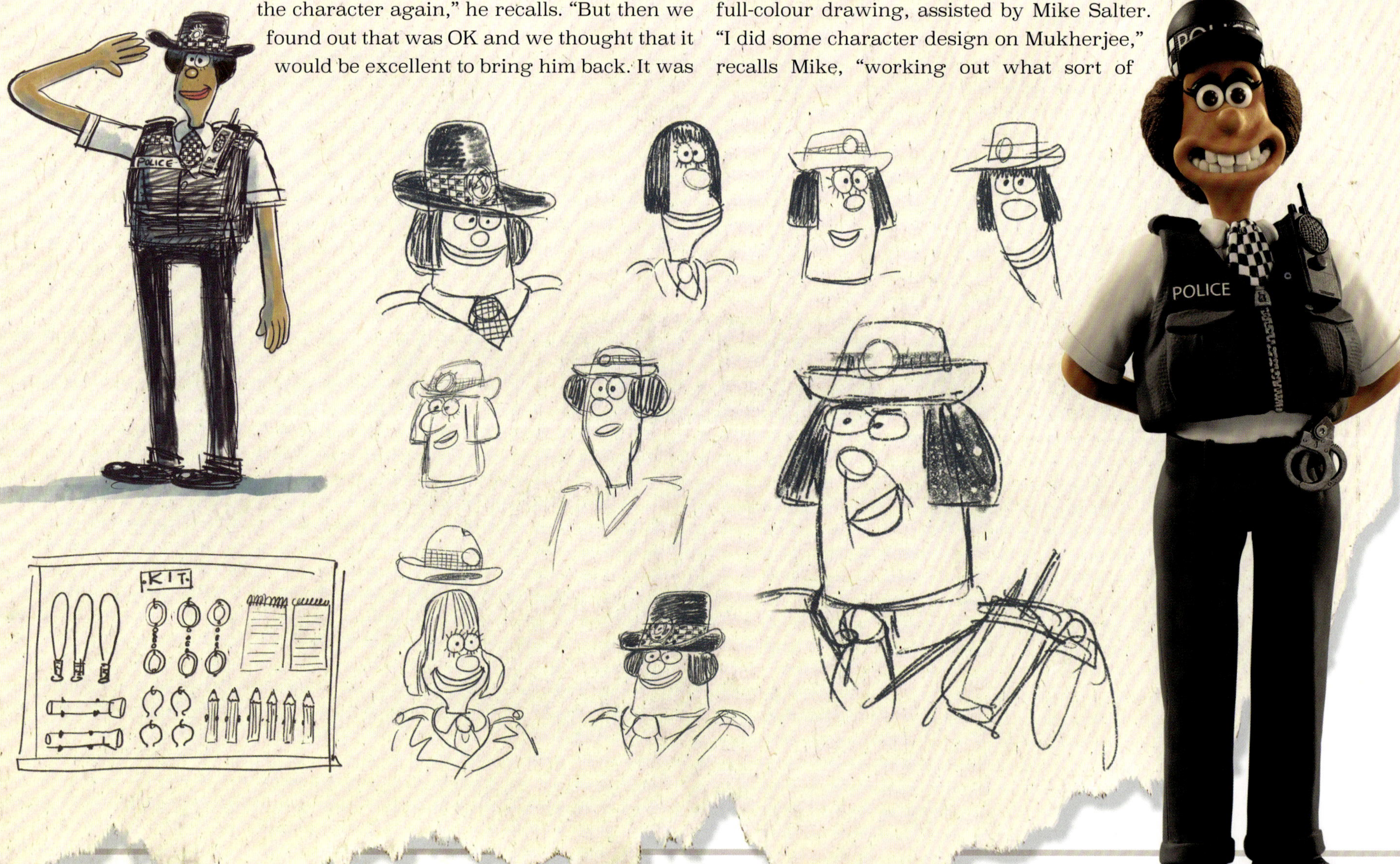

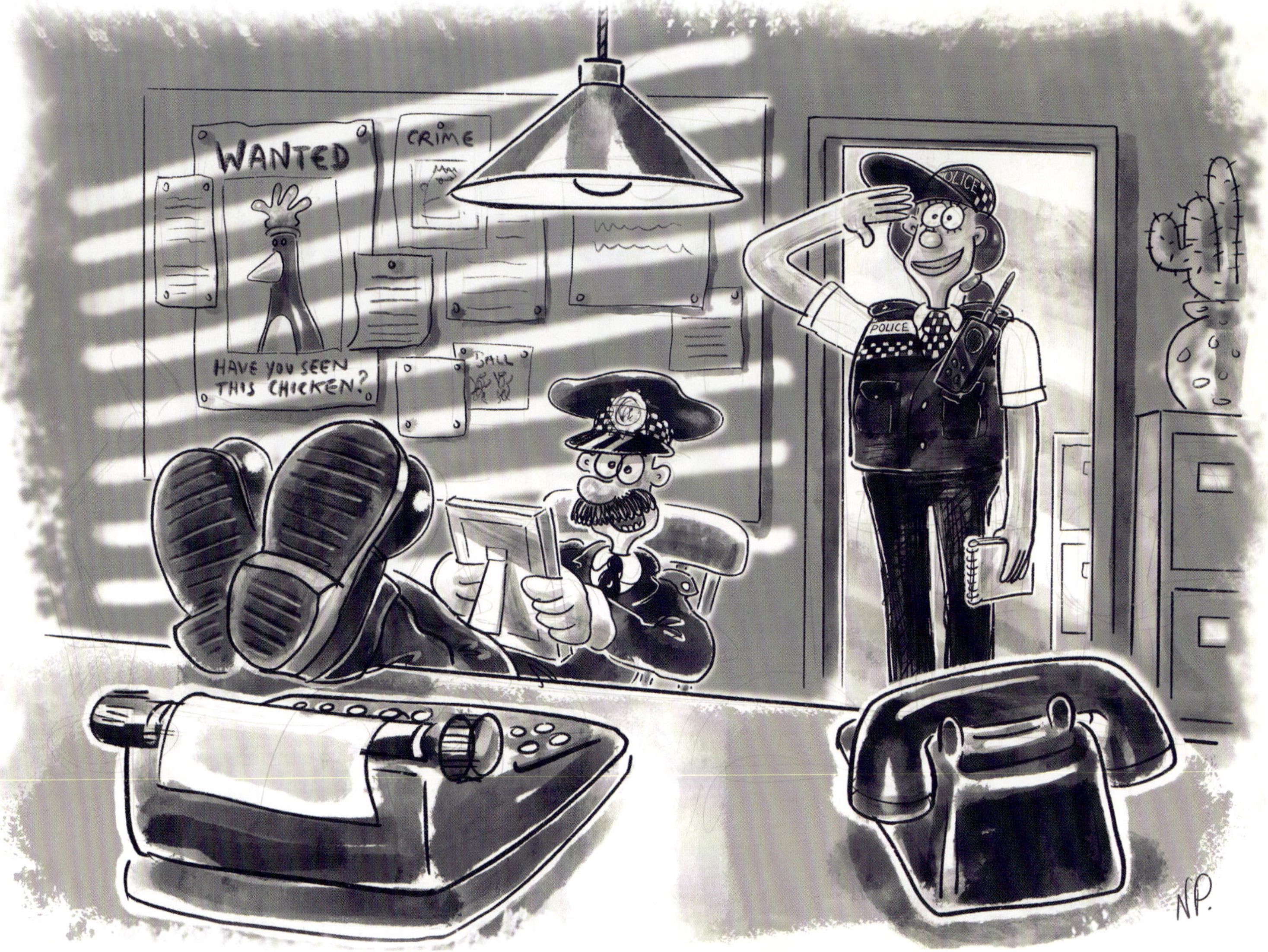

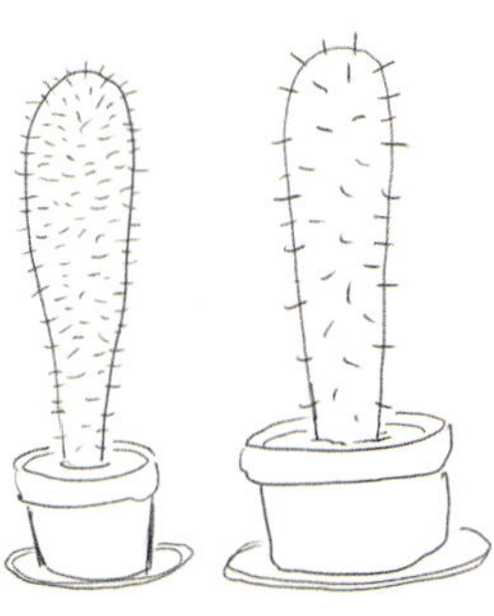

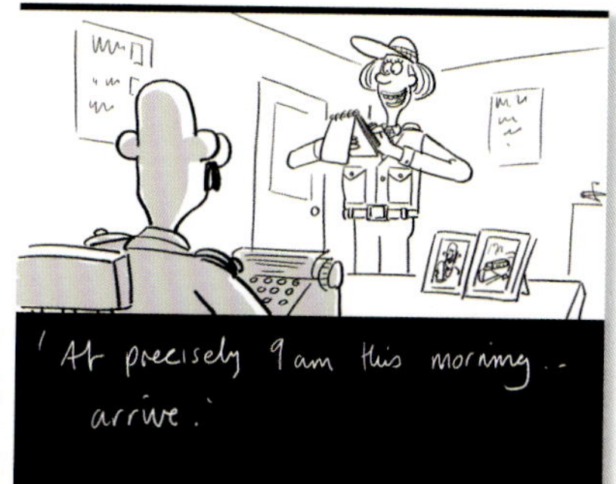

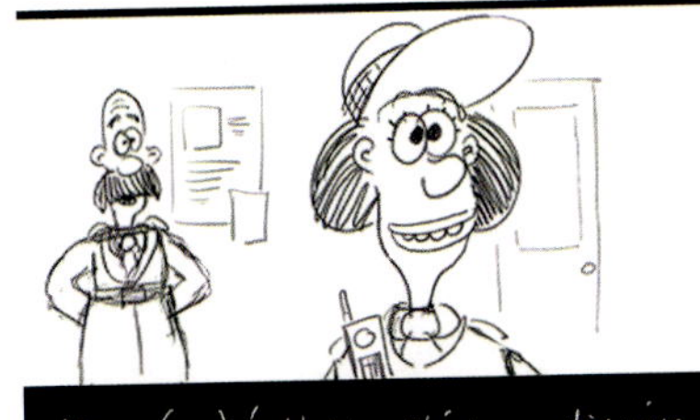

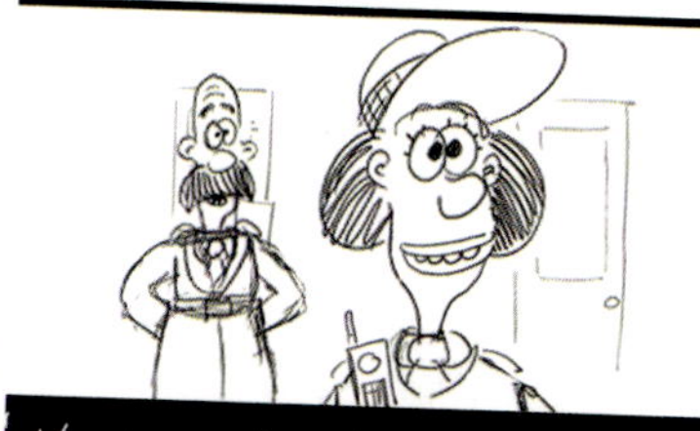

Above | Nick Park's sketch of Mukherjee reporting for duty.

Left | Early thumbnails for the scene in Chief Inspector Mackintosh's office.

police hat she was going to have, what sort of hair and so on. The design process is quite loose compared to the industrial-level turnarounds you get on CG films, especially in terms of what different people bring to the realisation of the characters."

Andy Spradbury then enters the picture to help create a clay sculpt that fully expresses the character. Along with the drawings, he is given a character brief. "They give you a description of what she does and what she wants to do, what's her position in the force and what's her personality. We'll have a meeting, the directors explain her connection with the film, and I work from that. Mukherjee was quite hard because Nick and Merlin had a couple of pictures that were similar. There were bits of them that they liked, bits of them they didn't like, so you had to sort of triangulate it. They know what they want, and somewhere in between these drawings is what they're actually looking for – it's for me to find the sort of effect they're after."

There then follows a series of exploratory sculpts to help define the look and personality. "I'll meet with Nick and Merlin once a week and they'll ask me to do amendments. Sometimes they'll just say, 'I don't like that', but that's part of the job, at least you're refining down what they don't want. It's a process! They might want more detail on it, or they want it smaller or bigger. You try not to address too many things at once; if you change too much, you get a tug of war where if you make his ears bigger, his eyes look smaller and you end up going backwards and forwards. There could be loads of concept sculpts; they're normally posed because it's

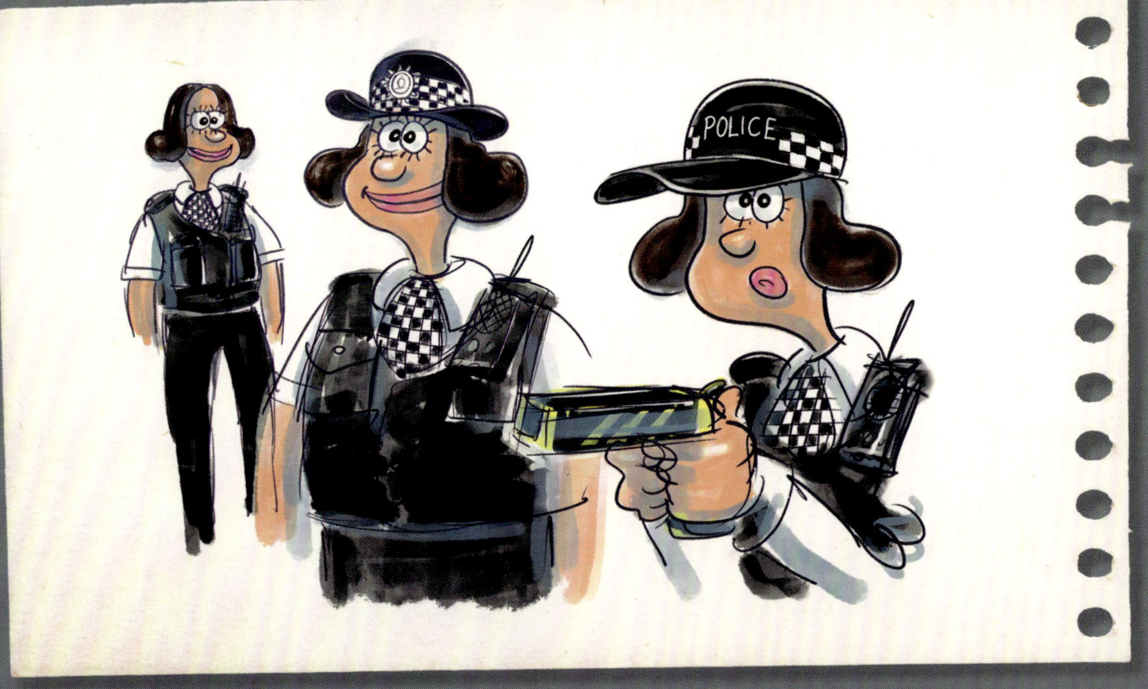

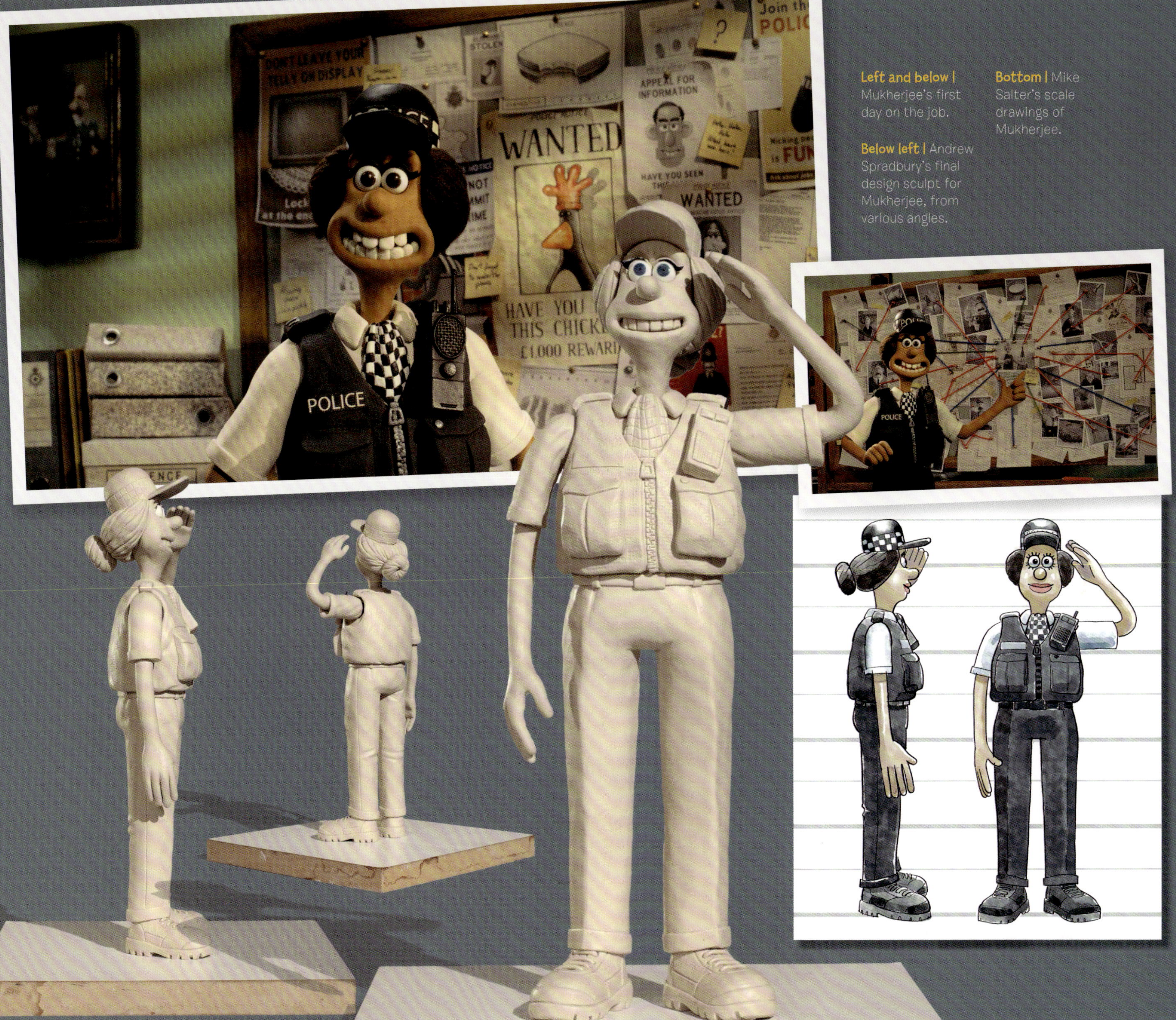

Left and below | Mukherjee's first day on the job.

Below left | Andrew Spradbury's final design sculpt for Mukherjee, from various angles.

Bottom | Mike Salter's scale drawings of Mukherjee.

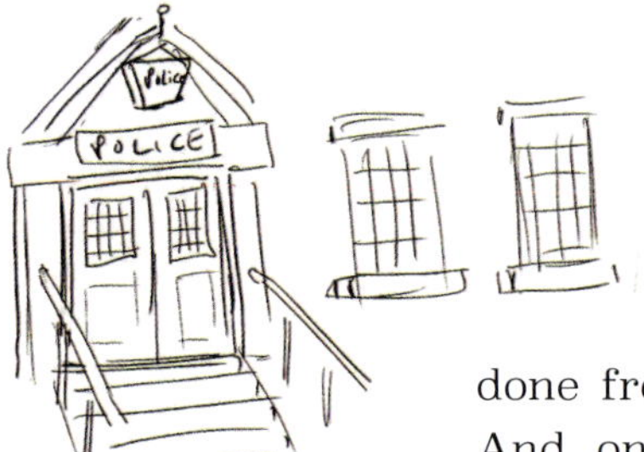

done from a drawing which has a pose to it. And once the directors like the proportions and what it looks like, then I'll do a production sculpt, which is a measured, symmetrical one that goes to Model-Making."

Chief Inspector Mackintosh himself underwent a process of evolution for this film. "I sculpted the *Were-Rabbit* one," recalls Andy. "He's changed a little bit – he's got a bit older, maybe a bit wiser, I have no idea. We spent a bit of time on his hat – he used to have a Bobby's helmet and when he took it off he had a really big bobbly head. Now we've had to make a flat cap but still make it look like he's got a bobbly head underneath. So he's

been promoted, but he's still got a silly head!"

"In addition to his cap, Mackintosh has got a few grey hairs in his beard now," observes marketing production manager Blair Brown. "His body shape has changed too, as Mukherjee tactlessly points out – he's definitely looking forward to retirement!"

The museum scenes provide a great opportunity for the prop department to display its artistry. While some of the exhibits dotted around might have originally been seen in previous productions, many were custom-made for this movie, with Aardman's customary propensity for visual gags fully on display. The suits of armour are prime examples. "There were two niches under the staircase

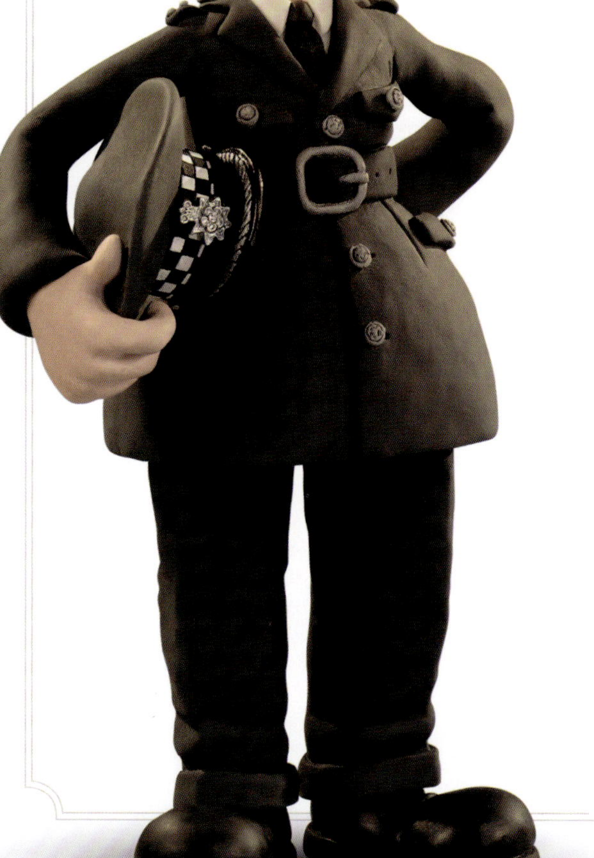

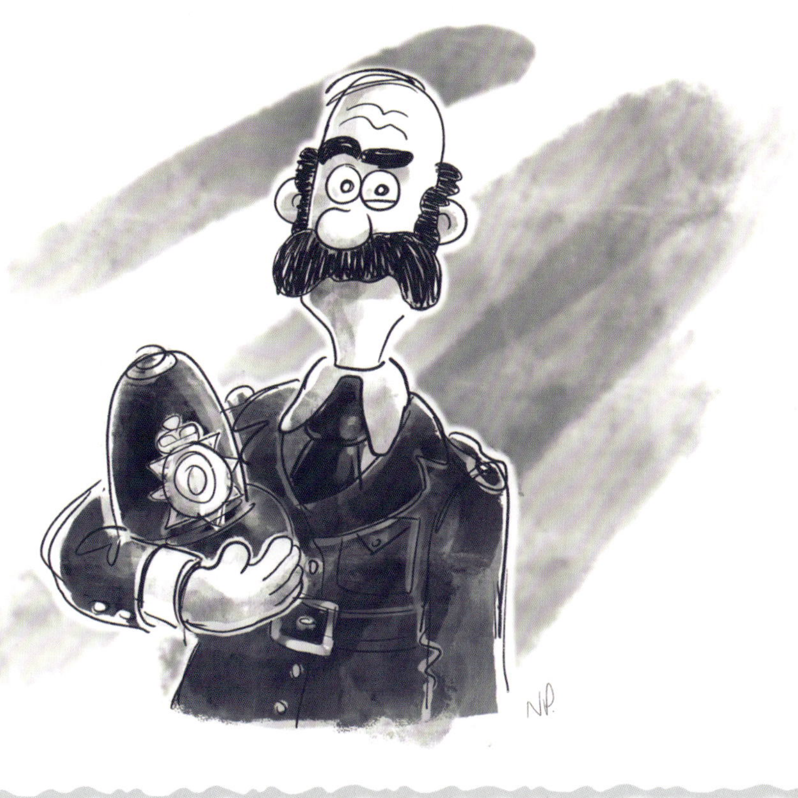

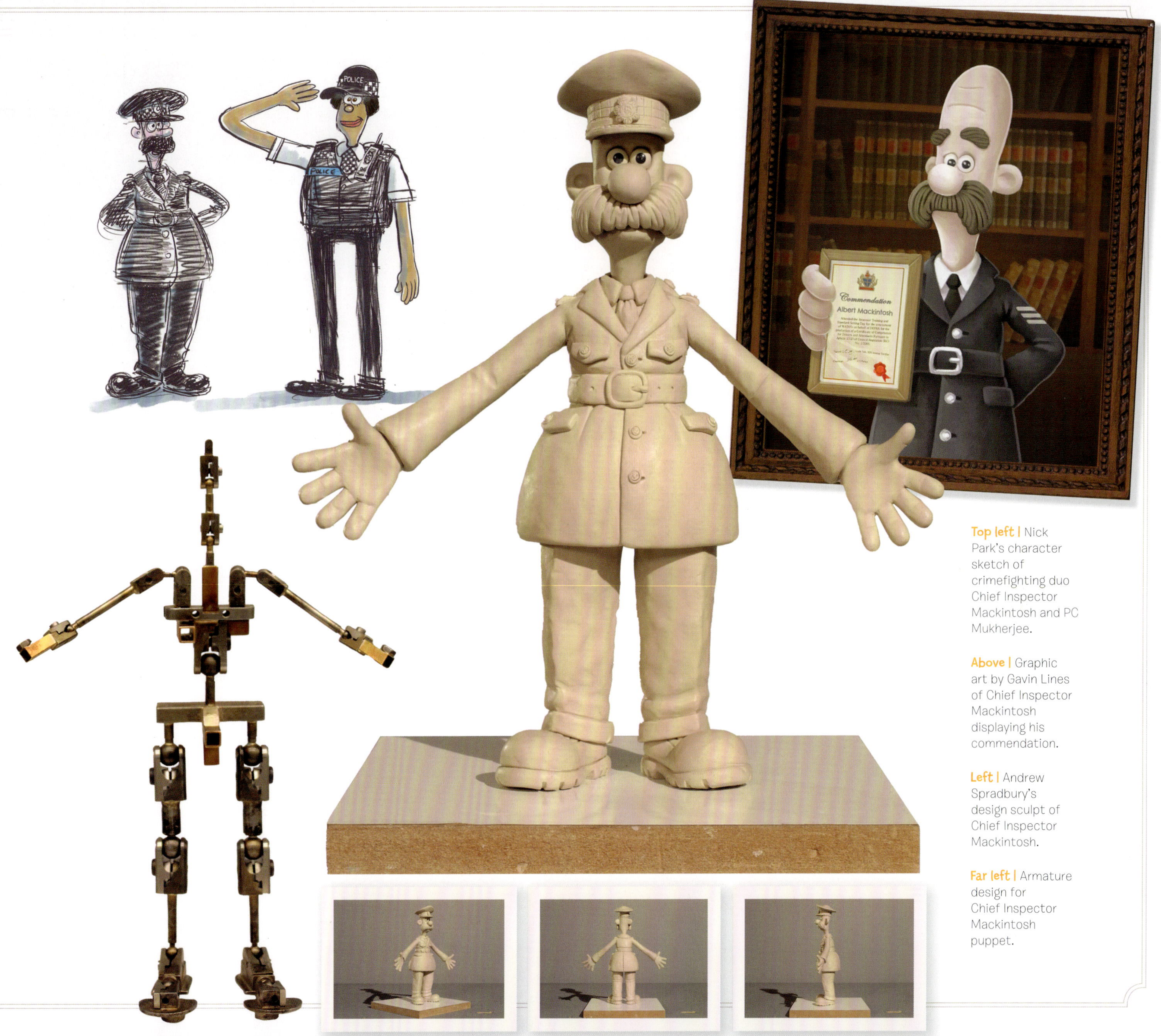

Top left | Nick Park's character sketch of crimefighting duo Chief Inspector Mackintosh and PC Mukherjee.

Above | Graphic art by Gavin Lines of Chief Inspector Mackintosh displaying his commendation.

Left | Andrew Spradbury's design sculpt of Chief Inspector Mackintosh.

Far left | Armature design for Chief Inspector Mackintosh puppet.

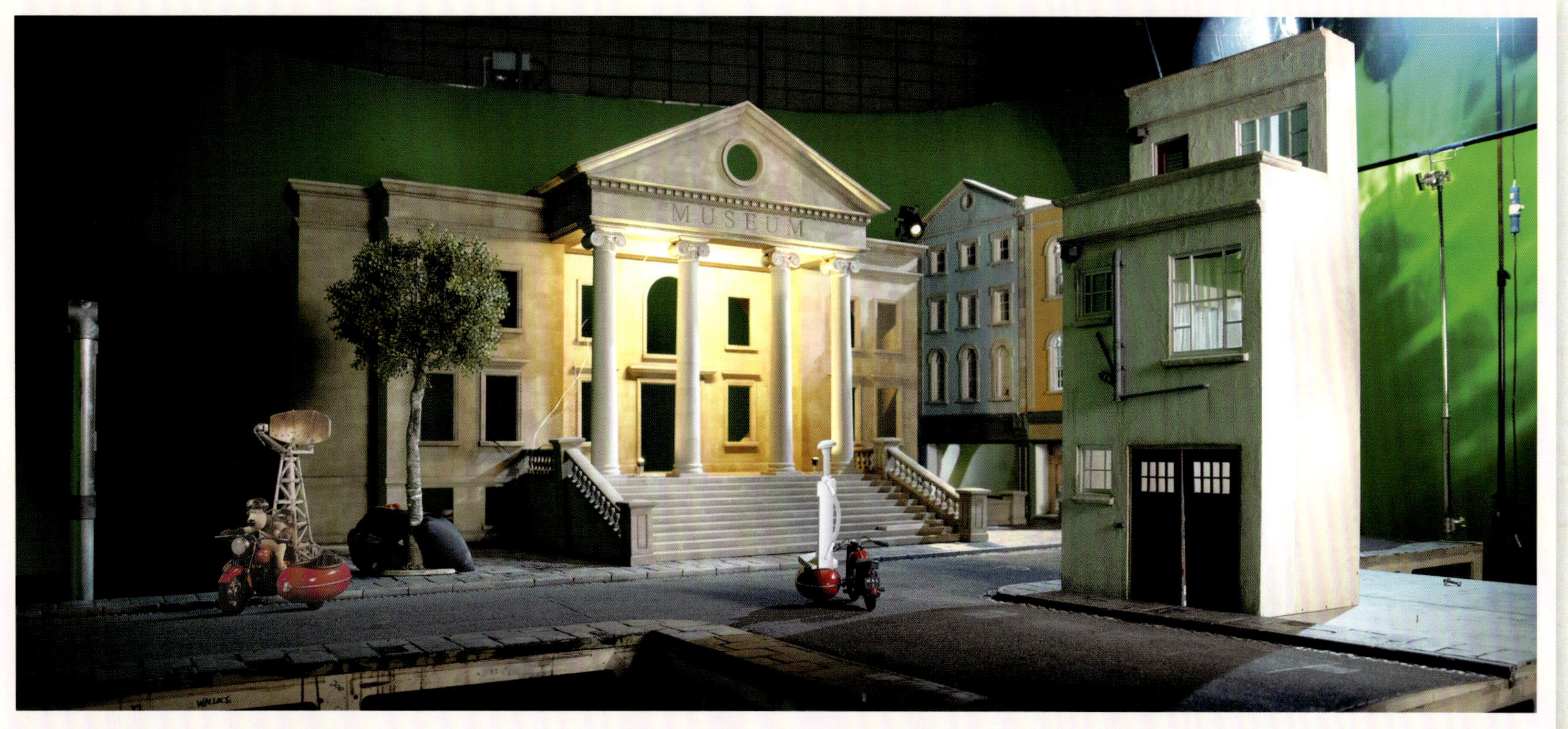

of the museum lobby," recalls art director for the scene, Richard Edmunds, "and we had to fill them with something interesting. We had a suit of armour we'd used before, but it was too big in scale, so we remade them. I thought it would be funny to have the chainmail look like a string vest and the codpieces like Y-fronts, so I proposed the idea to Nick and Merlin. They loved the idea, and Nick suggested the helmets could have sticky-out ears to make them more 'Wallace-like' so that's what we went with."

Prop maker Rosa Dodd describes the evolution of the helmets. "They were a lovely thing to make! Richard came up with the designs, which were a nod to Wallace with their big ears and woolly jumpers."

Even though the finished items are only

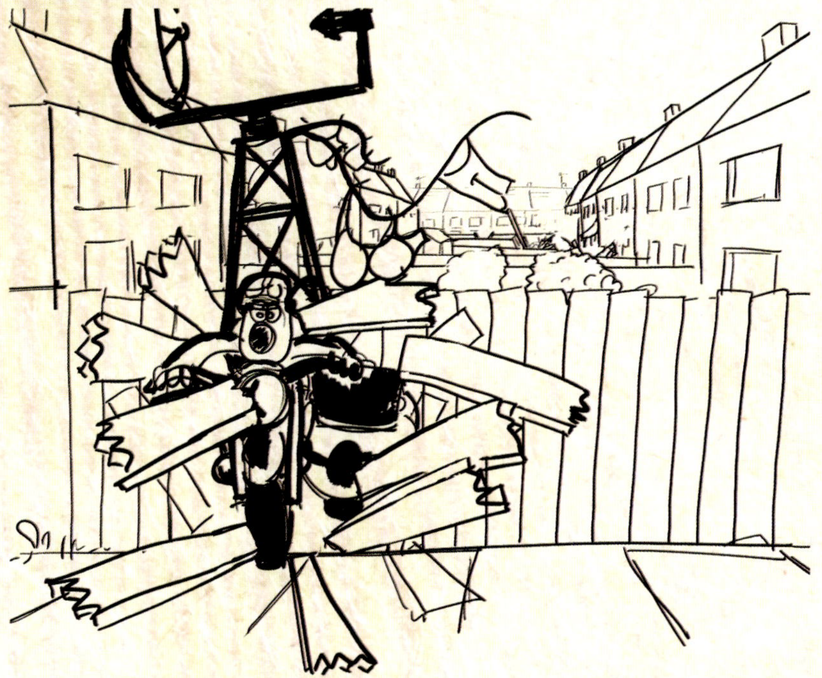

around six inches tall, a remarkable number of skills and techniques were required to create them. "They are on metal stands, so I need to solder steel to hang it all on," reveals Rosa. "I used a lot of plastic wood, which is really easy to shape and sand. I'd use the lathe saw to make the shape of the helmet, then I used the vac-forming machine to melt plastic and form it over the plastic wood to make a helmet. The vest, the pants – there are loads of vac-formed pieces. Then I needed something to use as the texture for the woolly jumper, and a dishcloth was the solution! There's always quite a bit of experimentation, so here I used a stretched dishcloth, which I dipped in fabric stiffener and wrapped around the former. We use loads of epoxy resin to do some of the additional sculpted detailing like the trims, the little rivets and the nose."

Then comes the painting. "It was mostly sprayed. We do a lot of dirtying down, picking out the detail. And we had some reference; I was looking at some armour references to base it on." The whole process takes about a week to make both the suits, even though the finished props will only be glimpsed in the background

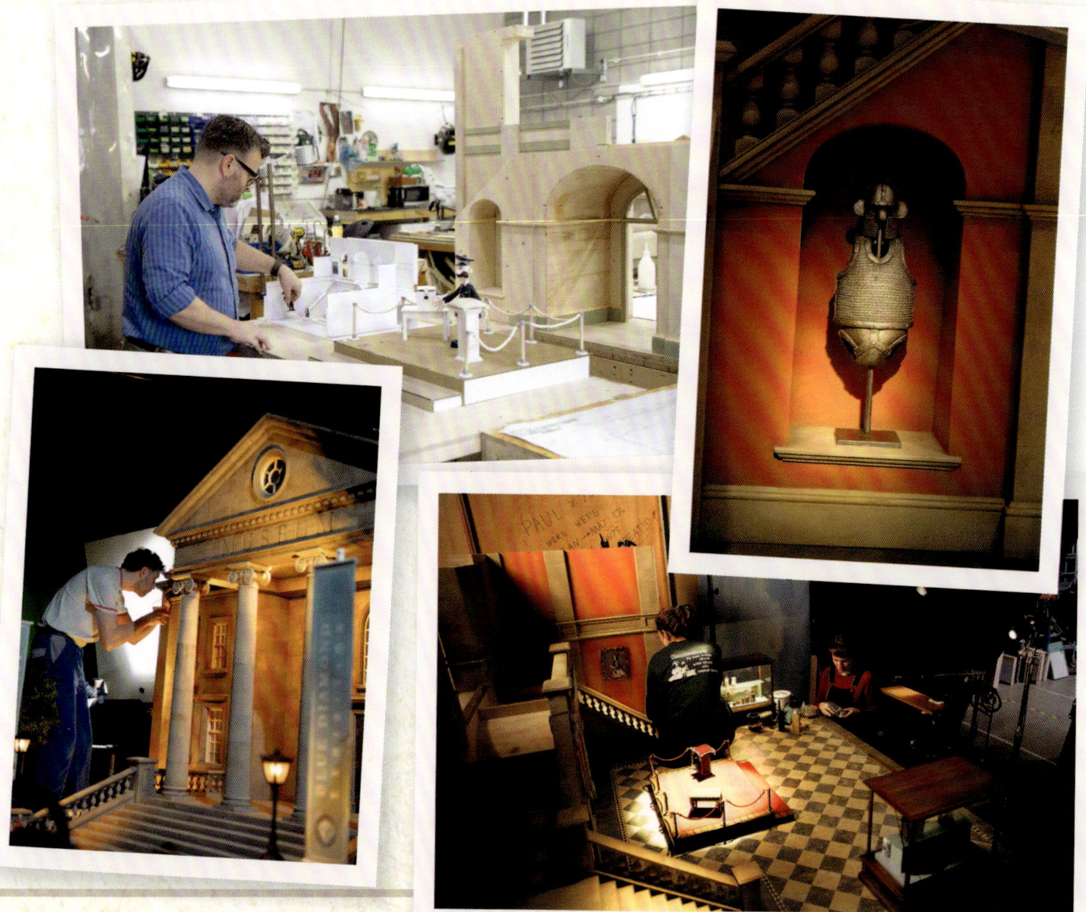

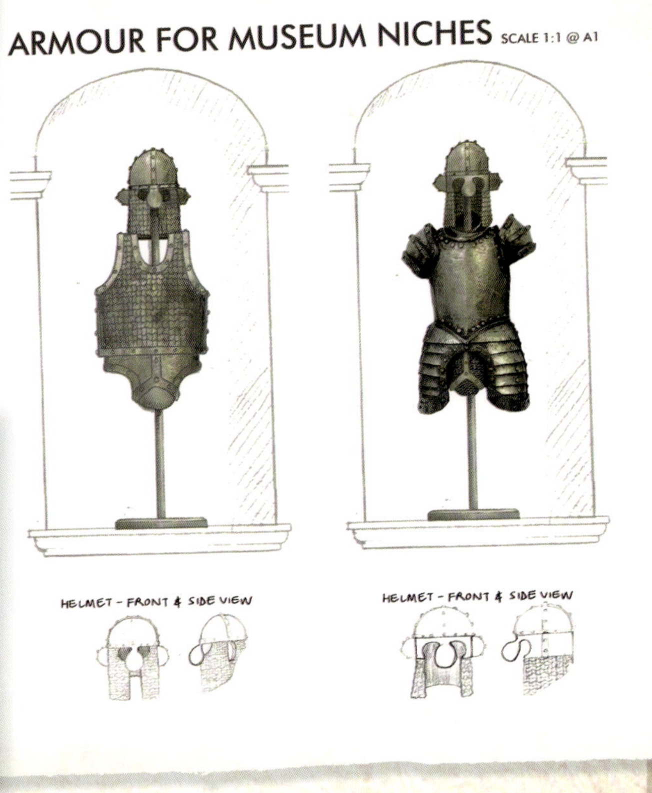

Below | Gavin Lines's messed-up masterpieces displayed on the walls of the museum - after Chalon, Munch and da Vinci.

Opposite top | Technical drawings by Richard Edmunds for the news crew's camera.

of a few shots. So viewers might require the use of freeze-frame to appreciate some of the finer details, such as the riveted underpants! "But that's the beauty of Aardman, isn't it?" says Rosa. "The fact that it's there."

Also adorning the walls of the museum are variations on well-known paintings by the likes of Canaletto and Munch, but given a special *Wallace & Gromit* twist. Like the armour, blink and you'll miss them, but the more eagle-eyed viewer may also spot a miniature of a canvas by Peter Crossingham – none other than Merlin's dad! – and even a cave painting featuring some familiar characters from Nick's last film…

The messed-up masterpieces are the work of graphic artist Gavin Lines, whose role encompasses producing the posters and newspapers that litter 62 West Wallaby Street, along with wallpaper, carpets, packaging – every element that requires some sort of graphic design. He has been part of the team since *Curse of the Were-Rabbit* and finds the possibilities for visual humour particularly appealing. "I get a chance to stretch my funny bone and add comedy to things," he explains. "Everything that I have to do, whether it's products on a shelf or a book cover or newspaper, is all done bespoke, so it's an opportunity to put a gag in everywhere I can. Anything can be funny: if it's a bottle of ketchup it can be funny, if it's a newspaper headline it can be funny, so I put as much humour as possible into everything I do. That's the company mandate – make sure that there's humour in everything."

While Gavin is a veritable fount of puns and visual gags, he also gets input from other members of the team. "I'll brainstorm ideas, I'll throw out a call to see if anyone has a funny suggestion for a jar of pickles or something, and

Opposite far right | Gavin Lines's Aardman-ised version of Wright's portrait of industrialist Richard Arkwright, Preston's (second) most famous son.

Opposite bottom | Technical drawings by Matt Perry for various elements of the museum set.

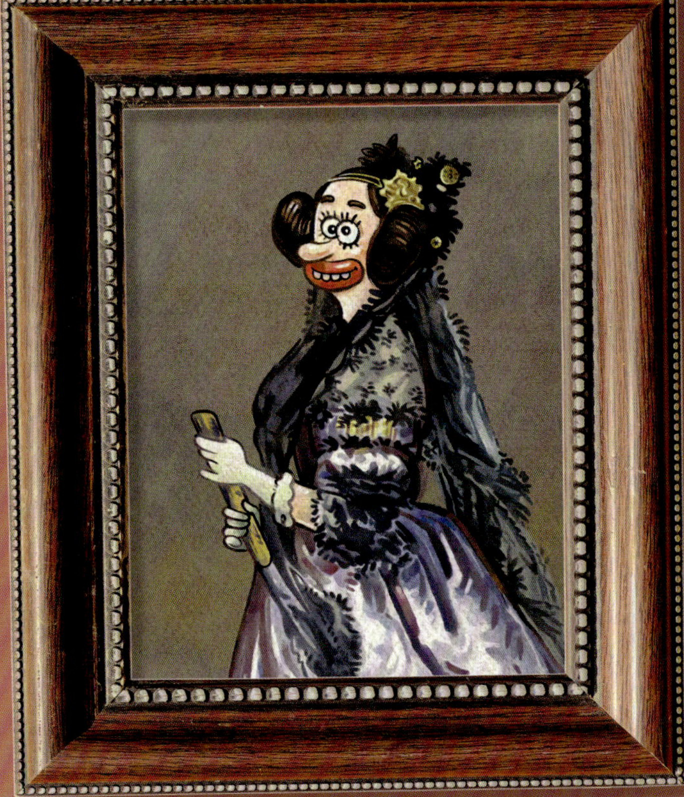

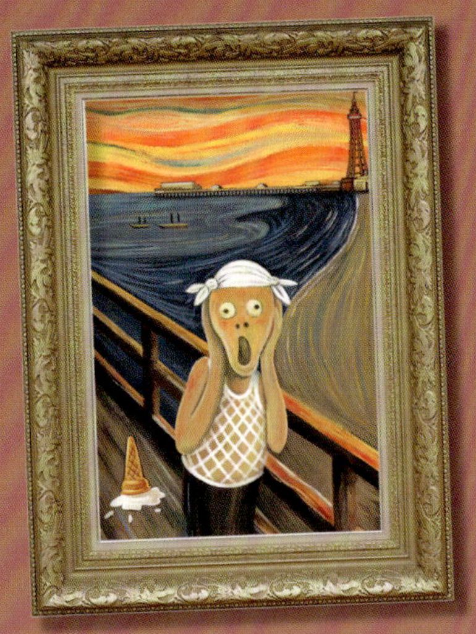

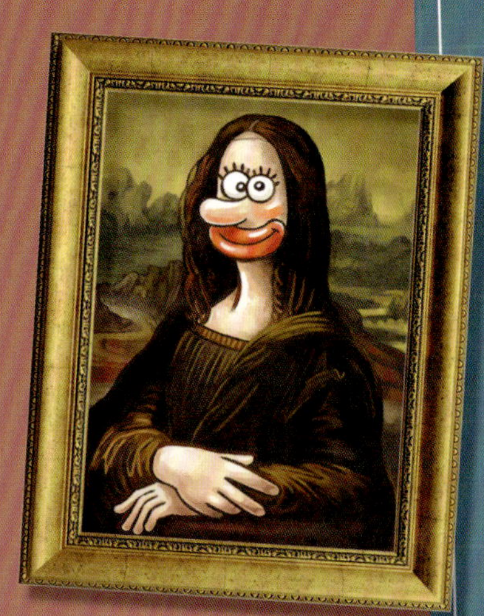

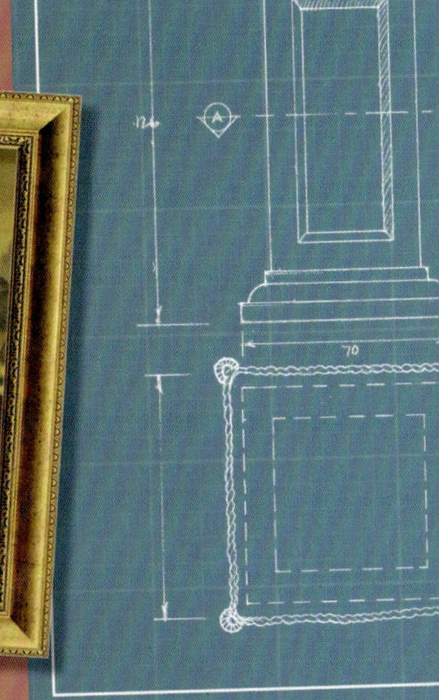

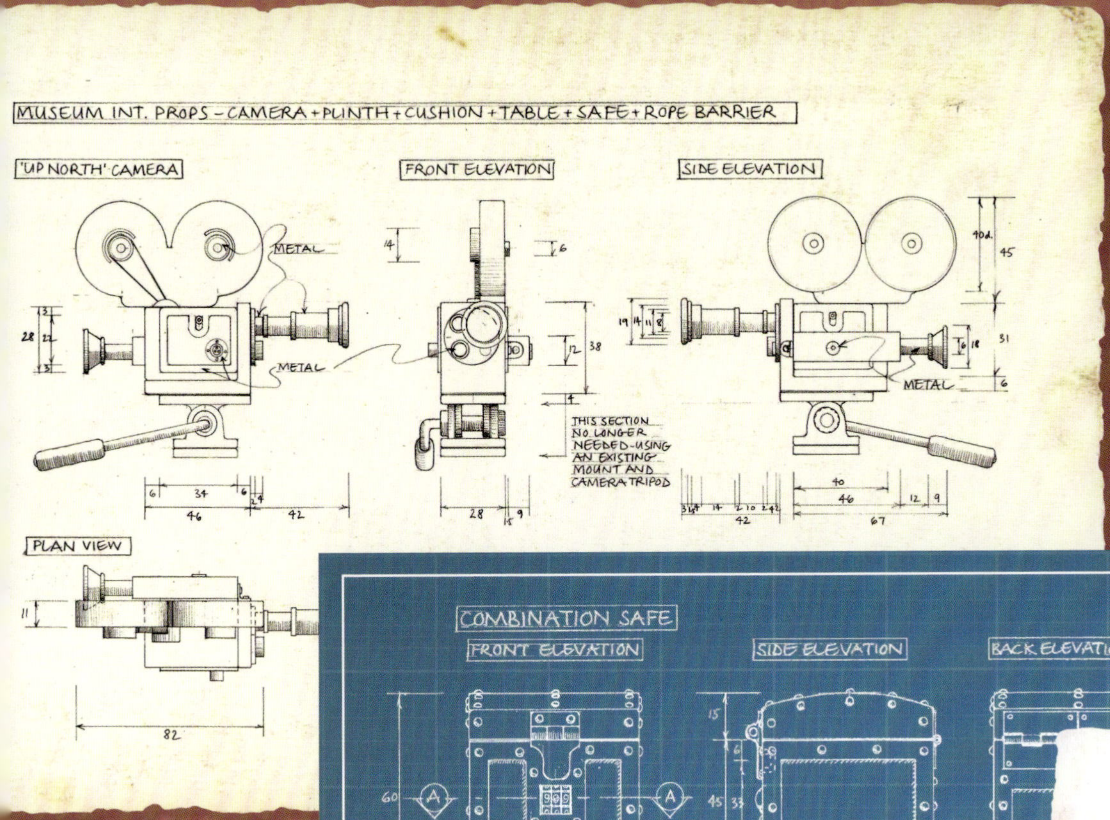

MUSEUM INT. PROPS – CAMERA + PLINTH + CUSHION + TABLE + SAFE + ROPE BARRIER

'UP NORTH' CAMERA

FRONT ELEVATION

SIDE ELEVATION

METAL

METAL

METAL

THIS SECTION NO LONGER NEEDED–USING AN EXISTING MOUNT AND CAMERA TRIPOD

PLAN VIEW

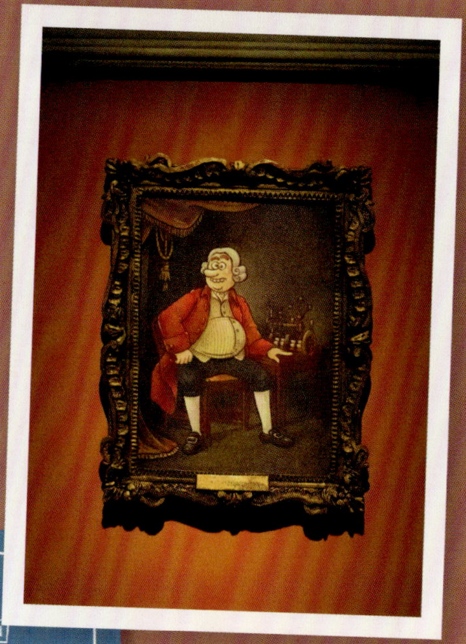

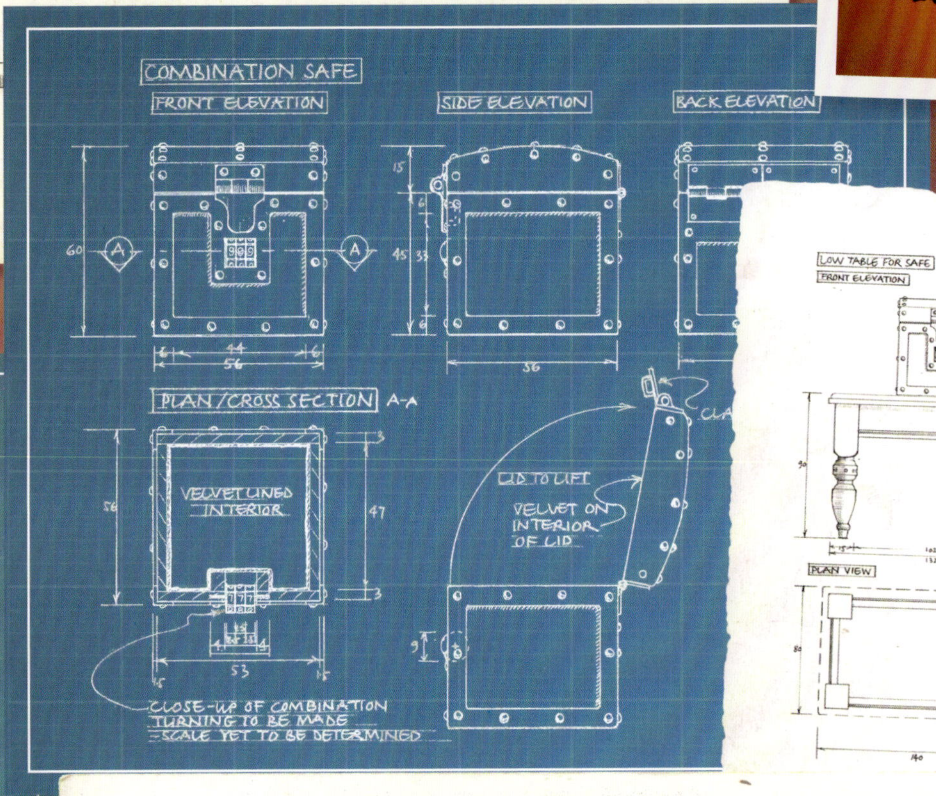

COMBINATION SAFE

FRONT ELEVATION

SIDE ELEVATION

BACK ELEVATION

PLAN / CROSS SECTION A-A

VELVET LINED INTERIOR

LID TO LIFT

VELVET ON INTERIOR OF LID

CLOSE-UP OF COMBINATION TURNING TO BE MADE –SCALE YET TO BE DETERMINED

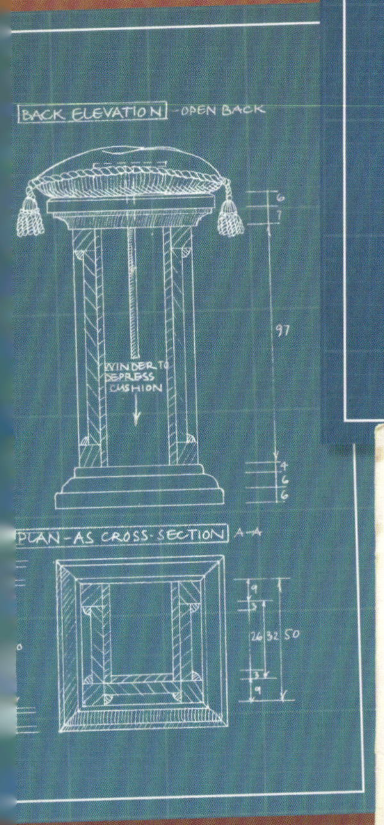

BACK ELEVATION –OPEN BACK

WINDER TO DEPRESS CUSHION

PLAN – AS CROSS SECTION A-A

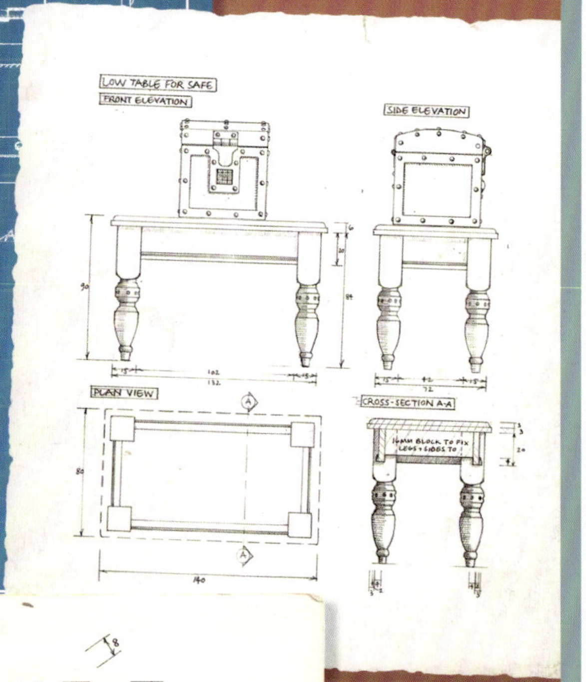

LOW TABLE FOR SAFE

FRONT ELEVATION

SIDE ELEVATION

PLAN VIEW

CROSS-SECTION A-A

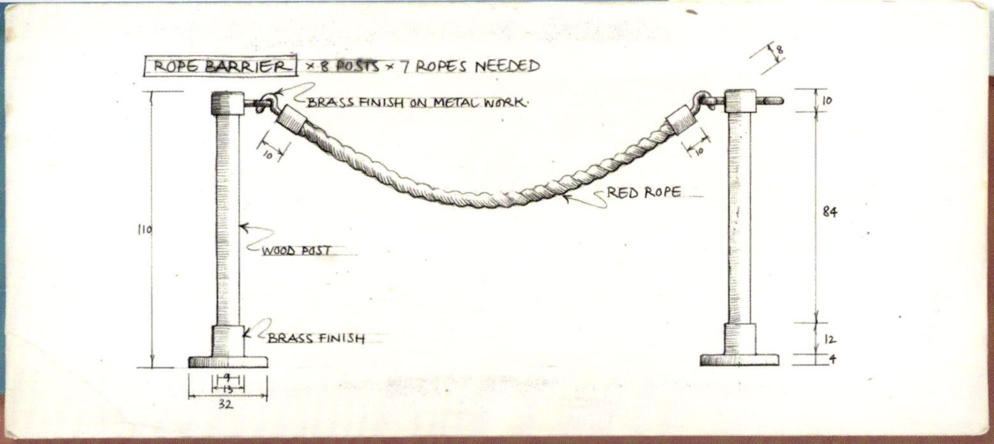

ROPE BARRIER ×8 POSTS ×7 ROPES NEEDED

BRASS FINISH ON METAL WORK

RED ROPE

WOOD POST

BRASS FINISH

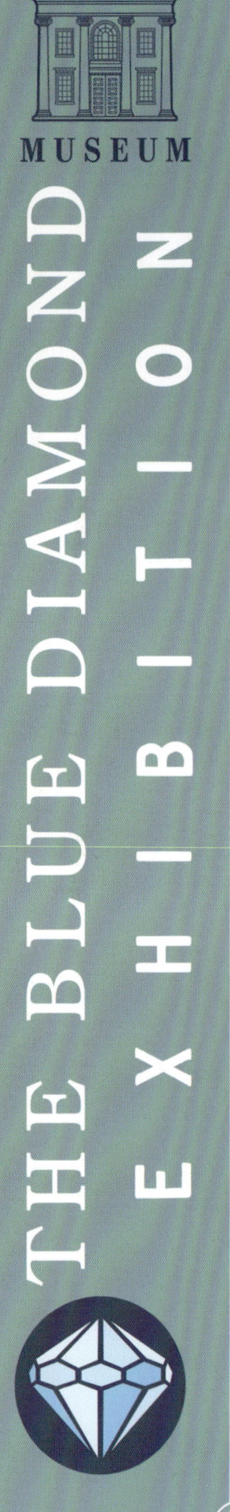

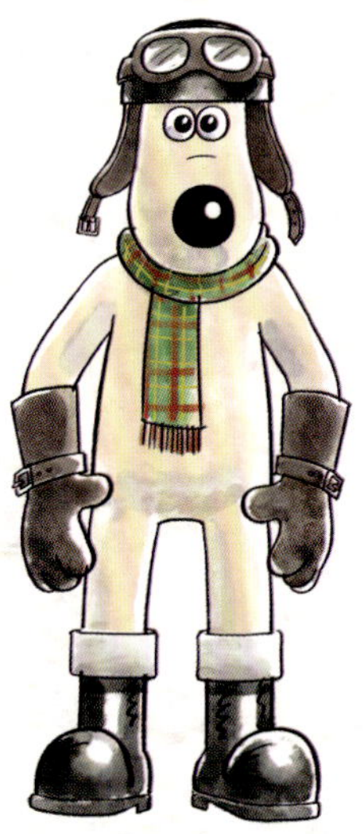

people will shout out ideas. Some gags come up from the script level, the storyboard guys will come up with ideas for gags. The directors give a lot of notes for the main 'hero' props, but with background details I feel they trust me. I've done it for a few years, and I get the company sense of humour. It's all very family friendly."

Having said that, Gavin does occasionally find that some of his ideas get vetoed. "It might not just be from the directors or the story team, it might come from the legal department saying 'We can't say that' or 'Do you want us to get clearance for that? It's going to cost money!' And we say, 'Don't worry, we'll just come up with a new idea.'"

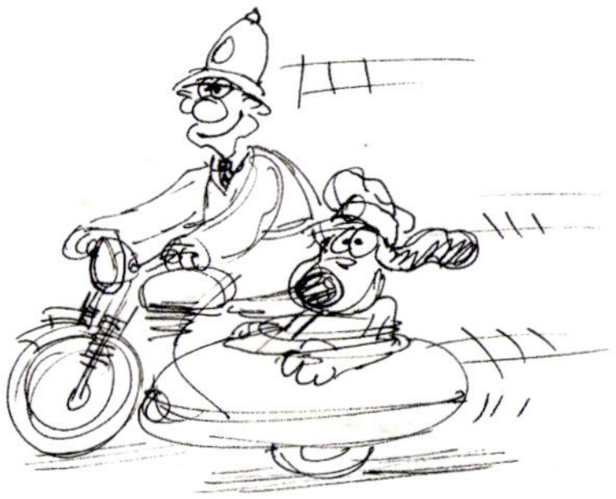

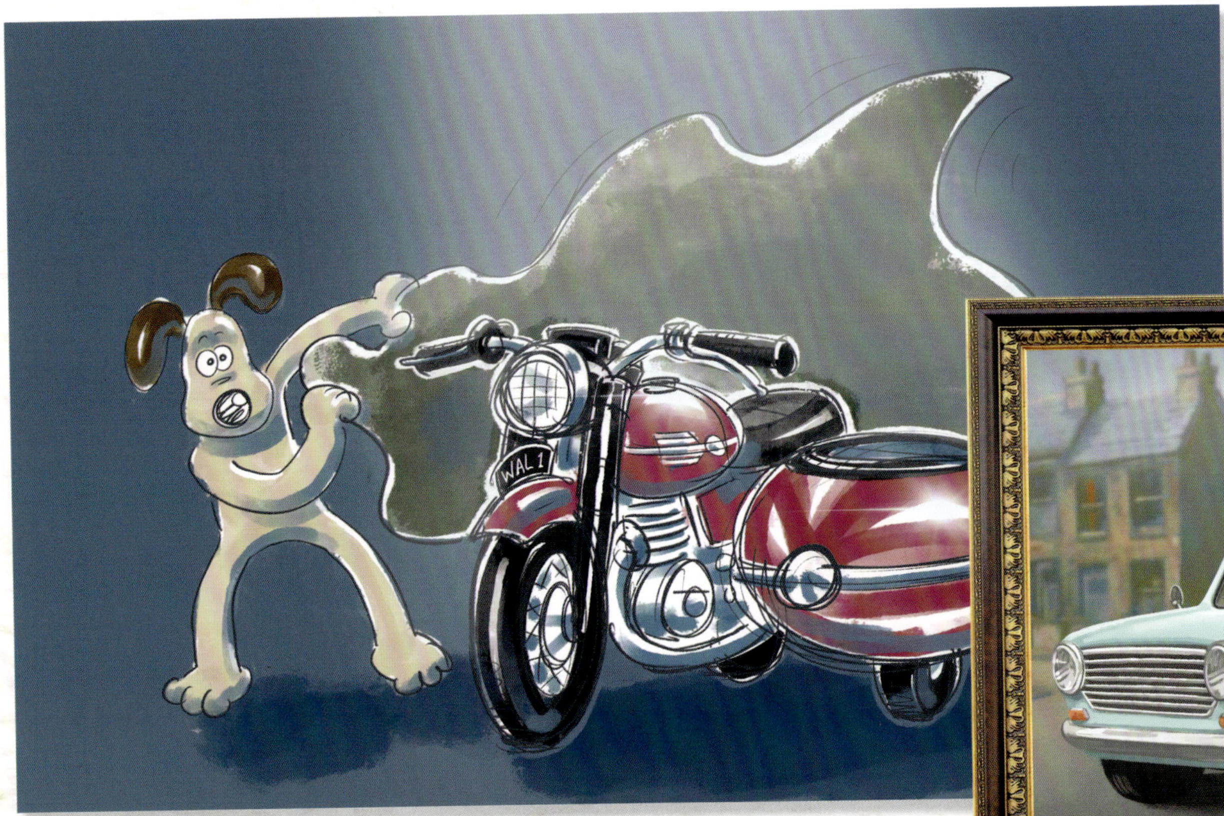

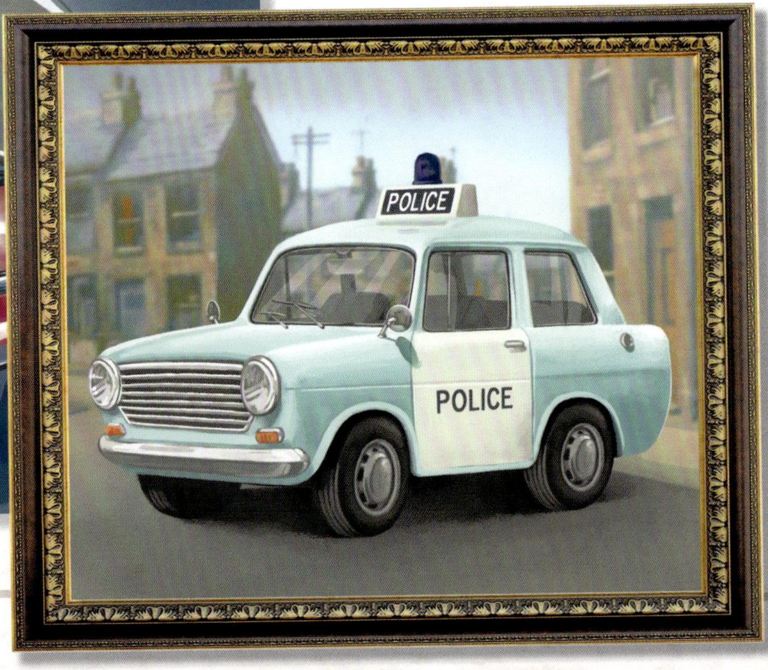

While many background gags go past in the blink of an eye, some of Gavin's visual comedy never gets seen at all. "Wallace at one point is reading a *Practical Inventor* magazine, and I did four or five spreads to go in it, and it's full of gags and funny images – character-based humour and wordplay. And all you see of it is one top right-hand corner, which is out of focus! That's a little advert for World of Grease, as it's an inventor's magazine. But it needed to be made, we need to fill out a magazine, so I'll just do it and make it funny because it makes me laugh while I'm doing it. And for the book

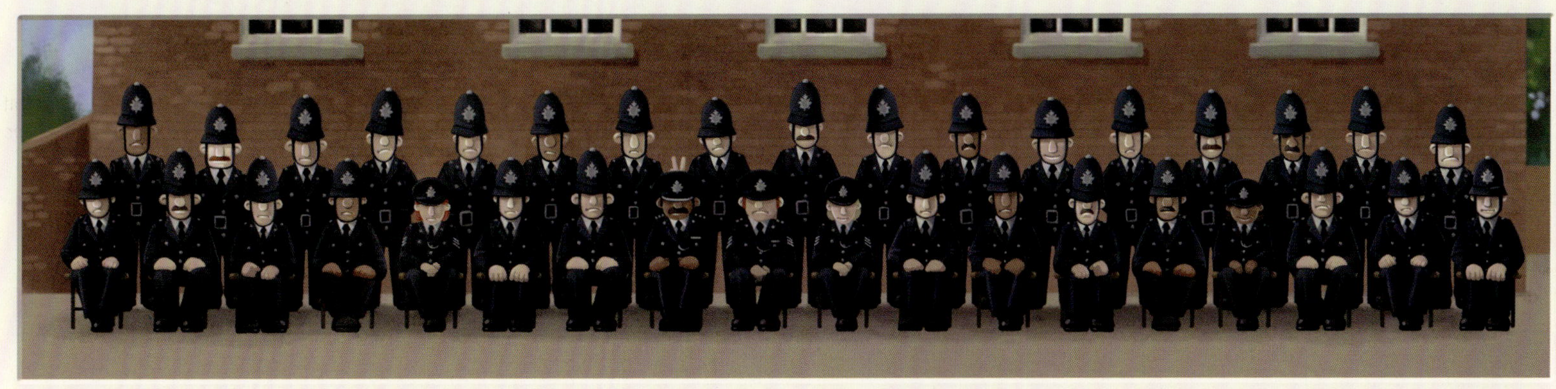

spines on Gromit's bookshelf I'll come up with a few pages of titles with dog puns on them, the legal department will pull out the ones where they're copyrighted, then we'll pass them on to the directors and they'll pick a few favourites. Then we'll get the book spine rubdowns [dry lettering transfers] ordered for the books."

But it's not just comedy that Gavin brings to the table – his compendious knowledge of graphics adds enormously to the period look of Wallace and Gromit's world. "Reference-wise, it's a case of looking at that Golden Age 50s and 60s packaging and design. It's the last great era of illustration, so it's nice to include that kind of reference."

His work is in evidence in almost every aspect of the movie, from the painted backdrop in the Penguin Pool right down to the litter on the floor of the enclosure. "Even with the boat chases, I did the graphics for the narrow boats. So my work may not be in every frame, but it's in every scene for sure."

There's a real sense of achievement when one of the team sees their gag make it to the final cut. "I managed to sneak in a book title, which was *A Room of One's Own* by Virginia Woof," recalls storyboarder Richard Phelan. "I was very proud that got through. It's always fun trying to get puns into Nick's films." Production meetings are also an opportunity to throw around ideas for gags. For example, there were intense discussions about what to put on the side of a cone delivery truck; after a few suggestions Merlin finally came up with 'Cone Brothers'!

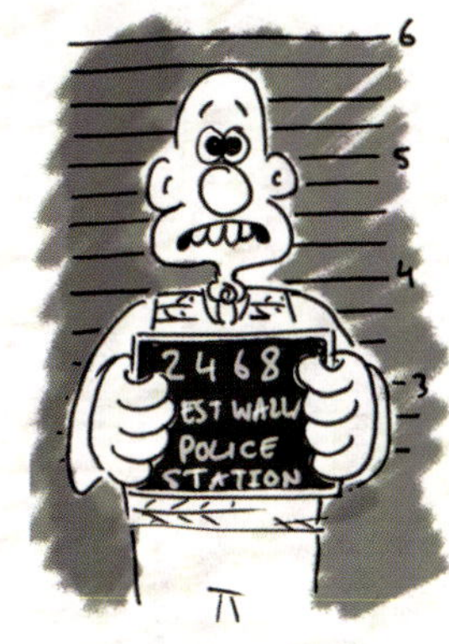

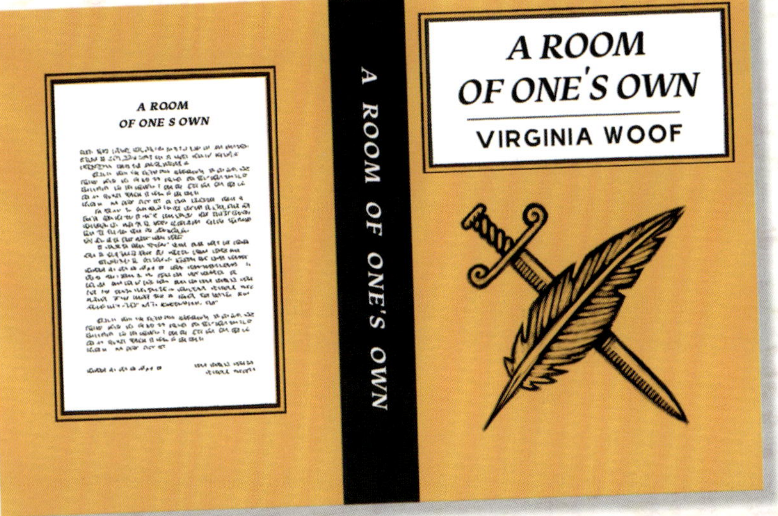

The 2D graphics used for Norbot's robo-vision also allowed Gav Strange to pepper the shots with visual humour. "Norbot's vision is reminiscent of '80s movies like *Terminator* or *Tron*: simple, effective graphics, glowing single colours. So as Norbot's scanning this stuff you have things like 'Garden Shed: Permanent Arachnid Dwelling, Non-Systematic Storage Facility'. The fact that the team are free and open for you to suggest something is fantastic."

Nick and Merlin's openness to ideas was particularly exciting for Gav. "Early on, when the hacking scene was being boarded," he recalls, "and Feathers changes Norbot's core protocol, originally he deletes GOOD and types EVIL. But I said, flippantly, 'Wouldn't it be funny if he selected from a drop-down menu', and Nick went 'Ah, that's a really nice idea'. When I next saw the board, there was the drop-down menu! That was a really special moment for me."

The virtual-reality simulation of the workings of Norbot's brain provided Gav with another opportunity. "Nick wanted to search around the brain and have gags on every level. So I've come up with ideas which we can replace or whatever, he wasn't super-prescriptive – we've got 'A Little Nervous System' or 'Short-Term Mem…', just these little silly things. They don't need to be there, but it all adds to the joy of the project."

He even managed to include a shout-out to his kids. "I've snuck their names into the sequence because you need to fill the screen with code all the time. It's super quick, but after all this technobabble you get 'Setting up the virtual matrix module', followed by my son's name and his date of birth. And my daughter and her

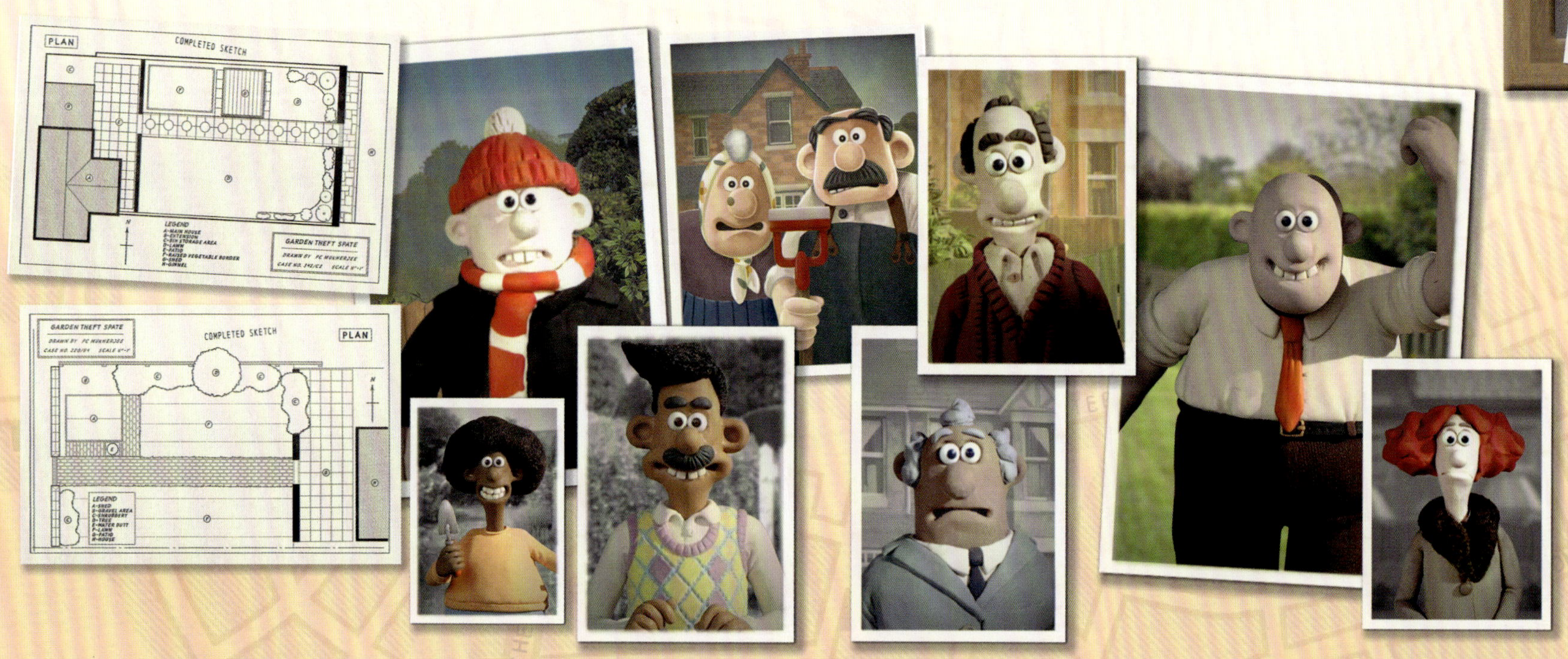

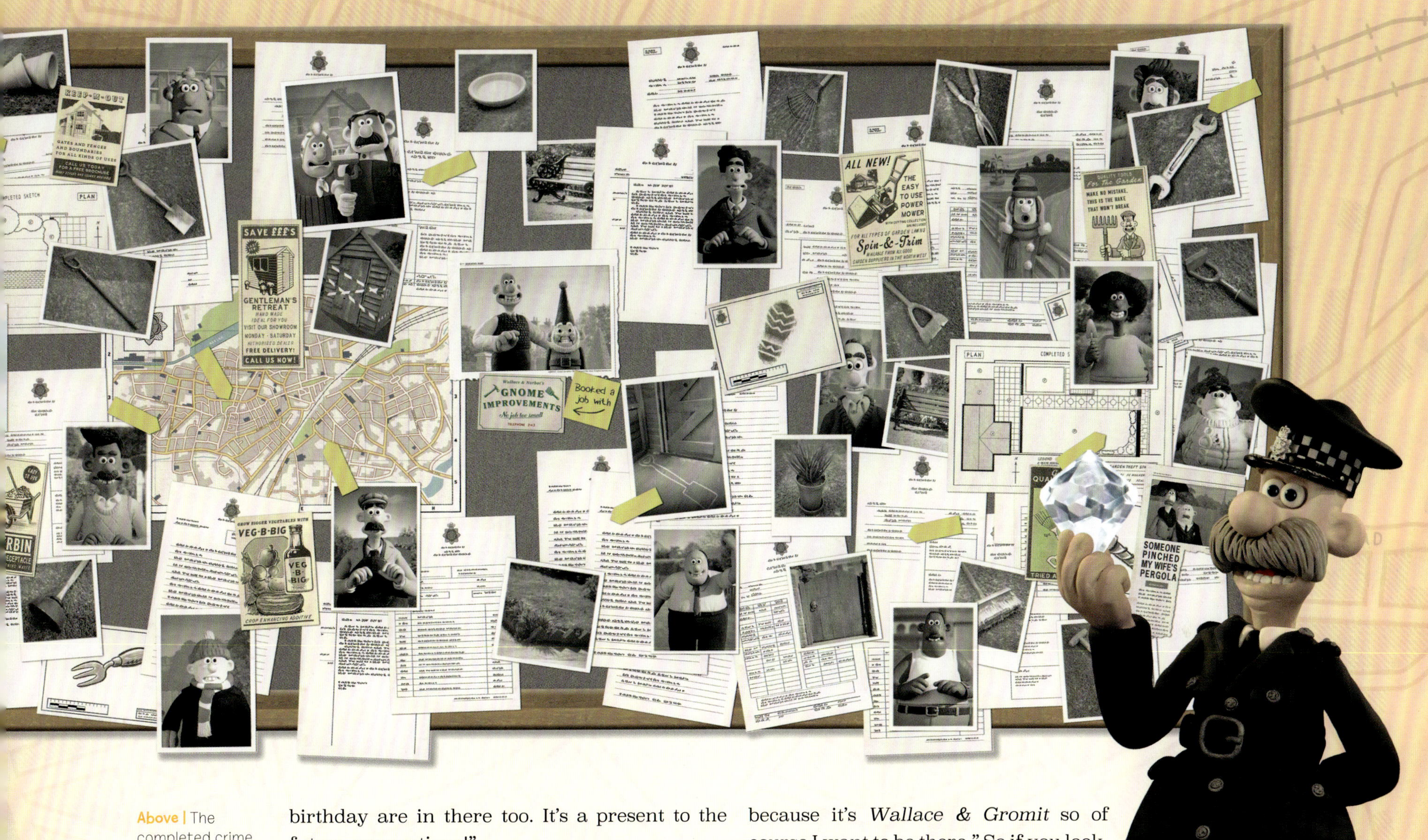

birthday are in there too. It's a present to the future generations!"

There are even some gags that work on a subliminal level, such as when Raul Eguia was animating the rubber glove hacking the computer keyboard. "I wanted to type a message like RAUL IS HERE," he explains, "but I couldn't do it because not all the keys were animatable. So I started with EVIL because the scene is about Feathers trying to turn the Norbot into an evil robot. Then I thought of adding my name because it's *Wallace & Gromit* so of course I want to be there." So if you look closely, you'll see the keyboard spell out 'EVIL RAUL'. And coincidentally, Raul also included a hidden message for his son. "I also had the animatable keys to type my son's name, so we are both there if someone wants to look at it frame by frame. He's only two years old now, but I thought it would be something to tell him when he's bigger: 'That's you there!'"

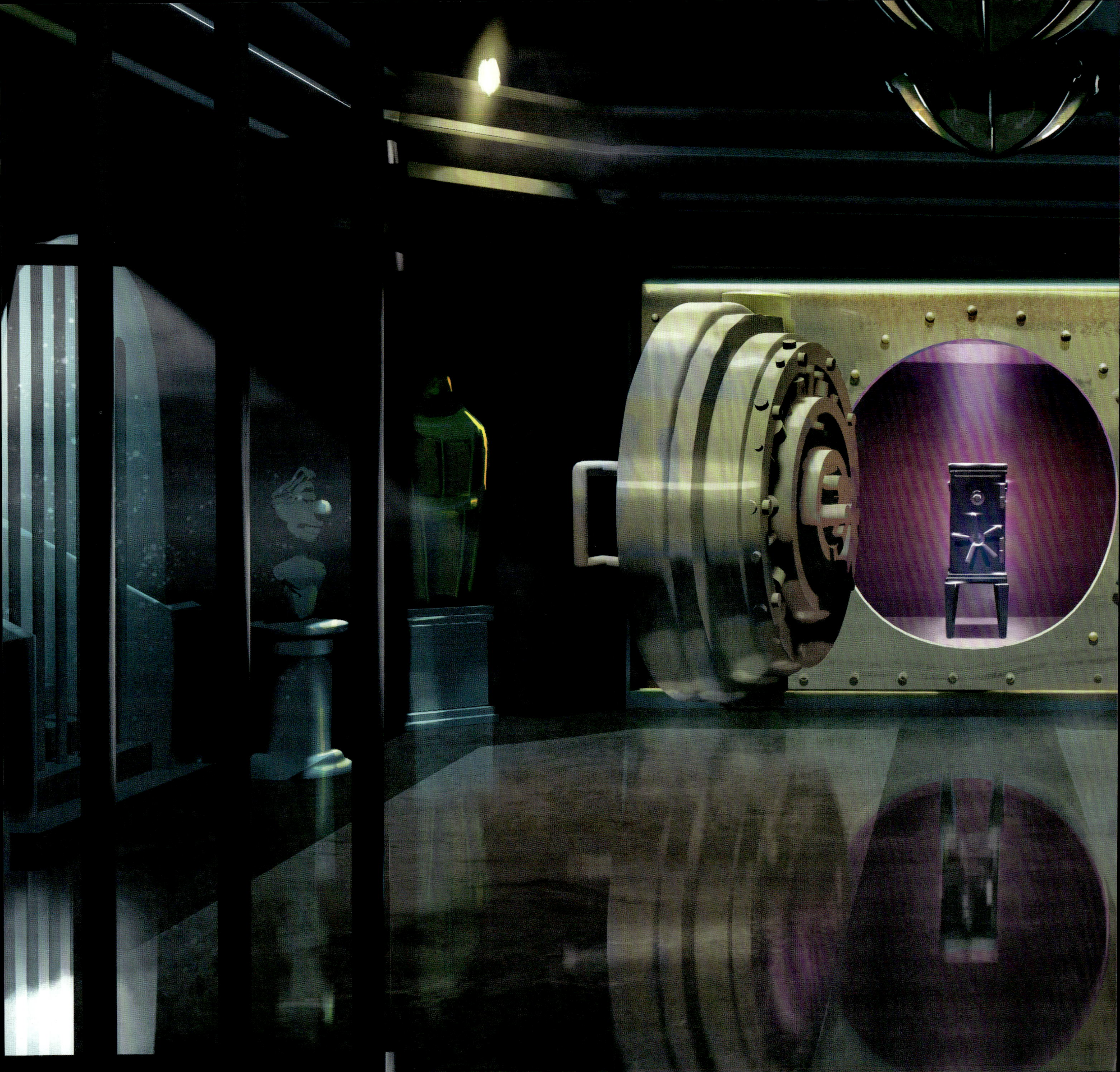

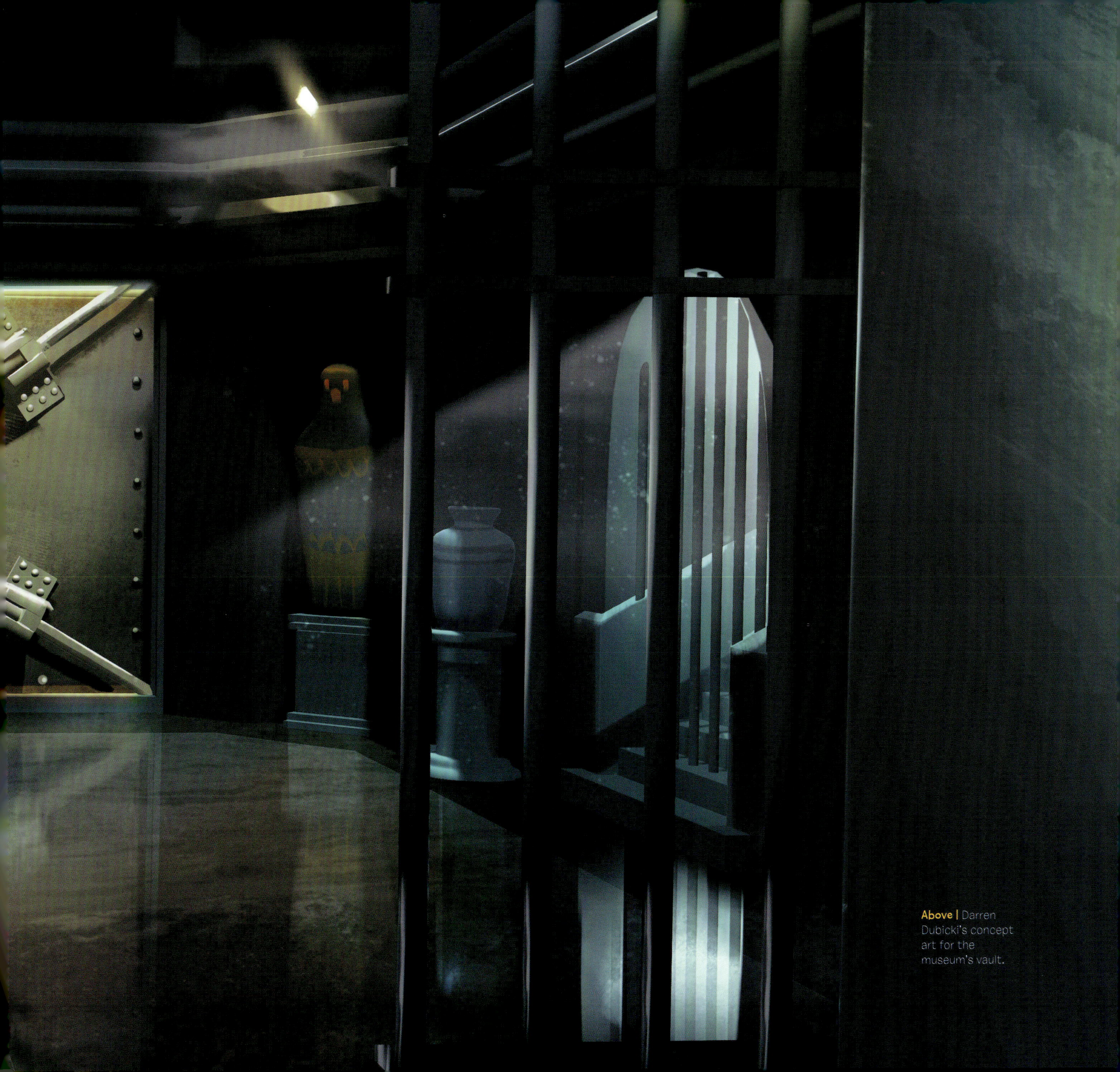

Above | Darren Dubicki's concept art for the museum's vault.

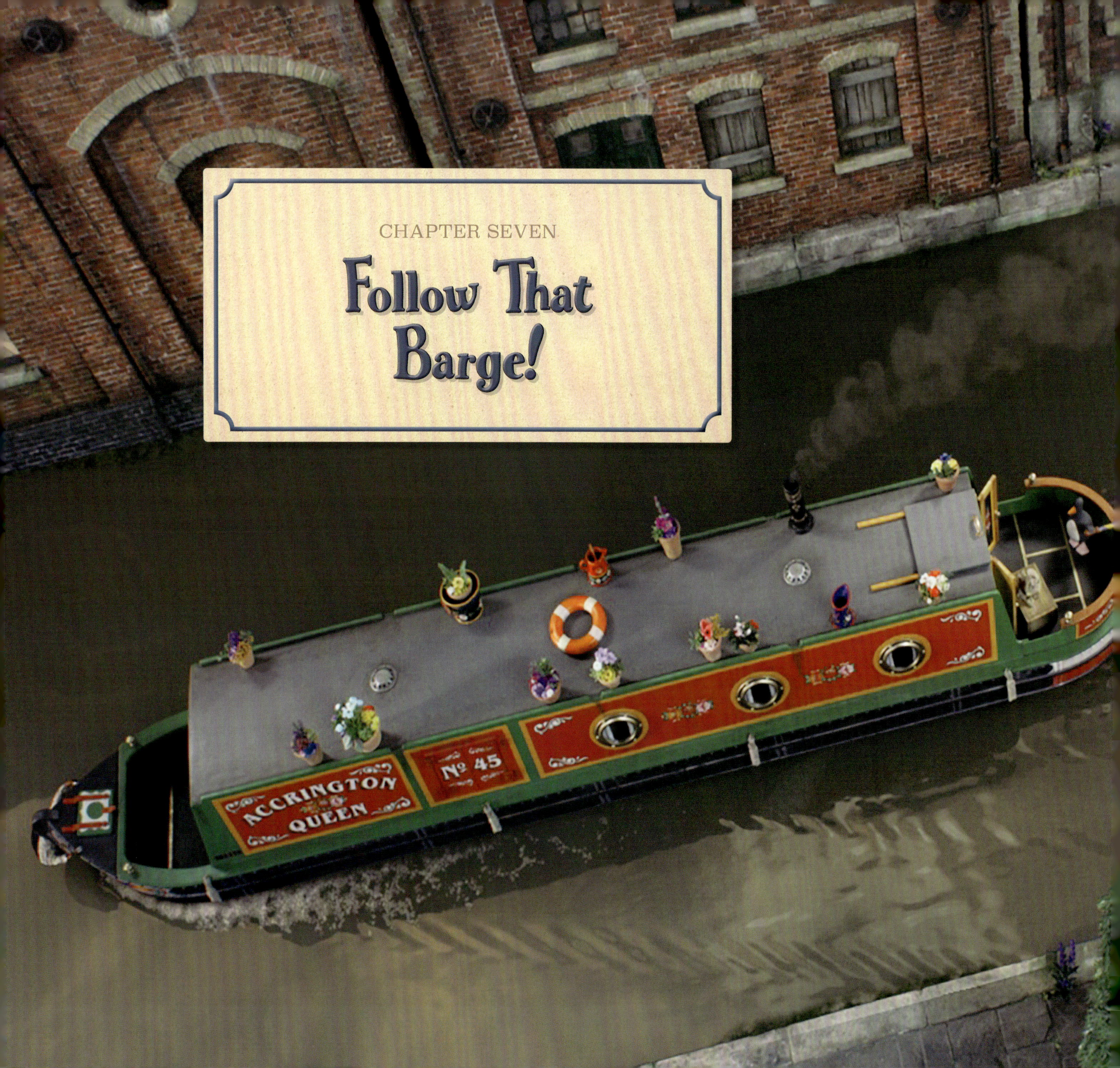
CHAPTER SEVEN
Follow That Barge!
ACCRINGTON QUEEN
Nº 45

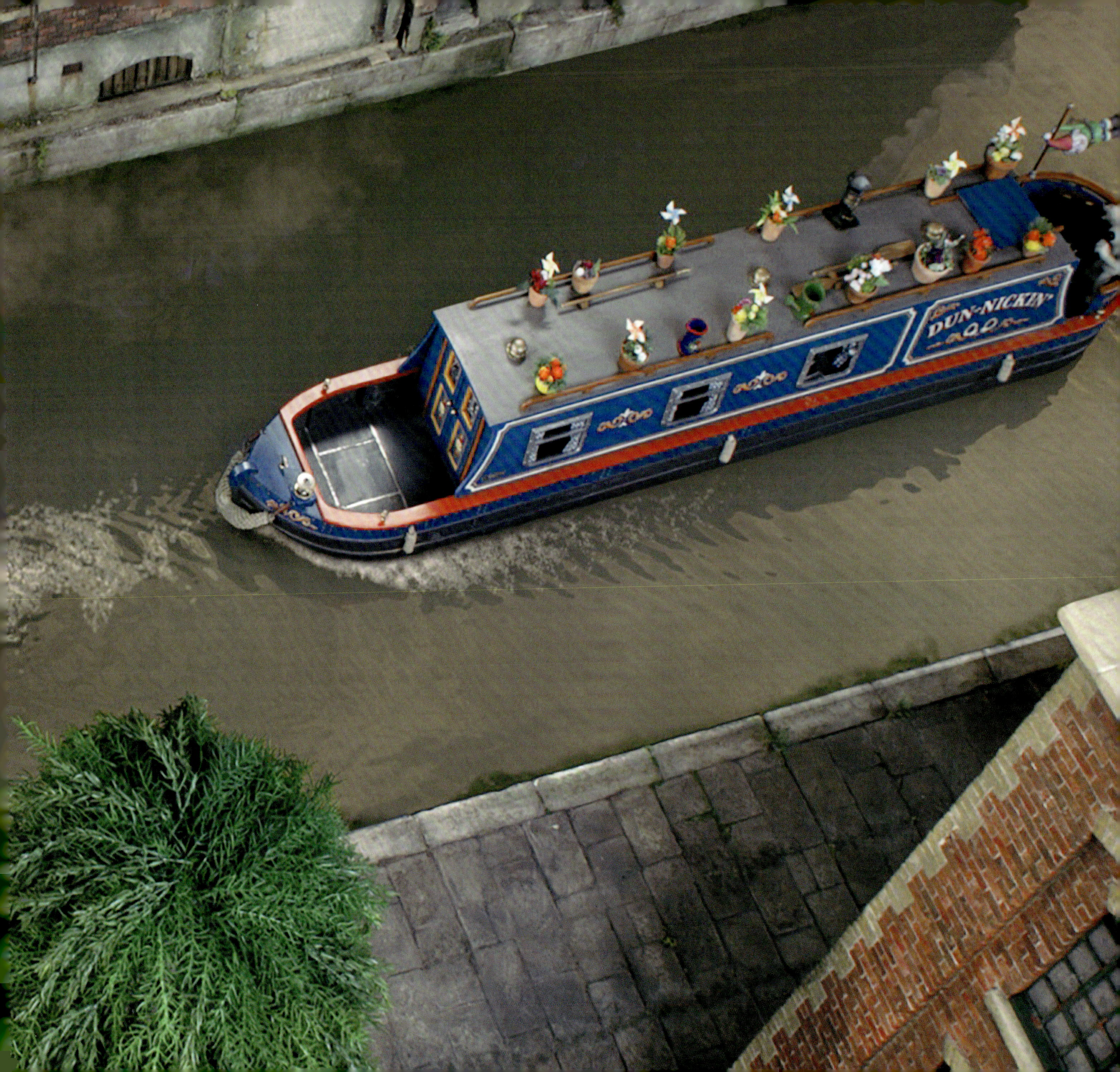

"DUN-NICKIN"

Follow That Barge!

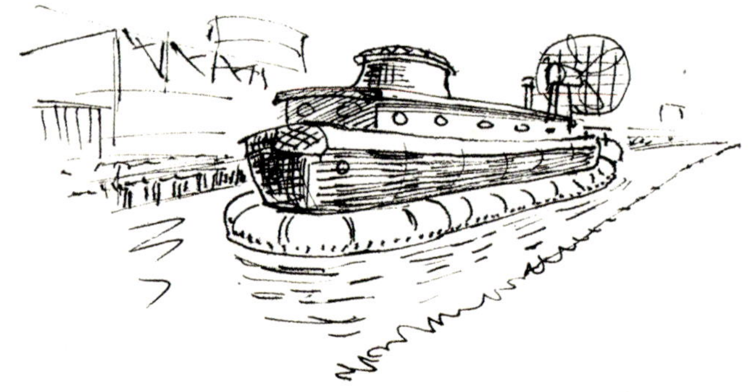

THE *WALLACE & GROMIT* MOVIES ARE renowned for their climactic chases, none more so than *The Wrong Trousers*, where Gromit desperately lays down track in front of a speeding toy train. Given that *Vengeance Most Fowl* is in many ways a companion piece to that film, how did Nick plan to top this now-classic sequence? With nothing less than the world's first slow chase scene, of course! "I've for a long time wanted to do something with British canals," he reveals, "the quaintness of it all and the quiet backwater feeling, the genteel lifestyle – but turning it into a high-octane Hollywood chase! It's a James Bond-type speedboat race on canal longboats. That idea had been floating about for quite a while, and when we had the idea of doing this as a 70-minute film it suddenly gave scope for a much bigger chase than could fit into a half-hour."

But the canal setting presented a new set of challenges for the art team. With its long

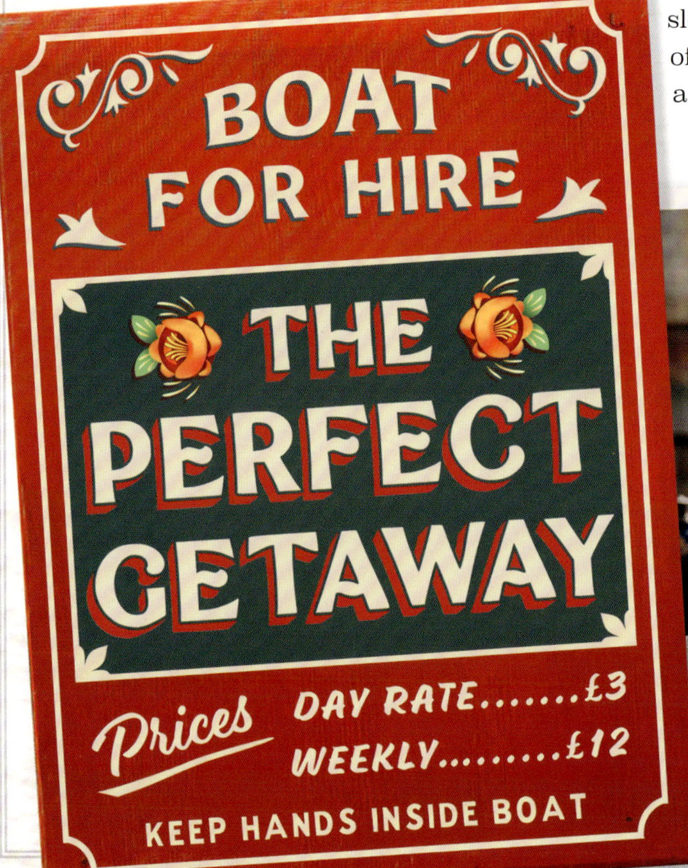

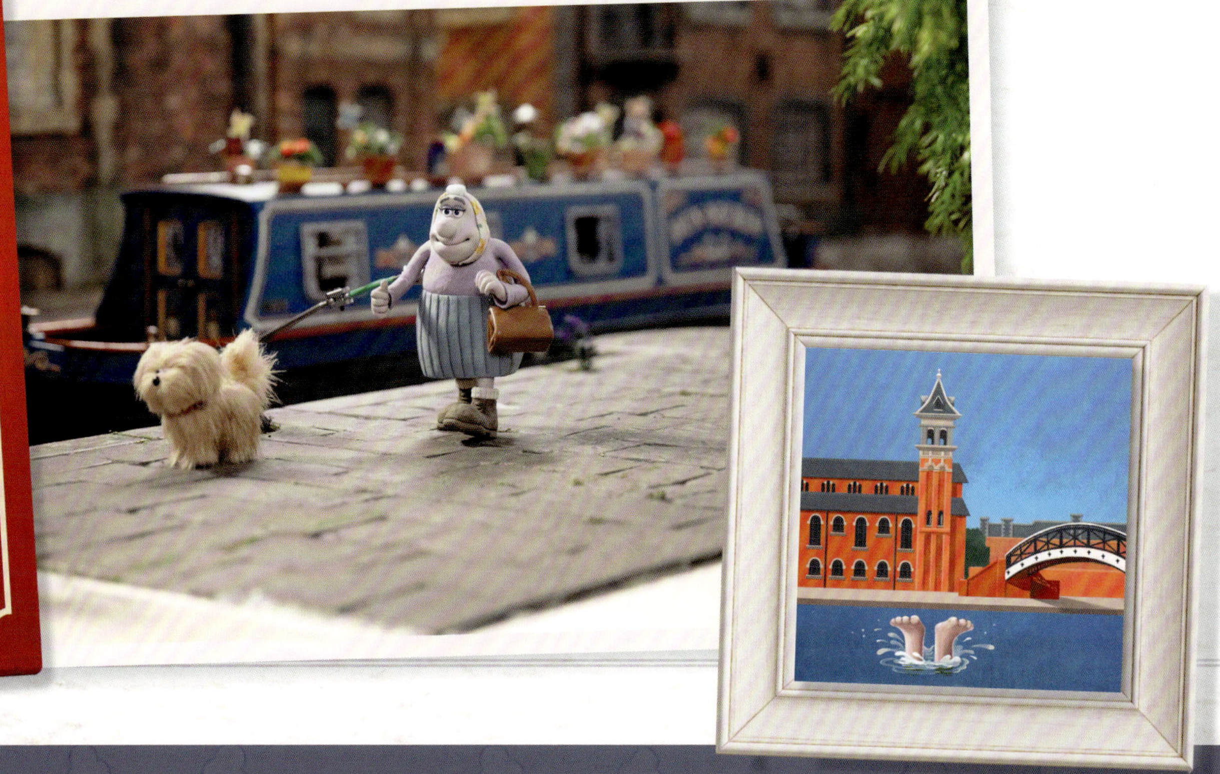

Above | Early Nick Park sketch for a hover-barge.

Bottom left | Graphic art by Gavin Lines for the sign that inspires Feathers's escape plan.

Bottom centre | The world's first slow chase scene.

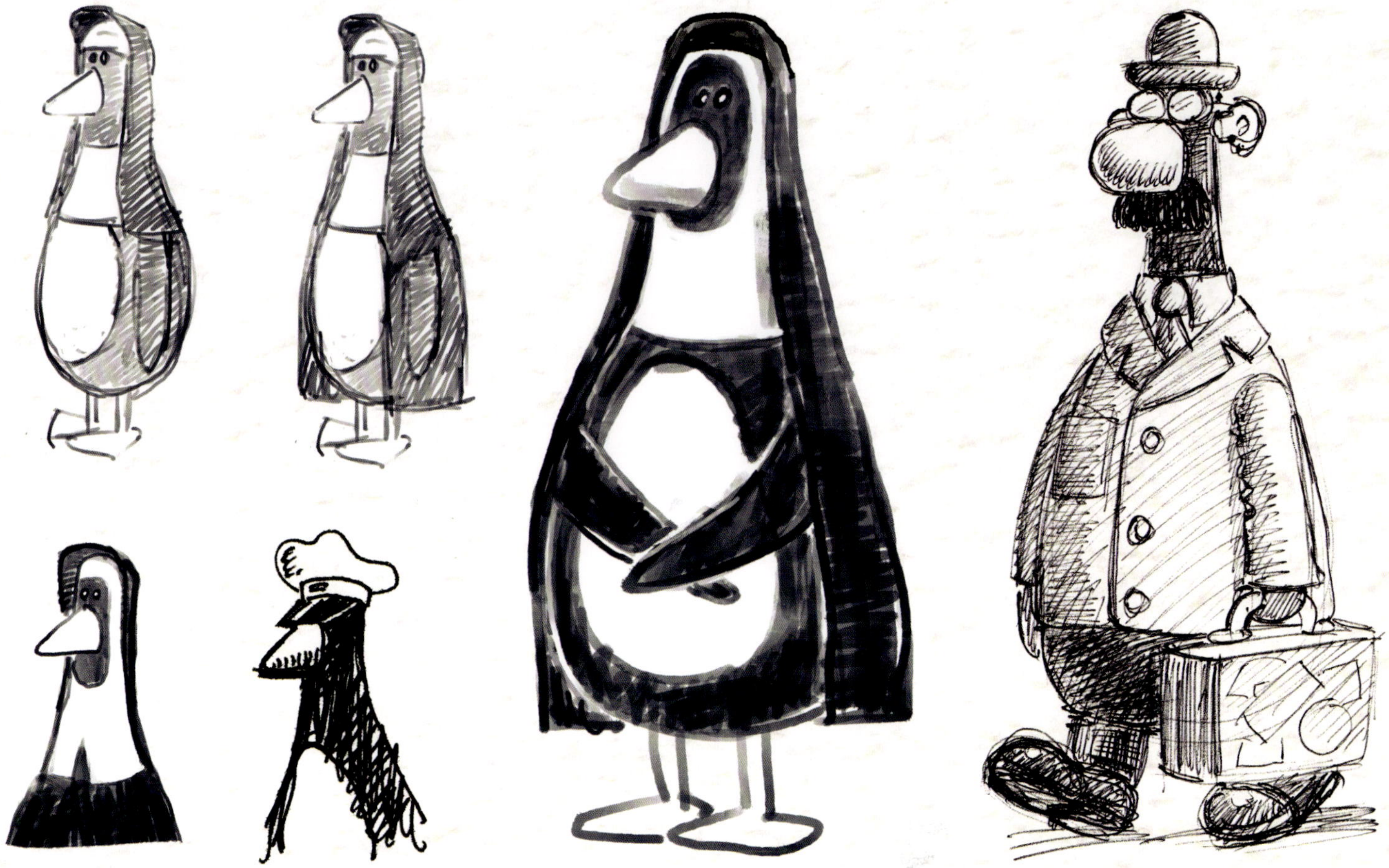

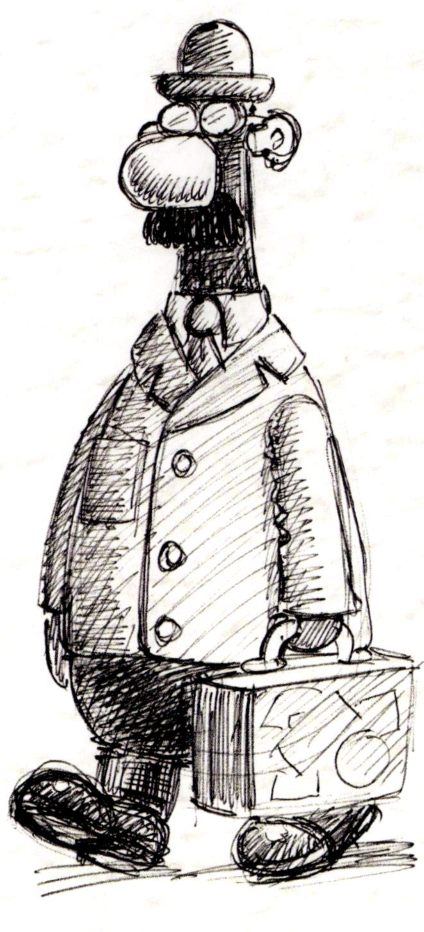
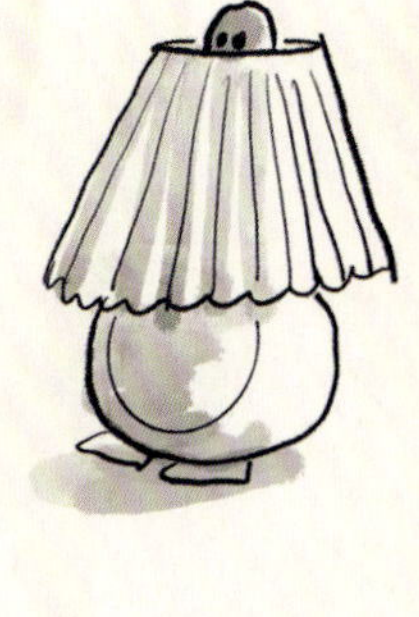
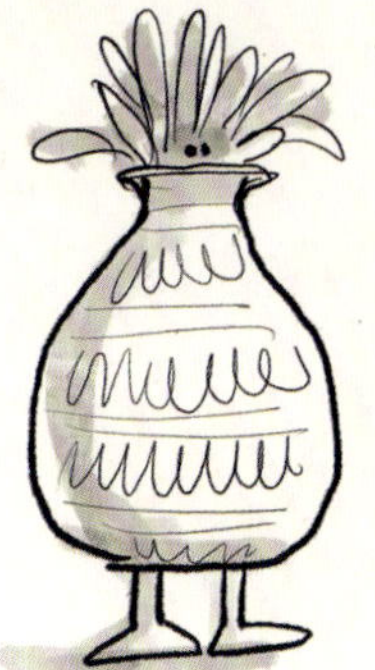
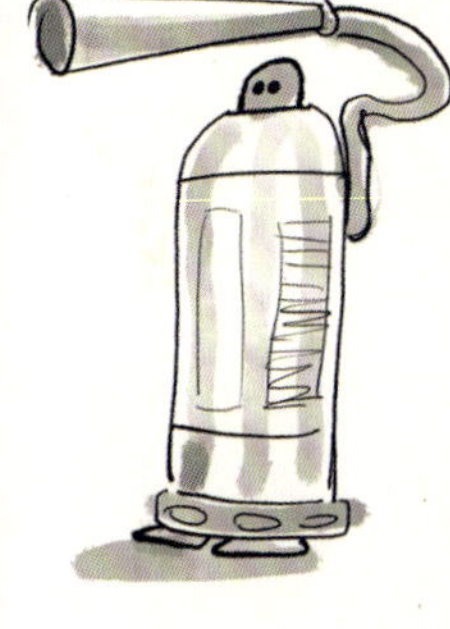
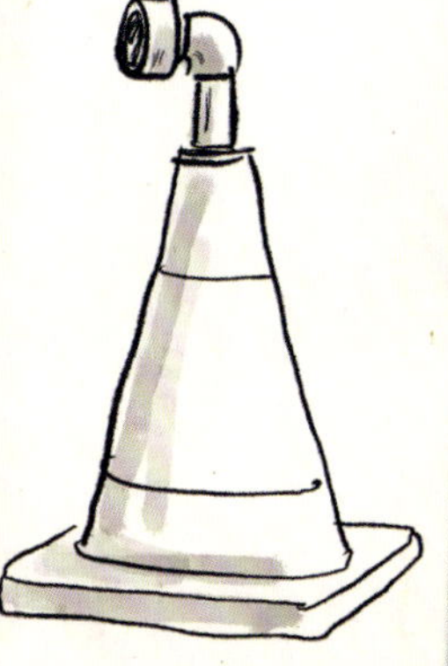

vistas and constantly changing backgrounds, it was exactly the wrong sort of sequence to attempt in stop-motion, where the sets have more in common with theatre than cinema – not to mention the amount of water involved, which is normally a no-go area for this style of animation. While using CG backgrounds and effects would nowadays be the conventional way to solve these problems, that would have gone against the production's ethos of trying to create as much of the movie as possible on the studio floor. Not only that, but the vast sets required would never fit within the confines of the physical studio and a budget which, while not ungenerous, was not on the full Hollywood scale of *Curse of the Were-Rabbit*.

If anyone was going to solve these logistical problems, producer Richard Beek was confident production designer Matt Perry was the man. "Matt is a logistical genius when it comes to putting things in order and working out how to get the most bang for your buck for sets," he explains.

Matt outlines the process used to achieve the near-impossible. "Nick was asking for what he wanted; his brief was at times quite tight, sometimes not so tight – it gets tighter the closer it gets to the studio floor.

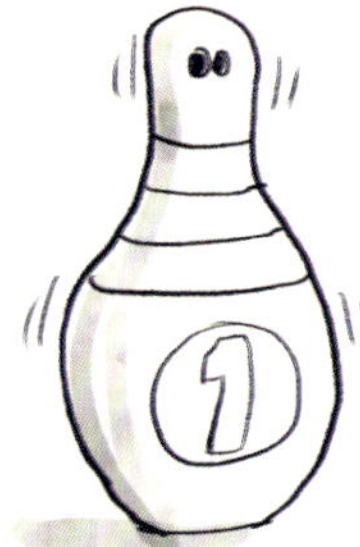

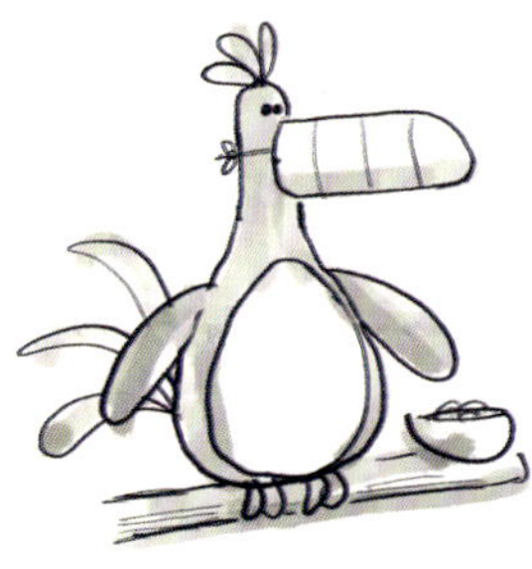

So I scribble away with sketches, then I've gone into building rough mock-ups in cardboard, then I go into sizing it, and then I go into previz [visualising the scenes on computer to create an idea of how they will look before filming]. For me to get any sense of the size that these are going to need to be I have to do a crude version in CG, just basic blocks."

The solution he hit on was to create a modular set that could be reassembled to create different locations along the canal. "I've designed it in a way that it's contained, so we're not out in big open countryside," he explains. "We've built the two sides of the canal, and every now and again there's a corner. We're using the same kit of parts that make this set to create all the locations. Once we get past the boatyard we make it more rural and we put loads of fences up on one side. Then we might use other bits of scenery that we've got around, or we'll purpose-build some to make it feel like we've moved out of the city. The first part will have greenhouses so it feels like allotments on one side, then there's a street running alongside it. But that will all go away and we'll end up in countryside for the final part of the chase."

But how did the team approach the problem of the ever-changing backgrounds as the canal winds its way through the town and out into the country? "We're stepping into a more technologically advanced production process here because the sets physically don't fit,"

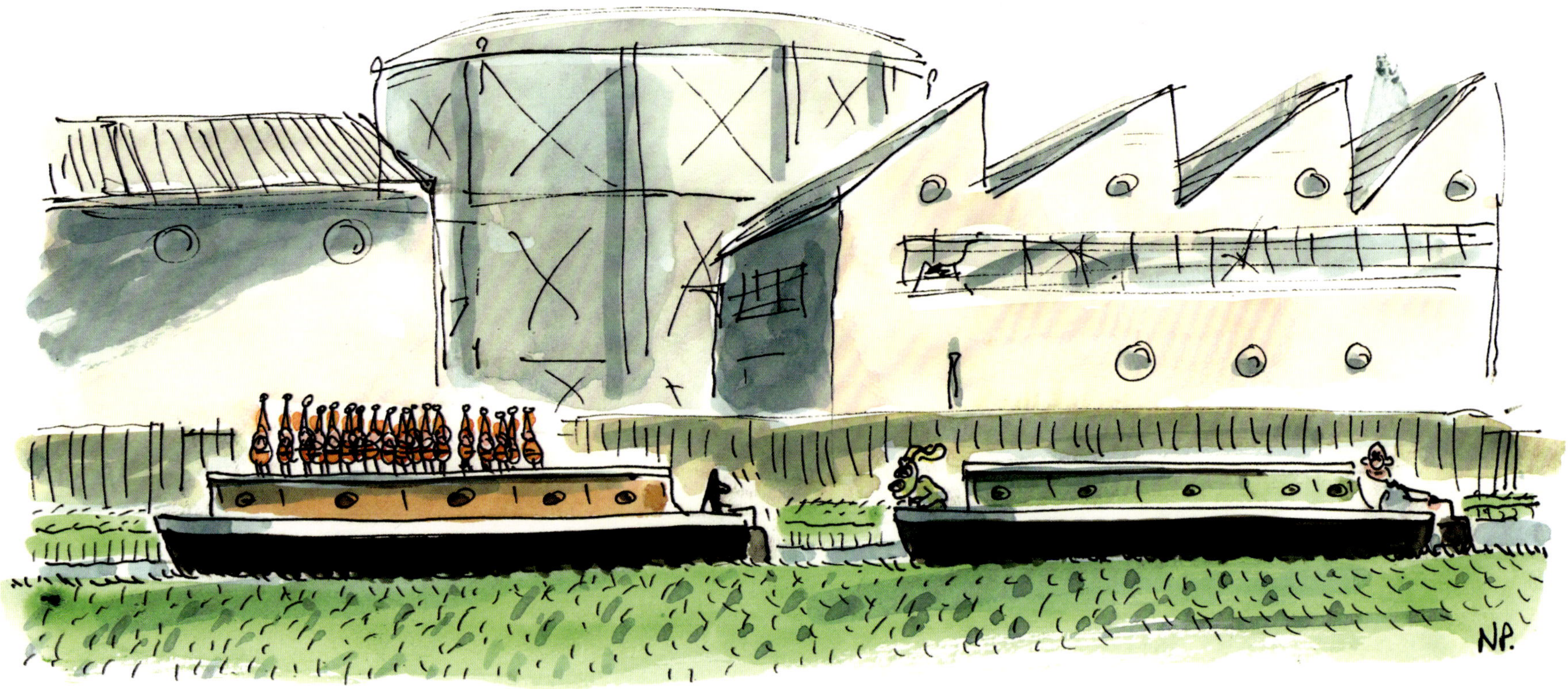

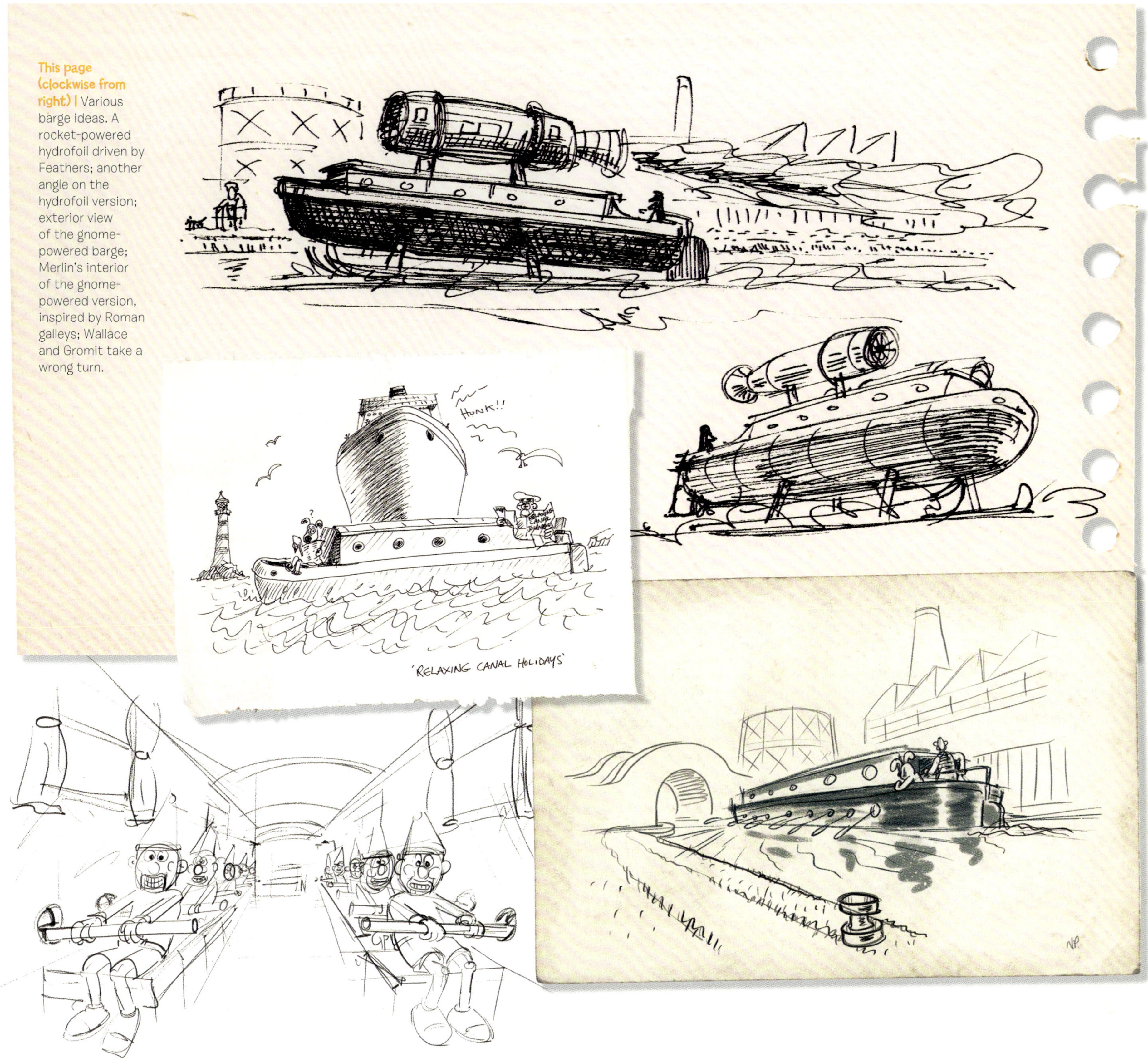

This page (clockwise from right) | Various barge ideas. A rocket-powered hydrofoil driven by Feathers; another angle on the hydrofoil version; exterior view of the gnome-powered barge; Merlin's interior of the gnome-powered version, inspired by Roman galleys; Wallace and Gromit take a wrong turn.

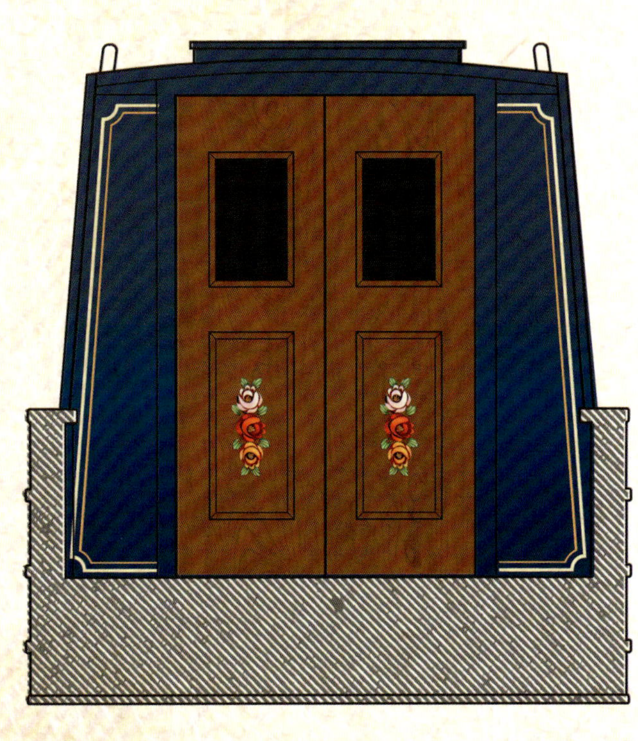
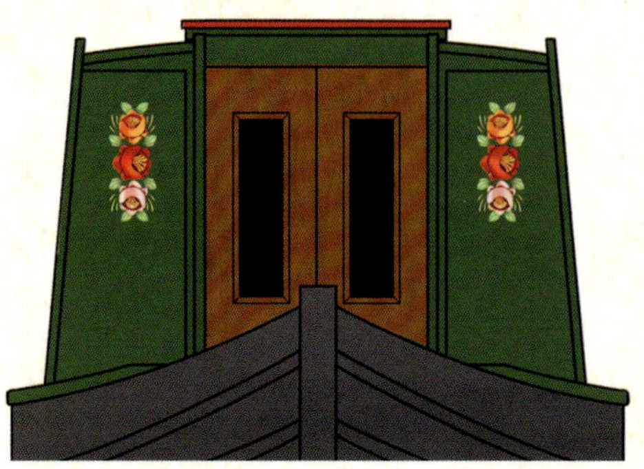
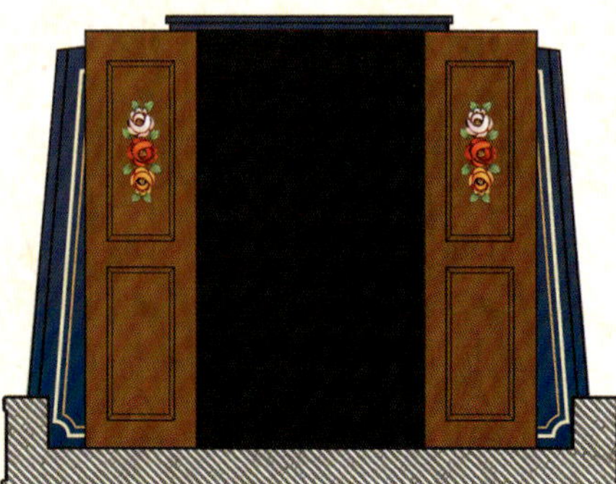

This page | Detail
of the graphic
design by Gavin
Lines for the
cabins, the sterns
and the sides of
the barges.

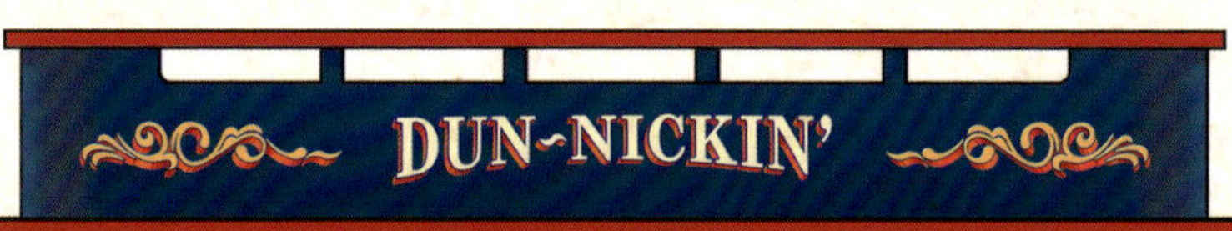

DUN-NICKIN'

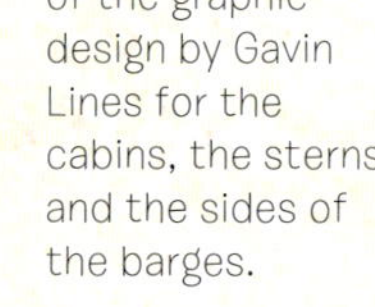

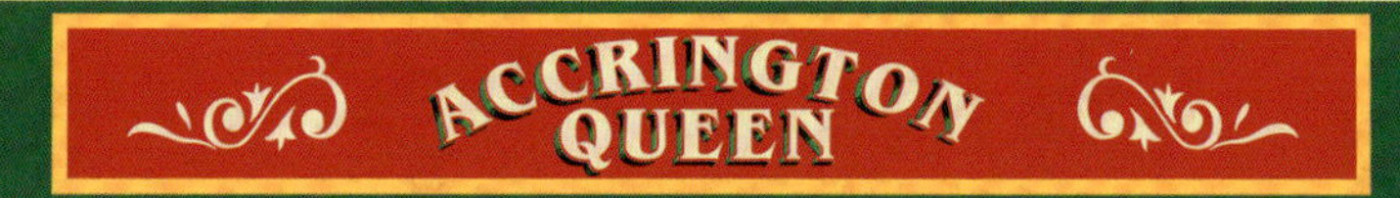

ACCRINGTON
QUEEN

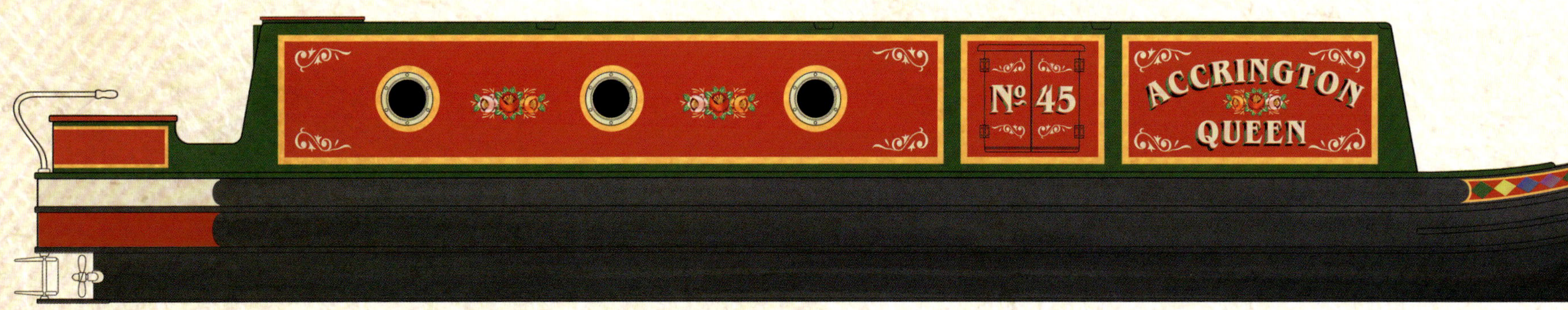

No 45
ACCRINGTON
QUEEN

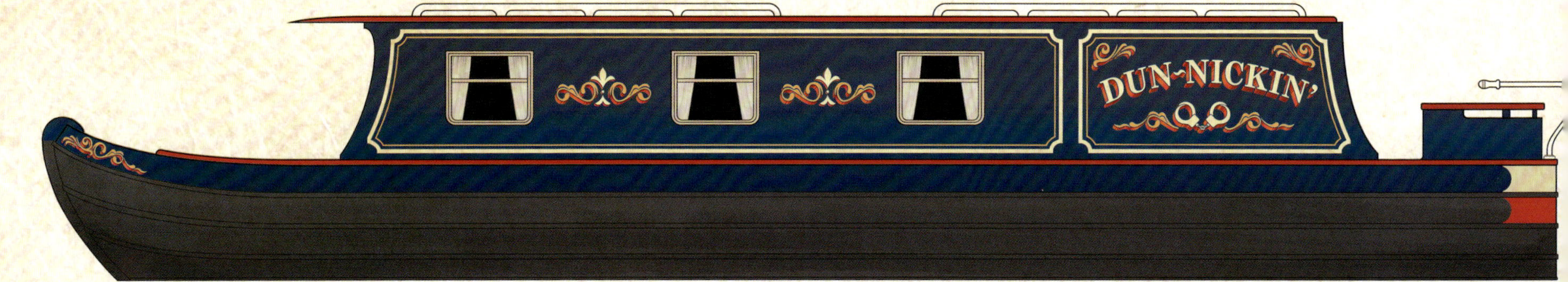

DUN-NICKIN'

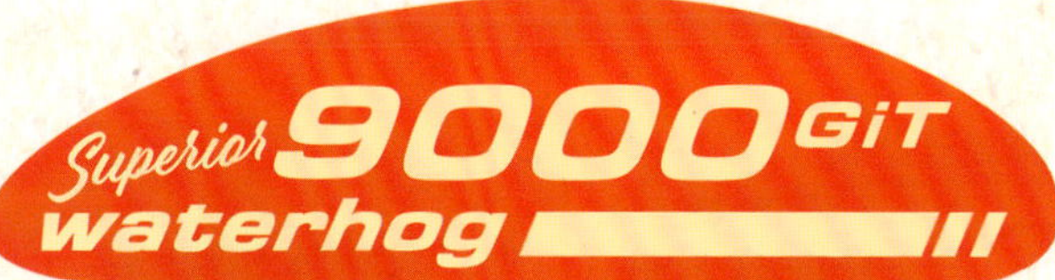

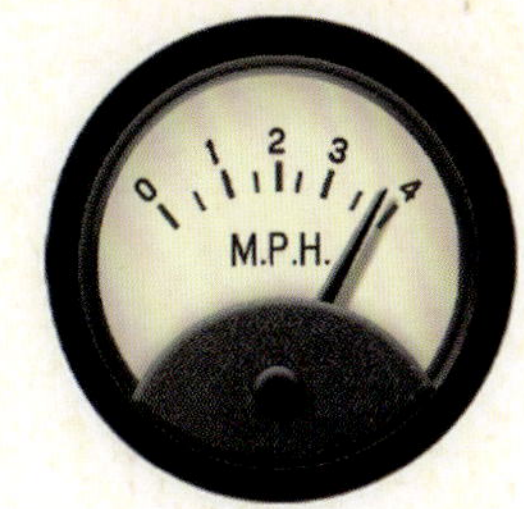
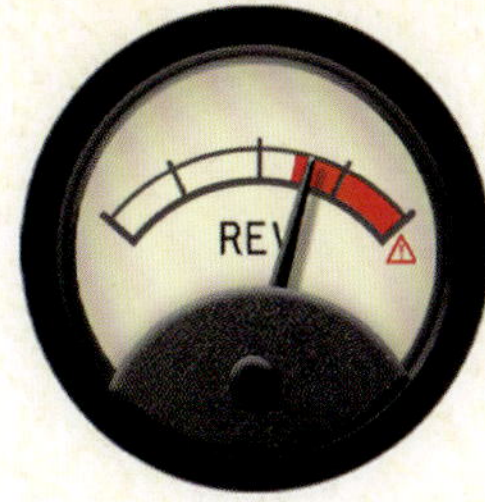

explains co-director Merlin. "We're embracing cutting-edge visual-effects technology where the digital team are not building a fully computer-generated environment, they're scanning a physical environment that the art department have built. So those sets exists digitally and we can point the camera anywhere we like. It's mind-boggling!"

Matt worked closely with the digital department to come up with this new approach for the backgrounds, known as 'array plates'. Howard Jones, VFX supervisor, explains: "Where we're on the top of the boat or it's side-on, it helps the floor to shoot on a smaller unit and put a blue screen behind rather than do everything on the one big unit. So we run a camera down the physical set, a bit like a 3D camera. We'll do this at three different heights to capture a massive 3D environment, then stitch the whole thing together in post to give us a 180-degree vista. Then you can shoot any way you want, but the quality will be the same."

"It's the same as running the camera along a real set for every single shot," adds Kirstie Deane, VFX producer. "You're just being more clever, more efficient about it."

Matt picks up the story: "If you did every single shot on a physical set it would take years. We've got a couple of shots where you specifically need the set there, but for everything else on the barge we're using array plates."

"Above the set there's a blue screen beyond the fence," adds Howard, "so we can put different buildings in for each pass. Once they've done the plates for one location we'll re-

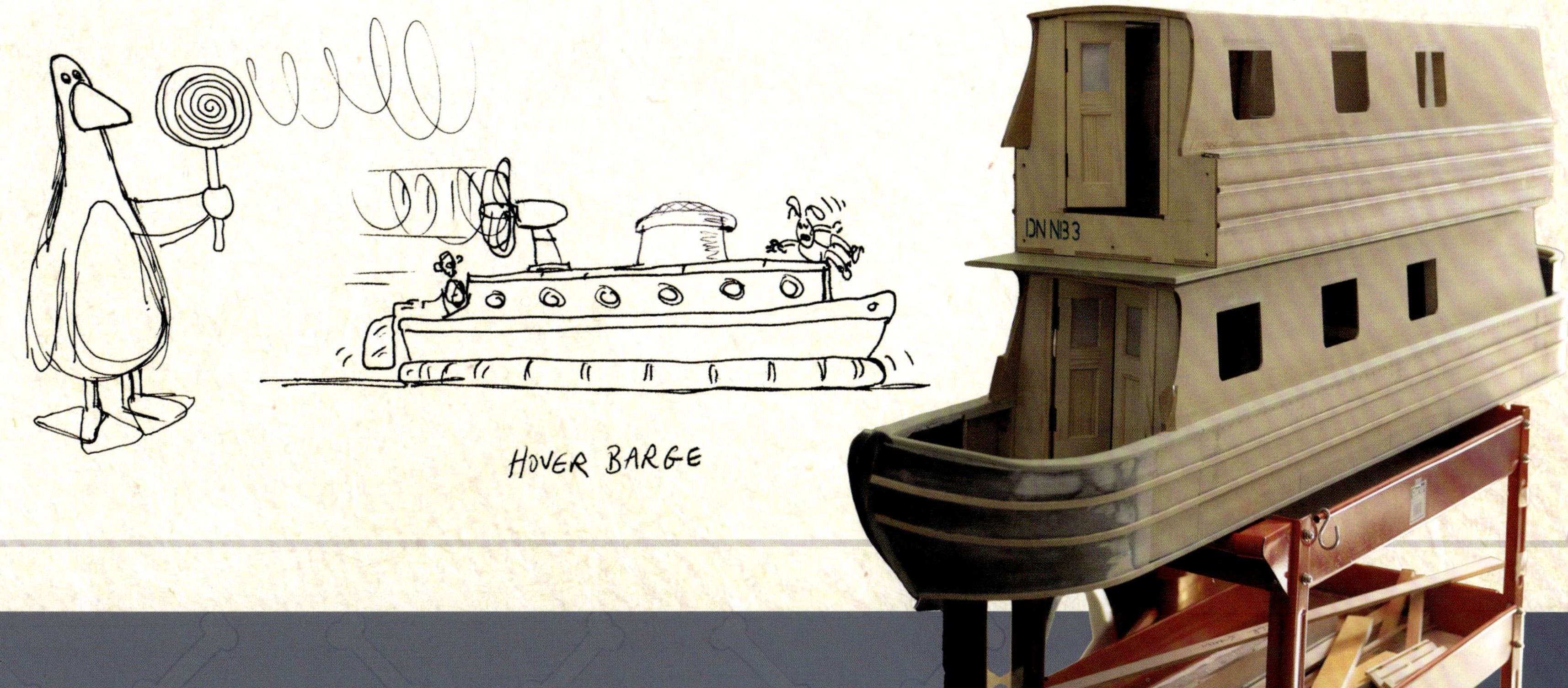

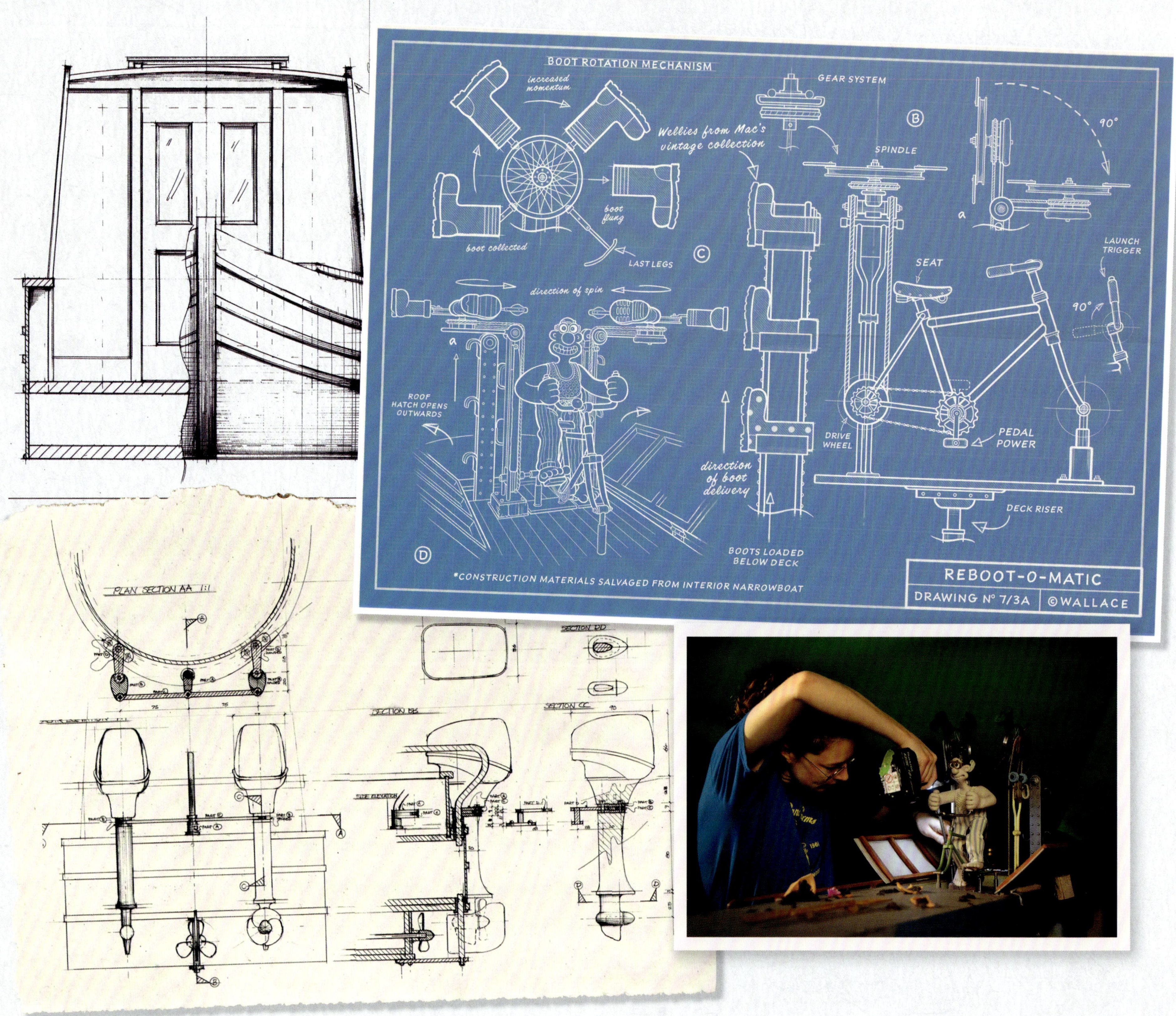

BOOT ROTATION MECHANISM
increased momentum
Wellies from Mac's vintage collection
GEAR SYSTEM
B
90°
boot flung
SPINDLE
boot collected
LAST LEGS
C
LAUNCH TRIGGER
direction of spin
SEAT
90°
ROOF HATCH OPENS OUTWARDS
a
DRIVE WHEEL
PEDAL POWER
direction of boot delivery
D
BOOTS LOADED BELOW DECK
DECK RISER
*CONSTRUCTION MATERIALS SALVAGED FROM INTERIOR NARROWBOAT
REBOOT-O-MATIC
DRAWING Nº 7/3A ©WALLACE
PLAN SECTION AA 1:1
SECTION DD
SECTION BB
SECTION CC
SIDE ELEVATION

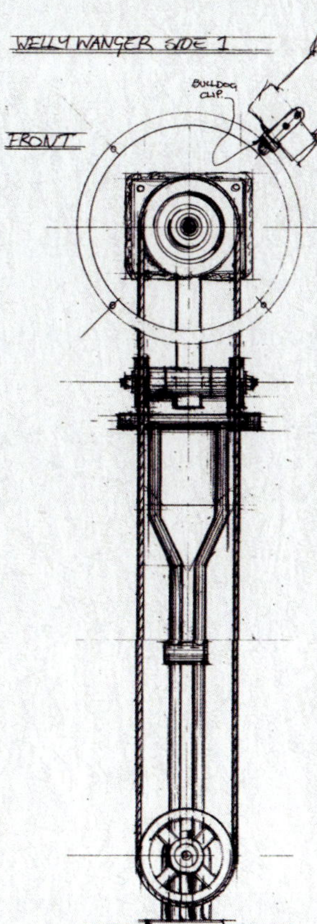

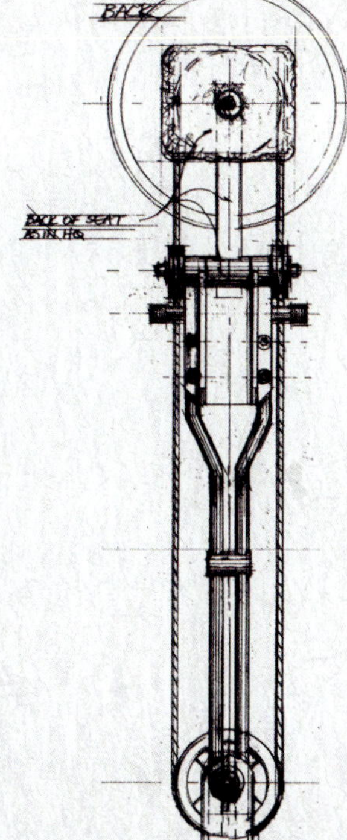

dress the set and then do a second plate of the new one. Then we can join them together and just keep repeating them." The one thing that can't be achieved on an array plate is a change in lighting, as the scene moves from night to early morning, but director of photography Dave Alex Riddett keeps a close eye on this in the final grade so that any changes needed can be achieved in post-production.

"As a rule, anything that can be done in camera or physically, we would always do that before we look to CG," explains Howard. "CG is always the fallback, if you like." But the water effects turned out to be another exception that proved this rule. "The canal boat and the water, you couldn't do all that with cling film!" observes Nick. "It would have its limitations – although we have still used cling film at times, for pouring tea and stuff like that."

"Normally in stop-motion you'd steer well away from water," adds Merlin, "but our whole Act 3 basically happens on a canal with characters interacting with water." To an extent, clever use of camera angles can minimise the amount of water shown, but where this was unavoidable the digital department came up with their own CG water effects.

"We've got two types of water," reveals Howard, "the canal water – dirty, muddy water with wind rippling across it – and then what I call the James Bond water, where it comes spraying out during the chase." In a fortuitous bit of timing, production co-ordinator Debs Price went on holiday near to an aqueduct just before work began on creating these effects. "She was able to take a load of pictures," recalls Kirstie. "It was pure luck. The sequence starts out quite dark, but as the sun comes up you have to start thinking about things like reflections and how muddy the water is. Our water is dirty but not disgusting!"

The CG water is only one component of the final sequences, and the complexity of all the elements that need to be combined can be illustrated by the wharf scene, where Wallace and co fly though the air and land on Chief Inspector Mackintosh's barge. This has to be factored in from the earliest stages of pre-production – line producer Steph Miller outlines the process: "First and foremost we look at the animatic to understand Nick and Merlin's creative vision for the shot, what they're hoping to see. So everyone involved, whether it's on the physical production side or the VFX team or Art,

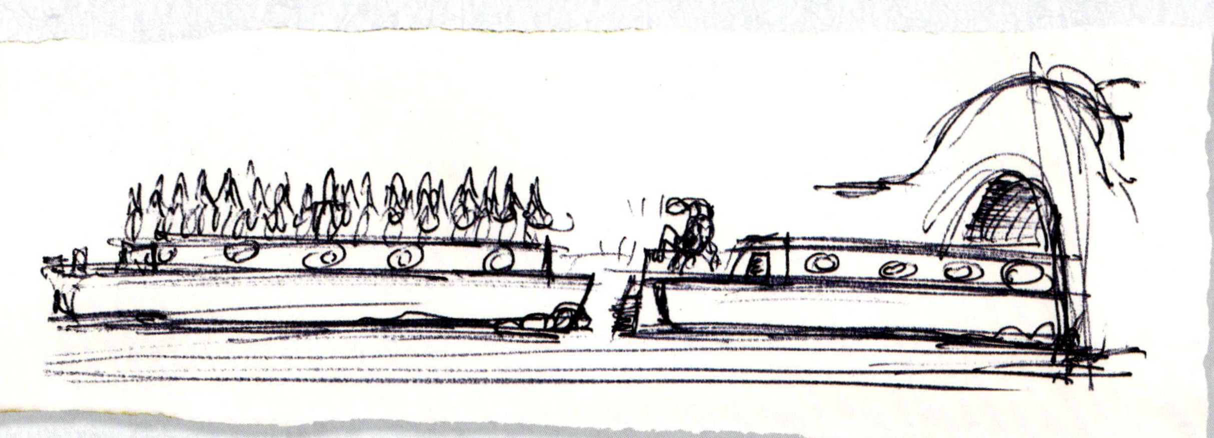

we plan meetings around these shots where we dissect the sequences to ascertain what are the layers, what are the processes, and we work out what order those processes need to be completed by so they can come together in comp at the very end. Then we work out which teams are involved and we schedule it like that. It's a real multi-team effort and there's an art in making sure it's all resourced properly with the correct talent."

Kirstie Deane takes up the story: "The next step would be a pre-production meeting where the VFX supervisor talks to the directors about the key shots and key effects, and we're able to break it down more – how we're going to construct the shot and scheduling everything on the studio floor. In the wharf scene, it's the first shot where you look down the canal and that's our key shot for the water effects, which has influenced the Look Dev of all the rest of the water shots in the film. It's also the first shot where you're seeing a big piece of sky – that's a DMP [digital matte painting]." Digital artist Jay Cassidy, based in Australia, provides the skies and distant backgrounds as digital matte paintings, the modern equivalent of the old glass matte painting used since the dawn of filmmaking.

There are multiple different 'plates' created in the composition of the shot. The key character animation is shot against a green screen, while the physical set is shot separately. Often the set is separated to give the animators access to the puppets, and different elements like the rocking canal barge and the curling rope are animated

as individual 'takes' as well. "Once these have been approved on the studio floor, all these elements are put together roughly into an Edit Cut Reference," Kirstie explains. "This gives the CG team the right timings and what elements from the floor to include. Then we have things like the 'silhouette pass', which helps us key out the animated figures in comp rather than having to rotoscope everything."

All the plates are then composited together with the CG water, the DMP sky and other effects, which is a very detailed and time-consuming process. "For a shot like this," says Kirstie, "you're adding in all these elements and the compositors have to make sure all the edges are super-neat and you can't see the join. Then they have to do the rotoscoping and something called tracking – we have a version of the barge that exists only in CG and one of

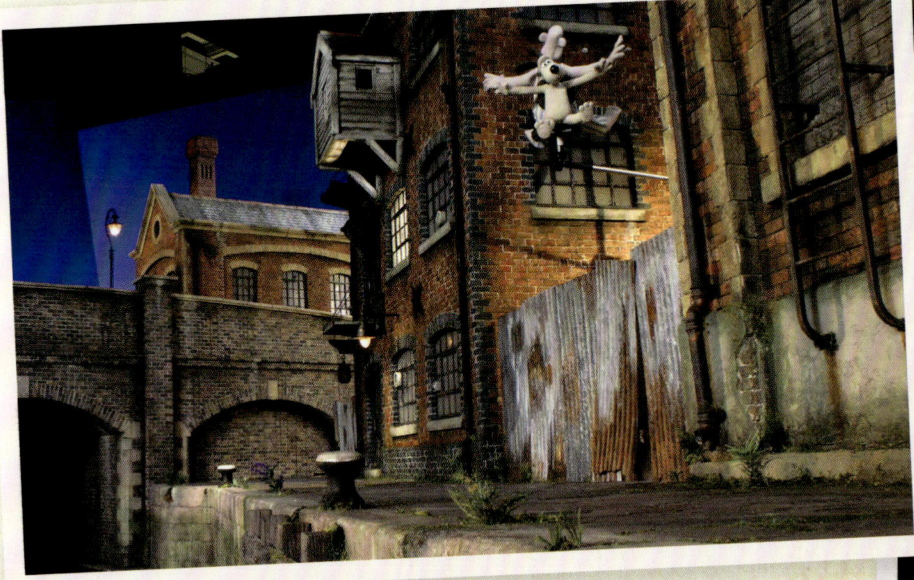

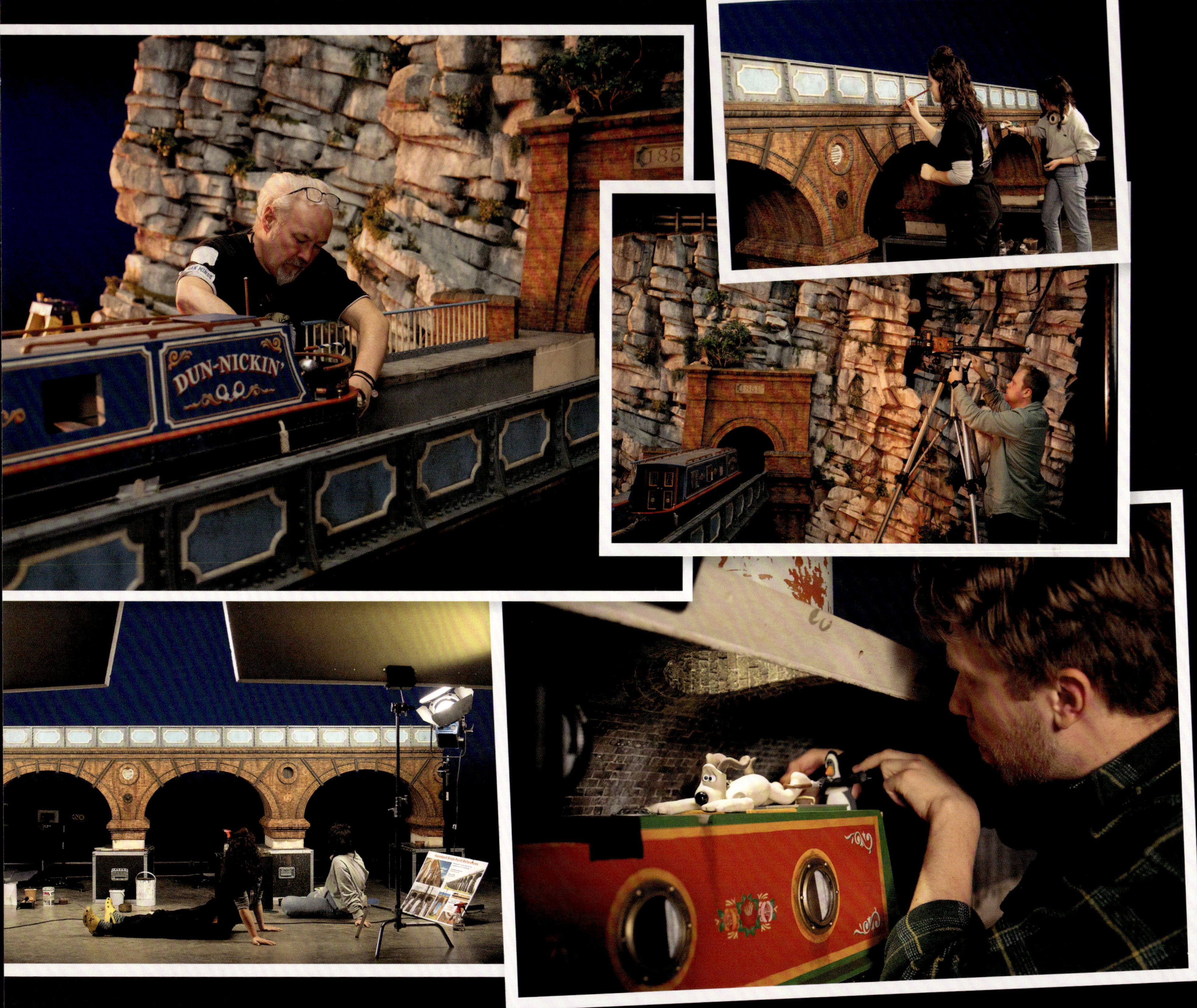

DUN-NICKIN'

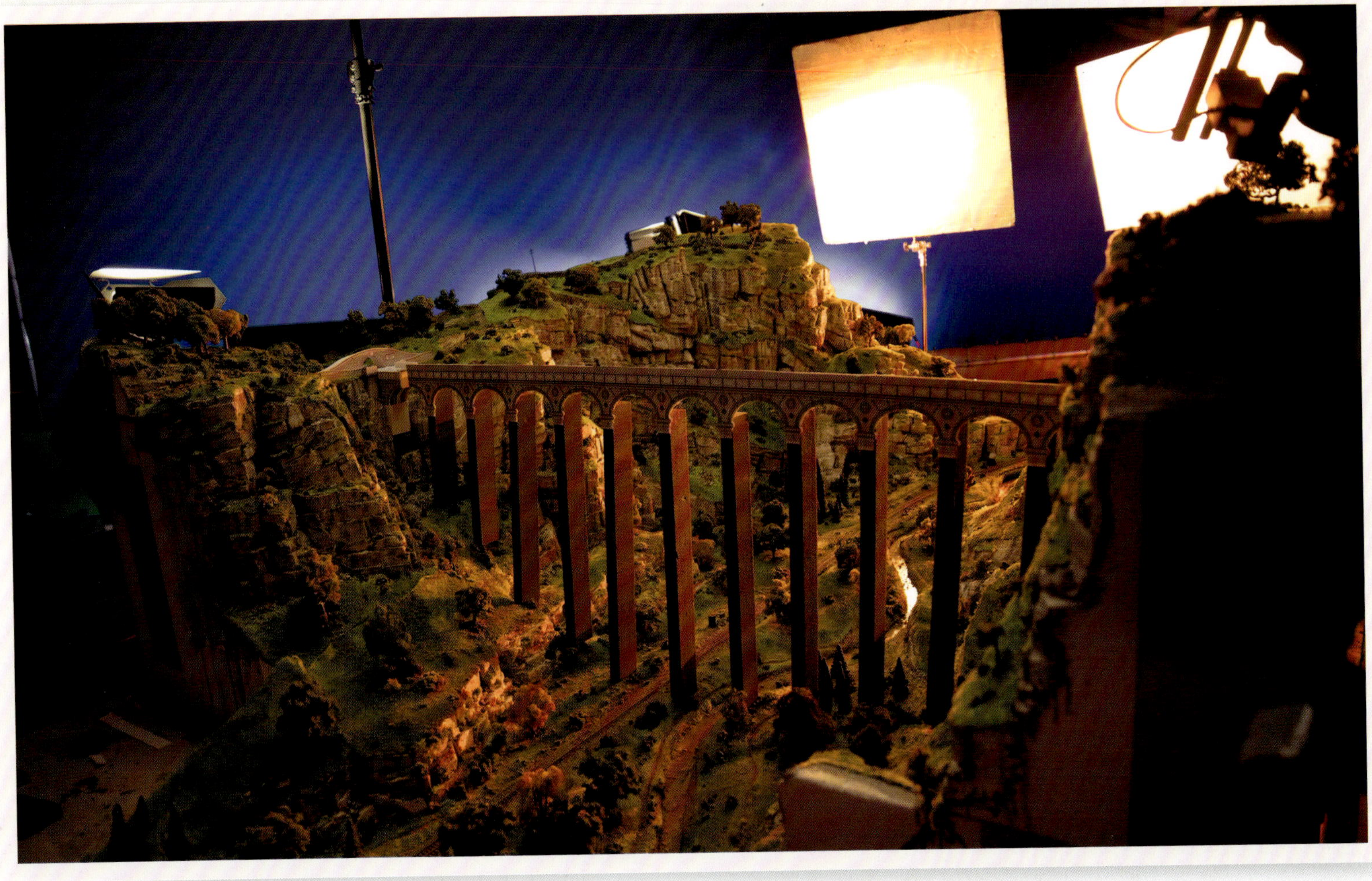

the really smart guys in our CG team tracks the physical barge with the CG barge so that when the CG water hits it, it can react to it – you have to create the physics in CG. It's a lot of work!"

At least all the animation for the wharf scene was shot at the same scale, but the aqueduct for the big finale demanded a different set of solutions. Set within a vast valley, the canal emerges from a tunnel and crosses the aqueduct over a river, while hundreds of yards below a train line runs into the far distance across the Yorkshire border. "To build this massive aqueduct with all its arches," explains Matt Perry, production designer, "we decided to only make three physical arches in close-up. We're using a miniature of the valley, but the aqueduct, when it sits within this, is going to be a virtual one. They scan our physical arches to create various extensions for long shots, and drop that into the set."

Art director Matt Sanders researched the detail. "I looked at British aqueducts," he recalls, "and there aren't a lot of them and they aren't necessarily in the style that

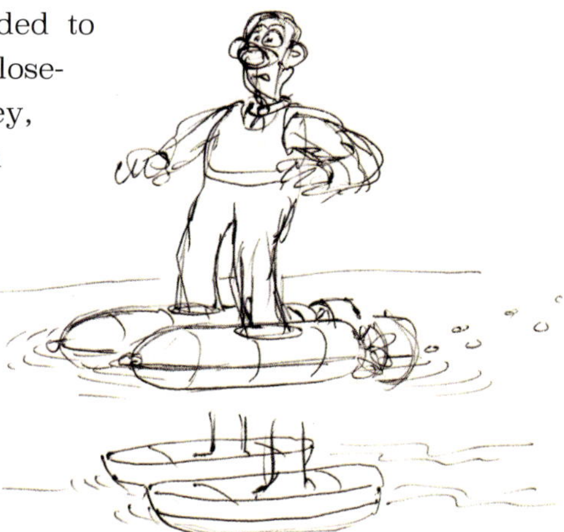

you might want. So the metal parts, the channels and the railings were based on an aqueduct from Wales. But the arches on that one were a bit boring, so our brick arches were actually based on a railway viaduct from the Ouse Valley; but the shapes of the arches are different, elliptical instead of semi-circular. Often you get a lot of reference and it's a bit of this one and a bit of that one which you Frankenstein together."

The construction department then builds the arches from Matt's drawings, and his reference is handed over to set painter ??? . "I paint the brickwork, then age it to make it look 200 years old," she explains. "Then we'll scan it on so it can be replicated digitally. I'll produce differently painted versions for different plates so when it's put together it won't look like it's endlessly replicated, it will look more organic. The pillar legs are going to be really tall – they're a complete cheat!" The legs of the aqueduct are in fact the only entirely CG element of set in the entire movie – their scale was so vast it was either that or raise the roof of the Aztec West studio…

The valley itself is constructed in three different scales. For the long shots there is a miniature set, produced entirely by Matt Sanders. There is then a middle-scale version at five times the size, and the section of the valley where the aqueduct disappears into the cliff face is built to ten times the scale of the miniature, in proportion to the puppets, for close-up action shots. Set dresser Kitty Clay worked on the two larger scale versions, taking her lead from Matt's intricately detailed miniature, his reference material and technical drawings. The construction department produced polystyrene

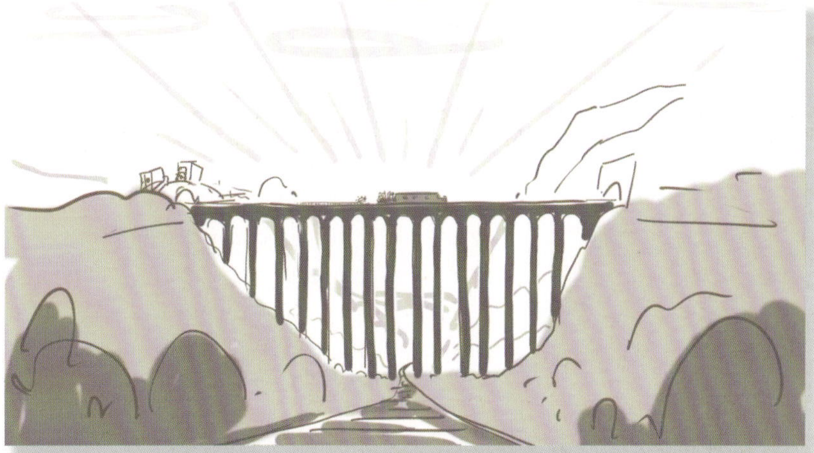

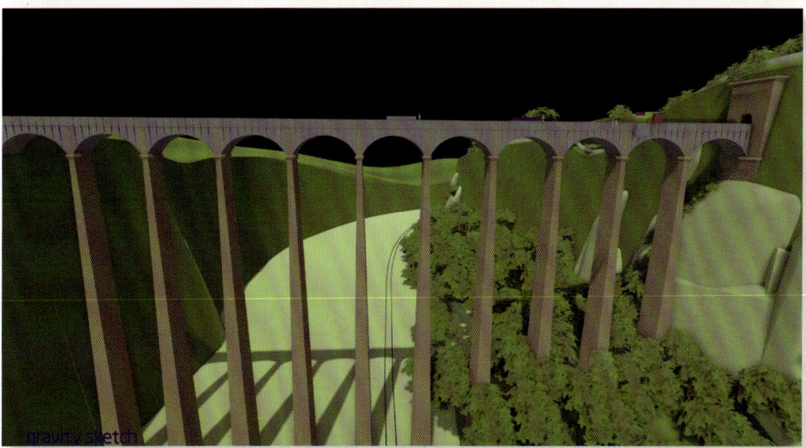

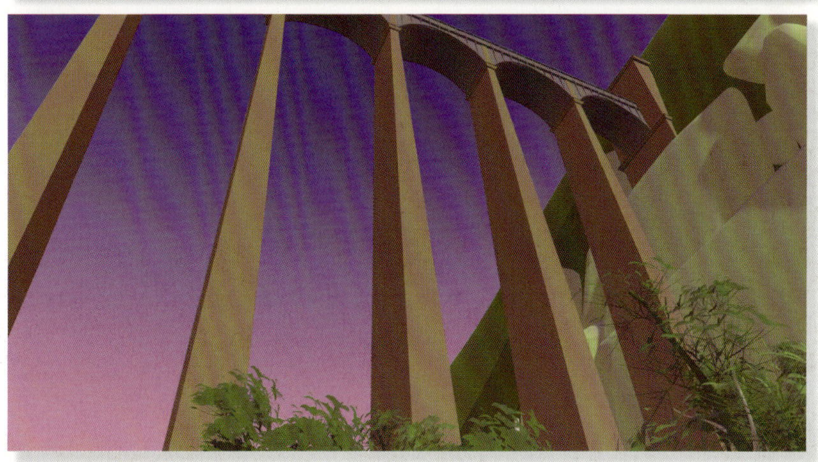

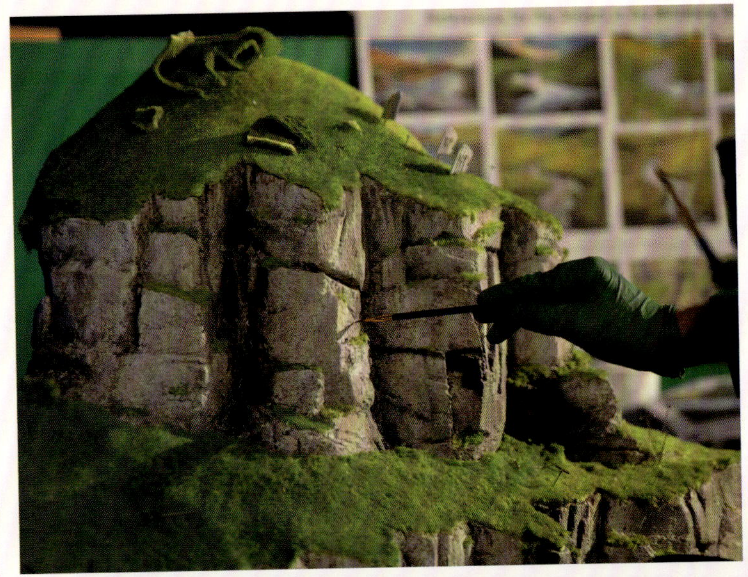

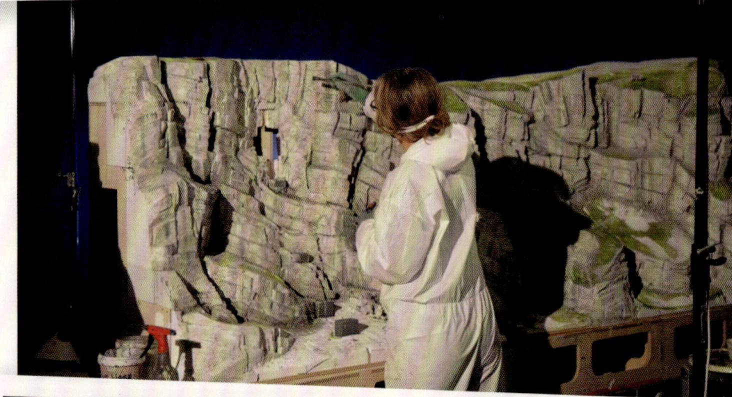

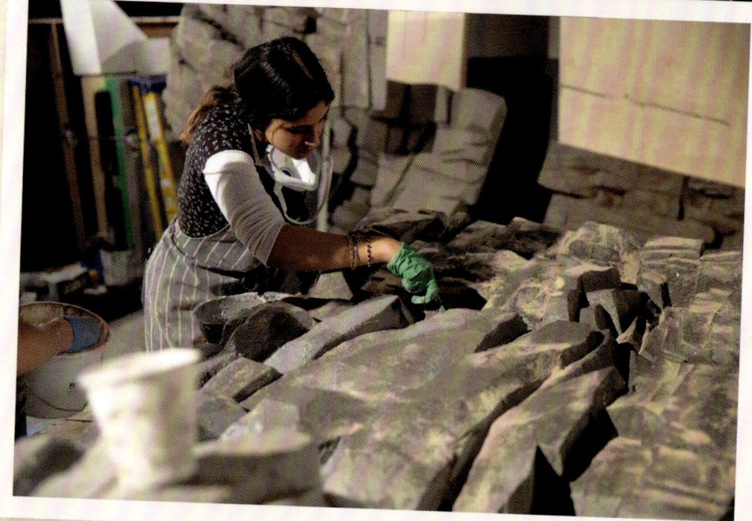

blocks in the rough shape of the rocks, then Kitty set about these with a kitchen knife to carve them into accurate cliff faces.

The modular approach again minimises the amount of set-building required. "It's very clever," says Kitty. "Instead of having to make the whole valley, which would take five or six weeks to dress and build, the sections actually move around so you're not going to have to build the whole thing. Once I've done a rough block-out of the rocks, I put a mucky wash on so I can visualise it as I start getting into it. Then I'll fine-tune all the carving, and then I'll render the whole thing, using an eco-friendly texturing as an alternative to plaster. Then I lay on a very thin fleece, which is painted green, then I plant in the trees and bushes and all the little details such as the leaves and the gravel between the train tracks." The trees and track are sourced from model railway suppliers, but are not always ideal. "The foliage looks a bit like candy floss, so we need to tease it all out to make it look more natural, and spray it a different colour as well. People always forget the finessing, that's what Aardman is so famous for."

Subtle use of CGI blends all the elements of the scene, physical and virtual, into a seamless whole, a process referred to by the digital team as the 'CG glue'. "This is really to make sure that it all sits together," says Howard. "The main bit of CG glue will be the legs of the aqueduct. They've built a section of the leg for the roadways, but the whole of the legs will always be in CG, and the glue bit will be where the legs land into the set. We'll paint in CG trees and foliage so we can get it to fit imperceptibly into the miniature."

"It's about marrying the two but making it look like it sits within the same world," agrees Kirstie. "It's trying to achieve this so it feels seamless and doesn't feel like one stop-frame team have done this bit and the VFX team have done that bit. It needs to feel like it's really cohesive."

Are the directors worried that the inclusion of modern technology could be seen as a betrayal of *Wallace & Gromit*'s stop-motion roots? "We're using CG quite a lot," says Merlin. "But it's a question of the best toys to tell the story. At no point have we insisted it's all in front of the camera and nothing else. That's where the heart and soul of *Wallace & Gromit* is, but if we need a better way to do it then that's what we're going to do. So we have the luxury of all the toys, but we don't use them all the time. That means you really pay attention when you do use them, and make sure you use them properly. Sometimes being able to do everything isn't the best way anyway. Restrictions can actually make it better."

With all these hi-tech elements and different departments involved, how do the directors keep on top of the filmmaking process to ensure that their vision is maintained? "Part of it is just trusting that the people on the team are at the top of their game and know their onions," says Merlin. "But a large part of it is being comfortable yourself – experience, you know? Nick has made a lot of feature films now, so you know what's going to work. Every single sequence has its own challenges, whether that's animation or art department or visual effects, all of them have got something. And that's what makes it exciting. It's when it's difficult that the reward is most satisfying."

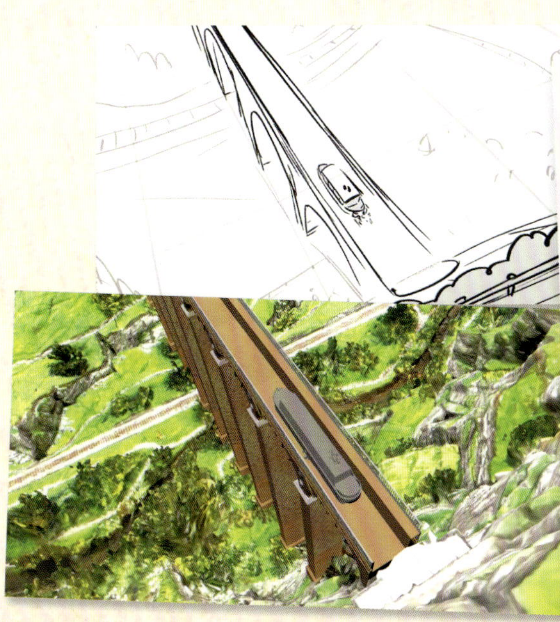

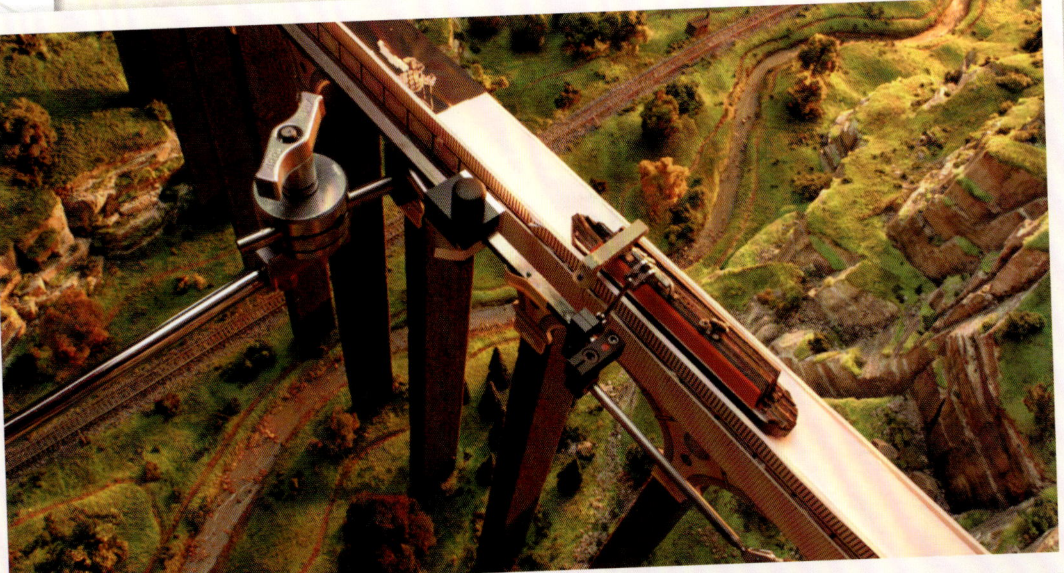

Elements of a Composite Shot

Top left | The original storyboard for the shot.

Centre left | A shot of the scene with 'water line marker' added as a guide for the CG water.

Bottom left | The shot with CG water added, both canal water with ripples and 'action' water thrown up by the skis.

Opposite page | A working final shot with all the elements composted, awaiting directors' approval and a finalised DMP sky.

Top right | The animation take, with character animation shot against the physical set and rigging for the puppet still visible.

Centre right | The puppets and set are recreated as CG geometry to interact with the water effects.

Bottom right | Background sky added as a Digital Matte Plate, with additional lighting.

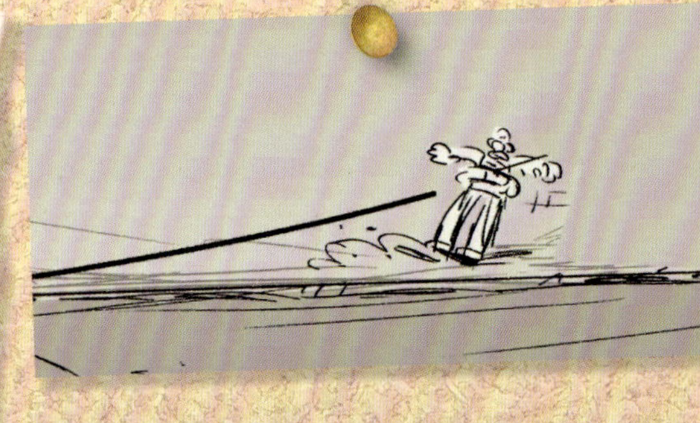

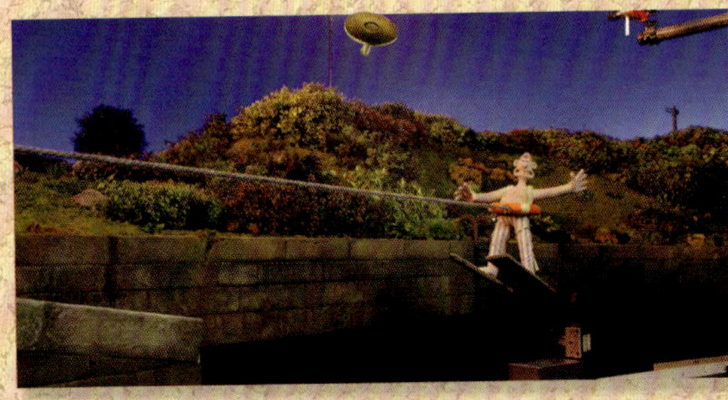

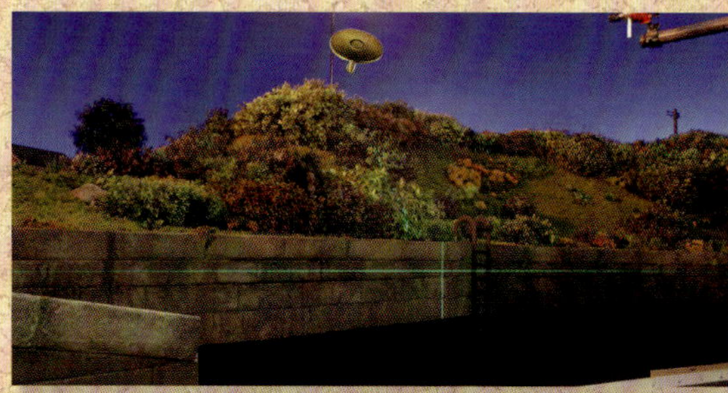

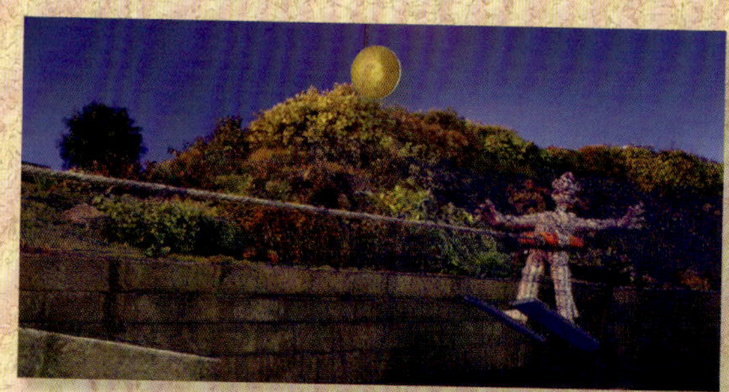

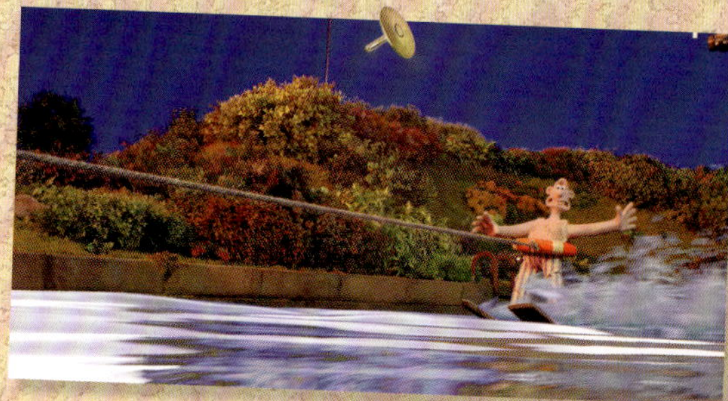

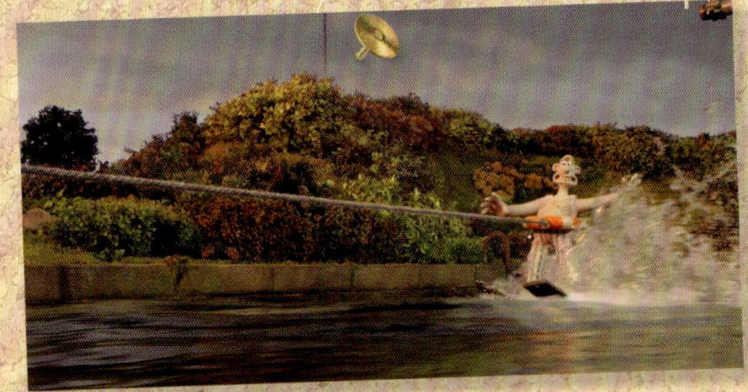

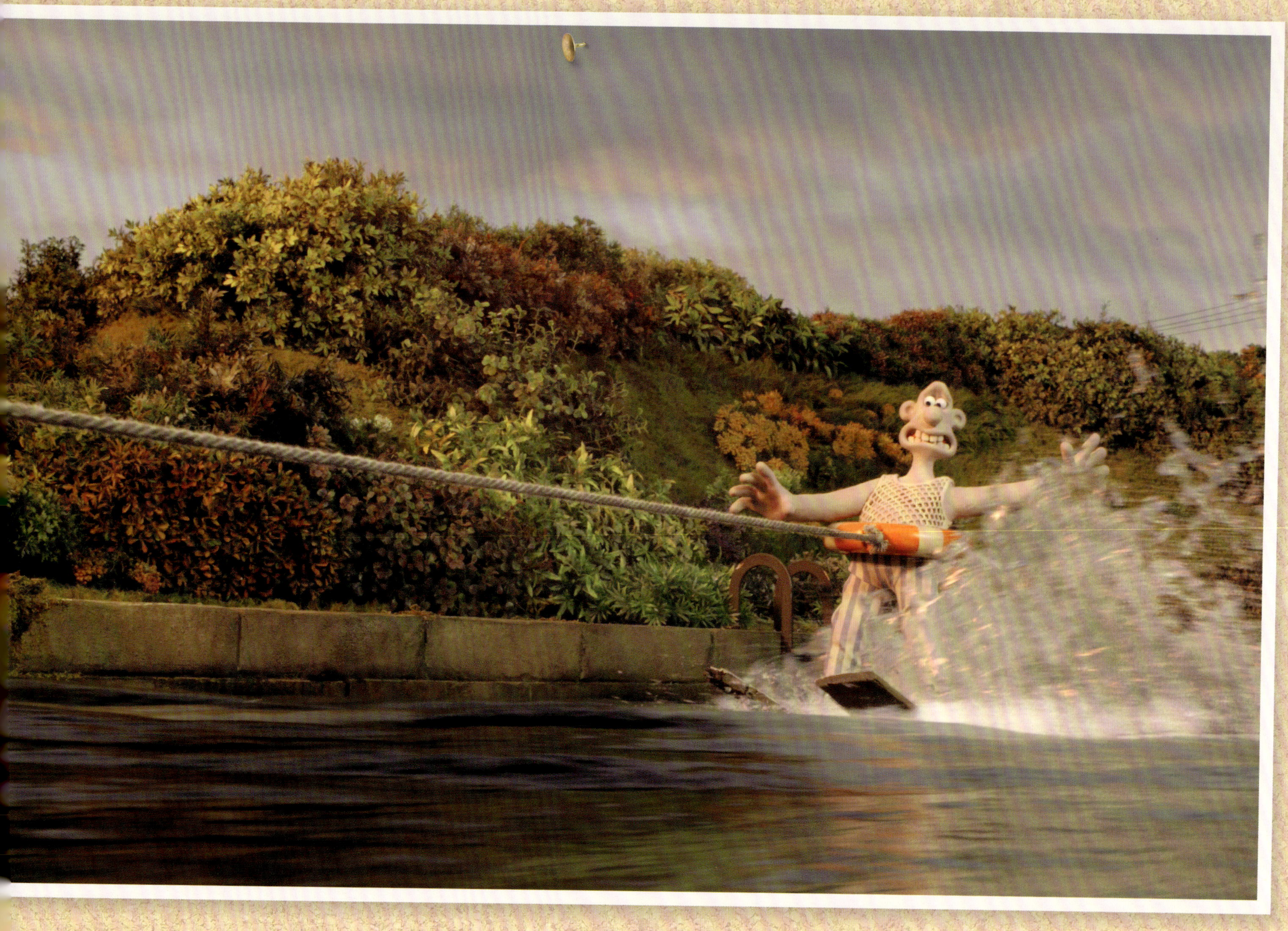

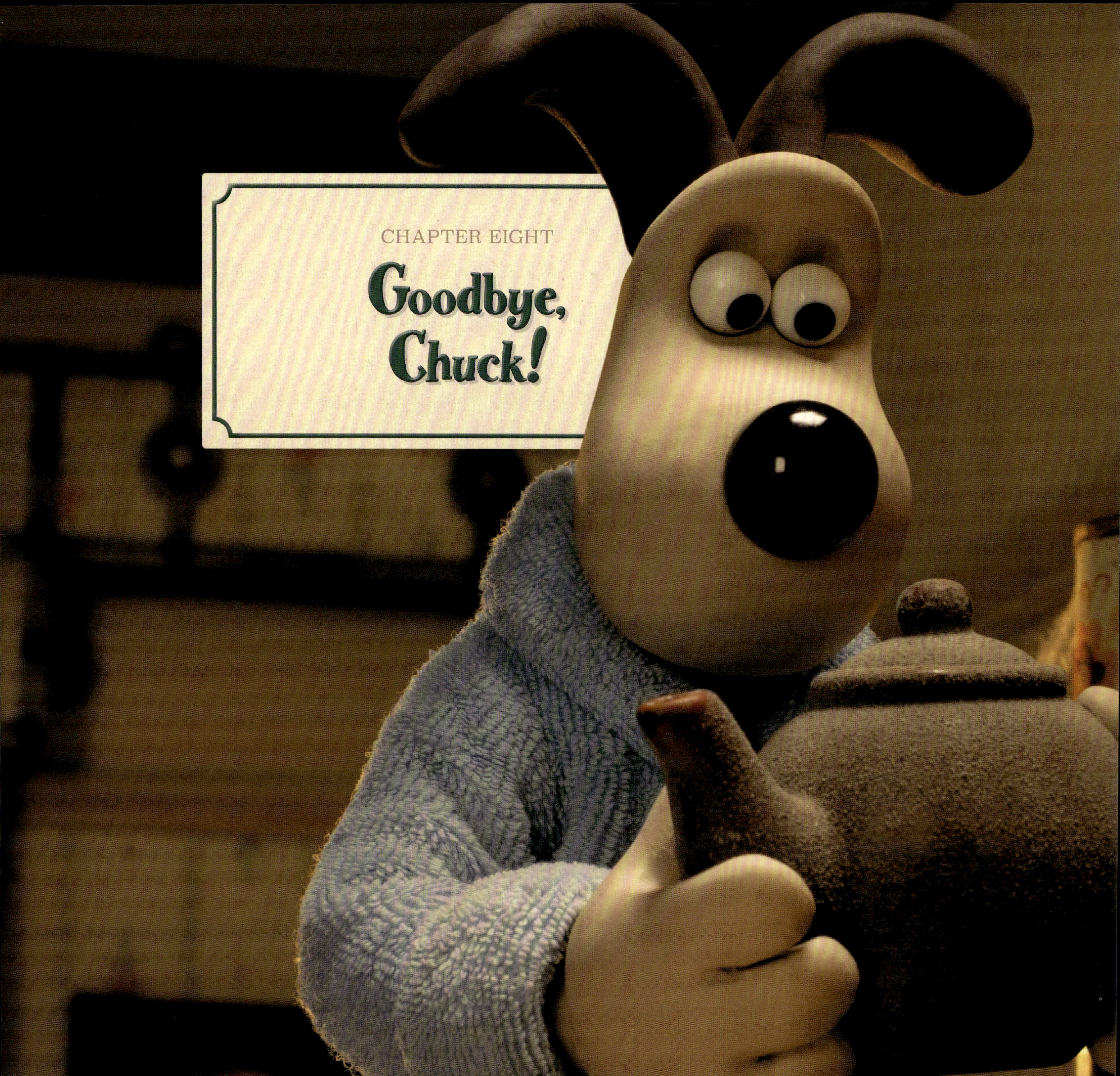
CHAPTER EIGHT
Goodbye, Chuck!

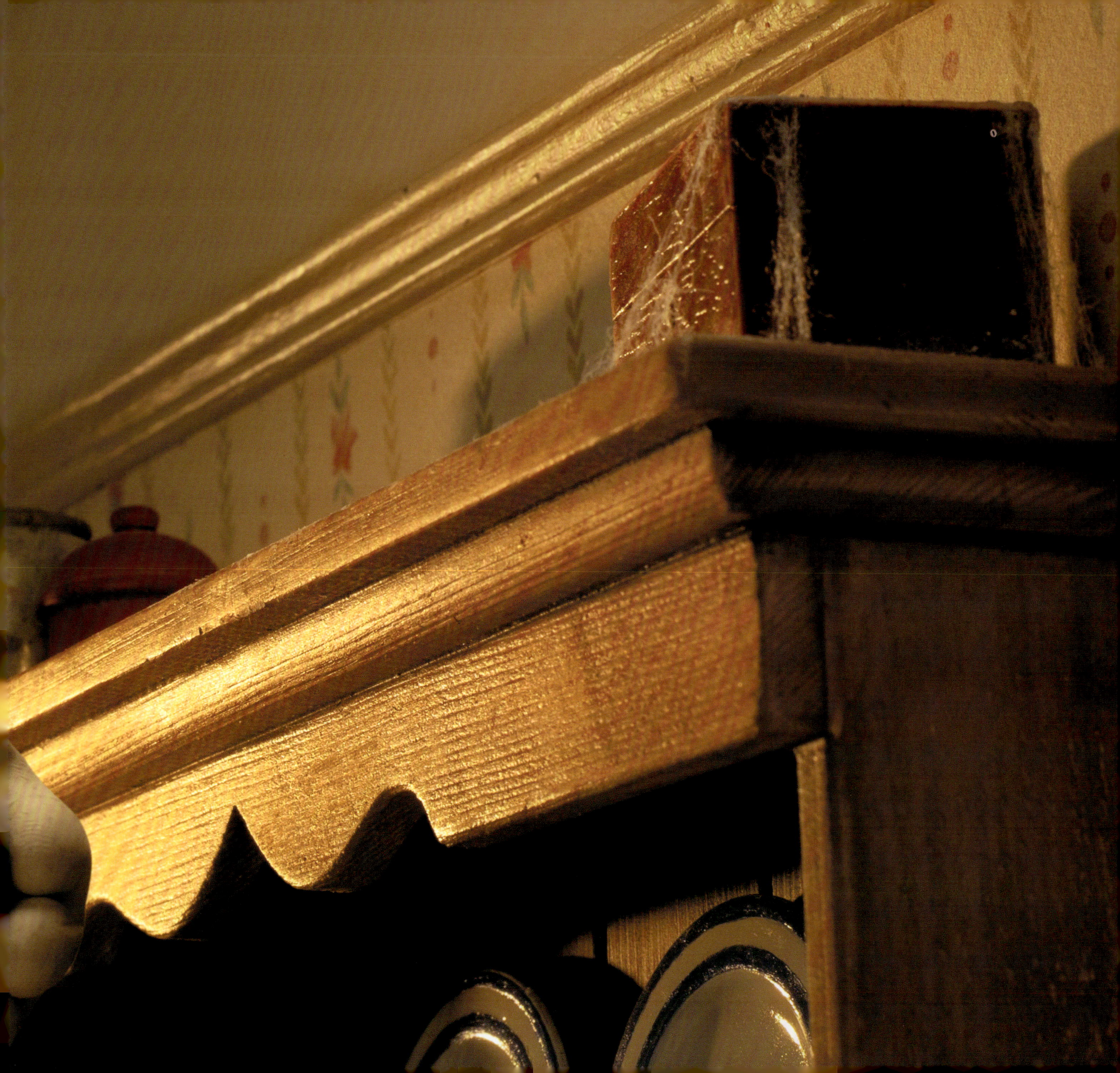

Goodbye, Chuck!

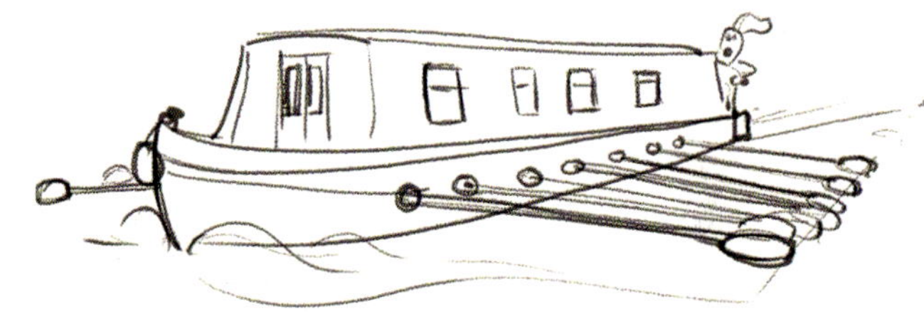

IT WOULD BE FAIR TO SAY THAT *VENGEANCE* *Most Fowl* finds Aardman firing on all cylinders as a studio. Its various departments have embraced the latest innovations in visual technology, combined with classic stop-motion techniques that go back to the late 19th century. But whatever the method of production, the aim is to keep the traditional hand-crafted look that makes the *Wallace & Gromit* style so unique.

"All the animators are very good sculptors," points out animation supervisor Will Becher, "to the point where they're almost too smooth. So we're trying to push them back to that Nick Park style – fingerprints and rough sculpts and confident boldness."

"We've had to be careful not to go too much into perfection," agrees Anne King. "We make sure the silicon looks like clay, retaining all the fingerprints from the sculpt. We have the unevenness and the lumpiness and the texture on there keeping things kind of wonky. You could easily smooth it out and make it all perfect, but then it would look like CG animation."

The same goes for the effects work. "*The Wrong Trousers* was very notable in that it had no special effects beyond opticals," recalls Dave Alex Riddett. "We superimposed the rain as a double exposure, the laser beams we did on a rostrum camera; there wasn't the digital technology then, it was all shot onto film. And that gave it a certain look – everything was hand-crafted, you could see how the world was built. But I think we did it sufficiently well that you accepted that was the world you were in and that things had a certain look because of it. And on this project it's the same mentality."

"It's a really nice reflection of Aardman in 2024," says Gav Strange, "that hybrid approach. The creative industries have come so far in terms of VFX, of CG, of compositing, of camera

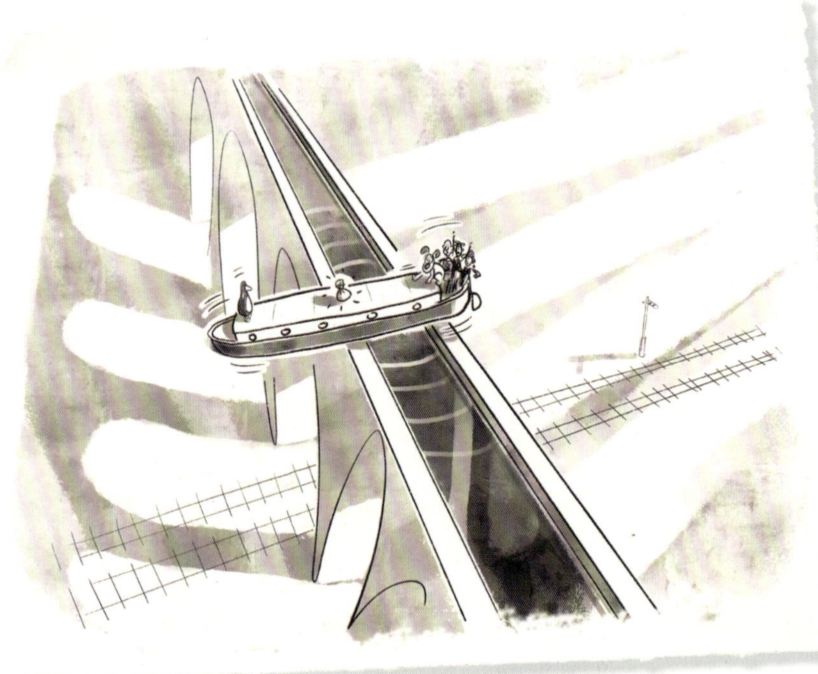

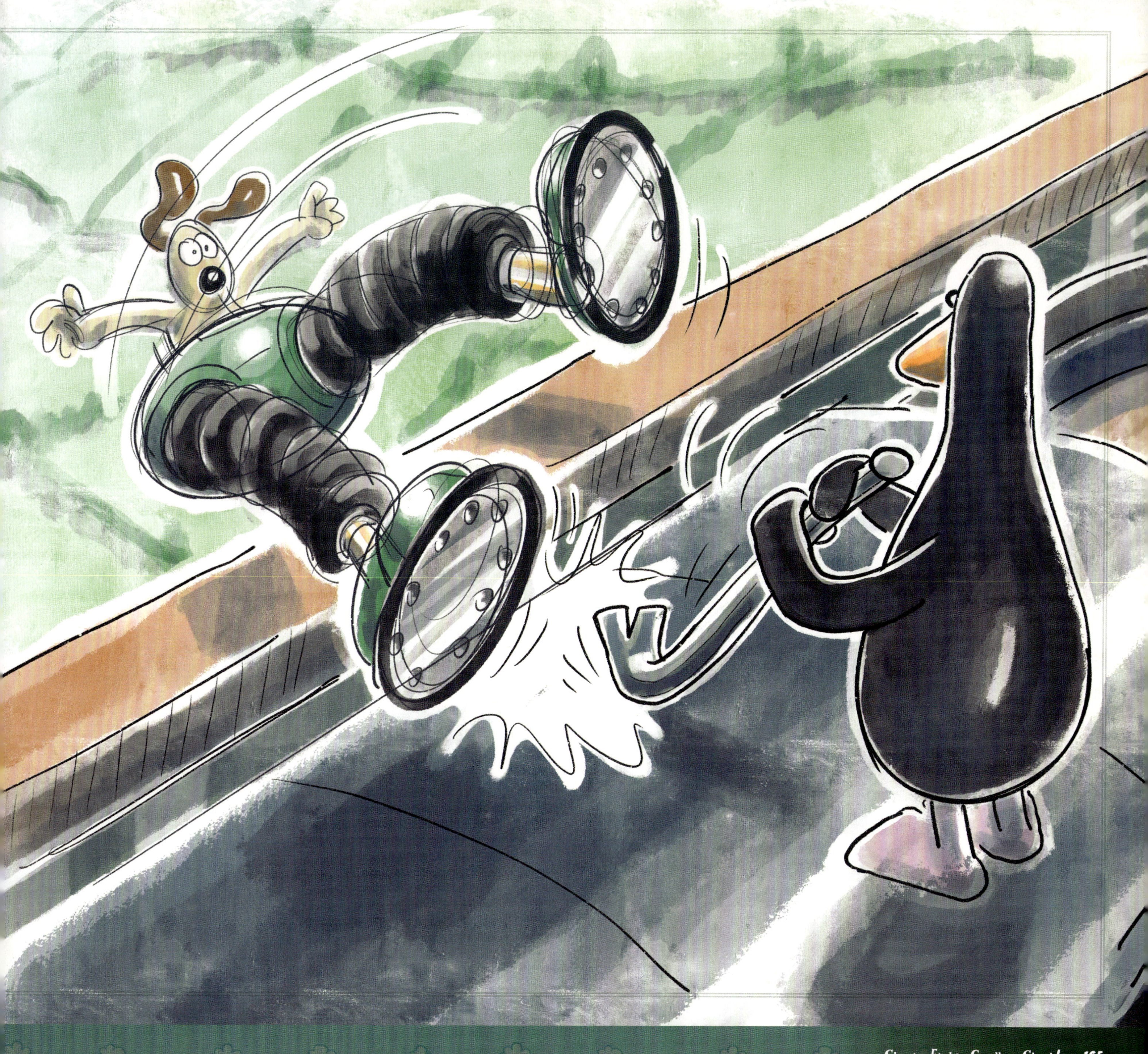

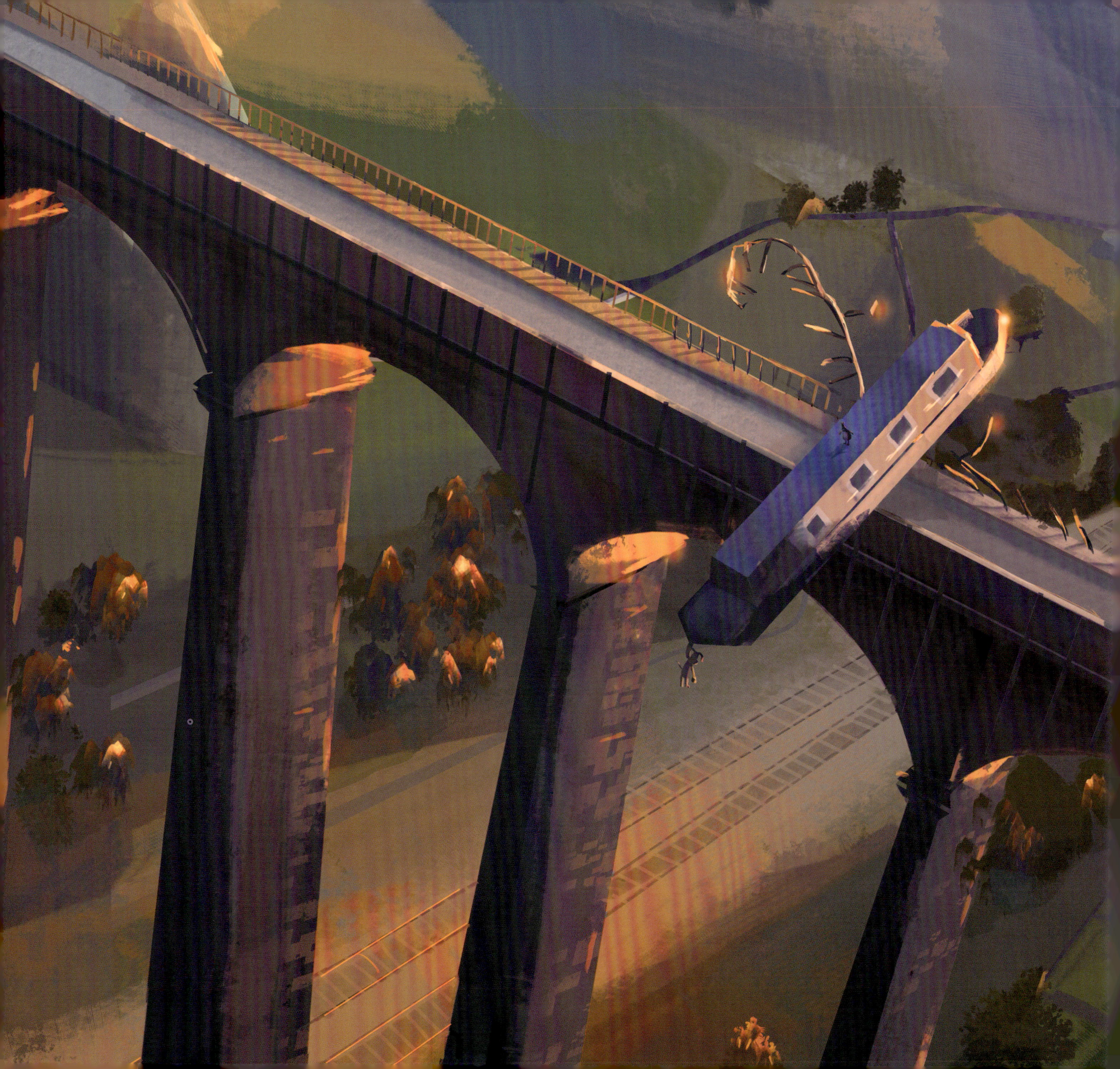

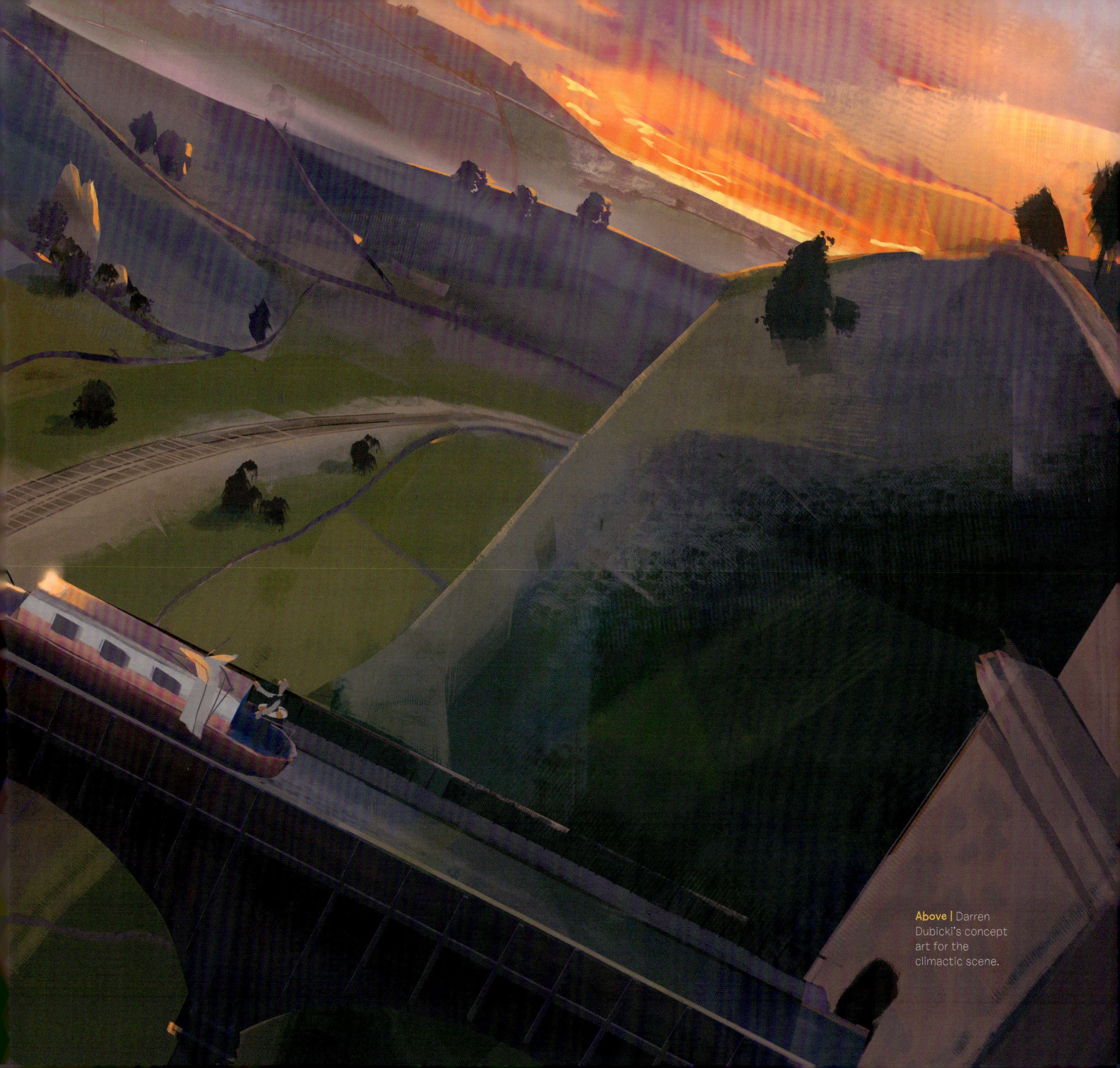

Above | Darren
Dubicki's concept
art for the
climactic scene.

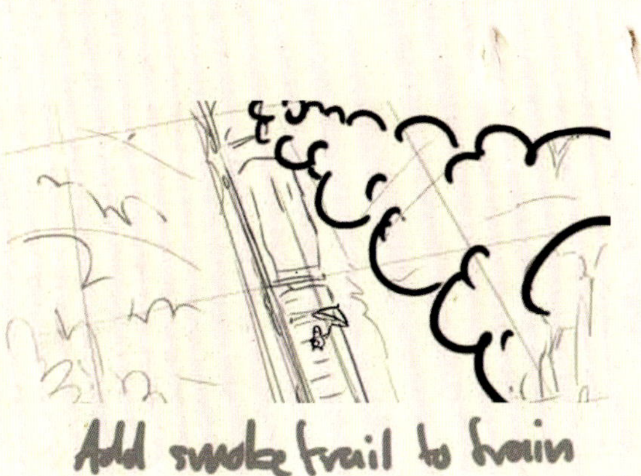

Add smoke trail to train
to help link shots.

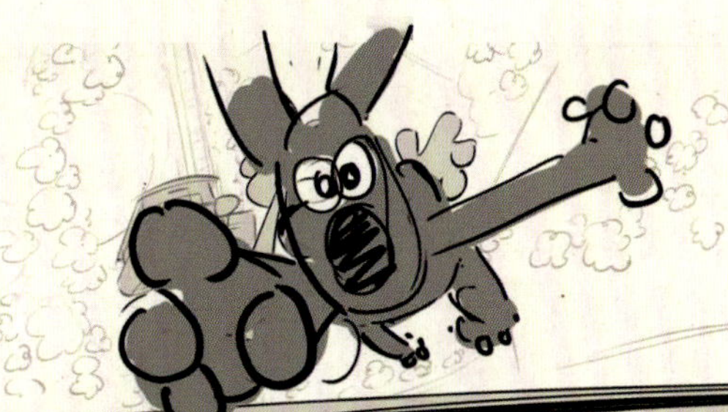

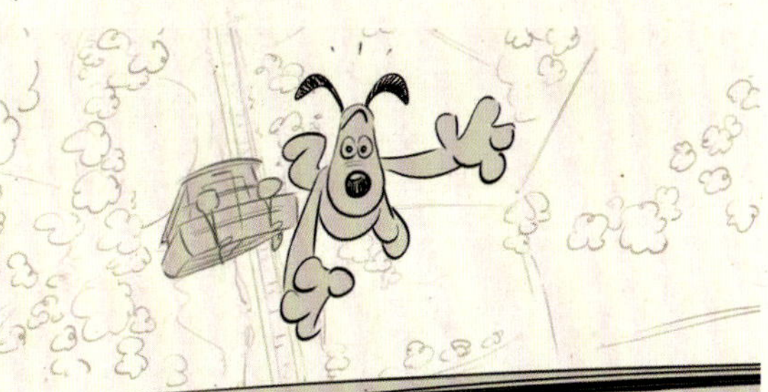

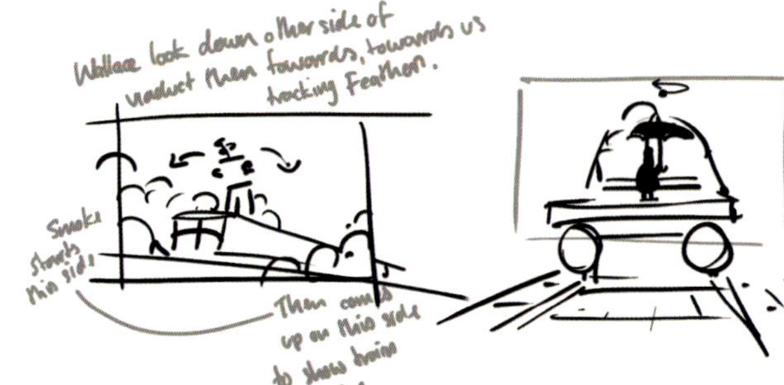

Both hands come
into shot.
Hands touch - fingertips
grip for a brief moment -
then disengage as Gromit
falls. Want to think there
might be hope for a split second.

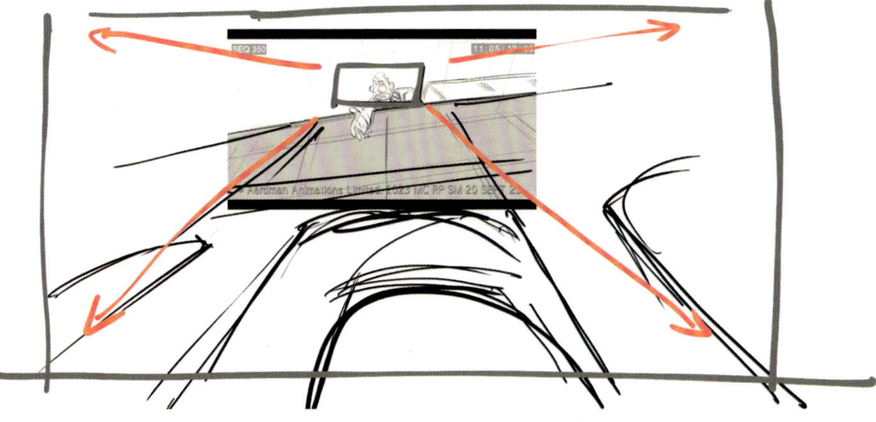

Start closer - end wider.

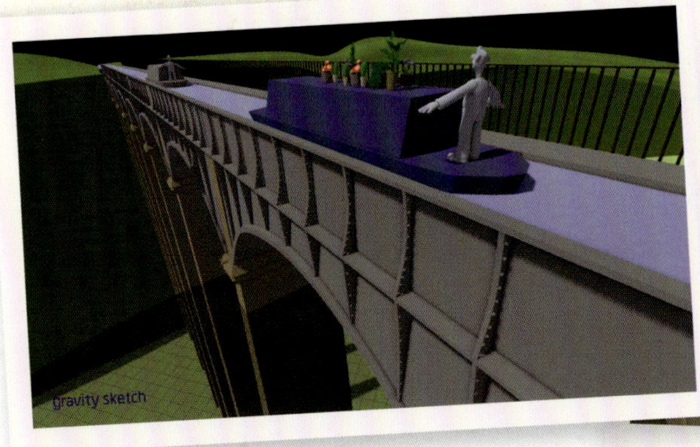

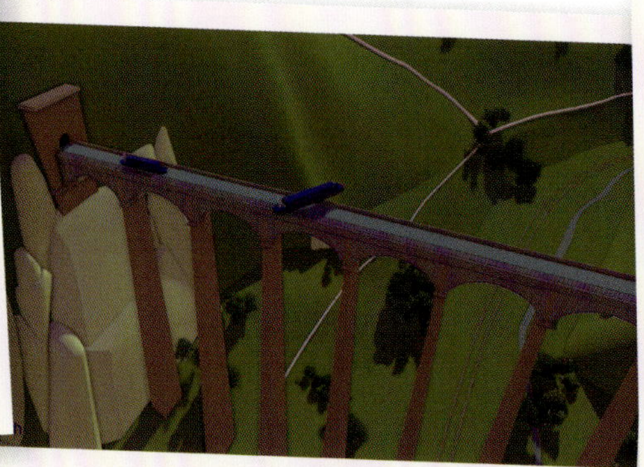

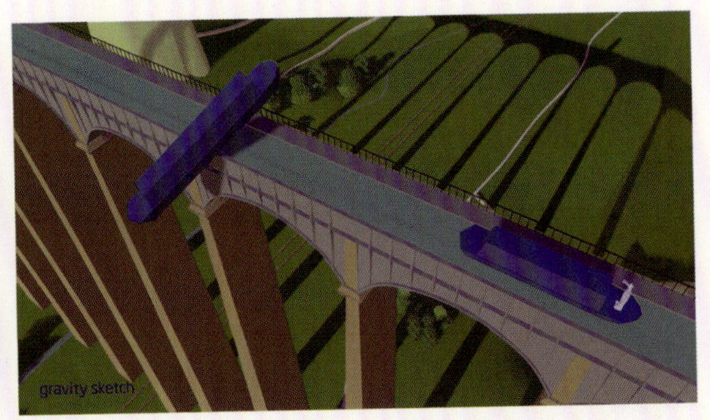

techniques and stop-motion, so Aardman can ask: 'What's the right tool for the job?'. They know what aesthetic they want for the project and can then use all the best bits to achieve it. All those teams are pulling in the same direction and everyone has awe for each other. Everyone is world class at what they do, but it still is that homemade cottage industry. It's hard to categorise it, which I guess is what makes it so special."

Forty years on from Aardman's first production, and with several of its founding members now proudly sporting bus passes, the company is still being constantly refreshed by new talent coming on board. "The standard of animation these days…!" enthuses Nick. "It's funny because in an age where you think CGI is going to take over, the expertise of animators now in stop-motion and clay is higher than I've ever known it. I think that's because so many people have watched our stuff when they were young and have dreamed of working here, so you couldn't have a happier bunch. And they're so good at what they do as well. We have some animators now who are real rising stars."

And it's an exciting opportunity for them to work alongside experienced Aardman crewmembers too. "What's great is that so much of the crew have worked on *Wallace & Gromit* before," adds Nick, "so it's not like you're teaching people from scratch. Dave Alex Riddett was on *The Wrong Trousers*, there's Julian Nott who has been our composer since *A Grand Day Out*, and Adrian Rhodes on sound design who I've worked with since the National

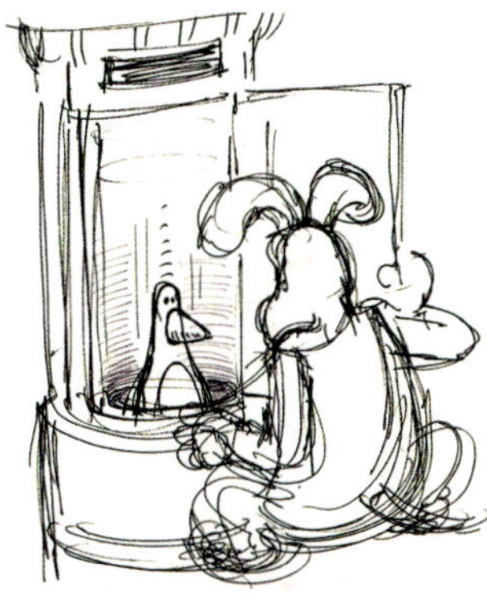

Film and Television School too."

So what are the qualities that Aardman looks for in its animators? There are different skills that each individual brings to the team. "You've got all-rounders who are good at everything, but wouldn't necessarily specialise," notes Will Becher. "Then you have some that are very good at character performance, very nuanced stuff. And then you've got the broad comedy – some people are just funny, so we give them the funniest shots and they deliver. It's very hard to find the team, there aren't many animators in the world who would do this style. Clay is a big part of it; if we have a really brilliant animator who's never worked with clay, it's a question mark – will they be able to manipulate the clay to find the performance required? And comedy is the other big thing. Comedy is about timing, and timing is something you can't teach."

An in-house training scheme, the Aardman Academy, provides a regular source of talent, with some of its graduates going on to join the team. "They come in with a limited amount of experience, but some experience of animating," recounts Will. "They do a 12-week course, which sees them do a lot of tests. Some of them become assistants and that's where they learn a lot more about sculpting clay. If you can have an animator who's been an assistant, that's the best way in."

Despite the wide variety of skills now involved in making each movie, there is a reluctance to

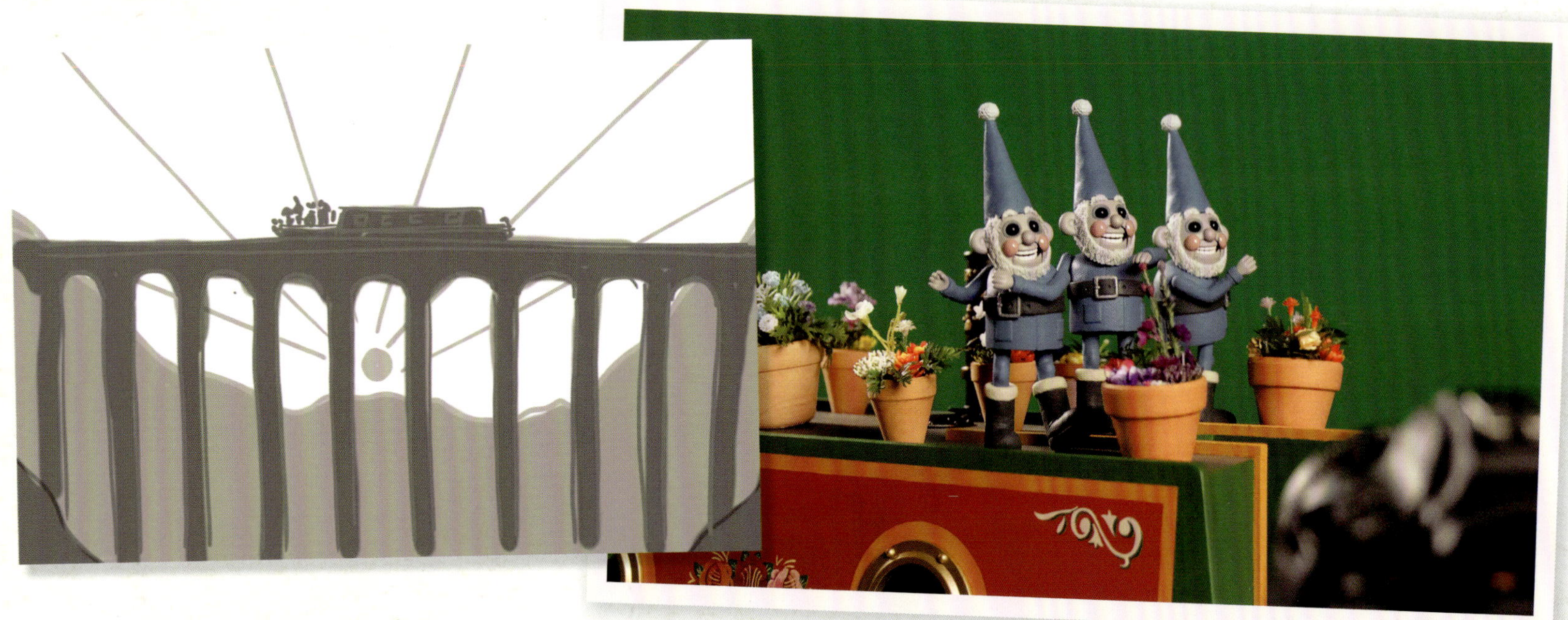

send the work out to other studios. "Farming out some of the visual effects to third-party production companies was something we looked at," admits producer Richard 'Beeky' Beek, "but we felt we had the skillset and capacity internally. And the good thing is that they know Nick, they know Merlin, they know the world of *Wallace & Gromit*. Third parties often do amazing work, but there is always a learning curve if you're working with a completely new company, of them understanding what it is we do, so that helps shortcut things quite significantly."

Stop-motion animation is such a hands-on and collaborative craft that it makes a big difference having all the departments under one roof (or two roofs if you count the CGI work done at the Gas Ferry Road site). Problem-solving can be shared, allowing the best solutions to be found by the people who actually have to do the work. "At pre-production meetings we get together and look at the boards," explains Howard Jones, "and everyone comes up with a theory of how

their department would approach it. With the digital department we can offer solutions, but because the ideal is to shoot things 'in camera' we're waiting to see if the floor can solve it first. We've got one shot of the van with the Norbot legs coming out of the bottom, and it was going to be a real nightmare to animate in terms of accessing the puppets, so I said, 'We can put CG legs in if you want', and everyone said, 'Oh, thank god for that!'"

The studio tries to avoid running on a top-down model with the directors calling all the shots, and the entire crew is appreciative of the latitude they get to bring their own contributions to Nick and Merlin's vision. "It's very important that everyone who is creating something has agency to bring a bit of themselves to it," explains Merlin, "otherwise there isn't any creative process. It's just a dictatorship and that never really works."

And that's the way the production team likes it too. "No-one is trying to out-Nick or out-Merlin them," says Gav Strange. "It's your chance to

Alternative sketch by Merlin of the sun rising behind the aqueduct.

 Behind-the-scenes shot of the Norbots being animated against a green screen for the canal chase (photo by Richard Davies).

play in the *Wallace & Gromit* sandbox, and you want to add to the sandpile purely out of love and respect for them both."

With so many different elements and departments involved in the filmmaking, the role of the production team is absolutely paramount too. "I'm incredibly lucky that I've got a great line producer with Steph Miller," says producer Beeky, "and also Ben Barrowman as production manager, who's got lots of experience working at this scale. I feel we're in very safe hands production-wise."

The directors' lives are made a lot easier by the smooth running of the production side too. "That's all credit to the heads of department and the teams," says Merlin. "They bring a wealth of experience to the project, but it's not just feature film experience. It's having made commercials and TV series, it's the best bits of all of those that are coming together. The tail can't wag the dog, but you also need to know what each paw is doing!"

How does it feel for Nick to be the captain of this vast ocean-going liner, compared to the little dinghy he skippered on *The Wrong Trousers*? "We've done a few features, I guess, but it's still quite daunting," he admits. "It's great partnering up with Merlin on it, to take half of it and share the burden of it. I put pressure on myself: I'm always thinking 'Oh, it's got to be better, you can't let people down, it's got to be funny'. You're constantly pushing that – 'How can we make it funnier?' So I've got to be careful. It's like perfectionism – that can be a real burden and a bad thing, but it's having that belief that makes it the standard it is."

To end this look at the art of *Vengeance*

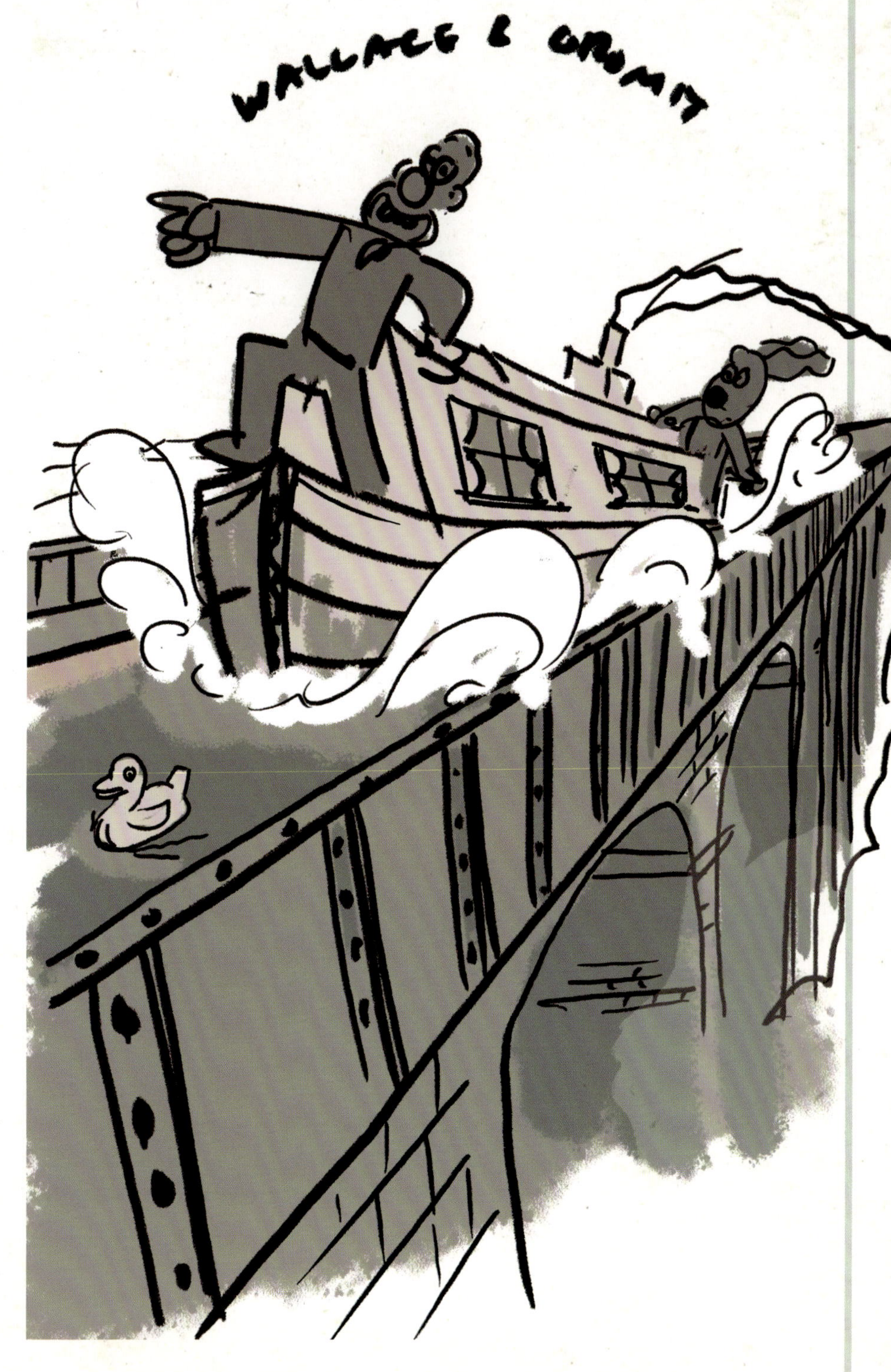

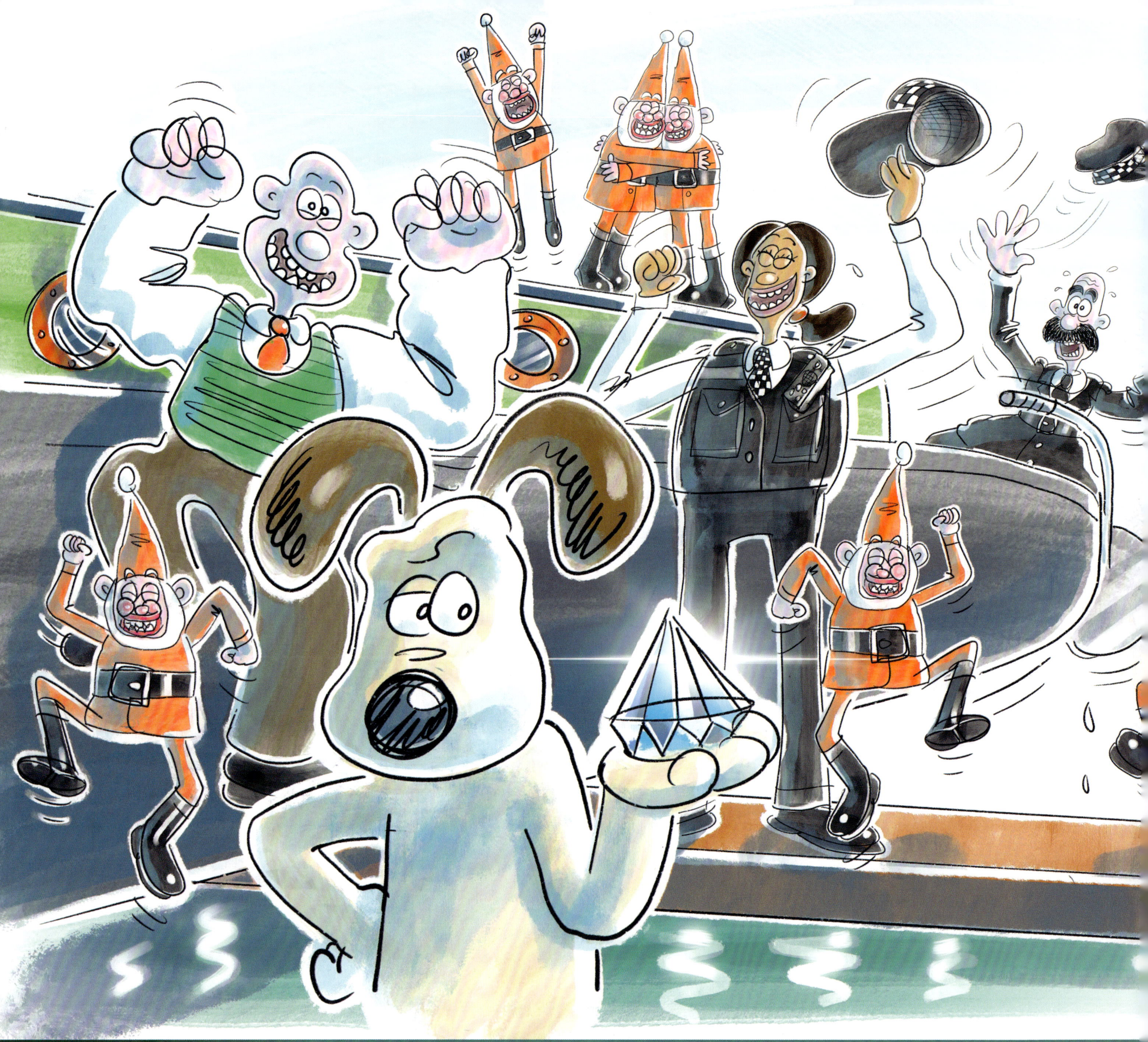

Most Fowl, how would the team sum up what we have been referring to throughout this book as that unique Aardman look? "I think it's just charming," says art director Matt Perry. "It's sweet and naive. It's got that nostalgic thing to it. That's possibly its appeal – it's lovely and quaint and just plain silly."

Graphic designer and gag-meister Gavin Lines echoes the sentiment. "It's friendly and amusing, and it's just kind of comfortable. It's homely in its look. It's never going to be an offensive thing or risqué. It's nice to immerse yourself in that kind of environment."

"And they are caricatures," adds cinematographer Dave Alex Riddett. "It's crazy, but you have to live in that world. It's another world that you've created, but it's as important as real life."

"It's hard to put your finger on it," says Merlin. "It's like a synergy, it's the fact that they are stop-motion, it's the fact that their relationship as characters resonates with kids, with adults, with married couples, with couples who bicker, with people who are loyal, with people who aren't. Together with the fact that they are both sophisticated stories and then also not sophisticated: there's stupid slapstick. All of these things are in a melting pot and hopefully we find the balance to bring them all together so that we embrace a wide audience. It's also the human touch. You can tell… not that they're hand-crafted, but that this world has been made by people. It's the same with Disney's *Jungle Book* where you see the sketch lines of the animators' touch on the characters; when they moved into

smoothing things out, they had to work much harder to create that emotional connection with the characters. Part of the challenge of using modern technology is that we maintain the feel, the DNA, that we don't put too much polish on it, that we keep a little bit of the roughness around the edges."

The last word, of course, has to go to *Wallace & Gromit* creator Nick. "It's about clay," he explains. "It's about thumbprints. Because some people's idea of good animation is to make it slicker, and we don't want it slicker. We want it to look like it has a signature, that there's an individual artist behind it all, and it's all from the same stable. That's very important."

And with the unique thumbprints of Nick, Merlin and the entire team all over *Vengeance Most Fowl*, audiences will undoubtedly be looking forward to being entertained by Aardman's artistry for many years to come. So with that, what better way to take our leave of West Wallaby Street than with the immortal words of Wendolene Ramsbottom?

"Goodbye, Chuck!"

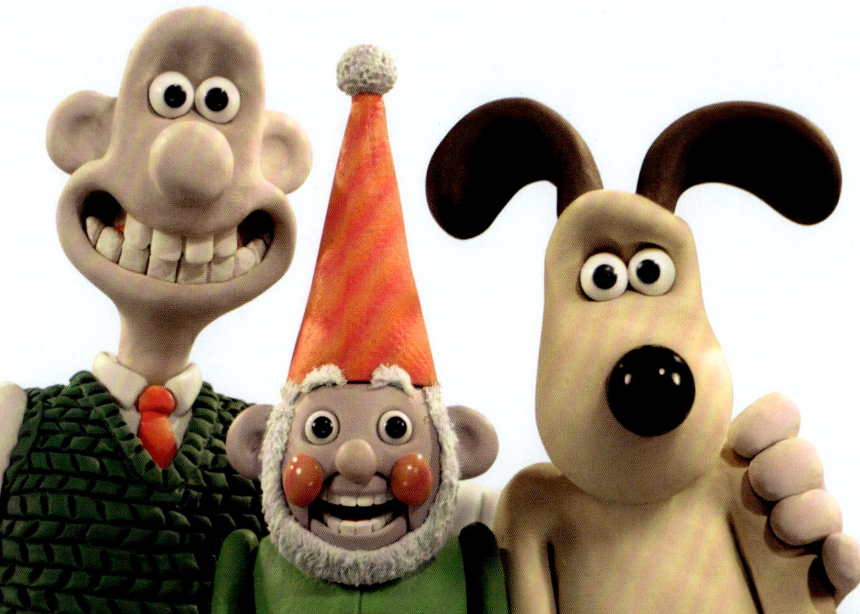

Opposite | Nick's colour concept drawing for the grand finale as the Blue Diamond is rescued.

Thank you from the Directors

IT MAY SOUND RIDICULOUS, BUT HERE IN A creative powerhouse like Aardman it's easy to take for granted the sheer number of gifted and inventive people surrounding us, in one company, on a daily basis. And the level of their innovation and ingenuity, in all departments, on a film like this is both mind-boggling and humbling, helping us and challenging us to realise our vision to the maximum degree.

All of this creativity, humour, passion and inventiveness has been lovingly and painstakingly folded into our film *Vengeance Most Fowl*. We hope it shines out for you in the movie and is self-evident for you in this book.

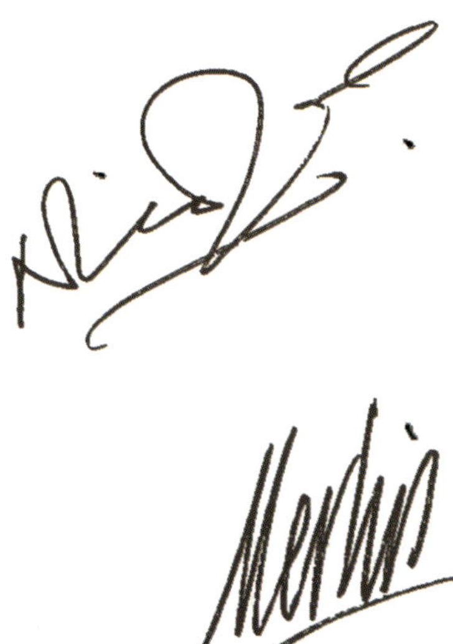

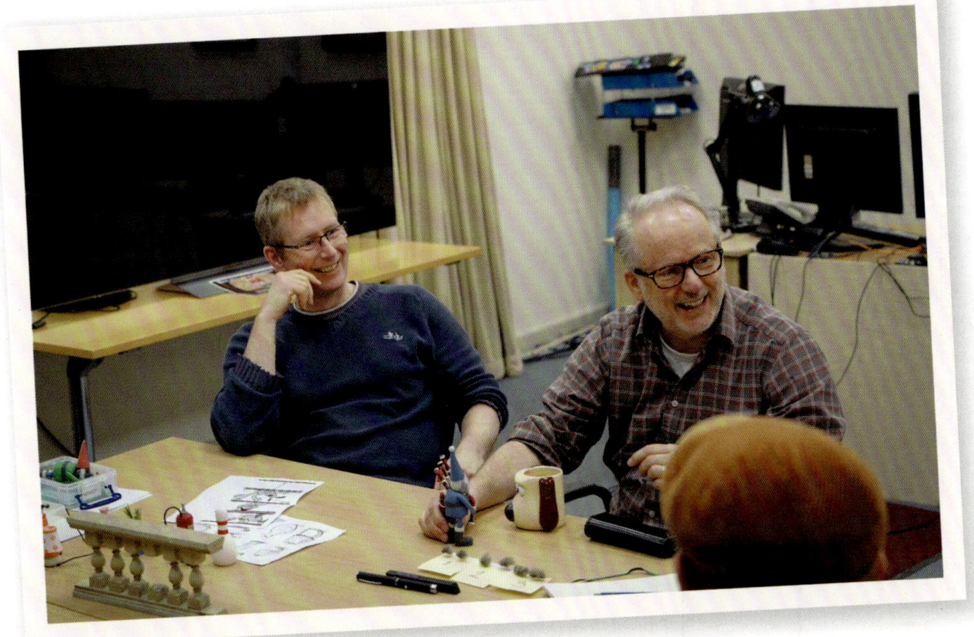

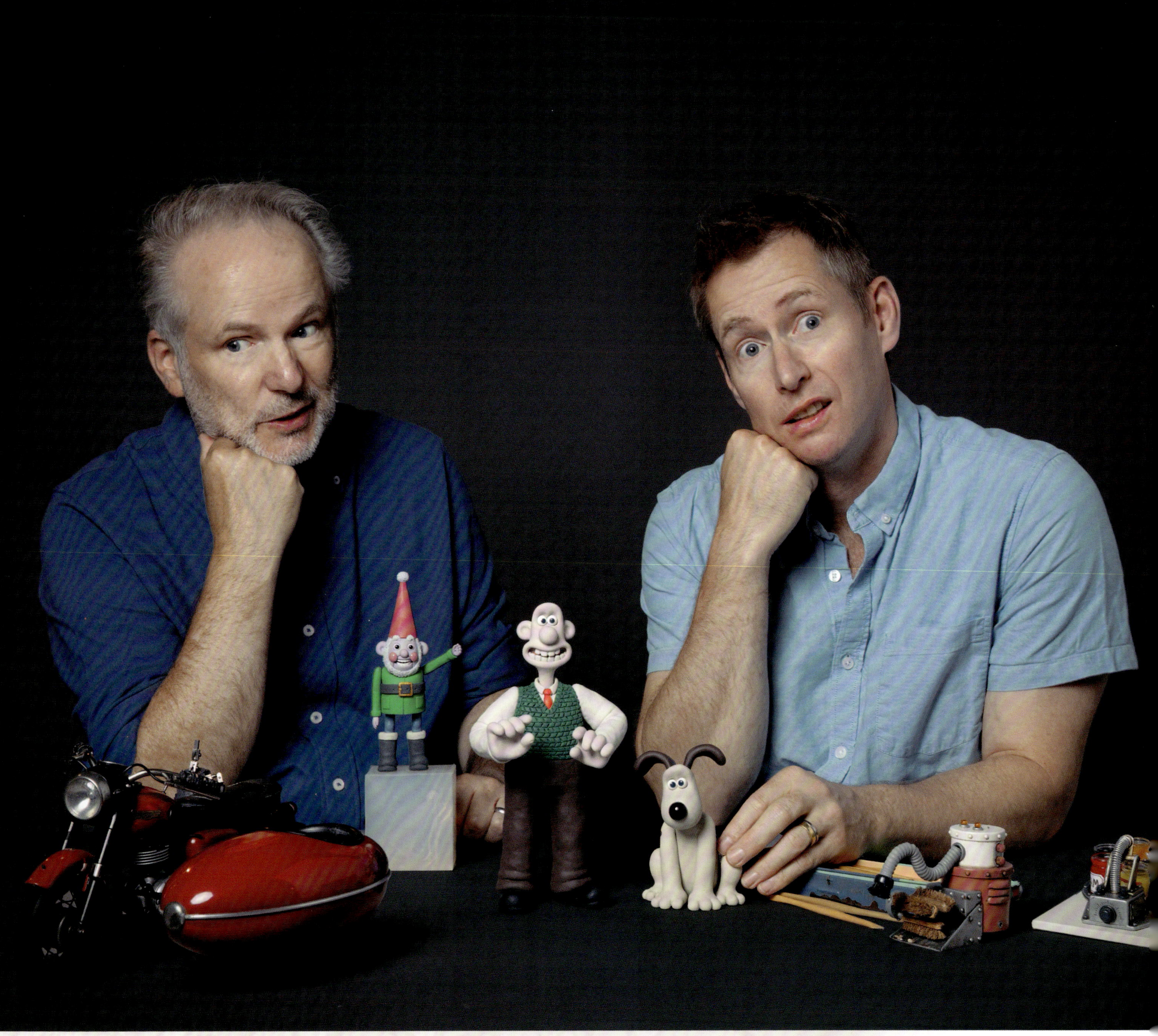

Acknowledgements

THE AUTHOR WOULD LIKE TO THANK THE following people for their assistance with this book: Angie Last, Blair Brown, Lucy Wendover, Ben Townsend, Susan Bolsover at Aardman, as well as the contributors, and Tina Pepler.

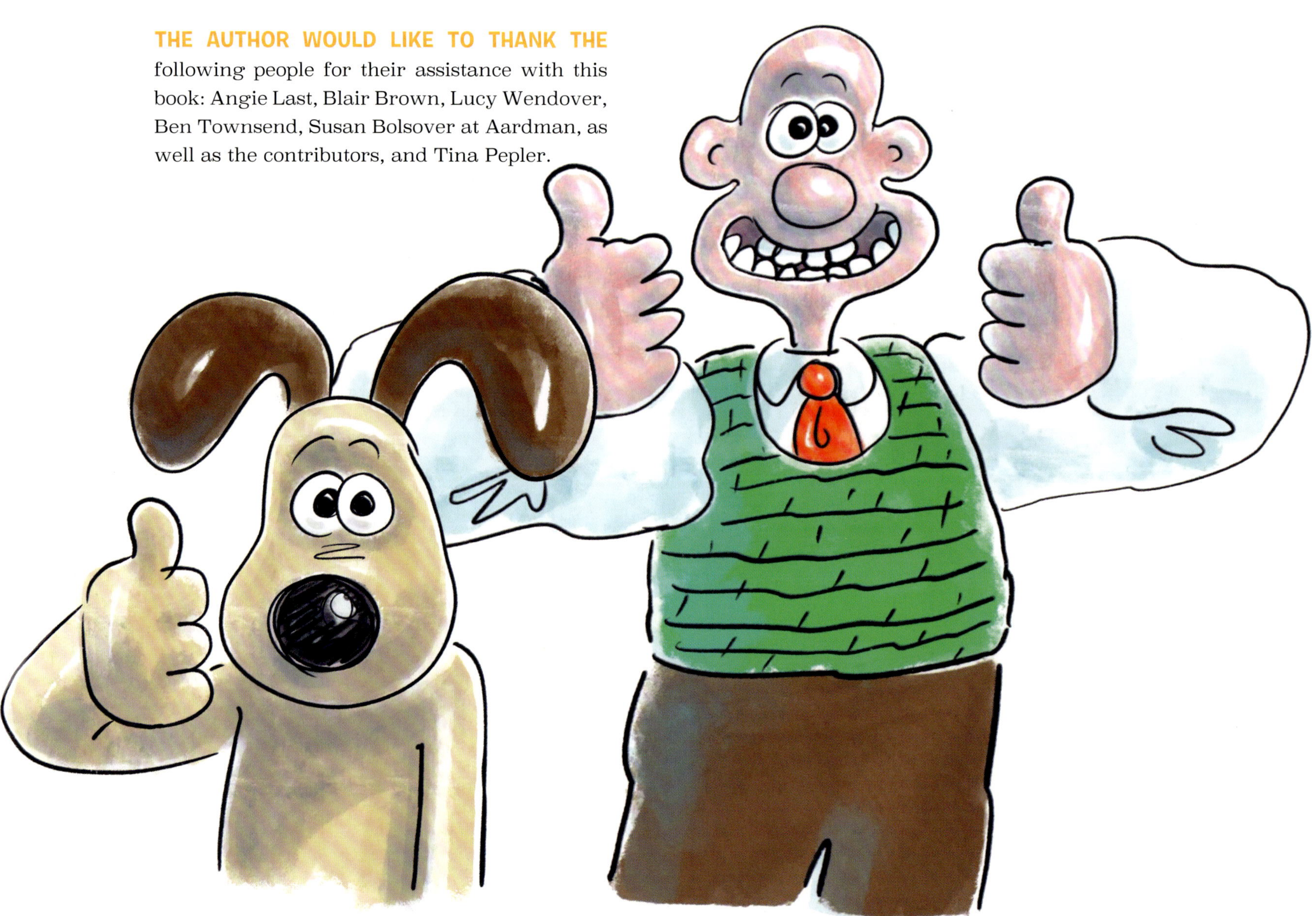

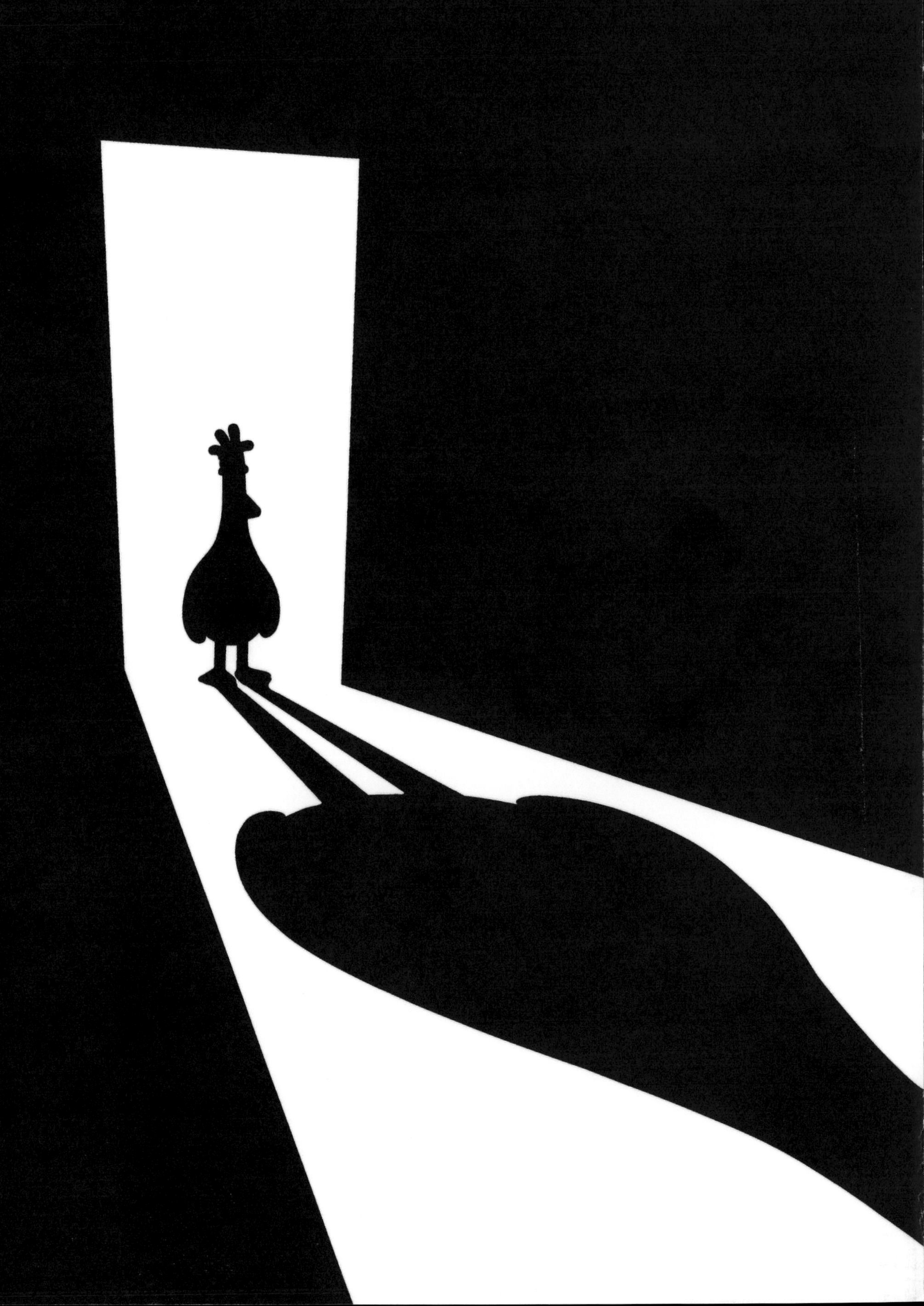